COGNITIVE PSYCHOLOGY
An Overview for Cognitive Scientists

Lawrence W. Barsalou
University of Chicago

LEA LAWRENCE ERLBAUM ASSOCIATES, PUBLISHERS

1992   Hillsdale, New Jersey   Hove and London

Lawrence Erlbaum Associates, Inc., Publishers
365 Broadway
Hillsdale, New Jersey 07642

Library of Congress Cataloging-in-Publication Data

Barsalou, Lawrence W.
   Cognitive psychology : an overview for cognitive scientists /
Lawrence W. Barsalou.
      p.   cm.
   Includes bibliographical references and indexes.
   ISBN 0–8058–0691–1 (hard). — ISBN 0–89859–966–0 (pbk.)
   1. Cognitive psychology.   I. Title.
BF201.B37   1991
153—dc20   91–37192
                                                                             CIP

Printed in the United States of America
10   9   8   7   6   5   4   3   2   1

to Claire Hodnett
for her love and companionship

CONTENTS

PREFACE

This book presents the basic concepts of modern cognitive psychology in a succinct and accessible manner. Rather than listing experiments and models exhaustively for each significant area of research, I have tried instead to produce a coherent overview of its central constructs. My primary goal is to equip readers with a conceptual vocabulary that will acquaint them with the general approach of cognitive psychology and allow them to follow discussions of it elsewhere. In presenting basic constructs, I cover a wide variety of experiments, theories, and issues. Although my coverage of an area is never exhaustive, I include specific examples of experiments and theories that provide a concrete sense of relevant research. I address not only current work relevant to cognitive science but also traditional work central to modern thinking. Given the constraints of an overview, I have, of necessity, failed to acknowledge much quality work of importance. Interested readers can find this work through the extensive references provided.

I have written this book for several audiences. First, it is for researchers in the other disciplines, besides psychology, that constitute the cognitive sciences, including computer science, linguistics, philosophy, anthropology, neuroscience, and so forth. I assume that many of these readers wish to acquaint themselves with cognitive psychology but are not prepared to invest extensive time in reviewing research literatures. Readers who subsequently wish to explore cognitive psychology further will find that the basic concepts developed here lay the groundwork for more detailed and technical presentations elsewhere. Little in the way of prior technical knowledge is necessary for understanding this book.

Second, I have written this book for proseminars, courses, and course sequences on cognitive science that cover methods and contributions from cognitive psychology. Similarly, this book can be used in courses and seminars that focus on neighboring disciplines (e.g., artificial intelligence, linguistics, philosophy), or on specific research areas (e.g., categorization, memory, learning, language, problem solving), where some perspective on cognitive psychology is desirable or necessary. Although many students in such courses may already have a strong background in cognitive psychology, some may have little or none. Rather than requiring these latter students to take a course on cognitive psychology or read a lengthy text, instructors could have them read this overview instead. Because this presentation of cognitive psychology is relatively brief and nontechnical, it can be covered quickly, leaving much time for other material.

Third, this book can serve as an introductory text in courses on cognitive psychology, providing students with a coherent overview of the field. Prior to lectures on specific experiments or theories, students could read relevant sections as background. This text could also provide background for additional course readings that emphasize themes, trends, and methods the instructor deems interesting or important. References throughout offer numerous examples of journal articles, edited chapters, and research monographs that could serve as detailed examples of research in particular areas.

Finally, I have written this book for lay readers interested in learning about current trends in scientific psychology. No background in psychology, methodology, or statistics is necessary for following this book. As much as possible, I try to avoid jargon, to use concrete examples from everyday life, and to make experiments and theoretical constructs intuitive. In addition, I attempt to define all technical terms as they become relevant.

Because the cognitive approach to psychology is somewhat subtle, often misunderstood, and sometimes controversial, I spend considerable time addressing the assumptions that underlie it. Three of the eleven chapters therefore address the "meta-assumptions" that govern research and theory in cognitive psychology. In the introductory chapter, I address the nature of cognitive constructs and their relation to information-processing constructs in computers and to the neuronal structure of the brain. In the chapter on representation, I address theoretical relations between cognitive theory and the brain, and between the brain and the physical world. In the final chapter, I address assumptions of the ecological, laboratory, formal, and computational approaches to cognitive psychology. These three "meta-chapters" enable a deeper understanding of the content areas and convey a general sense of what cognitive psychologists are trying to accomplish.

To facilitate readability and comprehension, I use extensive cross-referencing to connect related sections of the text. Every section has a numerical reference code, such as **6**.3 and **10**.4.1, where the first number represents the chapter and the following numbers represent subsections. These internal cross-references remind the reader that the current topic receives further coverage elsewhere, and they provide addresses for finding this material quickly. Should one want to review the cross-referenced material before proceeding further, it can be done easily. Another purpose of this cross-referencing is to promote integration of related topics distributed throughout the text. By reminding readers of the connections between various topics, cross-referencing should foster high-level, integrative connections, thereby providing a more coherent view of the field.

I am grateful to Andrew Ortony and Donald Norman for the opportunity to write this book and for their guidance in developing it. I am also grateful to the students in my courses on cognitive psychology over the last ten years. They have frequently challenged and developed my views in ways that I never anticipated. This book largely reflects the outcome of that process. I am also grateful to the Lilly Foundation for providing me with the opportunity to revise my course on cognitive psychology in 1984-85, and to the National Science Foundation (IST-8308984, IRI-8609187) and the Army Research Institute (MDA903-90-K-0112) for supporting my work over the last eight years. Lawrence Erlbaum Associates exhibited commendable patience with me as I worked to complete this book, although I imagine that they have had much practice. During this time, Judi Amsel and Julia Hough provided me with useful guidance. I am grateful to William Bechtel, Christopher Hale, Robert Kass, Dorrit Billman, and the Georgia Tech students in Professor Billman's 1989 undergraduate course and my 1990 graduate course on cognitive psychology for their comments on earlier drafts of this book; to Kathryn Bock for comments on chapters 7, 8, and 9; to Deborah Frisch for comments on chapter 10; to Edward Smith for comments on chapters 7 and 10; to Chava Casper for superb copyediting; and to Art Lizza for a steady hand on production. Any remaining errors are mine. Finally, I am deeply indebted to Gordon Bower, George Mandler, Douglas Medin, Brian Ross, and Edward Smith for the opportunities, support, and guidance that they have given me over the course of my career.

Lawrence W. Barsalou

1

INTRODUCTION

Imagine that an alien spaceship leaves Earth after a short visit and mistakenly abandons several robots as it heads for other exotic points in the universe. Several days later, a hiker discovers the robots, which are rushed to a research university. Over the next few months, scientists and engineers from around the world converge to dismantle one. To their amazement, they discover that the robot's internal structure far exceeds current scientific understanding. Neither the robot's components nor their organization resemble anything ever seen on Earth before. Moreover, the complexity of the robot's intricately related components is overwhelming. After extensive examination, the scientific community concludes that decades, if not centuries, of research will be necessary to explain the robot's physical structure.

Inability to understand the robots physically does not prevent understanding them in other ways. First, scientists could attempt to understand the robots behaviorally. How do the robots behave when placed in particular situations? When placed in sunlight, for example, the robots might "sunbathe" for several hours before actively pursuing goals. After being placed in darkness for long periods, the robots might seek sources of light. By discovering systematic relations between situations and the robots' responses to them, scientists can learn much about the robots' behavior.

Second, scientists could attempt to infer internal mechanisms in the robots that produce these behaviors. For example, sunbathing and light seeking suggest that the robots have a rechargeable solar battery. Although scientists might not be able to identify the physical system in the robots that captures,

1

stores, and utilizes solar energy, their behavioral experiments may consistently show that the robots have such a system. Further behavioral research might identify the system's functional parameters, such as the amount of light it stores, the wavelengths of light it absorbs, the rate at which it absorbs light, and so forth.

Behavioral research could also provide insights into other aspects of the robots, such as their perceptual abilities. Scientists could present the robots with different types of perceptual information and observe which types produce responses. For example, the robots might respond to visual, tactile, and kinesthetic information but not to auditory, olfactory, and gustatory information, leading scientists to conclude that the robots have perceptual systems for seeing, touching, and moving but not for hearing, smelling, and tasting. Further studies could assess specific aspects of the robots' perceptual abilities. What wavelengths of light do the robots' visual systems detect? Do the robots detect the same wavelengths of light as humans? Do the robots perceive different wavelengths as different colors? Do the robots detect other wavelengths not visible to humans, such as infrared light?

Behavioral research could assess whether the robots have a memory. Imagine that scientists place a robot in a dimly lit maze and that the robot eventually discovers a path out of the maze to sunlight, after initially running into several dead ends. Further imagine that scientists later place the robot in the same maze and that it exits the maze faster than it did the first time, avoiding the dead ends and immediately retracing the direct path to sunlight. Faster time to exit the maze the second time would indicate that the robot has memories of the paths that produced failure and success on the previous occasion. If the robot learns to be more efficient, it must store information from previous experiences and use it to improve later performance. Further studies could assess specific aspects of the robot's memory. Does it remember visual information that marks the path? Or does it remember the movements that led to sunlight? If the robot remembers its movements, it should find its way even when visual information along the path changes. But if the robot uses visual information to find its way, then changes in visual information should worsen performance. By manipulating aspects of the task in this manner and observing the robot's behavior, scientists can develop increasingly detailed accounts of the robot's memory.

After much behavioral research, scientists might develop a fairly complete account of the robots' abilities, including extensive accounts of the internal mechanisms that underlie these abilities, without having any knowledge of their physical bases. Knowledge of these internal mechanisms could nevertheless be extremely useful both scientifically and practically. It could explain the robots' past behavior. It could predict the robots' future behavior. It could allow people to use and interact with the robots optimally. It could allow people to keep the robots from getting into dangerous situations. It could guide explorations of the robots' internal structure, perhaps suggesting that scientists look for physical systems that store solar energy, detect particular kinds of perceptual information, and store particular kinds of memories.

As you have no doubt been thinking, this scenario is similar to the problem psychologists face with respect to humans. Ultimately, psychologists seek to understand the physical structure of the human nervous system and how it operates to produce intelligent behavior. Although many important facts about the brain and its peripheral nervous system have been discovered, they constitute only a very small proportion of what there is to know. For example, scientists have learned much about the local behavior of neurons, but they have learned little about how large collections of neurons generate the more global brain activities that underlie intelligence. Scientists have learned little about how the brain produces memory, learning, language, and thought.

Yet, for about a hundred years, psychologists have studied human behavior scientifically, knowing little about its physical basis in the brain. In the process, they have collected bewildering amounts of data that describe behavior in its myriad aspects. The scientific study of psychology began in several different European movements. In the late 19th century, a group of scientists known as introspectionists attempted to describe the contents and composition of conscious experience systematically (Boring, 1953, 1957; Dellarosa, 1988; James, 1890; Titchener, 1910). At the same time, another group of scientists known as psychophysicists attempted to describe systematic relations between conscious experience and physical information in the environment (Atkinson, Herrnstein, Lindzey, & R.D. Luce, 1988a; S.S. Stevens, 1975). In the early 20th century, gestalt psychologists attempted to describe how people organize fields of information during perception, memory, and thought (Duncker, 1945; Koffka, 1935; Kohler, 1940; J.M. Mandler & G. Mandler, 1964; Wertheimer, 1945/1982). Concurrently, behaviorists attempted to describe how humans and other organisms adapt to their environments (Bower & Hilgard, 1981; Domjan & Burkhard, 1986; Honig & Staddon, 1977; Rachlin, 1970; Skinner, 1953; Watson, 1930). For a good review of the developments that led to cognitive psychology, see R. Lachman, J.L. Lachman, and Butterfield (1979, chaps. 1-3).

Since these early movements, scientific psychology has flourished. Today, most universities and colleges have sizable psychology departments that promote psychological research and train graduate students as future scientists. Extensive literatures on nearly every aspect of human behavior have evolved, as several generations of experimental psychologists have refined their empirical and theoretical methods. Developmental psychologists have described the behavioral development of humans from birth through old age (M. Cole & S.R. Cole, 1989; Heatherington & Parke, 1986; Sroufe & R.G.

Cooper, 1988). Social psychologists have described human behavior in groups and various social settings (R. Brown, 1986; Shaver, 1987). Clinical psychologists have described abnormalities in human behavior (Goodwin & Guze, 1984; Kaplan & Sacuzzo, 1984). Perception psychologists have described how humans pick up physical information from the environment (Atkinson et al., 1988a; Boff, Kaufman, & Thomas, 1986; Bruce & P. Green, 1990; E.B. Goldstein, 1989; Sekular & Blake, 1990). And cognitive psychologists have described how humans store, manipulate, and use information (J.R. Anderson, 1990; Atkinson, Herrnstein, Lindzey, & R.D. Luce, 1988b; Ellis & R.R. Hunt, 1989; Glass & Holyoak, 1986; Lindsay & Norman, 1977; Neisser, 1967, 1976; Reed, 1988; Solso, 1988). By no means are these behavioral accounts complete, and a comprehensive theory of psychology remains elusive. Nevertheless, experimental psychologists have learned a tremendous amount about behavior in all of these areas, and their theoretical formulations are becoming increasingly sophisticated.

Most behavior remains poorly understood at the physical level. Scientists typically have little understanding of the underlying neuronal mechanisms that produce specific behaviors. Nevertheless, our understanding of the brain has also proceeded at a rapid rate. During the 20th century, physiological psychologists and other neuroscientists from biology, chemistry, physics, and medicine have made important advances in understanding the human nervous system (Adams & Victor, 1989; F.E. Bloom & Lazerson, 1988; N.R. Carlson, 1986; Heilman & Valenstein, 1985; Kolb & Whishaw, 1980; Lezak, 1983; Pinel, 1990). In certain areas, scientists have established close ties between behavioral phenomena and physical mechanisms. In perception, for example, the behavioral properties of sensory systems have become increasingly understood in neurological terms. Most scientists expect our understanding of the relations between the brain and behavior to grow extensively in coming years. Currently, however, relatively sparse relations exist between these two levels of theory.

1.1 INTERNAL CONSTRUCTS IN PSYCHOLOGY

As we saw in the robot example earlier, behavioral data often suggest internal constructs, independent of physical evidence for them. Similarly, in the absence of physical evidence, psychologists have proposed a wide variety of internal constructs to explain their behavioral observations of humans. Freudian theory provides a well-known example. On the basis of behavioral evidence observed clinically, Freud (1933) postulated the id, ego, and superego as internal mechanisms that produce behavioral normalities and abnormalities. Since then, scientific psychologists in virtually every area except behaviorism have proposed internal mechanisms to explain behavior.

In most cases, psychologists had no neurological evidence on which to base these mechanisms, but proposed them solely on the basis of behavioral evidence.

Proposing internal mechanisms in psychology has been quite controversial. In fact, this issue has dominated the history of modern psychology, dictating research and theory in fundamental ways. In the early years of this century, a group of psychologists known as behaviorists argued that internal constructs were unscientific. Because psychologists can not observe these constructs directly, behaviorists believed that including them in scientific explanations produced only unrigorous and shoddy science. Behaviorists proposed instead that psychological theories should exclusively address the physical stimuli that an organism encounters and its observable behavioral responses to them. Theoretical explanations should abandon internal constructs in favor of functional laws that express mathematical relations between observable stimuli and responses.

Typically, such laws in behaviorism have been the laws of classical and operant conditioning. In classical conditioning, a conditioned stimulus (e.g., a bell), associated with an unconditioned stimulus (e.g., food), comes to produce a conditioned response that is normally produced by the unconditioned stimulus (e.g., salivation). In operant conditioning, a reinforcer (e.g., food), associated with an arbitrary behavior (e.g., press the left response key), comes to control the behavior when a cue signals the reinforcer's availability (e.g., a light is on). Traditionally, behaviorists characterized the organism as a *tabula rasa* or blank slate, whose behavioral habits and skills primarily reflected the particular environmental events that occurred in conjunction with behavior. Thus, behaviorists argued that a complete learning history of an organism's behavioral responses to environmental stimuli should, in principle, be sufficient to explain its behavior (Bower & Hilgard, 1981; Domjan & Burkhard, 1986; Honig & Staddon, 1977; Rachlin, 1970; Skinner, 1953).

Behaviorism dominated scientific psychology in the United States from about 1910 to 1950. During this period, postulating internal constructs was taboo: Research did not address the presence of internal constructs, and theories rarely included them. The behaviorist edict to eschew internal constructs has few parallels in the history of science. Researchers across the sciences have nearly always proposed internal constructs that they could not observe directly. In the early history of genetics, for example, no one had ever observed a gene. Yet, this construct produced a revolution in biology, because it greatly improved biologists' ability to account for data, to generate new research, and to develop useful applications. The direct observation of genes years later was not surprising, given the tremendous amount of indirect support that the construct had accumulated. Similarly, physicists have frequently proposed theoretical constructs for non-observable entities. Although no one has ever observed quarks and other subatomic particles, these theoretical entities perform important scientific functions. The presence of unobservable theoretical constructs is certainly not unique to psychology. Unobservable constructs have a venerable history of success across the sciences (Hacking, 1983; G. Maxwell, 1964; McMullin, 1978; Toulmin, 1961).

Although the stature of behaviorism has declined considerably over the last 40 years, it nevertheless remains a central and important part of psychology. Classical and operant conditioning have been observed in a wide range of species and capture fundamental aspects of how organisms adapt to their environments. Moreover, behaviorists developed experimental design and control to a high art, and the quality of research in virtually every other area of experimental psychology has benefited from these advances (**11**.2). The sense of rigor and skepticism that behaviorists brought to experimental psychology has made it a stronger science throughout.

Three developments around the middle of this century greatly reduced behaviorism's influence on psychology and led to what many have termed "the cognitive revolution." One important development occurred in linguistics. When the eminent behaviorist, B.F. Skinner (1957), tried to explain language learning from a behaviorist perspective, a young linguist, Noam Chomsky (1959), wrote what was considered a devastating critique. Chomsky's arguments convinced many that a theory of language learning must include internal constructs. A theory that only considers the observable stimuli and responses in linguistic interaction is not sufficiently powerful to account for the structural properties of human utterances.

Chomsky proposed alternatively that the systematic patterns in human language primarily reflect the presence of an internal grammar. To explain language behavior, researchers must study this internal grammar empirically and include accounts of it in theory. Even though Chomsky had no physical evidence for such a grammar in the human brain, he argued that behavioral data provided a compelling argument for it. This proposal was heresy from the behaviorist perspective and was received as such. Many psychologists, however, had become worried that the behaviorist framework was not yielding progress in understanding the higher cognitive functions of language, memory, and thought. Chomsky's ideas not only provided a provocative theory of language, they also suggested that addressing internal mechanisms would be necessary to account for the higher cognitive functions. The formal elegance and rigor of Chomsky's particular theory also convinced many that, in general, theories of psychology could have these qualities (Chomsky, 1957, 1965; Chomsky & G.A Miller, 1963; G.A. Miller & Chomsky, 1963).

Information theory constituted a second important development that contributed to the demise of behaviorism and the rise of cognitivism. During the 1940s, applied mathematicians developed information theory to model electronic information systems, such as sonar and radar (Shannon & Weaver, 1949). An information theory account of a system typically assumes that a transmitter sends a message through a channel to a receiver, with different information systems varying in the characteristics of these basic components. For example, transmitters vary in their rate of transmission, messages vary in their complexity, channels vary in their signal-to-noise ratio, and receivers vary in their rate of decoding. By combining such variables mathematically, information theorists described important aspects of information processing.

During World War II, many experimental psychologists assisted the military in optimizing the ability of human operators to interact with electronic information systems. These psychologists found it natural to view an operator's ability to transmit and receive information in terms of information theory. They observed, for example, that human operators were limited in their rates of transmission and decoding, as well as in the complexity of the messages they could process. Moreover, an operator's limitations in transmitting and receiving appeared to reflect innate constraints rather than insufficient learning experience. No matter how much operators practiced transmitting and receiving, their performance approached asymptotic levels, suggesting internal limits on information processing.

Accounting for these internal limits theoretically seemed impossible in a framework that only considered the stimuli and responses in a learning history. Similar to Chomsky's conclusion about language, applied information theorists concluded that internal constructs are essential for explaining how humans process information. After the war, psychologists returning from their exposure to applied information processing were ready for Chomsky's argument that behaviorist approaches were fundamentally unable to account for important human abilities. Many of these psychologists applied their new insights about information processing in humans to basic research, and some of the seminal work in modern cognitive psychology ensued (Broadbent, 1958; Fitts & Posner, 1967; see also Card, Moran, & Newell, 1983; C.D. Wickens, 1984).

Computer science constituted the third development that contributed to the demise of behaviorism and the rise of cognitivism. The advent of the modern digital computer provided a rich theoretical metaphor for theorizing about human information processing: People, like computers, acquire information from the environment; both people and computers store information and retrieve it when applicable to current tasks; both are limited in the amount of information they can process at a given time; both transform information to produce new information; both return information to the environment. The information processing architecture of computers strongly framed much early thinking in modern cognitive psychology. The components of cognitive theories were often strikingly similar to computer components, as was their organization. Research projects frequently aimed at verifying and articulating this theoretical perspective (Atkinson & Shiffrin, 1968; Broadbent, 1958; Newell & Simon, 1972).

Critics of cognitive psychology sometimes argue that people are really not all that similar to computers. Most cognitive psychologists now agree. For example, cognitive theories typically assume that the human brain performs many kinds of parallel processing not currently found in most computers. Although models of memory retrieval in humans typically assume that the search for a particular piece of information occurs simultaneously across many information sources (e.g., J.R. Anderson, 1983; Gillund & Shiffrin, 1984; Hintzman, 1986, 1988), most current computers cannot perform these types of parallel search and rely instead on serial search. Similarly, most current computers typically store a given piece of information in a single memory location, yet recent memory theories assume that a piece of information can be distributed over many memory locations (e.g., Bechtel & Abrahamsen, 1990; McClelland, Rumelhart, & the PDP Research Group, 1986; Ratcliff, 1978; Rumelhart, McClelland, & the PDP Research Group, 1986).

The central theme that still unites cognitive psychology and computer science is information processing: Both disciplines focus on how systems acquire, store, retrieve, transform, and produce information to perform intelligent activity. Ironically, the relation between the two has taken something of a twist recently. Whereas computer architecture once defined theories of human cognition, advances in psychology are poised to redefine computer architecture. The potential of parallel, distributed memory models in cognitive psychology and neuroscience has stimulated the development of comparable architectures in computer science. Rather than modeling humans in the image of computers, it would not be all that surprising if we eventually fashion computers in the image of ourselves. Because attempts to make computers act intelligently have proceeded much more slowly than once anticipated, the study of information processing in humans may accelerate the development of intelligence in artificial systems (Hillis, 1985; Mead, 1989).

1.2 THE NATURE OF COGNITIVE CONSTRUCTS

Throughout the history of psychology, theorists have ascribed to humans a wide variety of internal constructs in the absence of physical evidence. Freudians ascribe dynamic forces, such as the ego and id. Personality theorists ascribe traits, such as extroversion and aggressiveness. Social psychologists ascribe attitudes, such as being against deforestation. Philosophers ascribe mental states, such as knowledge and belief. In everyday life, people ascribe emotions, motives, and numerous other states to each other as they try to explain and predict behavior. Ascribing internal states is a fundamental human activity in both mundane and scientific affairs.

The internal constructs of cognitive psychology tend to be of a very specific type: Almost always, they concern information processing, describing how the brain processes information. Some cognitive constructs correspond to mechanisms in the brain that pick up information from the environment; others to mechanisms that store information in memory; and still others to mechanisms that retrieve information from memory, transform information in memory, and send information back into the environment. As we shall see, nearly all cognitive constructs describe information processing mechanisms. In most cases, little if any physical evidence derived from neurological research is available to support these constructs. Instead, their plausibility rests primarily on their ability to explain behavioral data.

Cognitive constructs—as I will call internal constructs in cognitive psychology—typically do *not* represent conscious mental states. Instead, they typically represent unconscious information processing. Most cognitive psychologists do not try to explain conscious experience. In fact, cognitive psychology has embarrassingly little to say about subjective mental life. Rather than addressing conscious experience, cognitive psychology primarily addresses how the brain processes information. In this sense, cognitive psychology is closer to neuroscience than it is to more mentalistic forms of psychology that address conscious experience.

An analogy to computers may make this clearer. One way to explain a computer's behavior is in terms of its electronic circuitry. At the electronic level of analysis, physical components, such as resistors, condensers, and silicon chips, constitute the central explanatory constructs. These components enter various physical states, depending on the physical forces that emanate to them from other components, and together they determine computer operation.

A second way to explain a computer's behavior is in terms of its information flow structure. At this level of analysis, abstract entities such as commands, files, and directories constitute the central explanatory constructs. During computer operation, commands operate on files to perform various operations, such as search, multiplication, and inference. Although tremendous amounts of electronic structure and activity underlie these operations, the information processing level of analysis captures little of it. Instead, this level represents computer operations and entities only in terms of their information processing properties. For example, informational capacity in bytes represents the size of a file, and a string of characters represents its content; the underlying electronic circuitry that represents a file is typically irrelevant. Similarly, a name and a string of acceptable arguments represents a command; the underlying sequence of electronic events usually plays no role in its conceptualization and use.

Clearly, both the electronic and information processing accounts are essential for an adequate description of computers. The electronic account is necessary for building computers and for controlling them precisely, but is much too detailed and unwieldy for many other important uses, such as programming and word processing. Moreover, the electronic account does not readily capture the global processing abilities of computers. In contrast, the information processing account describes computers at a level that is suitable for the needs of most users, and it provides a global view of how computers process information. Without it, users could not see the forest for the trees and would get bogged down in unnecessary electronic details.

Neurological mechanisms and cognitive constructs in the brain are analogous to electronics and information processing in computers. Whereas neuroscience attempts to provide a detailed account of the brain's physical components and their operation, cognitive theory attempts to provide a more global account of how these physical components process information. Each level of analysis plays a different but complementary role (Bechtel, 1988a; Dennet, 1978; McCauley, 1986). Both are necessary for a complete understanding of the brain. Currently, our understanding of the brain's information processing abilities probably exceeds our understanding of the neuronal mechanisms that produce them. Ultimately, however, theory at both levels will become more complete and more closely interrelated. I return to the relation between neurological and cognitive constructs later in **3.3**.

Note that nothing in this two-level account of the brain corresponds readily to the subjective nature of consciousness. Rather than capturing conscious experience, cognitive constructs typically describe the brain's global, information processing properties. Because information processing accounts of computers imply nothing about computers having conscious experiences, information processing accounts of the brain typically have little to say about people's conscious experiences. Clearly, we have conscious experiences, but cognitive psychology has shed little light on how the brain produces them. Ultimately cognitive psychology will have to explain consciousness if it is to succeed, but present theories focus primarily on how the brain processes information to perform the fundamental tasks of intelligence. It is in this regard that cognitive psychology is closer to neuroscience than to more mentalistic forms of psychology that address conscious experience. For work in cognitive psychology that does address consciousness, see Ericsson and Simon (1984), Finke (1989), Johnson-Laird (1983, chap. 6), G. Mandler (1975, 1985), Marcel (1983a, 1983b), and Shepard and L.A. Cooper (1982).

Cognitive constructs play many important roles in psychology, besides providing a global account of the brain's information processing abilities. First, cognitive constructs allow psychologists to explain fundamental facts about human behavior that behaviorist theories can not explain, including numerous aspects of perception, memory, language, and thought. Cognitive constructs have expanded the scope of explanation in psychology considerably.

Second, cognitive constructs have motivated tremendous amounts of research. In the process of attempting to discover cognitive mechanisms and distinguish between various accounts of them, cognitive psychologists have greatly extended the empirical data that describe human behavior. If cognitive psychology were to disappear, it would leave behind a huge empirical legacy for any subsequent theory to explain. In this regard, cognitive constructs have been highly stimulating to the science of psychology and have produced a major contribution to its heritage. To get a sense of the tremendous amount of research that has been performed in mainstream cognitive psychology, peruse any of the journals cited frequently in the reference section of this book.

Third, cognitive constructs are producing useful applications in industry and education. Many cognitive psychologists aid in the design and assessment of communication systems, computers, and interfaces for complex transportation and industrial systems (Card et al., 1983; C.D. Wickens, 1984). Others aid in the design and assessment of educational and training programs (Glover & Bruning, 1990; Glover, Ronning, & Bruning, 1990; Mayer, 1987). If cognitive constructs did not capture something essential about human nature, they would not have such extensive application value.

Fourth, cognitive constructs provide hypotheses that guide exploration into the brain's physical structure. Knowledge about the brain's information processing abilities suggests the existence of corresponding neurological mechanisms that produce them. Currently, researchers in many areas are attempting to establish closer relations between cognitive and neurological mechanisms. Without guidance from a global analysis of information processing, exploration of the brain would be substantially less constrained and correspondingly more difficult. Because neuroscientists would have fewer ideas of mechanisms to look for in the brain, they might consider many incorrect hypotheses that cognitive theories would have ruled out as implausible. Conversely, findings from brain research are having increasing effects on cognitive theory, providing major constraints on the constructs of information processing. Because neurological findings constrain the cognitive mechanisms that are plausible, cognitive psychologists waste less time considering implausible mechanisms. This interplay between neurological and cognitive theory will probably become increasingly pronounced and mutually constraining as both areas develop.

Finally, cognitive constructs have had a widespread influence in other areas of the academic world besides cognitive psychology. Within psychology, cognitive constructs have found their way into most subdisciplines, including developmental, social, and clinical psychology (in developmental psychology, see Flavell, 1985; Siegler, 1986; in social psychology, see

Fiske & S.E. Taylor, 1991; in clinical psychology, see Beck, 1976; Mahoney, 1974; Meichenbaum, 1977). Outside psychology, cognitive constructs have also had widespread influence, with cognitive approaches developing in computer science, linguistics, philosophy, anthropology, and neuroscience (in computer science, see Newell & Simon, 1982; Schank & Abelson, 1977; Schank, 1982; in linguistics, see Chomsky, 1957, 1965, 1968; Lakoff, 1987; Langacker, 1987; in philosophy, see Bechtel & Abrahamsen, 1990; Dennet, 1978; J.A. Fodor, 1975; Thagard, 1988; in anthropology, see Dougherty, 1985; D. Holland & Quinn, 1987; Stigler, Shweder, & Herdt, 1990; in neuroscience, see Gallistel, 1990; Shallice, 1988; Squire, 1987). A cognitive revolution has indeed occurred during the last 30 years.

1.3 OVERVIEW

The remaining chapters address research in well–established areas of cognitive psychology. In each chapter, I discuss fundamental issues, empirical findings, and theoretical views. In the process, I review many behavioral findings of import and the cognitive constructs proposed to explain them.

Chapter 2 addresses people's ability to categorize entities in the environment. Of interest is how perceptual processes that extract information from the environment converge with expectations inferred from knowledge in memory to categorize a perceived object. Categories also figure centrally in other areas, including discussions of knowledge (**7**), semantics (**8**.6), speech perception (**9**.1), and induction (**10**.4). Chapter 3, on representation, further discusses the nature of cognitive constructs, focusing on the fundamental assumptions of representation that underlie them. I discuss representation after categorization, because categorization provides good examples of representation. Representation, in turn, will assist interpreting cognitive constructs in the remaining content areas. Chapter 4 on the control of information processing addresses various types of procedural knowledge, including mechanisms of automatic and strategic control. Automatic control of processing resurfaces at many later points, including discussions of concepts (**7**.2), lexical access (**9**.2), and automatized problem solving (**10**.6.3). Strategic control of processing also resurfaces frequently in memory encoding (**6**.1), memory retrieval (**6**.3), and thought (**10**).

Chapters 5, 6, and 7 address memory, in one form or another. Chapter 5 deals with the temporary storage of information in working memory. Various roles of working memory become important throughout the remaining chapters, especially in sentence processing (**9**.3), discourse processing (**9**.6), and thought (**10**). In Chapter 6, I discuss cognitive mechanisms that underlie the long–term retention of information. These mechanisms resurface repeatedly throughout later discussions of knowledge (**7**), language processing (**9**), and thought (**10**). Chapter 7 addresses human knowledge, and in particular the declarative knowledge that underlies concepts, categories, and conceptual systems. Here I introduce frames as the fundamental organizational unit of knowledge. Frames serve to organize later discussion of propositions (**8**.7.4, **8**.7.5), semantic strategies (**9**.3.3), sentence memory (**9**.5), discourse processing (**9**.6), and thought (**10**.1).

Language is taken up in chapters 8 and 9. Chapter 8 briefly reviews structural properties, largely from linguistics and philosophy, that are essential to understanding psychological work on language. Chapter 9 then reviews the wide variety of topics that cognitive psychologists have addressed in language processing, ranging from speech perception to lexical access to discourse processing. In chapter 10, I address various forms of human thought, including decision making, induction, deduction, and problem solving. Across these forms of thought, I illustrate the pervasiveness of non-formal mechanisms, especially similarity, availability, and framing. Finally, chapter 11 describes different approaches to cognitive psychology and their relations to one another.

The topic of learning receives extensive discussion throughout this book. Chapter 2 introduces the models and phenomena of category learning (**2**.3.1, **2**.3.2). Chapter 4 addresses the learning that produces automatic and strategic mechanisms of control (**4**.1.2, **4**.2.1, **4**.3). Chapter 5 describes the chunking of new information in working memory (**5**, **5**.2.4). Chapter 6 outlines the episodic learning that underlies long-term memory. Chapter 7 presents the knowledge that results from extensive experience and interaction with the environment. Chapters 8 and 9 sketch the acquisition of propositional information from discourse. Chapter 10 enumerates the many forms of learning that occur during induction (**10**.4) and problem solving (**10**.6).

Before proceeding to specific topics, I briefly note several important points about methodology. Cognitive psychologists are experimental psychologists, which means that they use scientific methods to draw conclusions about human nature. As I discuss in chapter 11, cognitive psychologists employ both descriptive and experimental methods to provide evidence for cognitive mechanisms. Descriptive methods measure systematic patterns in people's behavior and its environmental context (**11**.1). From observing human behavior in this manner, cognitive psychologists develop hypotheses about the underlying cognitive mechanisms that produce it. Experimental methods then serve to assess these hypotheses more rigorously (**11**.2). If researchers can control a proposed cognitive mechanism in the laboratory, confidence in its existence increases. A large well-developed literature describes the many methodological tools of the experimental psychologist (e.g., Kantowitz & Roediger, 1984; Robinson, 1981; Rosenthal & Rosnow, 1984).

As cognitive constructs accumulate empirical support, they play increasingly central roles in theory. As I discuss in chapter 11, cognitive psychologists often pursue two approaches to theory. First, they construct formal models of behavior using mathematical and logical languages (**11**.3). In these models, formalized versions of cognitive constructs play a central role in deriving empirical predictions, which are then tested in further research. Second, cognitive psychologists construct computational models of behavior using programming languages (**11**.4). These computer simulations attempt to reproduce the underlying cognitive processes that generate a particular behavior. To the extent that a simulation can perform the behavior the same way as a human, the cognitive constructs it implements gain credibility. Ideally, computationalists try to include only those mechanisms in their simulations that have received support from empirical research.

As we shall see, the interplay between data collection and theory development is often complex and takes many forms. Moreover, cognitive psychologists often disagree on the optimal approach for studying cognition. Such disagreement is not surprising, given that cognition is an incredibly complex topic and is still in its infancy as a science. Chapter 11 discusses methodology, theory, and approaches to cognitive psychology in greater detail. Readers who wish to learn more about these general topics before beginning the coverage of specific research areas in Chapter 2 may want to read chapter 11 before proceeding further.

2

CATEGORIZATION

People often take for granted cognitive abilities that seem simple but are actually amazingly sophisticated. The ability to categorize is one example. Upon walking into a home, people know instantly what is present. They recognize chairs, stereos, plants, dogs, friends, guacamole, wine, and just about everything else they happen to perceive. When people walk around outside, they recognize houses, cars, trees, dogs, mountains, birds, and clouds. When people interact, they recognize friends, facial expressions, actions, and activities. When people read, they categorize letters and words. Categorization occurs in all sensory modalities, not just vision. People categorize the sounds of animals and artifacts, as well as the sounds of speech; they categorize smells, tastes, skin sensations, and physical movements; and they categorize subjective experiences, including emotions and thoughts.

Categorization provides the gateway between perception and cognition. After a perceptual system acquires information about an entity in the environment, the cognitive system places the entity into a category. For example, an auditorally perceived entity might be categorized as the letter *b*, or a visually perceived entity might be categorized as a *chair*.[1] These categories are

---

[1] I use quotes to indicate linguistic forms and italics to indicate meaning. Whereas "dog" might represent the physical utterance of this word, *dog* represents the meaning that underlies it. My use of these markings is not entirely imprecise, as measured by linguistic conventions: Whereas a linguist might distinguish between an utterance of "dog," the written form of "dog," and the word for "dog," I use quotes to indicate all three. If I do intend a difference, it should be clear in the specific context. Similarly, whereas a linguist might distinguish between the semantic meaning of *dog* and conceptual knowledge of *dog*, I generally use italics in referring to both. Wherever I intend a difference, again it should be clear from the context. For a careful system of linguistic notation, see Lyons (1977a,b).

representations, because they are structures in the cognitive system that stand for perceived entities in the environment. For example, the category *p* is a representation in the cognitive system that stands for certain auditory stimuli; similarly, the category *chair* is a representation that stands for certain visual and tactile stimuli. As we shall see in chapter 3, the actual form of a representation in the brain need not look anything like its referent or linguistic label. For example, the brain represents *chair* with brain states defined over large populations of neurons, not with brain entities that literally look like a physical chair or the linguistic label "chair." Nevertheless, these brain states are representations in the sense that they stand for their referents in the environment and can be manipulated by cognitive mechanisms that reason about the environment. In chapter 3, I further discuss the relations between representations in the brain and their corresponding entities in the environment.

The representations assigned to entities during categorization play central roles in subsequent cognitive processing: They may be stored in memory. They may be combined with other representations. They may be transformed into new representations. They may trigger cognitive processes, such as the intention to achieve a goal. In general, many cognitive psychologists assume that the representations assigned during categorization constitute the fundamental units of cognitive processing. As we shall see in subsequent chapters, most cognitive processes begin with some form of categorization.

People typically perform categorizations effortlessly and unconsciously. Although a tremendous amount of cognitive processing underlies categorization, we are rarely aware of it. Instead, we simply know the outcome of this processing, namely, the categories of entities present in the current environment. Because categorizations typically occur effortlessly and unconsciously, the cognitive mechanisms producing them might seem simple and obvious. If these mechanisms were straightforward, a modest amount of scientific investigation would yield a satisfactory understanding of them. But after years of study, cognitive psychologists have gained more of an appreciation for the human categorization ability than an understanding of it.

A barometer of how well cognitive psychologists understand an intelligent ability is their proficiency at simulating it in artificial systems (11.4). If a cognitive theory provides an accurate, coherent, and complete account of an ability, then cognitive psychologists and other cognitive scientists (e.g., computer scientists, linguists, philosophers) should be able to use this theory as a blueprint to build an artificial system that performs this ability as humans perform it. Yet, the categorization abilities of current artificial systems do not begin to approximate this ability in humans or, for that matter, other species of the animal kingdom. Although a complete understanding of human categorization remains distant, cognitive psychologists have nevertheless made progress. They have identified important characteristics of this ability in humans, they have established a general framework from which more successful work may develop, and most importantly, they have developed a sense of what it is about categorization that has made understanding it so difficult.

2.1 THE ENVIRONMENT

The natural place to begin an analysis of categorization is with the question: What is it that organisms categorize? Because organisms have evolved in particular environments over millions of years, their categorization abilities have become tailored to these environments. Analyzing the entities that an organism has evolved to categorize might provide hints about its cognitive mechanisms that perform categorization.

One approach to this problem is to examine the sensory modalities on which a species makes categorizations. For example, humans classify visual, auditory, tactile, gustatory, olfactory, and proprioceptive information. Having identified a species' perceptual modalities, we can begin careful analyses of the physical stimuli that impinge on each, identifying the physical properties that determine perception. Because physical properties such as shape, size, texture, and wavelength determine the perception of visual stimuli, developing accounts of these physical properties is relevant to psychological theory. Using these analyses, for example, researchers can develop hypotheses about the roles of physical properties in categorization. We shall see one example of this approach shortly in Gibson's ecological analysis of vision.

An alternative approach is to consider the ontological categories that constitute the physical world, until recently mostly a philosophical endeavor (Bechtel, 1988a; Keil, 1979; Sommers, 1959, 1963). Ontological categories constitute the fundamentally different kinds of things in existence. Depending on the particular ontological analysis, ontological categories might include *locations, times, actions, animals, plants, artifacts,* and *thoughts.* Sometimes researchers examine even more specific types of categories, such as *speech sounds,* because their analysis is central to understanding an important phenomenon (e.g., language comprehension). Upon selecting a type of category for study, researchers analyze the relevant entities, developing hypotheses about the roles of their physical properties in categorization. We shall see two examples of this approach in analyses of speech sounds and artifact categories.

Ecological optics.   The theorist who most strongly emphasized study of the environment was James Gibson. In his *ecological optics,* Gibson (1950, 1966) performed careful analyses of the visual and tactile information available to organisms in the environment. In vision, for example, he catalogued the types of entities, surfaces, textures, and movements normally present. He then analyzed the patterns of light reflecting off of these various entities to identify the *ecological invariants* that determine these entities' perceived properties. Consider, for example, the size of the two high-rise buildings and the radio antenna in Fig. 2.1. Which of the three is tallest? People generally perceive the antenna as tallest and the buildings as equal in height. Researchers have shown that *horizon ratio* is central to these judgments. If two entities are of the same height, then the proportion of each that lies above the horizon will be constant at all points on a flat terrain. For example, the two buildings appear equally tall from all points, because the proportion above the horizon remains constant for both. In contrast, a much larger proportion of the radio antenna always lies above the horizon, thereby indicating its greater height. As this example illustrates, the horizon ratio is an ecological invariant that determines the perceived height of an entity, relative to other entities in the visual field.

Such analyses are physical, not psychological, because they simply characterize the ecological invariants that are available to organisms and the conclusions that they allow. For example, the horizon ratio is available to organisms and specifies the relative height of entities. However, these analyses do not specify how organisms process this information. In fact, Gibson was strongly opposed to considering cognitive mechanisms at all. He believed that cognitive mechanisms had received premature and excessive attention and that theorists, by failing to perform environmental analyses first, had gone astray. Moreover, Gibson believed that analyses of cognitive mechanisms were unnecessary. Instead, he argued that specifying the ecological invariants associated with environmental entities would be sufficient to explain the categorization of their properties (e.g., an object's relative height). Because organisms have evolved to detect these invariants, he believed, psychologists simply needed to discover them and the conclusions they afford.

Gibson's emphasis on the environment has had substantial impact on cognitive science (**11**.1). Researchers have begun performing much more extensive and careful analyses of environments, and their theories have focused increasingly on the role that invariant patterns of physical information play in categorization. However, only Gibson's most ardent followers still share his antipathy for cognitive explanations. Most theorists now believe that accounting for *how* organisms represent and process these patterns of physical information is essential. Otherwise, a theory of categorization is incomplete.

Speech. The sounds of speech constitute a specific type of category whose physical properties have received careful analysis. Linguists have been extremely successful at characterizing the properties of speech sounds in terms of the motor movements in the vocal tract that produce them (**8**.2).

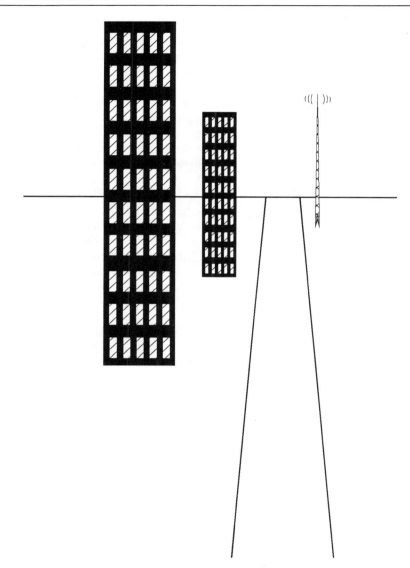

Figure 2.1. An example of the horizon ratio invariant.

Consider the speech sound [b], which has the properties of being a *stop*, *bilabial*, and *voiced*.[2] *Stop* refers to the complete blockage of air through the

---

[2] Following standard linguistic notation, the brackets in [b] represent the sound of this letter produced by a person's vocal tract, as opposed to its other possible properties, such as visual form, linguistic meaning, and so forth. (**8**.2, **8**.3).

vocal tract at some point during articulation of the sound; *bilabial* refers to the air blockage that results from pressing the upper and lower lips together; and *voiced* refers to the vocal chords vibrating at some point during the sound. Using articulatory features like these, linguists have described the sounds of particular languages quite successfully.

Engineers and psychologists have also performed careful analyses of speech categories. Instead of describing how the vocal tract produces a speech sound, engineers and psychologists attempt to describe a speech sound's acoustic properties. To see this, consider the speech spectrogram in Fig. 2.2. A speech spectrogram represents the pitches that compose a speech sound, along with their amplitudes, over time. As can be seen in Fig. 2.2, the pronunciation of "bab" produces four bands of pitch—or *formants*—with the lowest formant at about 500 Hz and the highest at about 3000 Hz. Because the lower two formants are darker than the upper two, the lower formants are louder. As can be seen from comparing the spectrograms for "bab," "dad," and "gag" in Fig. 2.2, the acoustic properties of different words vary. As discussed further in section **9**.1.2, engineers and psychologists have identified various patterns in spectrograms that correspond to the perceived characteristics of speech.

One might think that psychologists, armed with these highly detailed accounts of speech sounds from linguistics and engineering, should be able to explain how people categorize them. Moreover, one might think that engineers should be able to implement these analyses in artificial categorization devices. Yet, psychologists are far from having a satisfactory theory of speech categorization, and engineers' attempts to build speech categorization sys-

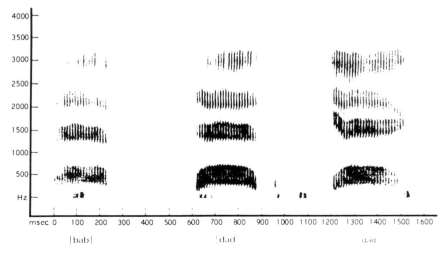

Figure 2.2. Examples of speech spectrograms from Ladefoged (1975), reproduced by permission.

tems have met with limited success. Although we have excellent tools for describing speech sounds, we have acquired only a limited understanding of the psychological mechanisms that categorize them.

Extensive analyses of spectrograms have provided insight into why a satisfactory understanding of speech categorization has been so elusive. Imagine that engineers construct a spectrogram for each of the [d] speech sounds that two speakers utter during a conversation. Not only would none of these spectrograms be identical, they would differ substantially in their acoustic properties. It turns out that the acoustic properties of a speech sound are heavily influenced by the speech sounds that precede and follow it. The vocal tract adapts each speech sound so that it follows easily from previous speech sounds and facilitates those that follow (9.1.2). Given the wide variety of contexts in which a given speech sound can occur, the forms it takes are legion. Consider the simplified spectrograms for [d] shown in Fig. 2.3. The acoustic properties of [d] vary widely, depending on the vowel that follows it. The variability in Fig. 2.3 only represents the beginning of the variability problem. The acoustic properties of a given speech sound also vary substantially both between speakers (across sex, age, and dialect) and within speakers (across deliveries, from whispering to talking to yelling). Taken together, the

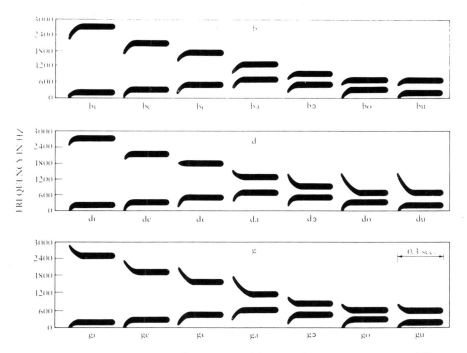

Figure 2.3. Examples of how the first and second formants for a consonant vary in different vowel contexts. From Delattre, Liberman, and F.S. Cooper (1955), reproduced by permission.

variety of forms that a speech sound can take make the attempt to explain their categorization a humbling experience.

One way that speech theorists have tried to tackle this problem is to find acoustic invariants associated with a given speech sound (9.1.3). Even though instances of a particular sound may differ widely in their properties, perhaps there are a few properties that occur for all instances and facilitate their classification. Identifying such invariants is similar to what Gibson had in mind for visual perception. The problem is that quite often a category simply has no invariants—no single property occurs for all category members.

Even if we could identify the properties that signal each speech sound category, we would still need to explain how people process these properties during categorization. To account for speech categorization, a theory must explain how cognitive mechanisms identify key properties in the speech signal and how they use this information to access categories. Having an account of the physical domain is not sufficient. Without an additional account of the cognitive mechanisms that process physical information, a theory of speech categorization is incomplete, and an artificial system that categorizes speech sounds cannot be built (for a recent collection of articles in this area, see Harnad, 1987).

Artifact categories.   Analyses of artifact categories have further empha-sized the point that categories are rarely neat and tidy. The philosopher Wittgenstein (1953) was the first to point this out with his classic analysis of the category *game*. He argued that finding definitional characteristics of *game* is impossible, and no one has yet shown him wrong. No property appears true of all games. Different games take a wide variety of forms, with this variety being loosely organized in what Wittgenstein termed a "family resemblance." Each game shares properties with some other games but not with all. More recently, investigators have observed a similar phenomenon in other artifact categories such as *vehicle, furniture, clothing*, and *tool* (Hampton, 1979; Rosch & Mervis, 1975). Rather than having clear-cut definitions, these categories contain exemplars that are only related by loose organizations of shared properties.

In summary, the tremendous variety of exemplars that instantiate a cate-gory, coupled with their lack of defining properties, would seem to make categorization difficult. Yet humans categorize effortlessly and accurately. A central challenge for categorization research is to specify the cognitive mech-anisms that enable humans to classify non-optimal categories so successfully.

2.2 CONTRIBUTIONS OF THE ORGANISM

Organisms are often born knowing categories relevant to their ecological niche (Eibl-Eibesfeldt, 1972; Grier, 1984). Certain rodents, for example, are born knowing how to categorize shadows of predatory birds flying above them. If rodents had to learn this category, they probably would not survive long enough to do so. Rather than building up knowledge of these categories through experience, organisms have such knowledge built in from birth. Categories of facial expressions, such as smiles, frowns, anger, and fear, are likely candidates for innate categories in humans (Eckman, 1982; Eckman & Oster, 1979). Although such categories are often largely innate, no category in any organism is completely innate. Instead, experience with the environment shapes all innate categories, with some innate categories being more malleable than others (4.1.1).

Some of the most important innate categories are those for the primitive perceptual properties that constitute complex stimulus configurations. For example, a chair is a complex configuration of simpler properties, such as a back, seat, arms, and legs. Moreover, each part of a chair is a smaller but nevertheless complex configuration of geometric solids, planes, and lines. At some level of analysis, certain primitive properties provide the elemental pieces of perception. For example, the primitive properties of vision might include lines, planes, and solids, whereas the primitive properties of audition might include pitch and loudness.

Psychologists typically assume that humans have innate detectors for categorizing the primitive properties of perception, whatever they might be. The Nobel Prize-winning work of Hubel and Wiesel (1959, 1962) provided strong evidence for innate mechanisms that categorize primitive properties in vision. These researchers inserted electrodes into the visual cortexes of animals and found that particular neurons only responded to certain visual properties. Some neurons responded to horizontal lines, others to vertical lines, others to dots. Some fired when their eliciting property was at a particular retinal location; others were location–independent. Still other neurons responded to particular movements of these visual properties, such as left–to–right translation. Later studies found that the behavior of these neurons does not result from learning but primarily reflects genetic origins. These findings have had a major impact on theories of categorization for the past 30 years.

Humans appear to have many innate property detection systems. In vision, these include systems for categorizing basic sensory dimensions (color and brightness), global shapes (low spatial frequency), details (high spatial frequency), simple solids (geons; Biederman, 1987), and complex information about textures and layouts (Gibson, 1950, 1966). The human auditory system has innate detection systems for loudness and pitch. The gustatory system has innate detection systems for sweetness, saltiness, sourness, and bitterness. The detection systems for touch and smell are not as well understood, but they are undoubtedly innate to an important extent. Much is known about these perceptual abilities. In fact, perception is arguably the best-developed domain of experimental psychology (Atkinson et al., 1988a; Boff et al., 1986; Bruce & P. Green, 1990; E.B. Goldstein, 1989; Sekular & Blake, 1990). Although this work is extremely relevant to cognitive psychology, and indeed is part of cognitive psychology, I will not address it further.

Structural Descriptions. Upon encountering an entity, a perceptual system provides information about the entity's primitive perceptual properties. Such output is *not* just a simple property list. If the output for a visually presented *t* were simply *horizontal line* and *vertical line*, the visual system would not be able to discriminate between *t*, +, and other configurations of these two properties. Consequently, perceptual systems must produce structural descriptions that specify, not only properties, but also the relations between properties (Palmer, 1975b). Specifying that the midpoint of a horizontal bar intersects a vertical bar in its upper half uniquely specifies the letter *t*. Structural descriptions are essentially instantiated frames, as I discuss later in 7.2.2 and 8.7.4.

People rarely perceive entities in isolation. Instead, entities are almost always perceived in contexts. Visually perceived chairs often occur in rooms that offer tremendous amounts of additional visual information or "clutter," including walls, people, and other furniture. Similarly, spoken language is often perceived against a background of other sounds including machinery, traffic, weather, human movement, and other conversations. These backgrounds create serious problems in forming structural descriptions. In an entire array of detected properties, which properties belong to one structural description, and which belong to another? Where do the visual properties forming a chair begin and end relative to a sofa and a wall behind it? Although human perceptual systems rarely err in forming these groupings, artificial categorization systems have serious problems, indicating that scientific theories of grouping are far from satisfactory (P.H. Winston, 1975). Numerous experiments have shown that the human brain imposes powerful forms of organization upon perceptual properties (Koffka, 1935). For example, the brain tends to group together properties that are close in proximity to one another, that form a continuous path, or that form a closed boundary. Although psychologists have frequently documented these robust organizational tendencies in perceptual behavior, they have experienced only modest success in specifying the mechanisms that underlie them (e.g., Egeth, Virzi, & Garbart, 1984; Treisman, 1982; Treisman & Gelade, 1980). However, most theorists believe, given the consistency of organizational tendencies across individuals, that these mechanisms must have a strong innate basis.

Although an incomplete understanding of perceptual primitives and structural descriptions greatly limits current theories of categorization, sufficient evidence exists to convince most theorists that innate perceptual detectors exist and that they form the basis of more complex categorizations. However, accounts of the information that these innate detectors provide are far from complete. Similarly, accounts of structural descriptions and the innate mechanisms that construct them remain sketchy. To the extent that theories do not explain the extraction and organization of information relevant to categorization, they fail to account for fundamental aspects of this ability.

2.3 CATEGORY REPRESENTATION AND PROCESSING

At least in advanced organisms, most categories are learned. People are not born knowing how to classify different kinds of objects, animals, and events. Instead, children spend much time learning categories during early development and refining this knowledge during later development (Carey, 1985; Keil, 1989; Markman, 1989). Consequently, another important contribution of the organism is its ability to acquire categories. This section addresses how people establish category knowledge in memory and use it during categorization.

As Fig. 2.4 illustrates, the first step in categorizing an entity is to form a structural description of it (2.2). The second step is to search memory for category representations similar to the structural description. If the entity is a chair, for example, representations for *chair, sofa, stool,* and *table* might all receive consideration, given their perceptual similarity. Third, a decision procedure selects the category representation best suited for classifying the entity, in this case the representation for *chair.* Fourth, relevant inferences about the entity are drawn from category knowledge. Because the entity is a chair, for example, the perceiver infers it can be sat upon. It is important to note that the primary purpose of making categorizations is to support inferences relevant to the perceiver's goals: Categorization is usually not an end in itself (7.2.1; Barsalou, 1990a). Finally, information about the categorization is stored in memory to update the category representation. Later categorizations may benefit from this memory, and memories of enough categorizations may eventually lead to expert classification performance.

2.3.1 Models of Categorization

Much recent work on categorization has addressed the search and selection stages of categorization in Fig. 2.4. Theorists have proposed a wide variety of categorization models to explain these stages, including exemplar models, prototype models, classical models, and mixed models (Medin & E.E. Smith, 1984; Mervis & Rosch, 1981; Oden, 1987; E.E. Smith & Medin, 1981). As we shall see, each type of model makes different assumptions about the representation of categories in memory and about the processes that operate on these representations to produce categorizations. In this section, I present the

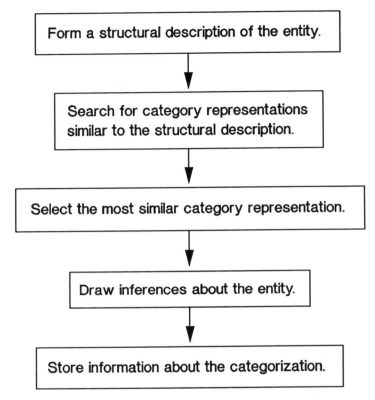

Figure 2.4.   A flow chart for processing during categorization.

basic assumptions that underlie these models. In section **2.3.2**, I present detailed examples of how they explain basic categorization phenomena.

Exemplar models.   One possible way to represent a category is with memories of its specific exemplars. According to this view, people represent a category with memories of exemplars that they encounter in daily experience (Brooks, 1978, 1987; Estes, 1986; Hintzman, 1986, 1988; Jacoby & Brooks, 1984; Medin & Schaffer, 1978; Nosofsky, 1984). For instance, the category of *bachelor* might be represented with memories of specific bachelors one has known. According to the exemplar view, people do *not* abstract generalizations from exemplar memories to form abstract category knowledge. For example, people do not abstract the generalization, *unmarried adult human male*, to represent *bachelor*. Instead, people's representation of *bachelor* is simply a loose collection of exemplar memories, each associated to the category name.

The exemplar view further proposes that exemplar memories are central to the categorization of unknown entities. To categorize an entity, the cognitive system attempts to find the exemplar memory that is most similar to the entity. Most theories assume that the cognitive system uses *parallel search* to find the most similar exemplar in memory, with this search proceeding automatically and unconsciously. Specifically, the cognitive system compares the structural description of the unknown entity to all exemplar memories across all categories simultaneously—not one after another, as would occur in *serial search*. Upon finding the most similar exemplar memory, the cognitive system assigns the category associated with it to the unknown entity. For example, if a perceiver is trying to classify something whose structural description is most similar to the memory of a previously experienced bachelor, then the perceiver classifies the unknown entity as a *bachelor*. The essential assumption is that categorization is most likely to be correct when a perceiver assigns an entity to the category having the most similar exemplar.

Actually, an infinite variety of exemplar models exists. Rather than basing categorization on the single most similar exemplar in memory, the cognitive system could use other decision rules. For instance, the category whose exemplar memories are most similar *on the average* could be assigned to the unknown entity. Or the category with the *highest number* of similar exemplars could be assigned. Moreover, if exemplar memories are increasingly forgotten with the passage of time, specific exemplar memories may have decreasing effects on categorization as their accessibility decreases.

The primary advantage of exemplar models is their ability to account for people's acquisition of poorly specified categories, such as the speech sound and artifact categories discussed earlier (**2**.1). Exemplar models can learn categories that exhibit tremendous variety and that do not have clear definitions. Exemplar models learn these categories by simply storing enough exemplars so that any subsequently encountered exemplar is more similar to exemplars of the correct category than to exemplars of incorrect categories. Similarity to exemplar memories provides a simple yet powerful categorization mechanism. Knowing an abstract rule for the category is not necessary for successful categorization performance.

One possible problem with the exemplar view is its assumption that the cognitive system stores a tremendous amount of idiosyncratic exemplar information for categories. Perhaps human memory is incapable of storing so much information. Nevertheless, many theories of memory assume that people store immense amounts of information and that none of it is ever forgotten (**6**.2.2). Moreover, no one has yet observed a limit on people's ability to acquire new information. Even when the older exemplars of a category are forgotten, exemplar models can still work well using recently encountered exemplars. As long as remembered exemplars are sufficiently similar to later category members, categorization proceeds smoothly. Researchers have even shown that exemplars affect categorization when people claim not to remember them (Jacoby & Brooks, 1984; T.O. Nelson, 1971, 1978; Squire & Butters, 1984).

A more serious problem with exemplar models is that people clearly know numerous abstractions about categories that they induce from exemplars. Exemplar models have little to say about the formation of these abstractions, their content, or their use. The next two types of categorization models are much more oriented toward abstraction.

Prototype models.   Rather than representing categories with exemplar memories, prototype models represent categories with prototypes. A prototype is a single, centralized, category representation. According to most prototype models, the cognitive system abstracts properties that are representative of a category's exemplars and integrates them into a category prototype (Barsalou, 1990b; Elio & J.R. Anderson, 1981; B. Hayes-Roth & F. Hayes-Roth, 1977; Homa, 1984; Posner & Keele, 1968; Reed, 1972; Reitman & Bower, 1973). Most models assume that the extraction and integration of prototypical information occurs automatically and unconsciously.

Prototypes can include many kinds of information, including averages of particular dimensions across exemplars (e.g., the average *height* and *weight* of *dogs*) or the most frequent properties across exemplars (e.g., *brown* as the most frequent color of *dogs*). Moreover, if prototypes are viewed as structural descriptions, then they can include average or frequent relations. For example, the prototype for the letter *t* could include the average vertical placement of the horizontal bar. Similarly, the prototype for *bird* could include a correlation between *small* and *sings*, given that small birds typically sing. Prototypes can also include information about the distribution of properties. If *brown*, *black*, and *white* all occur frequently for *dogs*, then the prototype might include information about all of them, as well as their relative frequencies. In all cases, prototypes contain centralized category information that has been abstracted from exemplars, rather than memories of specific exemplars.

According to prototype models, the categorization of an unknown entity proceeds as follows. First, the cognitive system compares the entity's structural description to the prototype associated with each possible category. Upon finding the prototype that is most similar to the structural description, the cognitive system assigns the prototype's category to the corresponding entity. As with exemplar models, the essential assumption of prototype models is that maximizing similarity—in this case between an unclassified entity and a prototype—optimizes classification accuracy. Also as with exemplar models, prototype models can learn poorly specified categories. Prototype models work well for categories whose exemplars vary widely and have nothing in common. If all members of a category are more similar to its prototype than to the prototypes of other categories, then all members will be categorized correctly. All members of a category can be similar to a prototype without any particular properties defining membership.

One problem with some prototype models is that they fail to store information about specific exemplars. People often appear to remember exemplars, indicating that *abstract* prototypes do not provide a full account of category knowledge. However, other prototype models store both exemplar-level information and abstract information about categories and do not have this problem (Barsalou, 1990b). Another problem for prototype models is that they often fail to specify constraints on the abstraction process (see Goodman, 1955). In principle, the cognitive system could abstract an infinite number of properties for a given category. Consequently, prototype models must place principled constraints on abstraction, such that they abstract only those properties relevant to goals of the cognitive system (7.3.1, **10**.2.3, **10**.4.1).

Classical models. According to the classical view of categories in philosophy and linguistics, rules underlie categorization. Although rules can take a variety of forms, the ideal rule specifies properties that are individually necessary and jointly sufficient for category membership (Katz, 1972; E.E. Smith & Medin, 1981). A property is necessary for membership, if all category members must have it. A set of properties is jointly sufficient for membership, if any entity having them belongs to the category. For example, the properties *human, male, adult,* and *unmarried* are individually necessary and jointly sufficient for membership in *bachelor.* Many other rules are possible. For example, some rules contain disjunctions of individually sufficient properties, none of which is necessary. Consider the category of *strike* in baseball. One independently sufficient condition for strike is: *the ball goes through the strike zone.* Another independently sufficient condition is: *the batter swings and misses.* Still another is: *the batter swings and fouls.* If any of these properties is true, the pitch is a *strike,* even though none is necessary. Rules can be even more complicated. For example, the biconditional rule states that an entity belongs to a category either if it has two criterial properties or it has neither. Consider the category of *gay relationship.* A romantic relationship is gay if either *both partners are male* or *both partners are not male.*

Whereas similarity underlies categorization in exemplar and prototype models, it has nothing to do with categorization in classical models. In classical models, an entity belongs to a category only if it strictly satisfies the category's rule. Either the entity satisfies the rule, or it does not. An entity cannot be a category member if it is similar to a rule but must match the rule perfectly. Unlike prototype and exemplar models, no partial satisfaction can occur. Instead, category membership in classical models is all-or-none. All exemplars are equivalent in membership, because all exemplars strictly and equally satisfy their category's definitional rule.

Much research has found, however, that exemplars vary continuously in how well they match their category prototype, a phenomenon researchers often refer to as *graded structure, typicality,* or *goodness of exemplar* (**2**.3.2, **7**.3.2). Whereas some exemplars are highly similar to the prototype, others are only moderately similar, and still others are somewhat dissimilar. For example, *chair* is similar to the prototype of *furniture,* but *painting* and *refrigerator* are less similar. When exemplars are highly similar to the prototype, their membership is relatively certain, but as exemplars' similarity to the prototype decreases, their membership may become increasingly uncertain (Hampton, 1979; McCloskey & Glucksberg, 1978). Nevertheless, weak similarity to a prototype is often enough for category membership; a strict match is not necessary. The pervasiveness of graded structure in natural categories has raised serious doubts about the viability of classical models as accounts of human categorization (E.E. Smith & Medin, 1981).

Another serious problem for classical models is that many categories do not have clear definitions. As we saw earlier (**2**.1), many speech and artifact categories do not have properties that are either necessary or sufficient for category membership (**2**.1). Consequently, classical models are not as widely applicable as exemplar and prototype models. Even when categories do have definitions, prototypes often seem more important than rules. Consider *bachelor.* People hesitate to include monks and gay males in *bachelor,* even though these exemplars fit its necessary and sufficient conditions. Because monks and gay males are not similar to the prototypical *bachelor,* they do not seem to belong in the category, even though technically they do.

Rules may be important primarily when payoffs for correct categorizations are high. When you meet someone at a singles bar who matches the prototypical *bachelor,* you may classify him as such, if the costs for making a mistake are low. On the other hand, a tax collector would never use the prototype for *bachelor* to classify someone during an audit. Because being married carries important financial implications, a tax collector must adhere strictly to the rule for *bachelor* when classifying tax payers.

Mixed models.   Researchers have performed numerous experiments to assess exemplar, prototype, and classical models. Across this large body of research, evidence can be found for the use of exemplars, prototypes, and rules in categorization. Categories often appear to have multiple representations, each of which operates in certain settings. Consider *bachelor.* You can remember specific bachelors you have met, and these memories may help classify similar people by analogy at later times. You know prototypical properties of bachelors that may be useful in reasoning about them following categorization (**7**.2.1). You know the rule for *bachelor* and can use it to minimize errors when correct categorization is important.

This variety of possible category representations further increases the difficulty of studying categorization. Because people represent categories in so many different ways, identifying the conditions surrounding each type of representation is complicated. Moreover, it is often difficult, if not impossible, to determine empirically whether people use exemplars, prototypes, or rules to represent categories. Because many different processing assumptions can accompany each type of representation, a wide variety of models exists, and theorists can construct exemplar and prototype models that account equally well for observed data (Barsalou, 1990b). Category representations receive further discussion throughout the remainder of this book, especially in chapters 3, 7, 8, 9, and 10.

2.3.2 Basic Categorization Phenomena

Over the course of a lifetime, a person develops extensive knowledge of natural categories, such as facts about *cats*, *houses*, and *cars*, along with numerous memories of their exemplars. Moreover, different people acquire different knowledge and memories for a given category from their idiosyncratic experiences with it. As a result, researchers typically don't know what knowledge particular people have for a category, nor how they have organized it. As we shall see throughout this book (and especially in Chapter 7), researchers have developed methods for estimating a person's knowledge at a given point in time. To establish high degrees of control over category knowledge, however, researchers often teach people simple artificial categories in the laboratory and then study their use in categorization. Because all learning of these categories occurs in the laboratory, an experimenter completely determines the knowledge that subjects acquire. In this way, researchers can study basic categorization phenomena without having to worry about other aspects that vary between subjects or that are irrelevant to the hypotheses being tested. The subsequent generalization of findings from controlled laboratory settings to the real world is indeed important, but researchers have typically found that phenomena in artificial categories occur in natural categories as well (Medin & E.E. Smith, 1984; Mervis & Rosch, 1981; Oden, 1987; E.E. Smith & Medin, 1981). Consequently, artificial categories provide a powerful scientific tool for exploring basic categorization phenomena observed initially in natural categories.

To get a feel for this type of research, consider two artificial disease categories: *plurosis* and *multinomia*. Figure 2.5 presents 12 imaginary patients (i.e., training exemplars) who have these two imaginary diseases. Each patient has three symptoms: a *skin* condition, an *eye* condition, and a *breathing* condition. For example, patient K.I., who has *plurosis*, exhibits *skin rash*, *dry eyes*, and *shallow breathing*. As can be seen from examining the training exemplars in Fig. 2.5, the prototype for *plurosis* is *skin rash*, *dry eyes*, and *rapid breathing*, because these symptoms occur most frequently across the patients

PLUROSIS				MULTINOMIA			
PATIENT	**SKIN**	**EYES**	**BREATHING**	**PATIENT**	**SKIN**	**EYES**	**BREATHING**
			Training exemplars				
K.I.	rash	dry	shallow	**E.W.**	scaly	puffy	shallow
S.J.	rash	red	rapid	**R.M.**	scaly	sunken	labored
W.A.	sores	dry	rapid	**D.T.**	oily	puffy	labored
G.N.	rash	sunken	uneven	**W.P.**	scaly	cloudy	uneven
P.F.	spots	dry	wheezing	**A.R.**	sores	puffy	wheezing
R.R.	oily	cloudy	rapid	**N.D.**	spots	red	labored
			Tests for a graded structure effect				
P-HIGH	rash	dry	rapid	**M-HIGH**	scaly	puffy	labored
P-MEDIUM	rash	dry	uneven	**M-MEDIUM**	scaly	puffy	uneven
P-LOW	spots	sunken	rapid	**M-LOW**	spots	sunken	labored
K.I.	rash	dry	shallow	**E.W.**	scaly	puffy	shallow
			Tests for an exemplar effect				
P.F.'	spots	-	wheezing	**A.R.'**	sores	-	wheezing
P-NONE	sores	-	uneven	**M-NONE**	oily	-	uneven
			Tests for attribute weighting				
P-SKIN	rash	-	-	**M-SKIN**	scaly	-	-
P-EYES	-	dry	-	**M-EYES**	-	puffy	-
P-BREATH	-	-	rapid	**M-BREATH**	-	-	labored

Figure 2.5. Artificial categories that demonstrate graded structure effects, exemplar effects, and attribute weighting.

having this disease. Similarly, the prototype for *multinomia* is *scaly skin, puffy eyes*, and *labored breathing*. Some patients closely approximate their respective prototype (e.g., K.I. for *plurosis*, E.W. for *multinomia*); other patients are less typical (e.g., R.R. for *plurosis*, N.D. for *multinomia*).

A standard categorization experiment contains a *training phase* followed by a *test phase*. Consider an experiment in which subjects learn about *plurosis* and *multinomia*. In the training phase, subjects receive the descriptions of the 12 training exemplars in random order. For example, subjects might receive A.R. first, then P.F, then K.I, then R.M., and so forth. As subjects receive each patient's description, they decide whether the patient has *plurosis* or *multinomia*, and the experimenter provides feedback about the correctness of their diagnosis. For the first few patients, subjects must guess, because they have no prior knowledge about these imaginary diseases, but as they store information about the first few patients, they begin to learn how to categorize later patients correctly. Subjects usually perform the training phase for several cycles until they can categorize most or all of the patients without error.

Having learned the categories in the training phase, subjects then perform the test phase of the experiment. In the test phase, the experimenter presents additional patient descriptions, and subjects attempt to diagnose these patients. Unlike the training phase, however, the experimenter usually does not provide feedback about the correctness of subjects' diagnoses. Instead of trying to increase subjects' learning through additional feedback, the experimenter attempts to test hypotheses about the cognitive mechanisms that underlie categorization performance.

Graded structure.   No other categorization phenomenon is more widespread or fundamental than graded structure (Barsalou, 1985, 1987; Homa, 1984; Posner & Keele, 1968; Rosch & Mervis, 1975; E.E. Smith & Medin, 1981). Every category exhibits graded structure, and no other variable goes as far in accounting for categorization performance (7.3.2). Graded structure results from exemplars varying in how representative they are of their category (2.3.1). Some exemplars are highly representative, providing much information about most category members. For example, *robin* provides much information about what most *birds* are like. In contrast, other exemplars provide much less information—and in a sense are misleading—about most category members. *Ostrich*, for example, does not provide representative information about most *birds*.

Many experiments build graded structure into artificial categories and observe its effects on categorization performance. Consider the tests for a graded structure effect in Fig. 2.5. P-HIGH is the most representative exemplar of *plurosis* possible, because all three of its characteristics occur frequently across the training exemplars (*rash, dry, rapid*). In contrast, P-MEDIUM is less representative, because only two of its symptoms occur frequently across the training exemplars (*rash, dry*), with one symptom occurring infrequently (*uneven*). P-LOW is still less representative, because only one of its symptoms occurs frequently across the training exemplars (*rapid*), with two symptoms occurring infrequently (*spots, sunken*). Similarly, M-HIGH, M-MEDIUM, and M-LOW decrease in representativeness for *multinomia*. Note that subjects would not receive any of these test exemplars during the training phase of the experiment but would see them for the first time during the test phase.

Many experiments have found that subjects classify test exemplars less accurately, less confidently, and less rapidly as their representativeness decreases. For example, subjects would categorize P-HIGH better than P-MEDIUM, which they would categorize better than P-LOW. This decrease in categorization efficiency illustrates the graded structure effect so pervasive in human categorization. Furthermore, if subjects received a training exemplar such as K.I. in the test phase, they probably would not categorize it as efficiently as P-HIGH, which they have never seen before!

These findings suggest that subjects learn prototypes for the categories during training and use them subsequently to categorize test items. Prototype acquisition explains the graded structure effect, and it explains why subjects may classify an exemplar not seen previously better than they classify an exemplar seen previously. In each case, the ease of classifying an exemplar—regardless of whether it was seen in training or not—increases as it approximates more closely the prototype acquired during the training phase. Consider how well each of the test exemplars for *plurosis* matches the prototype acquired for this disease: *skin rash*, *dry eyes*, and *rapid breathing*. P-HIGH matches the prototype perfectly on all three symptoms and is therefore categorized most efficiently. P-MEDIUM matches the acquired prototype on two symptoms and is classified less efficiently. P-LOW only matches the acquired prototype on one symptom and is classified least efficiently of all. K.I. matches the acquired prototype on two symptoms and is therefore classified worse than P-HIGH, even though subjects saw K.I. in the training phase but not P-HIGH. As these examples illustrate, the degree of match between a test exemplar and a prototype provides a natural account of graded structure effects.

Exemplar effects.   The standard results for graded structure suggest that subjects do not use exemplar memories in categorization. If subjects did, then they should classify exemplars seen previously better than they classify exemplars not seen previously. It is hard to imagine how exemplar memories could underlie categorization, if subjects categorize an exemplar not having a memory better than an exemplar having one.

However, theorists have developed ingenious exemplar models that explain graded structure effects (Brooks, 1978, 1987; Estes, 1986; Hintzman, 1986; Jacoby & Brooks, 1984; Medin & Schaffer, 1978; Nosofsky, 1984). These models assume that subjects compute the overall similarity of the test exemplar to all of the exemplars in each category and assign the category whose overall similarity is highest. Imagine subjects trying to categorize P-HIGH in the test phase. According to these exemplar models, subjects would compute the similarity of P-HIGH to memories for all six training exemplars of *plurosis* and to all six training exemplars of *multinomia*. As can be seen from examining Fig. 2.5, P–HIGH is more similar to the six exemplars of *plurosis* than to the six exemplars of *multinomia*. Specifically, P–HIGH shares two symptoms each with K.I., S.J., and W.A., and it shares one symptom each with G.N., P.F., and R.R. Overall, P–HIGH has nine matches with the training exemplars for *plurosis*. In addition, P–HIGH shares no symptoms with any exemplar for *multinomia*. Because P–HIGH is more similar to the members of *plurosis* than to the members of *multinomia*, subjects diagnose it as *plurosis*.

Next consider the categorization of K.I. during the test phase. K.I., too, is more similar, on average, to the six exemplars of *plurosis* than to the six exemplars of *multinomia*, but it is not as similar overall to the exemplars of *plurosis* as is P–HIGH. K.I. shares three symptoms with its memory from the training phase; it shares one symptom each with S.J., W.A., G.N., and P.F.; and it shares no symptoms with R.R. In addition, K.I. shares one symptom with a training exemplar for *multinomia* (*shallow* for E.W.). Sharing this symptom with *multinomia* makes classifying K.I. more difficult, because K.I. shares a symptom with the incorrect category. Overall, then, K.I. has seven matches with the training exemplars for *plurosis*, and one match with the training exemplars for *multinomia*. In contrast, P–HIGH has nine matches with *plurosis* and no matches with *multinomia*. Consequently, subjects categorize P–HIGH better than K.I as a member of *plurosis*. As this example illustrates, a model that only contains exemplar memories and no prototypes may categorize an exemplar that was seen previously more poorly than an exemplar that was never seen!

Exemplar models make additional predictions that provide more direct support for people's use of exemplar memories in categorization. Consider the tests for an exemplar effect in Fig. 2.5. P.F.′ is the same as P.F. but lacks a symptom for *eyes*. As can be seen from examining Fig. 2.5, P.F.′ has an overall similarity of two to the training exemplars of *plurosis* (i.e., two matches with P.F.). P–NONE also has an overall similarity of two to the training exemplars of *plurosis*. However, its two matches come from two different exemplars (i.e., one each from W.A. and G.N.). As many experiments have demonstrated, subjects categorize test exemplars better to the extent that they match one training exemplar well than when they match multiple training exemplars weakly. For example, subjects would be more likely to categorize P.F.′ as *plurosis* than P–NONE, because P.F.′ matches one exemplar of *plurosis* highly, whereas P–NONE matches two exemplars of *plurosis* weakly. Although P.F.′ and P–NONE match the training exemplars of *plurosis* equally well overall, the higher match of P.F.′ to one training exemplar causes people to place it in this category more often. Such results suggest that people retrieve exemplar memories during categorization and use them in categorizing new exemplars.

One might think that exemplar effects provide evidence against prototype theories, yet theorists have developed prototype models that can explain these effects (Barsalou, 1990b). Consequently, exemplar effects do not entail that people use exemplar models during categorization. Instead, people could use prototypes that contain specific information about exemplars, as well as the more general information true across exemplars. For example, the prototype for *plurosis* could state that category members occasionally have the properties of *oily* and *shallow*, along with the more frequent properties of *rash*, *dry*, and *rapid*. In addition, prototypes could contain information about the cooccurrences of properties. For example, the prototype for *plurosis* could state that *spots* and *wheezing* cooccur occasionally for exemplars. If prototypes contain idiosyncratic properties and cooccurring properties, they can readily account for exemplar effects. Consequently, it is difficult to determine whether people use exemplars or prototypes in categorization. Nevertheless, exemplar results demonstrate that people store very specific knowledge about exemplars in memory. Regardless of whether people store specific information from exemplars as exemplar memories or integrate this information into prototypes, these results illustrate that they acquire very specific information from exemplars and use it in subsequent categorizations.

Attribute weighting.   People rarely weight attributes equally in performing categorizations. Consider the attributes for *skin*, *eyes*, and *breathing* in Fig. 2.5. Subjects could weight these attributes equally. If they did, then a match on any attribute would count an equal amount toward categorization. On the other hand, subjects could weight these attributes differently, such that a match on one attribute counts more than a match on another.

Consider the tests for attribute weighting in Fig. 2.5. As can be seen, the P-SKIN test only specifies a value for the *skin* attribute (*rash*) and does not contain a value for any other attribute. Similarly, the P-EYES and P-BREATH tests only contain a value for their respective attribute. If subjects learned to weight attributes equally in the training phase, then they should categorize these three test exemplars equally accurately, confidently, and quickly at test. However, if subjects learned to weight the attributes unequally, the three test exemplars should vary in categorization efficiency. The test exemplar for the attribute with the highest weight should be categorized most efficiently, followed by the test exemplar for the attribute with the next highest weight, and then the test exemplar for the attribute with the lowest weight. Across a wide variety of experiments, researchers have generally found that people weight attributes unequally; rarely do they assign equal weights to attributes when performing categorization (Goodman, 1955; Medin & Schaffer, 1978; Nosofsky, 1984; Ortony, 1979; Sutherland & Mackintosh, 1971; Trabasso & Bower, 1968: A. Tversky, 1977).

To see how prototype and exemplar models incorporate attribute weighting, consider the categorization of P-MEDIUM and P-LOW as members of *plurosis* in Fig. 2.5. When all attribute weights are equal, a prototype model predicts that P-MEDIUM should be categorized better than P-LOW, because P-MEDIUM matches the *plurosis* prototype on two attributes (*skin*, *eyes*), whereas P-LOW only matches it on one (*breathing*). An exemplar model makes the same prediction, because P-MEDIUM has seven matches with *plurosis* exemplars and one match with *multinomia* exemplars overall, whereas P-LOW has five matches with *plurosis* exemplars and two matches with *multinomia* exemplars.

Imagine now that people weight *breathing* twice as high as they weight *skin* and *eyes*. How does this affect categorization? Both a prototype model and an exemplar model predict no difference in categorization efficiency for P-MEDIUM and P-LOW. A prototype model makes this prediction because the two matches for P-MEDIUM on *skin* and *eyes* each count for half as much as the one match for P-LOW on *breathing*. In other words, the unequal weighting has made one match on *breathing* just as important as two matches on *skin* and *eyes*. An exemplar model also predicts no difference between P-MEDIUM and P-LOW. P-MEDIUM has a total of six matches with *skin* and *eyes* and one match with *breathing* across the training exemplars for *plurosis*. In addition, P-MEDIUM has one match with *breathing* across the training exemplars for *multinomia*. In contrast, P-LOW has a total of two matches with *skin* and *eyes* and three matches with *breathing* across the training exemplars for *plurosis*. In addition, P-LOW also has two matches with *skin* and *eyes* across the training exemplars for *multinomia*. If *breathing* has twice as much weight as *skin* and *eyes* (e.g., weights of 1, .5, and .5, respectively), these matches combine to make categorization of P-MEDIUM and P-LOW equally efficient (e.g., $6(.5) + 1(1) - 1(1) = 3$ for P-MEDIUM; $2(.5) + 3(1) - 2(.5) = 3$ for P-LOW). If *breathing* were weighted three times as much *skin* and *eyes* (i.e., weights of 1, .33, and .33, respectively), then P-LOW would be categorized more efficiently than P-MEDIUM (i.e., $6(.33) + 1(1) - 1(1) = 2$ for P-MEDIUM; $2(.33) + 3(1) - 2(.33) = 3$ for P-LOW). As this example illustrates, attribute weighting can override the overall number of attribute matches.

Why do people weight some attributes more than others? Researchers have found that people weight attributes unequally for a variety of reasons. Some attributes receive high weight because they are salient perceptually. For example, *shape* and *color* are salient attributes in visual categories, and people often focus on them, at least initially. Some attributes receive high weight because they are familiar: People often classify a piece of music according to the *instruments* played (e.g., piano, violin) and not its underlying *musical form* (e.g., sonata, fugue), because *instrument* is a more familiar attribute. Attributes receive high weight because they are salient in theories about the physical world: Physicians believe that *bacteria* and *viruses* are central to disease and therefore weight attributes involving their presence heavily in diagnostic categories. Other attributes receive high weight because they are more predictive of category membership than other attributes: One's view on *taxes* may be more predictive of *political affiliation* (e.g., Democrat vs. Republican) than his or her view of *campaign spending*.

As these examples illustrate, many factors underlie the unequal weights that attributes receive in categorization. However, predicting the relative weights of attributes prior to an experiment is a difficult and largely unsolved problem. Although researchers often learn from experience which attributes subjects weight more heavily than others, they have developed relatively little ability to predict attribute weightings a priori from theory. Developing a theory that predicts attribute weighting constitutes a major challenge to the study of categorization.

Correlated attributes.   So far, we have only considered the independent roles of attributes in categorization. If a test exemplar has *rash* as its value for *skin*, then the weight (i.e., importance) of *rash* in a categorization decision is unaffected by the exemplar's value for *eyes*. If *rash* matches the prototype, it receives the same weight, regardless of whether the value for *eyes* is *dry, red*, or anything else.

Values of attributes may act together, however, to determine categorization decisions, with the weight of one attribute value depending on the value of another attribute. Consider an experiment by Medin, Altom, Edelson, and Freko (1982) in which subjects learned about the imaginary disease, *burlosis*. In the training phase of this experiment, subjects received descriptions of several patients, each having five symptoms. As can be seen from examining the training exemplars in Fig. 2.6, the values for *eye condition* and *weight change* were perfectly correlated: Whenever *eye condition* was *puffy, weight change* was *gain*; whenever *eye condition* was *sunken, weight change* was *loss*. In the training phase of the experiment, subjects only saw exemplars that exhibited this correlation; they never saw exemplars having *puffy eyes* and *weight loss* or having *sunken eyes* and *weight gain*.

Consider the implications of such training on learning. If subjects did not acquire information about the correlation between *eye condition* and *weight change*, then they should have considered these two attributes independently in the test phase. Whether the values for these two attributes maintained the correlation or violated it should not have affected categorization decisions. To see this, consider one of Medin et al.'s tests for a correlation effect (Fig. 2.6). Subjects received the CORR and NO–CORR exemplars during the test phase and had to decide which was more likely to be an instance of *burlosis*. The critical difference between CORR and NO–CORR was that CORR

BURLOSIS

PATIENT	BLOOD PRESSURE	SKIN CONDITION	MUSCLE CONDITION	EYE CONDITION	WEIGHT CHANGE
			Training exemplars		
R.L.	low	rash	stiff	puffy	gain
L.F.	high	rash	stiff	puffy	gain
J.J.	low	spots	sore	puffy	gain
R.M.	high	spots	sore	puffy	gain
A.M.	high	rash	sore	puffy	gain
J.S.	high	rash	sore	puffy	gain
S.T.	high	spots	stiff	sunken	loss
S.E.	low	rash	sore	sunken	loss
E.M.	high	rash	sore	sunken	loss
			Test for a correlation effect		
CORR	high	rash	sore	sunken	loss
NO-CORR	high	rash	sore	sunken	gain

Figure 2.6. An artificial category that demonstrates an effect of correlated attributes. Adapted from Medin, Altom, Edelson, and Freko (1982), by permission.

maintained the correlation from the training phase, whereas NO-CORR violated it.

If subjects processed the attributes independently, they should have chosen NO-CORR more often than CORR as an instance of *burlosis*, because NO-CORR and CORR only differed in their value for *weight change*, with *weight gain* in NO-CORR occurring for six training exemplars but *weight loss* in CORR only occurring for three. As a result, NO-CORR had more overall matches with the training exemplars than CORR. Processing the attributes independently, subjects should have preferred NO-CORR over CORR, because of its higher number of matches.

On the other hand, if subjects acquired information about the correlation during the training phase, they should have used it to process *eye condition* and *weight change* interactively—not independently—in the test phase. Subjects should have considered the values of *eye condition* and *weight change* together for each test exemplar, determining whether they violated or matched the correlation observed during training. In evaluating NO-CORR, subjects should have counted its violation of the correlation as evidence against the correct categorization being *burlosis*. In evaluating CORR, subjects should have counted its match with the correlation as evidence for *burlosis* being the correct categorization.

The subjects in Medin et al.'s experiment chose CORR more frequently than NO-CORR as a member of *burlosis*, demonstrating their use of the correlation during the test phase. A number of other researchers have reported similar results, showing that people use correlations between attributes to perform categorization (Billman & Heit, 1988; Malt & E.E. Smith, 1984; Medin & Schwanenflugel, 1981; J.D. Martin & Billman, 1991; Wattenmaker, Dewey, T.D. Murphy, & Medin, 1986).

People are especially adept at discovering and using a correlation when they can construct a good explanation for why its two attributes covary. For example, subjects might explain the correlation between *eye condition* and *weight change* in Fig. 2.6 as follows: When people gain weight, they acquire additional flesh around their eyes, thereby producing puffy eyes; when people lose weight, they lose flesh around their eyes, thereby producing sunken eyes. In contrast, subjects might have more difficulty explaining a slightly different form of this correlation. If *weight gain* cooccurs with *sunken eyes*, and *weight loss* cooccurs with *puffy eyes*, subjects might not be able to explain why these pairs of attribute values cooccur. Subjects would therefore be less likely to learn the correlation and to use it in categorizations (L.J. Chapman & J.P. Chapman, 1967, 1969; G.L. Murphy & Medin, 1985; G.L. Murphy & Wisniewski, 1989).

Base rate effects and competitive learning.   Categories vary in how often their exemplars occur in the world. For example, most U.S. citizens experience exemplars of *robin* more frequently than exemplars of *woodpecker*. Imagine that someone tells you that there is a bird outside and that you are to guess if it is a *robin* or a *woodpecker*. Which would you choose? According to Bayes' theorem (**10**.3.2), you should prefer the category with the higher *base rate* or frequency of occurrence (Kahneman & Tversky, 1972; Kahneman, Slovic, & Tversky, 1982). Because *robin* occurs more frequently than *woodpecker* in your experience, *robin* is the best guess. As we shall see, people's categorization decisions sometimes follow base rates, and sometimes do not.

Consider an experiment performed by Medin and Edelson (1988) in which subjects learned about two imaginary diseases. As Fig. 2.7 illustrates, in the training phase, subjects saw three times as many patients having one disease (*baysonoma*) as having the other disease (*deltitis*). As Fig. 2.7 further illustrates, a given disease always exhibited the same symptoms: Patients with *baysonoma* always had *fever* and *tremors*, whereas patients with *deltitis* always had *fever* and *insomnia*. *Fever* occurred for every patient and therefore did not discriminate

TRAINING EXEMPLARS			TEST EXEMPLARS		
PATIENT	SYMPTOMS	DISEASE	PATIENT	SYMPTOM(S)	DISEASE
R.M.	fever tremors	baysonoma	B-ONLY	tremors	?
L.E.	fever tremors	baysonoma	D-ONLY	insomnia	?
J.T.	fever insomnia	deltitis	BD-BOTH	fever	?
R.S.	fever tremors	baysonoma	B-VS-D	tremors insomnia	?
M.A.	fever insomnia	deltitis			
J.M.	fever tremors	baysonoma			
S.J.	fever tremors	baysonoma			
S.F.	fever tremors	baysonoma			
A.W.	fever tremors	baysonoma			
D.O.	fever tremors	baysonoma			
J.S.	fever insomnia	deltitis			
F.A.	fever tremors	baysonoma			

Figure 2.7. Artificial categories that demonstrate base rate effects and competitive learning. Adapted from Medin and Edelson (1988), by permission.

between diseases. In contrast, *tremors* perfectly predicted *baysonoma*, and *insomnia* perfectly predicted *deltitis*.

After subjects learned the categories, they received a series of test exemplars. First consider the B-ONLY and D-ONLY tests. Subjects' categorizations of B-ONLY and D-ONLY were not surprising. For each, the symptom of the test exemplar specified a clear diagnosis: Because *tremors* only occurred for *baysonoma* during the training phase, subjects almost always categorized B-ONLY as *baysonoma*. Because *insomnia* only occurred for *deltitis* during the training phase, subjects almost always categorized D-ONLY as *deltitis*.

The BD-BOTH test exemplar provided a test of whether subjects used base rates in categorization. Because *fever* occurred for every case of *baysonoma* and *deltitis*, this symptom provides equally strong evidence for each category. Consequently, the only basis for subjects' decisions should be base rates. If subjects used base rates to categorize test exemplars, then they should have categorized BD-BOTH more often as *baysonoma* than as *deltitis*, because *baysonoma* occurred three times more often than *deltitis*. Medin and Edelson indeed found that subjects categorized BD-BOTH as *baysonoma* more often than as *deltitis*, indicating subjects' use of base rates in categorization.

Consider the final test exemplar in Fig. 2.7: B-VS-D. This exemplar contains the symptom that predicts *baysonoma* (*tremors*) and the symptom that predicts *deltitis* (*insomnia*). If subjects used base rates to categorize B-VS-D, they should have preferred *baysonoma* over *deltitis*. Because B-VS-D contains one perfectly predictive symptom for each disease, its symptoms provide equally strong evidence for each. The only basis for making a decision, according to Bayes' Theorem, is again the difference in base rates. Because *baysonoma* occurred three times more often than *deltitis*, subjects would be expected to categorize B-VS-D as *baysonoma*. Surprisingly, subjects generally categorized B-VS-D as *deltitis*, thereby violating the base rates prediction.

What underlies this violation? A number of theorists have suggested that *competitive learning* is responsible. Consider the relative predictiveness of *fever* for *baysonoma* versus *deltitis*. Across all of the training exemplars, 67% of *fever's* occurrences were for *baysonoma*, and 33% of its occurrences were for *deltitis*. As a result, *fever* is a good predictor of *baysonoma* but not of *deltitis*. Next consider the relative predictiveness of *tremors*. Across all of the training exemplars, 100% of *tremors'* occurrences were for *baysonoma*, so *tremors* provides a second good predictor of *baysonoma*. However, *baysonoma* already has one good predictor, namely, *fever*. If *fever* and *tremors* compete to predict *baysonoma*, then *tremors* should not develop as much of a role in predicting cases of *baysonoma* as it would if *fever* weren't already a good predictor. Finally, consider the relative predictiveness of *insomnia*. Across all of the training exemplars, 100% of *insomnia's* occurrences were for *deltitis*. Like *tremors*, *insomnia* is a perfect predictor of its category. Unlike *tremors*, however, *insomnia* does not have to compete with another good predictor. Because *fever* is not a good predictor of *deltitis, insomnia* doesn't have to compete with it to predict this disease. Moreover, *insomnia* has to override the tendency of *fever*, which always cooccurs with it in the training phase, to predict *baysonoma*. For both of these reasons, *insomnia* becomes a more powerful predictor for *deltitis* than *tremors* becomes for *baysonoma*. When subjects see *insomnia* and *tremors* together in the B-VS-D test exemplar, the strength that *insomnia* developed from competitive learning during the training phase dominates categorization, such that subjects fail to consider the base rates.

As these results illustrate, people sometimes follow base rates in categorization, preferring a more frequent category to a less frequent category. Under conditions of competitive learning, however, they may favor a category with a low base rate, because a potent predictor controls categorization (see also Gluck & Bower, 1988).

2.4 EXPECTATION

So far, we have only considered the role of perceptual information in categorization. According to prototype and exemplar models, information initially enters the cognitive system through vision, audition, and the other sensory modalities. Once the cognitive system forms a structural description from feature information, it projects this description to memory, trying to find the best matching prototype or exemplar(s). Theorists often refer to these operations in categorization as *bottom-up processing*, because information flows from the "bottom" of the system (perceptual modalities) toward the "top" (knowledge and procedures in memory).

However, categorization involves much more than bottom-up processing. During categorization, extensive information also flows in the other direction, thereby producing *top-down processing*. To get a sense of top-down processing, imagine being in a restaurant and having some friends arrive. If you were not expecting these friends, you might be slow to recognize them and might even fail to do so, but if you were expecting these friends, you would probably recognize them quickly. This sort of top-down processing from expectations to perception pervades categorization. Most entities in daily life occur when and where people expect to encounter them. People expect to see cars on roads, chairs in rooms, and dogs in yards.

An experiment by Palmer (1975a) demonstrates the roles of both bottom-up and top-down processing in categorization. On most trials, subjects viewed a scene for 2000 msec.[3] After a 1300 msec delay, subjects viewed an object for 20, 40, 60, or 120 msec, their task being to name the object. Across trials, subjects saw four types of scene-object pairs:

Related-context pairs. The scene and object in the pair were related (e.g., kitchen-bread).

Misleading-context pairs. The scene and object were unrelated, but the object had the shape of something typically found in the scene (e.g., kitchen-mailbox, where the mailbox had the same shape as a loaf of bread).

Unrelated-context pairs. The scene and object were unrelated, and the object did not have the shape of something typically found in the scene (e.g., kitchen-bugle).

No-context pairs. Objects occurred without scenes. These trials provided a baseline measure of how well subjects could classify objects in the absence of scene-produced expectations.

Figure 2.8 shows the probability that subjects correctly categorized the objects. First, note the general improvement in accuracy as an object's exposure duration increased. This improvement represents the role of bottom-up processing in categorization: The longer the subjects had to view an entity, the more perceptual information they extracted, and the better categorization became. The differences between the four functions represent the effects of top-down processing. Because accuracy was always higher for related-

---

[3] One millisecond (msec) is one thousandth of a second. Consequently, 2000 msec is 2 seconds.

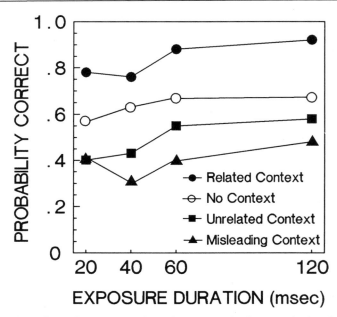

Figure 2.8. The effects of bottom-up and top-down processing in categorization. Adapted from Palmer (1975a), by permission.

context pairs than for no-context pairs, the scenes in the related-context pairs provided expectations that improved accuracy. Without scenes, and especially for short exposures, subjects frequently did not extract enough bottom-up information to be correct. When they had some idea of what to expect, however, the same amount of bottom-up information was more likely to converge on the correct category.

In contrast, accuracy was always less for unrelated-context pairs than for no-context pairs, indicating that expectations also interfered with categorization. Subjects did not expect to see these objects in these scenes and had trouble identifying them when they did. For misleading-context pairs, the objects' resemblance to expected objects created even more interference. The range of performance across pairs at each exposure duration demonstrates the powerful effects of expectation when bottom-up information remains constant.

Theorists generally assume that people's extensive world knowledge provides these expectations (7). In almost any situation, knowledge about the current context produces expectations about categories likely to be present. These expectancies facilitate the categorization of instances from these categories but interfere with the categorization of instances from unexpected categories. Research in cognitive psychology has probably demonstrated top-down processing at least as often as any other cognitive effect. In virtually any domain, researchers have found that people have expectations that influence their categorization performance. Expectation is a central facet of human cognition, and we shall see many further examples of it in later chapters (especially **9**.4).

2.5   SPREADING ACTIVATION MODELS

Many cognitive psychologists view categorization, and other cognitive abilities as well, in terms of a spreading activation framework (J.R. Anderson, 1983; A.M. Collins & E.F. Loftus, 1975; McClelland & Rumelhart, 1981; Morton, 1969, 1979; Quillian, 1968; Rumelhart & McClelland, 1982; Seidenberg & McClelland, 1989; see Ratcliff & McKoon, 1988, for an alternative view). Figure 2.9 depicts a simple spreading activation network for categorizing written instances of the word "butter." This network contains innate property detectors for line segments (e.g., |, —), which are grouped to form acquired detectors for letters (e.g., *b*, *u*), which are grouped to form acquired detectors for words (e.g., *butter*, *milk*). Each line, letter, and word

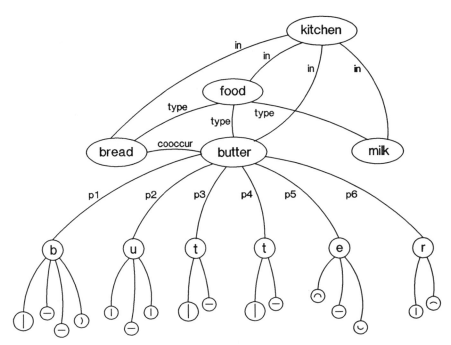

Figure 2.9.   An example of a spreading activation network. Detectors p1 through p6 represent the positions of letters in "butter" from left to right.

detector in Fig. 2.9 is a processing unit that can both send and receive activation (a useful analogy is to view activation like electricity). Consider how this account explains the categorization of "butter." Line detectors that correspond to the characteristics of "b" become active and begin sending activation to the *b* detector. Simultaneously, other line detectors begin sending activation to the letter detectors for other letters in "butter" (e.g., *u*). Note that each line detector also activates other letter detectors sharing that line. For example, the vertical line in "b" activates, not only the *b* detector, but also the *h* and *k* detectors (Fig. 2.9 does not show these pathways).

Figure 2.10 offers a more specific account of how a detector becomes active. Assume that the activation function in Fig. 2.10 corresponds to activation of the *b* detector. Prior to receiving any activation, the *b* detector rests at its baseline level of activation. Once a target is presented (i.e., a particular "b"), the *b* detector starts receiving activation from line detectors, and its activation begins to rise above baseline and approach threshold. A threshold is the critical amount of activation that a detector must have before its category can be assigned to a perceived entity. If the *b* detector crosses its threshold before any other letter detector crosses its threshold, the category *b* is assigned to the target. The activation function in Fig. 2.10 can similarly represent the activation of word detectors in Fig. 2.9, such as the detector for *butter*. As the *butter* detector accumulates activation from its letter detectors, its activation begins to rise above baseline. If the *butter* detector crosses threshold before any other word detector, it is assigned as the categorization of "butter."

Activation of hierarchically organized detectors in this manner illustrates

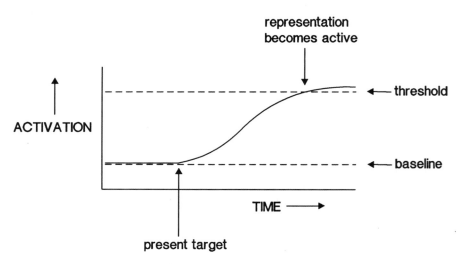

Figure 2.10. Activation of a category representation from baseline to threshold.

how spreading activation models represent bottom-up processing during categorization. When an entity is perceived, innate detectors become active, and in turn activate acquired detectors for groupings of innate detectors. These acquired detectors may in turn activate more abstract acquired detectors, which may in turn activate still more abstract acquired detectors, and so forth. Ultimately, this bottom-up activation converges on one high-level detector more than any other, such that its category becomes assigned to the perceived entity.

Spreading activation models also account for top-down processing during categorization. To see this, imagine that a person reads "bread." As the word detector for *bread* becomes active, activation spreads from it along pathways to related words, such as *kitchen, food, butter,* and *milk* (see Fig. 2.9). As activation reaches the detectors for *kitchen, food, butter,* and *milk,* their activations begin to rise above baseline. However, none of these categories is assigned to "bread," because the detector for *bread* receives more intense bottom-up activation and passes threshold first. However, the *priming* of the detectors for *kitchen, food, butter,* and *milk* lingers for a while and may affect their later processing. Such priming constitutes top-down processing, because the activation of one word (*bread*) produces expectations, via spreading activation, about other words that are likely to occur (*kitchen, food, butter, milk*).

Figure 2.11 illustrates the specific ways in which top-down priming affects the subsequent processing of detectors. First, consider how top-down processing primes the detectors for expected categories. When a category is expected, its detector's activation rises above baseline, even before an in-

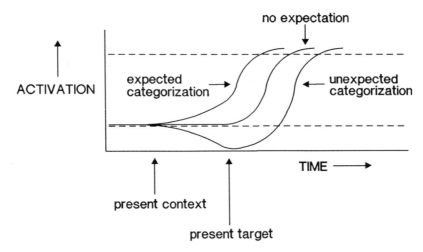

Figure 2.11. Activation of a category representation under different conditions of expectation.

stance of the category occurs (see the curve for *expected categorization* in Fig. 2.11). If an instance then occurs, less bottom-up activation is necessary for the detector to pass threshold, and it passes threshold sooner. Imagine, for example, that an instance of *bread* is categorized initially, thereby priming related detectors, such as the detector for *butter*. If "butter" is encountered subsequently, less perceptual information must be extracted to categorize it. Because the word detector for *butter* has already received top-down priming, it requires less bottom-up activation from its letter detectors. As a result, categorization is more likely to succeed, similar to Palmer's finding for related-context pairs (Fig. 2.8). As we shall see later, priming also increases the speed of categorization (**4**.1.2, **9**.4.1)

Consider now how top-down processing inhibits the detectors for unexpected categories. When a category is unexpected, its detector's activation falls below baseline (see the curve for *unexpected categorization* in Fig. 2.11). If an instance then occurs unexpectedly, more bottom-up activation is necessary for the detector to pass threshold, and it passes threshold later. Imagine that an instance of *hammer* is categorized initially, which inhibits unrelated detectors, such as the detector for *butter*. If "butter" is encountered subsequently, more perceptual information must be extracted to categorize it. The word detector for *butter* requires more bottom-up activation from its letter detectors to overcome its inhibition and cross threshold. As a result, categorization is less likely to succeed, similar to Palmer's findings for unrelated- and misleading-context pairs (Fig. 2.8). Not surprisingly, inhibition also decreases the speed of categorization (**4**.1.2, **9**.4.1)

Theorists have proposed many different kinds of spreading activation models, whose characteristics vary widely. The version presented here captures some of the more standard assumptions in these models. As you may have noticed, this standard model essentially implements a hierarchical arrangement of prototypes (**2**.3.1). Each detector functions as a prototype for two reasons: First, a detector can cross threshold, even when one of the detectors that feeds into it is inactive. The word detector for *apple* could fire, for example, even if a letter is missing from an instance (e.g., "a_ple" or "appl_"). Thus, no particular property must be present for a detector to fire. A detector does not embody a rule that requires every property to be present, but instead, similar to a prototype, can cross threshold upon receiving sufficient activation from a subset of its detectors.

The detectors in a spreading activation net are prototypes for a second reason as well. As we saw in **2**.3.2, the exemplars of a category vary in typicality, with typical exemplars being categorized more efficiently than atypical exemplars. Spreading activation models capture this by assuming that typical exemplars feed more activation into the detector for their category than atypical exemplars. To the extent that an exemplar exhibits all of a category's properties (i.e., it is typical), the maximum number of property detectors activates the category detector. To the extent that an exemplar exhibits few of a category's properties (i.e., it is atypical), fewer property detectors activate the category detector. For example, the letter string "apple" is more typical of the word *apple* than is the letter string "a_ple" and activates the word detector to a higher extent. Because different exemplars of a category can activate its detector to different extents, spreading activation networks constitute one of the many possible implementations of prototype theory.

As we saw earlier, people are sensitive to attribute salience, correlated properties, and competitive learning in categorization (**2.3.2**). Theorists can add various mechanisms to spreading activation networks to account for these phenomena. To account for attribute salience, theorists make some pathways in a network stronger than others. As pathways become stronger, they transmit activation more rapidly, giving them more control over the activation of detectors. Thus, if people weight the first letter of a word more than the second letter, the pathway from the detector for the first letter of a word to the word detector could be stronger than the pathway from the second letter. As a result, the first letter contributes more activation to the word detector than does the second letter. In general, more salient attributes have stronger pathways to their categories. Stronger pathways can also result from competitive learning. To the extent that one property wins out in predicting its category, its pathway becomes strong and dominates processing (Gluck & Bower, 1988).

To handle exemplar effects, spreading activation models can include property detectors for idiosyncratic properties. Rather than only having detectors for prototypical properties, spreading activation models can include detectors for atypical properties as well. Upon categorizing an exemplar with novel properties, the network connects detectors for these properties to the category. Later, if another exemplar exhibits these properties, these detectors feed additional activation to the category, thereby facilitating categorization and producing an exemplar effect. To the extent that these properties continue to occur across exemplars, their pathways become stronger and their influence on categorization increases.

To account for correlation effects, spreading activation models can include pathways from one property detector to another. If there is a correlation between *t* and *h* in the first two letters positions of words, a pathway could connect these two detectors directly. When the detector for *t* becomes active, it begins to activate the detector for *h*, and vice versa. As a result, these two letters become active more quickly and send activation to the word level more rapidly. Adding such pathways between cooccurring detectors is much in the spirit of the connectionist models, to be discussed next.

Connectionist models. The recent development of connectionist models in cognitive science has made spreading activation networks significantly more powerful (Bechtel & Abrahamsen, 1990; McClelland & Rumelhart, 1981; McClelland et al., 1986; Rumelhart & McClelland, 1982; Rumelhart et al., 1986). One important change has been to increase the number of connections between the detectors in a network. As we just saw, a network can include facilitatory connections between two detectors that cooccur frequently. In connectionist models, the entire set of detectors that becomes active for a given category develops an extensive set of facilitory relations between them. Consider the line, letter, and word detectors that represent *butter* in Fig. 2.9, along with all of *butter's* associates, such as *bread*. Because all of these detectors tend to be active at the same time, many facilitory connections develop between them, forming a closely interrelated pattern of cooccurring detectors. When an instance of the category occurs and activates some of these detectors, these facilitory relations begin to activate other detectors in the pattern. As a result, the entire pattern of detectors for the category becomes active quickly and dominates other possible patterns of detectors in the network.

Besides adding facilitory connections between detectors that tend to cooccur, connectionist models also add inhibitory connections between detectors that tend not to cooccur. In Fig. 2.9, for example, the letter detector for *b* in *butter* would be negatively related to the word detector for *food*, to indicate that *food* should be inhibited if a *b* is detected. Similarly, the word detector for *butter* might be negatively related to the letter detector for *h*, to indicate that if *butter* is expected, *h* is unlikely to occur. As these two examples illustrate, negative relations between hierarchical levels can help inhibit detectors that are unlikely to provide categorizations in the current context. However, negative relations can also exist within a hierarchical level. For example, the letter detector for *b* at the first position in a word might be negatively related to all other letter detectors in the first position, such that the activation of *b* inhibits its competitors. As all of these examples illustrate, the negative relations within a connectionist net assist a network in converging on the correct categorization: While facilitory connections unite to activate the detectors for a category, inhibitory connections unite to inhibit competing detectors, thereby making the task of the facilitory connections easier.

Theorists have also developed sophisticated learning procedures for connectionist networks that provide them with impressive learning abilities. These schemes essentially allow connectionist nets to extract prototypical information across many exemplars, while simultaneously storing idiosyncratic information about individual exemplars. Consequently, connectionist models capture important aspects of both prototype and exemplar models. Moreover, connectionist models categorize extremely well when given only partial property information for an uncategorized entity. Because these models store so many relations between detectors, partial patterns of information are often able to activate related properties and inhibit irrelevant ones, such that correct categorizations can occur.

Connectionist networks have tremendous potential as models of categorization. Moreover, their basic architecture is *somewhat* similar to the architecture of the brain, although many important differences exist as well. Each neuron in the brain activates and inhibits thousands of other neurons, similar to the inter-connected organization of detectors in a connectionist network. This similarity suggests that cognitive theory, as expressed in connectionism, may develop important insights about how the brain works. Conversely, insights from neuroscience are likely to continue having beneficial effects on cognitive theories. Much remains to be learned about connectionist models, and many unresolved issues about their properties remain (4.4; for critiques of connectionism, see J.A. Fodor & Pylyshyn, 1988; McCloskey & N.J. Cohen, 1989; Pinker & Prince, 1988).

CONCLUSION

Although psychologists and other cognitive scientists are far from having an adequate theory of categorization, much has been learned about it: The exemplars of a natural category often exhibit tremendous complexity and often lack defining properties. Innate mechanisms extract primitive perceptual properties and integrate them into structural descriptions. People use multiple forms of category representation, including exemplars, prototypes, and definitions. Top-down expectations greatly facilitate expected categorizations and inhibit unexpected categorizations. Although cognitive scientists have yet to develop a powerful theory of categorization, they have come to understand why the problem is so formidable: Describing the physical exemplars that constitute a category is difficult because exemplars are often diverse and lack defining characteristics. Developing an account of innate categorization mechanisms is difficult because researchers have not been able to specify the complete set of innate property detectors, nor the mechanisms that integrate them into structural descriptions. Modeling category representation is difficult because people use so many different types of category knowledge. Developing accounts of bottom-up and top-down processing is difficult because these mechanisms process category representations in complicated and dynamic manners. At least researchers now recognize the fundamental problems that they must solve to produce a satisfactory theory of categorization. In addition, they have developed methodological tools that may eventually produce a comprehensive theory. We shall return to categorization many times in the coming chapters.

3

REPRESENTATION

One of the thorniest issues in cognitive psychology is the nature and role of representation. Because psychologists view representation in many different ways, and because it is often misunderstood, a careful analysis is central to any presentation of cognitive psychology. I have delayed discussing representation until now, because constructs from categorization provide excellent examples. I have chosen to digress at this point before continuing to further topics, because a sound grasp of representation is essential for a proper understanding of cognitive theory. Hopefully, this brief excursion will make the following chapters more meaningful and less ambiguous. In section **3**.1, I begin with a definition of representation developed by Palmer (1978). In section **3**.2, I apply this definition to three fundamental forms of representation in cognitive psychology. In section **3**.3., I consider implications of this definition for relations between cognitive psychology and neuroscience.

3.1 REPRESENTATIONAL SYSTEMS

According to Palmer (1978), a representational system satisfies the following five conditions:

1. There is a target domain.
2. There is a modeling domain.
3. A subset of the structure in the target domain is relevant.
4. A subset of the structure in the modeling domain is relevant.
5. A systematic correspondence exists between the relevant structure in the modeling domain and the relevant structure in the target domain.

Consider the realization of these five conditions in Fig. 3.1:

1. The target domain contains three rectangles.
2. The modeling domain contains three line sets.
3. The relevant subset of the structure in the target domain is rectangle height—rectangle width is irrelevant.
4. The relevant subset of the structure in the modeling domain is number of lines—line height is irrelevant.
5. The systematic correspondence between the modeling and target domains is that number of lines increases as rectangle height increases.

The modeling domain in Fig. 3.1 captures information about the target domain and therefore supports the answering of questions about it. If the target domain is absent, yet someone wants to know whether rectangle X is taller than rectangle Y, he or she can answer correctly by consulting the modeling domain (i.e., seeing if line set x has more lines than line set y). In this manner, the modeling domain represents the target domain. Typically, the modeling domain does not represent all of the structure in the target domain; nor must all aspects of the structure in the modeling domain represent some structure in the target domain. The structure of the two domains is only identical in a perfect isomorphism. As we shall see for representation in cognitive psychology, the structural overlap between the two domains is always partial: The modeling domain, using some of its structure, represents some of the structure in the target domain.

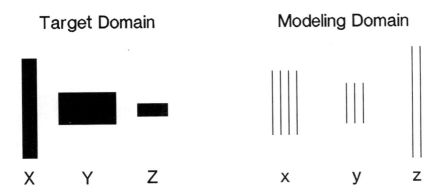

Figure 3.1.   Example of a representational system. Adapted from Palmer (1978), by permission.

It is essential to see that the individual characteristics of each domain are irrelevant to the correspondence that constitutes representation within a representational system. Consider Fig. 3.2. Modeling domain A and the target domain in Fig. 3.2 are identical to the modeling and target domains in Fig. 3.1: Increasing numbers of lines represent increasing rectangle height. Now consider modeling domain B in Fig. 3.2. Although modeling domain B looks a lot like modeling domain A, they capture completely different structure in the target domain. Whereas number of lines in modeling domain A captures information about rectangle *height* in the target domain, number of lines in modeling domain B captures information about rectangle *width* in the target domain. Two modeling domains can look similar but not have anything in common in terms of the correspondence that constitutes representation within a representational system. Representation cannot be equated with the appearance of a modeling domain or with its individual characteristics. The systematic relation between two domains determines the nature of a representation.

To see this important point more clearly, consider modeling domain C in Fig. 3.2. Although modeling domain C does not look anything like modeling

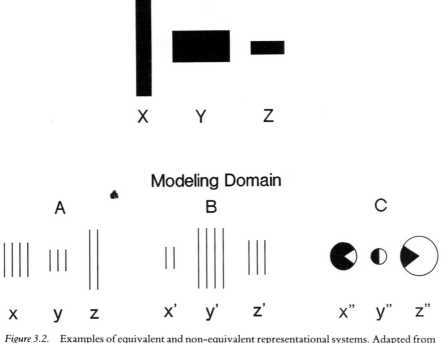

Figure 3.2. Examples of equivalent and non-equivalent representational systems. Adapted from Palmer (1978), by permission.

domain A, they are actually equivalent representations of the target domain. Modeling domain A captures rectangle height by number of lines. Modeling domain C captures rectangle height by the proportion of a circle that is shaded. Exactly the same questions can and cannot be answered about the target domain from modeling domains A and C. As these examples illustrate, the essential character of a representation cannot be equated with its individual characteristics. If it could, then modeling domains A and C should not be the same, given the substantial difference in their appearances. Rather, the essential character of a representation depends upon the systematic correspondence between the two domains. Because modeling domains A and C capture the same information in the target domain, they are representationally equivalent, even though they capture the information in different ways.

3.2 REPRESENTATION IN COGNITIVE PSYCHOLOGY

Equipped with a definition of representation, we can explore the nature of representation in cognitive psychology. Consider Fig. 2.4 and Fig. 2.9 from the previous chapter. Figure 2.4 contains a flow chart that describes the cognitive operations in categorization; Fig. 2.9 contains a spreading activation network that represents category knowledge. What do these two figures *represent*? Critics of cognitive psychology sometimes make the following argument: Cognitive psychologists believe that flow charts and networks like these actually exist in the human brain, yet it is ridiculous to believe that the brain contains flowcharts and networks. Furthermore, postulating such entities creates the impression that people are computers. Unfortunately, such criticisms reflect a profound misunderstanding of representation in cognitive psychology specifically, and of scientific theory in general.

The issue of representation spans three domains in cognitive psychology: the environment, the brain, and cognitive theory. Cognitive psychology addresses three representational systems that involve these domains:

1. The brain's representation of the environment.
2. Cognitive theory's representation of the environment.
3. Cognitive theory's representation of the brain.

First, consider how the definition of a representational system described in 3.1 applies to the brain's representation of the environment. Because people can accurately perceive, remember, and manipulate the environment, they clearly have the ability to represent it. The neuronal structure of the brain is capable of establishing systematic correspondences between subsets of its structure and subsets of structure in the physical environment. Not all structure in the brain—such as the subsystem that regulates blood flow—is relevant to representation; and not all structure in the environment—such as light beyond the range of human sensitivity (e.g., infrared)—is represented. Most importantly, the neuronal structure doing the representing looks *nothing* like the environmental structure being represented. By no stretch of the imagination do the neurons that represent a visually perceived chair look anything like the chair itself. Instead, the essence of the representation is a particular correspondence between the two domains.

Consider next how the definition of a representational system applies to cognitive theory's representation of the environment. Examples of such systems include Gibson's (1950, 1966) analyses of ecological optics, and speech theorists' analyses of the speech signal (2.1). Again, these theories are not psychological, because they do not address how organisms process information. Instead, they simply provide objective accounts of the information that organisms perceive. Often, these theories are expressed in formal languages. Gibsonian accounts of ecological invariants, for example, are sometimes stated algebraically. Not all structure in such a theory—such as the particular alphabetic characters used to express variables—is relevant to representation; and not all structure in the environment—such as the temperature of surfaces—is represented. Once again, the formal structure doing the representing (the algebra of the surface) looks nothing like the environmental structure being represented (the actual surface). The essence of the representation is the particular correspondence between the two domains.

Finally, consider how the definition of a representational system applies to cognitive theory's representation of the brain. Here we return to cognitive constructs, such as the flow chart in Fig. 2.4 and the spreading activation network in Fig. 2.9. Both the flow chart and spreading activation network represent aspects of the brain. Not all structure in these constructs—such as the size of boxes in the flow chart, nor the color of lines in the network—is relevant to representation; and not all structure of the brain—such as connections between individual neurons—is represented. The flow chart and spreading activation network capture very little of the brain's structure and represent different aspects of it. Most importantly, these cognitive constructs look nothing like the neuronal structure they represent. Instead, the essential character of their representation depends upon how they correspond to the brain. It is ridiculous to believe that either Fig. 2.4 or Fig. 2.9 looks like a neuronal mechanism. To think that cognitive constructs are literally "in the brain" is just as ridiculous as believing that the algebra of a Gibsonian analysis is "in the environment," or that a physical chair is "in the brain" perceiving it. The essence of a construct in cognitive theory has little to do with its appearance; its essence depends upon its correspondence to the brain.

The primary purpose of cognitive constructs, such as those in Fig. 2.4 and Fig. 2.9, is to represent psychologists' theoretical understanding of the brain as an information processing system. If psychologists believe that the brain contains a particular piece of information, they can include a construct in their theory to represent that belief. If psychologists believe that people know the appearance of *blue* but not of *infrared*, they can include a construct for the appearance of *blue* but not of *infrared* in their theory. Similarly, if psychologists believe that the brain organizes certain information together, they can organize the corresponding constructs in their theory together. If they believe that people organize knowledge of colors together, they can represent this as a spreading activation network that links categories of colors (2.5). If other psychologists believe that people do not organize colors together but instead organize them with object categories (*grass* is *green*, *carrots* are *orange*, *snow* is *white*), they can represent this with an independent network for each object that contains information about the object's color.

To the extent that cognitive constructs correspond to the actual state of affairs in the brain, psychologists should be able to use them to predict human behavior. Consider the two constructs just suggested for color organization: A single network of color categories versus separate networks for objects with relevant color categories embedded in each. If one of these cognitive constructs is correct, it should predict human performance. If not, both constructs' predictions should fail. As we shall see in later chapters, many methods exist in cognitive psychology for evaluating cognitive constructs like these. Using measures of memory and reaction time, for example, psychologists could determine whether color categories are integrated in a single color network, or whether they are distributed throughout object networks. Upon performing such experiments, psychologists might accrue more support for one construct than for the other.

As the predictions of a cognitive construct receive increasing empirical support, confidence that it corresponds to structure in the brain increases. If its predictions fail, confidence decreases. Most importantly, cognitive constructs could predict many empirical findings but not look anything like the physical contents of the brain. The success of these constructs reflects psychologists' ability to infer structure in the brain, to capture this structure in some language that expresses cognitive constructs (e.g., flow charts, networks, algebra, logic), and to use these constructs to predict behavior accurately. Although cognitive constructs do not look anything like physical mechanisms in the brain, they can correspond to these mechanisms and thereby serve scientific goals.

In summary, cognitive constructs represent cognitive psychologists' current understanding of how the brain processes information. Although these theoretical representations probably capture some structure in the brain, they undoubtedly fail to capture much other structure. Psychologists do have to start somewhere, however, and the reason for performing experiment after experiment, and developing model after model, is to articulate theories more precisely, so that the amount of brain structure they capture will grow.

3.3   RELATIONS BETWEEN COGNITIVE PSYCHOLOGY AND NEUROSCIENCE

In all of this talk about cognitive theory representing the brain, let us be clear that cognitive theorists are *not* modeling the detailed neuronal structure of the brain: They are modeling its information processing characteristics at a global level. Even connectionists, whose theories are closest to brain architecture, are careful to say that connectionist processing units do not necessarily correspond to neurons.

The following analogy to computers may be helpful. As we saw in 1.2, computer scientists represent computers at multiple levels. Most concretely, they represent the physical structure of a computer's physical components in terms of electronics and physics. Indeed, given computer scientists' ability to construct computers, they clearly have a complete understanding at this level. However, computer scientists also understand computers at more abstract levels. For example, they use flow charts to represent the flow of information through a computer's memories and processors, and high level programming languages to represent the flow of information as a computer reads, writes, stores, and transforms information. Most importantly, neither a flow chart nor a programming language captures the physical, electronic details of a computer; they represent only its global, information processing characteristics.

Many cognitive psychologists view the relation between neural and cognitive accounts of the brain as analogous to the relation between electronic and information processing accounts of computers (e.g., J.A. Fodor, 1975). In both cases, the information processing description fails to capture much structure in the physical description. In both cases, the two levels of description do not look anything alike. Instead, the information processing description *represents* the physical description partially through systematic correspondences between them.

It is important to draw two further implications of this analogy. First, a single information processing description may describe many different physical implementations accurately. In the computer domain, different computers may all share a single abstract architecture for information processing, while varying in specific hardware details (e.g., the large class of microcomputers that are compatible with the DOS operating system). A similar state of affairs exists for cognitive theory. Any given cognitive construct could be realized in many possible brain structures. Again, cognitive theories do not represent actual brain structure but represent general information processing accounts of what the brain might be doing.

The second implication is the converse of the first, namely, different information processing accounts can describe the same physical structure. In the computer domain, two different information processing accounts can represent the same structure in a computer. One programmer might use a high-level programming language such as FORTRAN to represent how a computer performs a particular task, whereas a second programmer might use assembly language to represent how the computer performs the same task. The same is true for cognitive theory: Theorists constantly propose different information processing accounts of how the brain performs a particular information processing task.

Given that psychologists can construct so many different information processing accounts of the brain, how do they establish preferences for particular ones? Standard considerations from philosophy of science enter here (Bechtel, 1988b). Psychologists generally prefer accounts that are maximally consistent with empirical findings; that make clear, and sometimes provocative, predictions; that are disconfirmable; that are precise, powerful, parsimonious, and not overly difficult to use; and that complement theories in related areas and disciplines.

A final point: Observers sometimes claim that cognitive theory will disappear once scientists fully understand how the brain works at the neuronal level (P.M. Churchland, 1990; P.S. Churchland, 1986; but see McCauley, 1986; Pylyshyn, 1984). Yet, consider computer science once again. Even though computer scientists fully understand computer electronics, they have not dispensed with information processing accounts of computers. Having to program a computer with only an electronic account of how it works would be extremely tedious. Having to program with an abstract account of files and programming commands is clearly more useful. Information processing accounts are indispensable to many goals of designing and using computers (**1**.2).

Cognitive psychologists believe that the same is true of neuroscience. Upon achieving a complete understanding of the brain, scientists will still need information processing accounts to discuss the brain's global operation. When discussing global information processing in the brain, they may want to avoid getting bogged down in the details about which neuron is activating which other neuron. Instead, scientists will need to have an information processing description that represents those aspects of the brain relevant to their goals. Having only a theory that represents every aspect of brain activity would be far too cumbersome for use in such situations.

Again, everything boils down to the problem of representation. Psychological theories systematically represent those aspects of the brain relevant to specific scientific goals. Because of the variety of scientific and applied goals that psychologists face in understanding the brain, multiple representations of how it works will be necessary. Cognitive psychology aims to represent how the brain processes information, thereby serving those scientific and applied pursuits that rely on this level of explanation.

4

CONTROL OF INFORMATION PROCESSING

Imagine being at a party. Although it's certainly the last thing you would want to think about in that situation—unless you're with some cognitive psychologists—what controls your information processing? What controls how your perceptual systems pick up and categorize information as you listen to a nearby conversation and recognize people coming through the door, while simultaneously carrying on your own conversation? What controls your bodily movements as you walk through a crowded room, consume hors d'oeuvres, and talk? What controls your thinking as you decide whether you've had too much to drink, as you plan how you're going to meet someone, and as you reconstruct a vague event that occurred long ago?

When explaining the control of information processing, psychologists must avoid the *homunculus*, the notion of a miniature man in the head. For centuries, the homunculus has served many purposes. He has been viewed as "inhabiting the reproductive cells and acting as an agent for genetic transmission, as a kind of gremlin in the body regulating morality, or as a little 'green man' in the brain governing decision-making" (Reber, 1985, p. 328). Presumably a female counterpart, the *homuncula*, plays similar roles. The obvious problem with this account is that it provides no explanation at all. If a homunculus controls an information processing system, what controls the homunculus? A homunculus within the homunculus? Such reasoning leads to a useless infinite regression.

Cognitive psychologists have spent much effort developing accounts of mechanisms that control information processing. Only by successfully doing so can they head off the criticism that homunculi dwell in theories of cognition. To the extent that psychologists specify well-defined mechanisms that control information processing, they fill the vacuum that homunculi would otherwise inhabit.

To get a sense of the problem, first consider *what* must be controlled. As Fig. 4.1 suggests, an information processing system must control perception, movement, memory, and thought. For perception, the cognitive system must control which sensory systems are attended to, including the eyes, ears, nose, mouth, skin, and proprioceptors. For movement, the cognitive system must control which motor systems are active, including those for the head, trunk, limbs, digits, eyes, and mouth. For memory, the cognitive system must control the encoding of information into long-term memory (6) and the

	TYPE OF CONTROL	
COGNITIVE ACTIVITY	**Automatic**	**Strategic**
Perception	innate learned	learned
Movement	innate learned	learned
Memory	innate learned	learned
Thought	? learned	learned

Figure 4.1. An overview of information processing control.

retrieval of this information into working memory (**5**). For thought, the cognitive system must control the processing of information in working memory (**10**). Appropriate behavior in many situations often requires carefully coordinated mixtures of perceiving, acting, remembering, and thinking.

Further consider the types of control that occur during information processing. Following current theories, Fig. 4.1 proposes that control can take both *automatic* and *strategic* forms (Posner & Snyder, 1975; Schneider & Shiffrin, 1977; Shiffrin, 1988; Shiffrin & Schneider, 1977). Whereas some cognitive operations occur automatically without being willed, others occur strategically as deliberate attempts to achieve goals. Figure 4.1 further suggests that both innate and learned mechanisms underlie automatic processing, whereas only learned mechanisms underlie strategic processing. The next two sections address automatic and strategic processing in turn, and the final section addresses their role in skilled performance. As we shall see in later chapters, automatic and strategic processing play extensive roles throughout cognition. Note that many cognitive psychologists refer to the control of information processing as *attention*, but because attention has been difficult to define, and because automatic and strategic processing have supplanted it to a large extent, I will not develop attention as a central cognitive construct.

4.1 AUTOMATIC PROCESSING

Simple stimulus–response mechanisms often control the cognitive system. When one of these mechanisms detects an eliciting stimulus, it initiates its response immediately and quickly, regardless of whether the person consciously intended to produce this response or not. Consider the reflexive response to avoid a rapidly approaching object (e.g., a rock hurtling toward your head). On perceiving that a rapidly approaching object is about to hit your body, you move immediately and quickly to avoid it. You do not have to reason about your action. It "just happens," subjectively speaking. Upon detecting an imminent collision, a simple stimulus–response mechanism takes control of the cognitive system and initiates motor movements to avoid the rapidly approaching object. People usually cannot inhibit the initiation of these responses, because the mechanisms that produce them have powerful abilities to wrest control away from willful intentions. For this reason, theorists often refer to these responses as "automatic."

By no means, however, must automatic performance occur without awareness or lie completely beyond deliberate control. Various aspects of an automatic process may be conscious. For example, people are typically aware that they are moving to avoid an object, although they are typically unaware of the mechanism that is producing the action. Furthermore, an automatic process may be modifiable and terminable at various points in its execution.

As people begin to realize that they are acting reflexively to a stimulus, they may begin to reason about what is happening, develop an intention to act differently, and initiate a different action. For example, someone who sees a rock hurtling toward his head might begin to duck automatically, but as he begins to realize that the "rock" is made of soft foam, thrown by a mischievous friend, he may reverse his ducking behavior and allow it to hit him harmlessly. As this example illustrates, "automatic" simply means that the categorization of an eliciting stimulus *initiates* a response. "Automatic" does not mean that the response must be fully executed or that it is unmodifiable.

Cognitive scientists often refer to the stimulus–response mechanisms that produce automatic responses as *production rules* or *productions* (J.R. Anderson, 1983; Newell, 1990; Newell & Simon, 1972; but see Logan, 1988, for an alternative view). Because productions represent simple stimulus–response relations, they are superficially similar to the stimulus–response associations of behaviorism (1.1). Actually, however, they are quite different. Whereas behaviorists view associations as external relations between physical stimuli and behavioral responses, cognitive scientists view productions as cognitive mechanisms that control information processing operations. Productions are *if-then* processing rules represented in long-term memory: If a production detects an eliciting stimulus, it becomes active in memory and attempts to take control of the cognitive system to execute its response. We shall see many examples of productions throughout this chapter.

Following the perspective on representation presented in Chapter 3, cognitive psychologists do not believe that productions exist literally in the brain. Instead, productions are theoretical representations of the brain mechanisms that actually control information processing. Theorists could represent control in other ways, but production systems have provided the most extensive and successful accounts of control thus far. To the extent that production systems do not provide optimal accounts of control, future research will develop new representations of the brain mechanisms that control information processing.

4.1.1 Innate Automatic Processing

Although theorists typically view productions as learned mechanisms of control, many types of innate control also have an if-then quality, very much in the spirit of the construct. Consequently, I use *production* more liberally to represent any form of condition–operation control, regardless of whether it is learned or innate. As we shall see, organisms are genetically endowed with a wide variety of innate productions. The particular productions found in a given species most likely reflect the environmental forces that have shaped its evolution. Such productions structure the control of information processing extensively, even in humans.

Perhaps the best known innate productions are simple motor reflexes. For example, an innate production controls the knee–jerk reflex, relating pressure on the knee to a kicking response. Similarly, people blink when a puff of air strikes an eye. Innate productions like these help an organism avoid threatening stimuli, although many *fixed action patterns* (as they are called in the ethology literature) also exist for activities such as reproduction and feeding (Eibl-Eibesfeldt, 1972; Grier, 1984; Rosenbaum, 1990).

Even these basic automatic processes, however, are not completely automatic. For example, the size of an eye blink depends on what the cognitive system is currently doing (Anthony & Graham, 1983). If the cognitive system is currently focusing on a visual stimulus, eye blinks are larger following a sudden light flash than following a sudden noise. Conversely, if the cognitive system is currently focusing on an auditory stimulus, eye blinks are larger following a sudden noise than following a sudden light flash. Furthermore, eye blinks are larger if the cognitive system is focusing on an interesting stimulus in either modality than if it is focusing on an uninteresting stimulus. If eye blinks were completely automatic, their size would remain constant across all of these manipulations. As these results illustrate, however, contextual factors alter even the most automatic of processes.

People also possess innate productions throughout their perceptual systems. For example, the cognitive system orients automatically to intense, unexpected, and/or changing stimulation in any perceptual system. A loud crash orients auditory processing toward the location of the crash. An unexpected movement in the visual periphery orients visual processing toward the location of the movement. An unexpected taste while eating but thinking about something else orients processing toward the mouth. Many other automatic characteristics of perceptual processing are genetically endowed as well. For example, the perception of color, the construction of structured descriptions against backgrounds (2.2), and the perception of depth depend largely on innate automatic mechanisms. These types of innate perceptual processing are automatic because they require no conscious intention, and because they are difficult to inhibit or alter. Much is known about the physiological and information processing mechanisms that underlie innate automatic processing in perception, and research efforts at these two levels of representation are often closely related (Atkinson et al., 1988a; Boff et al., 1986; Bruce & P. Green, 1990; E.B. Goldstein, 1989; Sekular & Blake, 1990).

Innate automatic processing also underlies memory to some extent. Although people often don't try intentionally to remember events as they occur, they nevertheless encode information about them into memory automatically (see *incidental learning* in **6**.1.2). People appear particularly sensitive to information about the frequency, location, and time of events. Consider frequency. You probably don't keep track intentionally of how often various words or letters occur in the English language, or of how often various kinds of accidents and diseases occur. Yet researchers have found that people provide surprisingly accurate estimates of these frequencies: People know that the word "book" occurs more often than the word "balk." Even though people don't deliberately keep running counts of word frequency, their cognitive systems nevertheless store information automatically that supports relatively accurate frequency estimates.

Numerous experiments in controlled laboratory settings have demonstrated people's abilities to store information in long-term memory automatically. To see how these experiments work, read through the following list of words. As you read each word, decide whether it refers to an animate or inanimate object. Perform each animacy judgment as quickly as you can and then move onto the next word:

tulip	apple	bottle	bicycle	hat
apple	horse	frog	ice	wheel
hat	tree	book	apple	juice
cabin	bicycle	hat	cup	apple

Take a piece of paper and cover the list before reading any further. Once you have covered the list, consider the following five words:

bicycle	ice	apple	roof	hat

Without deliberating, quickly write on a piece of paper your intuitive estimate of how many times each of these words occurred in the list. Now remove the piece of paper that covers the list and check your answers. Although your frequency estimates may not be exactly correct, they probably correlate highly with the correct answers. Specifically, your estimates for the more frequent words are likely to be higher than your estimates for the less frequent words. Interestingly, your ability to estimate frequency was probably not affected by whether you expected a frequency test. If you did not expect a frequency test, you probably performed just as well as someone who did.

Cover up the word list again, and test your knowledge of spatial location. Look at these words:

horse	juice	tulip	frog	ice

For each word, in which of the five columns did it occur? Again, don't deliberate. Just write your answer down as soon as an intuitive answer comes to mind. Now remove the piece of paper and check your answers. Although your estimates of spatial location may not be exactly correct, they probably correlate with the correct locations. To the extent that a word occurred toward the left, you probably estimated that it occurred toward the left. Once again, if you didn't expect a location test, you probably performed just as well as someone who did.

Researchers test memory for temporal position in a similar manner. Imagine that you heard a list of words, presented one at a time, with each word being presented only once. You later hear the words again, one at a time, in a new order. As each word occurs this second time, you must decide whether it occurred in the first, second, third, or fourth quarter of the original list. Although your temporal estimates would not be perfect, they would be highly correlated with the correct temporal position, and expecting or not expecting a test would again have little effect.

Hasher and Zacks (1979, 1984) reviewed research on people's ability to remember information about frequency, location, and time, assessing whether people performed more accurately under intentional learning conditions than under incidental learning conditions (6.1.2). In *intentional learning*, the experimenter informs subjects, prior to learning, that they will later receive a test on frequency, location, or time. As a result, subjects perform the learning phase of the experiment expecting to perform one of these tests. In *incidental learning*, subjects perform an irrelevant task on the acquisition material (e.g., animacy judgments), believing that this task constitutes the primary purpose of the experiment and not expecting to perform a subsequent test.

If the encoding of frequency, location, and time occurs automatically, subjects should encode this information even when they do not have the goal to do so. Incidental learning should be just as good as intentional learning. Across a wide variety of experiments, Hasher and Zacks found that the incidental learning of frequency, location, and time was generally as good as the intentional learning of this information. Because an intention to encode frequency, location, and time is not necessary for acquiring them, Hasher and Zacks concluded that people acquire these three types of information automatically.

Hasher and Zacks further found that the ability to store this information does not vary significantly across subject populations: Children, college students, and the elderly generally perform equivalently on these tasks, as do depressed and non–depressed individuals. In contrast, these populations differ considerably on non–automatic memory tasks that reflect subjects' strategies and effort (Hasher & Zacks, 1979). In *free recall*, for example, where individuals try to write down as many words as they can remember from a list they saw earlier (6.3.1), using good strategies and exerting much effort can greatly improve performance. Because children, college students, and the elderly vary widely in their strategies and effort, they exhibit large differences in free recall, as do depressed and non–depressed individuals. In contrast, the different strategies and effort that these populations exhibit play a much smaller role in remembering frequency, space, and time. Because automatic storage mechanisms dominate the encoding of this information, strategies and effort have little effect, and these populations acquire information about frequency, space, and time equally well.

Contrary to Hasher and Zacks' strong conclusion, more recent work has found that people can strategically control their ability to remember frequency, location, and time, at least to some extent (Barsalou & B.H. Ross, 1986; Begg, D. Maxwell, Mitterer, & Harris, 1986; Greene, 1984, 1986, 1988; Jonides & Naveh-Benjamin, 1987; Naveh-Benjamin & Jonides, 1986; K.W. Williams & Durso, 1986). The goals that people pursue while experiencing events do affect memory for these types of information. Similar to what we saw earlier for eye blinks, the storage of frequency, location, and time is not completely automatic. Rather, the processes that store this information adapt themselves to current contextual factors. Nevertheless, strategic control often appears to have a relatively small impact on the automatic performance of these innate encoding mechanisms. Regardless of what people intend to do deliberately, they nevertheless encode considerable information about frequency, location, and time automatically.

4.1.2 Learned Automatic Processing

All organisms have the ability to extend information processing beyond their genetic endowment. Whereas innate automatic processes optimize survival by accumulating the wisdom of evolution, the ability to acquire new automatic processes enables adaptation to local and unexpected environmental contingencies. Even organisms as simple as the amoeba can learn new behaviors. If an organism frequently pairs a novel stimulus with a particular response, it may acquire a production that eventually produces the response to the stimulus automatically. Imagine someone who always feeds her dog as soon as she hears the chimes at a local church ring five times for five o'clock. Normally, a dog begins to salivate upon perceiving food, but because the dog hears the chimes, and because the chimes signal food, they eventually cause the dog to salivate before food appears. In addition to having an innate automatic production that produces salivation to food, the dog acquires a learned automatic production that produces salivation to the chimes (**1.1, 10**.4.1). Numerous factors moderate the acquisition of learned automatic productions and have received intense study from behaviorists and others for decades (Bower & Hilgard, 1981; Domjan & Burkhard, 1986; J.H. Holland, Holyoak, Nisbett, & Thagard, 1986, chap. 5; Holyoak, Koh, & Nisbett, 1989; Honig & Staddon, 1977; Rachlin, 1970).

Humans, too, learn new productions. Frequently associating a stimulus with a response eventually produces a production having a relatively automatic status. Once such a production develops, perception of the stimulus produces the response with no deliberate intention to do so. Consider the word "hyalite." Although most people don't know that "hyalite" means *clear colorless opal*, they can learn to access its meaning automatically with practice. If "hyalite" and *clear colorless opal* cooccur frequently enough, perception of the word will eventually produce its meaning automatically.

What factors are critical to the development of a learned automatic production? One important factor is *frequency of cooccurrence*. To the extent that a stimulus and a response cooccur frequently, a learned automatic production may develop to produce the response upon perception of the stimulus. Without frequent cooccurrence, a learned automatic production will typically not develop. *Consistent mapping* is a second critical factor: To the extent that the stimulus only occurs with the critical response and with no other response, a learned automatic production may develop. If the stimulus sometimes leads to one response and sometimes to another, the responses compete and prevent the formation of a learned automatic production. Lack of consistent mapping prevents the formation of a learned automatic production, even when the stimulus cooccurs frequently with each of the responses (Logan, 1988; Schneider & Shiffrin, 1977; Shiffrin, 1988; Shiffrin & Schneider, 1977).

People acquire a wide variety of learned automatic productions. Consider movement. People often produce learned movements automatically with little or no intention. Experienced drivers can operate a vehicle for long stretches of time without thinking about what they are doing. They become engrossed in conversation or thought while their eyes, arms, and legs perform many of the operations necessary for controlling a car occur automatically without conscious intention. Consider people's responses to traffic signals. Because red lights cooccur so frequently with pressing the brake pedal, and because red lights are consistently mapped to pressing the brake pedal, an automatic production develops between them. Analogously, another automatic production develops between green lights and pressing the accelerator. Many other learned automatic productions underlie movement in a variety of other activities, including skilled typing and piano playing (Rosenbaum, 1990; Rumelhart & Norman, 1982).

Learned automatic processing in perception. Learned automatic productions underlie much perceptual processing. Some cause people to shift their attention to important stimuli in the environment, such as a speaker who utters your name (Moray, 1959). Everyone has had the experience of being deeply involved in a conversation at a party and hearing his or her name mentioned across the room in a different conversation. Although unaware of this other conversation before, hearing your name suddenly draws your attention to it. Because hearing one's name cooccurs so frequently with shifting attention to the speaker over the course of a lifetime, a learned automatic production becomes established between hearing one's name and shifting attention to the person who utters it. As a result, the production can produce an orienting response to another conversation, even in the absence of an intention to do so. Moreover, it would probably be difficult, if not impossible, to inhibit this response, at least initially. Interestingly, the advertising industry frequently takes advantage of learned orienting reflexes by inserting the sound of ringing telephones and doorbells into commercials. Because people also learn to shift attention to these stimuli automatically, advertisers use them to capture attention.

In a laboratory experiment, Shiffrin and Schneider (1977) demonstrated that learned automatic processing can produce perceptual orienting responses that conflict with subjects' intentions. In the training phase of this experiment, subjects learned to detect certain target letters automatically. Imagine that D, H, and X were the target letters for every trial of the training phase. On each trial, subjects watched a series of 20 frames flash by on a computer screen, such as those in the first column of Fig. 4.2. Each frame in the series replaced the previous frame at the same position on the screen. On some trials, 1 of the 20 frames contained 1 of the 3 targets (i.e., D, H, or X), but on other trials, no frame contained a target. If any frame contained a target, subjects were to respond immediately that a target was present. If none of the frames contained a target, subjects were to respond, following the final frame, that a target was not present.

As Fig. 4.2 illustrates, the first frame in the first column contains, J, S, M, and B, the second frame contains R, L, C, and Z, and so forth. Because the fifth frame contains one of the three targets (H), the correct response for this series of frames is "target present." The second column in Fig. 4.2 illustrates a series of frames containing no target, for which the correct response is "target absent." Subjects performed hundreds and hundreds of trials detecting the same targets. Because subjects always responded to a perceived target by responding "target present," they consistently mapped the target to the same response. As a result, subjects acquired learned automatic productions that enabled them to process the targets quickly and efficiently. Immediately upon detecting a target, the appropriate production fired, causing subjects to respond "target present."

In the test phase of the experiment, subjects performed a similar task. On each trial, subjects again saw a series of 20 frames flash by briefly. As in the training phase, some trials contained a frame with a target, and some trials did not. However, targets in the test phase differed in several important ways from targets in the training phase. First, the targets in the test phase were never the letters used as targets in the training phase (i.e., never D, H, or X). Second, the targets varied from trial to trial, with new targets being assigned just prior to each series of 20 frames. Third, the targets were not consistently

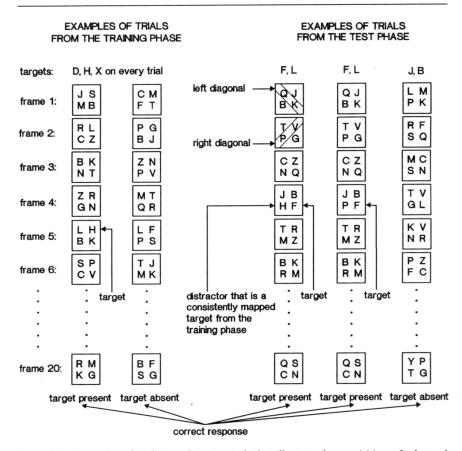

Figure 4.2. Examples of trials in a detection task that illustrate the acquisition of a learned perceptual orienting response. Based on an experiment performed by Shiffrin and Schneider (1977).

mapped to a response and therefore did not develop automatic productions. Instead, each letter sometimes served as a target and sometimes served as a distractor. To see this, consider the third column in Fig. 4.2. For this trial, F and L are targets, whereas J, B, and many other letters are distractors. For the trial in the fifth column of Fig. 4.2, however, J and B are targets, whereas F, L, and many other letters are distractors. As these two columns illustrate, the same letter sometimes mapped to "target present" and sometimes mapped to "target absent." Because letters were not mapped consistently to the same response, the task was harder, and automatic productions did not develop.

The training and test phases differed in one further way: Whereas subjects had to consider every letter in each frame during the training trials, subjects only had to search through letters on *one diagonal* during the test trials. Look at the first two frames in the third column of Fig. 4.2, which illustrate the left and right diagonals within a frame. During the test phase, subjects only had to search for targets on the left diagonal and could ignore letters on the right diagonal. Furthermore, targets only occurred on the left diagonal and never occurred on the right diagonal. In the third column of Fig. 4.2, subjects would only have to check Q and K in the first frame, because they lie on the left diagonal; they could ignore J and B, which lie on the right diagonal.

The third and fourth columns in Fig. 4.2 illustrate the critical manipulation in the experiment. The only difference between these two columns occurs in the fourth frame. As can be seen, this frame also contains a consistently mapped target from the training phase in the third column but not in the fourth column (i.e. H versus P). Whereas H was a consistently mapped target in the training phase, it is a distractor in the test phase, occurring on the right diagonal in some trials but not in others. This manipulation had a substantial effect on subjects' ability to detect targets on the left diagonal (i.e., F in the fourth frame of columns 3 and 4). When a consistently mapped target served as a distractor on the right diagonal, subjects' ability to categorize targets on the left diagonal was much lower than when a consistently mapped target did not appear.

On the basis of this result, Shiffrin and Schneider reached the following conclusion: When a consistently mapped target from the training phase serves as a distractor in the test phase, it produces an automatic orienting response to itself. For example, when H occurs on the right diagonal, it attracts attention to itself, thereby causing subjects to miss target F on the left diagonal. In the process of learning automatized productions for targets in the training phase, subjects learned to orient automatically to them before making a response. Consequently, when these targets serve as distractors on the right diagonal in the test phase, they pulled subjects' attention away from letters on the left diagonal. Even though subjects' intention was only to process letters on the left diagonal, automatic productions for targets from the training phase took control of the cognitive system and caused subjects to perform an orienting response that they did not intend. This illustrates the potent ability of automatic productions to control information processing, at least initially, even when they conflict with strategic processing. Actually, this makes much sense, because such productions can serve a useful purpose in attracting attention to important stimuli in the environment.

Learned automatic processing in memory. Learned automatic productions also underlie much processing in memory. Upon encoding a particular stimulus, people may activate information associated with it in memory automatically. The Stroop effect is a classic example (Stroop, 1935; see also J.D. Cohen, Dunbar, & McClelland, 1990; Logan, 1980; MacLeod &

Dunbar, 1988). Subjects in this type of experiment read words in colored ink, their task being to name the ink color out loud as quickly as possible. Upon seeing "window" in orange ink, for example, a subject says "orange." The critical manipulation concerns the meaning of the word. In the neutral condition, the meaning of the word is unrelated to its ink color (e.g., "window" in orange ink). In the consistent condition, the meaning of the word is the same as its ink color (e.g., "orange" in orange ink). In the inconsistent condition, the meaning of the word is a color different from its ink color (e.g., "purple" in orange ink). Of interest is whether the meanings of these different words affect how long it takes subjects to say that the ink color is orange.

In general, responses are fastest for consistent meanings, next fastest for neutral meanings, and slowest for inconsistent meanings. It is important to note that subjects don't have to attend to meaning in this task, because all they must do is name ink color. In fact, it's to their advantage to ignore meaning, yet subjects are typically unable to do so. Because they have paired words and their meanings over and over again for many years, productions associating these words and their meanings fire automatically. When the meanings are consistent with ink color, they help; when they are not, they interfere. Similar to Shiffrin and Schneider's finding that subjects can't ignore consistently mapped targets on the "off" diagonal, subjects in the Stroop task activate meanings, even when they have no intention of doing so and are even trying to inhibit them. If subjects receive much practice at this kind of task, they can learn to ignore meaning, but this simply shows that new automatic processes develop between ink colors and their names after much practice at the new task (Reisberg, Baron, & Kemler, 1980).

Neely (1977) provides a particularly powerful demonstration of learned automatic processing in memory. Subjects performed the *lexical decision task* (Meyer & Schvaneveldt, 1971), which has become a useful tool for studying a wide range of cognitive phenomena (see **9**.2 and **9**.4 for further examples; Henderson, 1982). Upon seeing a target string of visual letters, subjects must press one key if it forms a word (e.g., "floor") and another key if it does not (e.g., "floon"). Prior to each target string, subjects in Neely's experiment viewed a context string, such as "BUILDING" or "BODY." They were told that whenever they saw "BUILDING," names of *body parts* (e.g. "heart") would be more likely to follow as targets than names of *building parts* (e.g. "floor"). In contrast, whenever subjects saw "BODY" as a context, names of *building parts* would be more likely to follow as targets than names of *body parts*.

Subjects' intentions are crucial to the logic of this experiment. On seeing "BUILDING," subjects' intention should be to think of *body parts*. Because body part names are most likely to follow, thinking of them produces top–down processing that facilitates categorization when they appear (**2**.4,

2.5). Conversely, subjects' intention on seeing "BODY" should be to think of *building parts*.

Yet, learned productions overrode subjects' strategic intentions in Neely's experiment. When subjects saw "BUILDING" followed by "heart," their lexical decisions were actually slower than when they saw "BUILDING" followed by "floor." Even though subjects' intention was to think of *body parts*, the production between *building parts* and *floor* activated *floor* automatically when "BUILDING" was encoded. The frequent pairing of *building parts* and *floor* in subjects' prior experience had created a production that fired automatically when "BUILDING" was presented.

Actually, such activation only occurred in Neely's experiment when the target immediately followed the context. As Neely inserted increasing delays between the context and the target, the automatic activation of specific *building parts* (e.g., *floor*) from "BUILDING" declined, and subjects' intention to think of *body parts* upon seeing "BUILDING" began instead to activate specific *body parts* (e.g., *heart*). When subjects had sufficient time to implement strategic processing, they were able to overcome the initial automatic processing. The strategic control of processing in this manner is the topic of the next section.

4.2 STRATEGIC PROCESSING

Whereas automatic processing occurs without conscious intention, *strategic processing* is the pursuit of conscious intentions. Consider Neely's instructions to think of *body parts* whenever "BUILDING" is read. On reading "BUILD-ING," subjects activate *building parts* automatically, even though this is not their intention. In contrast, subjects don't activate *body parts* unless they intend to think of this category. If subjects were feeling lazy, they could just read "BUILDING" but not use it as a cue for *body parts*, or they could think of *fruit* instead if they wished. Subjects only activate *body parts* if that is their intention. Eventually "BUILDING" could come to activate *body parts* automatically, but only if subjects performed the task long enough to develop an automatic production relating these two categories.

Consider "hyalite" again. Did its meaning come to mind effortlessly? If not, trying intentionally to remember where you heard "hyalite" may be necessary for recovering its meaning. Moreover, if you don't feel like searching memory, you probably still don't know what "hyalite" means. To activate its meaning, you must have the goal of searching for it. Of course if you associate "hyalite" and its meaning frequently enough, strategic processing will no longer be necessary for activation to occur, nor sufficient to inhibit it, at least initially.

4.2.1 Mechanisms of Strategic Processing

At the most general level, strategic control determines the goal an organism pursues when several are possible. For simple organisms, this control may reside largely in innate automatic productions. In fish, for example, certain internal and external stimuli automatically trigger feeding, fighting, reproduction, flight, and so forth. What makes human information processing so much more complex is that people frequently achieve acquired goals in acquired manners (e.g., buying a house plant, writing a letter).

People have extensive knowledge about goals in long-term memory. As Schank and Abelson (1977) suggest, people have knowledge about *biological goals* (e.g., satisfying hunger), *achievement goals* (e.g., establishing a successful marriage), *entertainment goals* (e.g., going to a symphony), and *preservation goals* (e.g., keeping one's belongings from being stolen). People have tremendous amounts of knowledge about these goals, including knowledge about their enabling conditions, how to achieve them, and so forth.

Executive productions.   Executive productions provide one representation of the cognitive mechanisms that establish and execute acquired goals. Executive productions use knowledge of goals—together with information about the current context—to perform strategic processing. These productions have the same if-then quality as the productions that underlie automatic processing.

The primary difference between automatic and executive productions revolves around the experience of conscious willful control. Whereas automatic productions often seem to fire unconsciously and beyond the range of conscious control, executive productions seem intuitively to be the embodiment of deliberate free will. However, executive productions do not necessarily reflect the free will that people often believe underlies conscious control. Instead, the firing of executive productions may be just as inevitable as the firing of automatic productions, although conveying an illusion of free will or self control in the process. On a given occasion, the current states of the environment and the cognitive system may determine which executive productions fire in which order to pursue the high-level goals of the cognitive system. The subjective experience of control and free will may often accompany these firings but not be their cause. We shall return to these issues later in section 4.4.

Another important difference between automatic and executive productions concerns different limits on their firings. Whereas large numbers of automatic productions can fire simultaneously in parallel, the number of executive productions that can fire simultaneously is extremely limited. As we shall see in section 4.2.2, the centralized strategic resource that implements executive productions exhibits a limited capacity, such that only one, or possibly a few, executive productions can fire at once. In contrast, large numbers of automatic productions can fire at once in parallel, as their initiating conditions are perceived, because their implementation bypasses this limited strategic resource.

Consider some simplified examples of executive productions. One executive production might initiate a search for goals, when time exists to pursue them:

IF there is nothing to do,
THEN search memory for possible goals.

The operation of this production might retrieve various goals that the actor has had the intention of pursuing, like getting some long-needed sleep or making some phone calls. Subsequent executive productions might initiate assessment of the current situation and determine if conditions are right to pursue retrieved goals. For example:

IF the conditions for a retrieved goal are currently present,
THEN assign this goal a high likelihood of success in the current context.

If a person is in a hotel room with several free hours before a conference, then these conditions provide the goals of getting some sleep and making some phone calls with a high likelihood of success. Once feasible goals have been identified, further executive productions might determine the relative value of pursuing each and then select one to pursue. Many aspects of decision making in humans enter into these particular productions (e.g., the formal utility model in **10**.3.2). For example:

IF more than one goal is feasible,
THEN combine the costs and benefits of each to obtain its overall utility.

If both getting sleep and making phone calls are feasible, then their respective utilities are computed to see if one goal is more desirable than the other. Once the utilities for each feasible goal are available, further executive productions select the goal with the highest utility. For example:

IF the utilities for several feasible goals are available,
THEN pursue the goal with the highest utility.

If making phone calls has higher utility then getting sleep, then the goal to make phone calls dominates. Finally, people have other executive productions that protect goals achieved previously. For example:

IF current conditions threaten an achieved goal,
THEN determine if the achieved goal is more important than the current goal.

If a fire breaks out in the hotel, this production would help determine that protecting one's life and helping other hotel occupants protect theirs is more important than making a phone call. Subsequent productions would switch the goal to initiating relevant strategies, such as calling the fire department and avoiding fumes. Certainly the productions in these examples are vastly oversimplified. However, their purpose is simply to convey a sense of how productions can explain executive control. Many actual implementations of production systems in artificial intelligence demonstrate the clear feasibility of using executive productions to control the behavior of information processing systems (J.R. Anderson, 1983; Newell, 1990; Newell & Simon, 1972; Norman & Shallice, 1986).

An interesting issue to consider is the extent to which executive productions are learned versus innate. Certainly people have different goals. Moreover, people differ in when and how they achieve the same goals. Yet these differences may reflect people's *knowledge* of goals and how to achieve them, rather than the executive productions that operate upon this knowledge (i.e., declarative vs. procedural knowledge; 7.1). One factor that may make humans unique among organisms is their possession of innate productions that search, compare, and execute acquired goals. If this is so, then we must amend Fig. 4.1 to include innate processes as providing some type of strategic control.

Scripts.   Once executive productions select a goal, they may extract information from a script to achieve it. A *script* is a knowledge structure in long-term memory that specifies the conditions and actions for achieving a goal (Abbott, Black, & E.E. Smith, 1985; Barsalou & Sewell, 1985; Bower, Black, & Turner, 1979; Norman & Shallice, 1986; Schank, 1982; Schank & Abelson, 1977). Consider the script for doing laundry. This script specifies the initial enabling conditions that must be met if its goal is to be achieved (e.g., dirty laundry exists, a washer and dryer are available, enough laundry detergent is present, etc.). The script further specifies the sequence of actions that will achieve the goal (e.g., collecting dirty laundry, sorting it into piles, turning on the washer, placing detergent in the washer, putting clothes in the washer, etc.).

Executive productions perform a wide variety of operations on scripts during goal achievement. Once a script becomes active, executive productions may select possible actions from the script, assess whether their enabling conditions are met, initiate enabled actions, and monitor their success. If enabling conditions are not met, or if an action fails, then executive productions may decide to modify the script, terminate the script, initiate an alternative script, or initiate another script for getting assistance from others (Norman & Shallice, 1986). As discussed later, increased practice at performing an activity may eventually transfer control from executive productions to a more automatized form of the script (**4**.3, **10**.6.3).

Clearly, people do not achieve the same goal rigidly in the same way time after time. Instead, they constantly modify script-based behavior to reflect current contextual constraints. Consequently, most scripts are not rigid action sequences for goal achievement, as the name "script" unfortunately implies. Instead, scripts often contain a tremendous amount of information about how to handle the wide variety of factors that can arise when achieving a goal. When eating at a restaurant, for example, people don't always perform the same exact series of actions. Instead, their actions are guided by the nature of the restaurant (e.g. a fast food restaurant vs. a fine European restaurant), by specific events that occur unexpectedly (e.g., the main dish arrives cold), and by other goals being pursued simultaneously (e.g., celebrating an anniversary). The dynamic control of human information processing reflects scripts' powerful ability to support wide variations in how people achieve a particular goal. Further flexibility may also arise from the ability of executive productions to reorganize performance when script knowledge fails.

Remindings.   Most theorists assume that scripts arise from much experience at achieving a particular goal (**10**.6.2). But how do people achieve novel goals for which they have little experience (**10**.6.1)? In many such cases, they are reminded of past occasions on which they achieved a similar goal. For example, someone who needs to buy a car and has only done this once before might recall her previous purchase and use this information to guide current behavior by analogy. If she remembers having previously studied reviews of cars in trade journals, she might begin the next purchase the same way. Note that the use of remindings to control goal achievement is highly similar to the use of exemplars to control categorization (**2**.3.1); it is also highly similar to implicit memory, which we will consider later (**6**.3.3). In all cases, memories of specific events—not abstract knowledge—guide processing.

Consequently, another function of executive productions is to control the retrieval and application of reminded events. These productions search for memories of relevant prior events, examine a remembered event for relevant information, assess whether a past action will work, and modify past actions for current use. Remindings also occur frequently during the control of familiar activities. Because a familiar activity often takes unfamiliar twists, its script may not contain information relevant to handling particular variations, especially when they have only occurred occasionally. Successful control of behavior in these situations may be facilitated by extracting information from similar past events. Someone with a well-developed laundry script may be washing a shirt, for example, and be reminded of a time when pants made of a similar fabric melted in the dryer. Application of this reminding to the current situation would prevent making the same mistake twice.

As this example illustrates, people often retrieve remindings using task-relevant information. The information that produced the reminding—the shirt fabric—is relevant to washing the shirt correctly. If the launderer ignores the fabric, he may ruin the shirt, but by focusing on this task-relevant information, he may be reminded of the prior time he ruined a fabric of this type and initiate alternative actions.

However, not all remindings occur this way. On other occasions, remindings result from processing information irrelevant to the task at hand. Consider an experiment by B.H. Ross (1984), in which subjects learned to use a word processor on a computer. In the first phase of the experiment, subjects learned pairs of equivalent word processing commands, such as two equivalent commands for entering a word into a text: INSERT and APPEND. Subjects learned to use each command in the context of a particular type of text. Some subjects learned INSERT while editing a *grocery list* and learned APPEND while editing a *business memo*. Other subjects received the opposite assignments of commands to text types (e.g., INSERT for a business memo; APPEND for a grocery list). Note that these assignments are irrelevant to the task: Subjects could use either command to enter words into either type of text.

In the second phase of the experiment, subjects edited either another grocery list or another business memo. Of interest was whether subjects preferred to use INSERT or APPEND when entering a word into this new document. Ross found that subjects tended to use the command that they had used for the same type of text earlier. For example, if subjects had used INSERT to edit a previous grocery list, they tended to prefer INSERT for entering a word into a second grocery list. Similarly, if subjects had used APPEND to edit a previous business memo, they tended to prefer APPEND for entering a word into a business memo.

As this result illustrates, an irrelevant aspect of the task—text type—controlled subjects' strategic processing to some extent. If only relevant aspects of the task had determined performance, subjects should have used each command roughly 50% of the time, because each allows subjects to achieve the relevant goal. If subjects had favored one command over the other for some reason (e.g., ease of keystrokes), they should have favored the same command for *both* text types. Why, then, did subjects favor one command for one text type and the other command for the other text type?

Ross concluded that irrelevant factors in a task context often produce remindings. When performing a task in a particular context, people are often reminded of previous events from that context. As these memories from the same context become active, task-relevant information in them may guide strategic processing. In essence, the cognitive system is betting that past events in similar contexts offer solutions to current problems (see also Bassok, 1990; Bassok & Holyoak, 1989; Catrambone & Holyoak, 1989; Gentner, 1989; Gick & Holyoak, 1980, 1983; Holyoak & Koh, 1987; Holyoak & Thagard, 1989a, 1989b; Kolodner, 1988; Novick, 1988; B.H. Ross, 1987, 1989a, 1989b; B.H. Ross & Kennedy, 1990; Schank, 1982).

4.2.2 Performance Characteristics of Strategic Processing

Much work in cognitive psychology has addressed various aspects of strategic processing (Shiffrin, 1988). In the following sections, I address the limited capacity of strategic processing, the selectivity of strategic processing, and the processing of non-selected information.

Limited capacity.   Because people can only achieve a small number of goals at any one time, their ability to execute strategic processing is limited. Most people would have trouble balancing their checkbook, planning a vacation, and carrying on a conversation simultaneously. Theorists often assume that people's limited ability to perform strategic processing reflects a limited strategic resource of some kind. Reading a new recipe may require so much of this limited strategic resource, for example, that a cook is unable to do anything else simultaneously, and would be unable to follow a piece of music in the background. However, strategic tasks vary in the amount of the strategic resource that they require, with some tasks requiring less than others. When a primary strategic task does not require all of the strategic resource, a secondary strategic task may utilize the remainder. For example, making a recipe may require less of the strategic resource than reading it, such that simultaneously following a piece of music is possible. Some tasks may demand more of the strategic resource than exists. Playing a new video game may overwhelm novices because they can't process all of the relevant stimuli simultaneously.

A strategic task is *resource limited* if its performance depends upon the amount of the strategic resource available to it. As the availability of the resource decreases, performance on the task decreases as well. If enough of the resource is available to perform the task, performance may be good (e.g., following music while making a recipe), but if performing some other strategic task leaves less of the resource, performance may be poor (e.g., following music while having to read a recipe). Low availability of the strategic resource, then, limits task performance. A strategic task can also be *data limited,* if its performance depends on the quality of the information (data) available to it. As the quality of the information available for a task deteriorates, performance deteriorates as well. For example, the ability to process a phone message may deteriorate with increasing noise on the line, no matter how much of the strategic resource is allocated to it.

Researchers use *performance-resource functions* to represent how the strategic resource constrains task performance. Consider panel A of Figure 4.3. This panel plots the percentage of optimal performance on Task 1 as a function of the amount of the strategic resource allocated to it. For example, when people allocate 10% of the strategic resource to Task 1, they perform Task 1 at 40% of its optimal level. When they allocate 50% of the strategic resource to Task 1, they perform Task 1 at 93% of its optimal level. When they allocate 70% or more of the strategic resource to Task 1, they perform Task 1 at 100% of

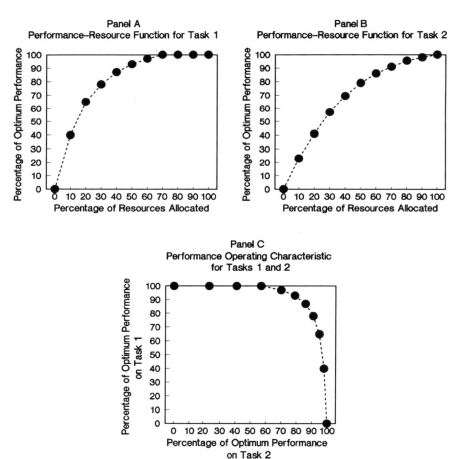

Figure 4.3.   Examples of performance-resource functions for two tasks (panels A and B) and their performance operating characteristic (panel C).

its optimal level. Look now at the performance-resource function for Task 2 in panel B of Figure 4.3. As can be seen, Task 2 requires more of the strategic resource than Task 1 for optimal performance. Whereas Task 1 requires at least 70% of the strategic resource for optimal performance, Task 2 requires 100%. As these performance-resource functions illustrate, the availability of the strategic resource constrains task performance, and tasks differ in the amount of the strategic resource that they require.

Panel C of Figure 4.3 shows the *performance operating characteristic* for Tasks 1 and 2 combined. This panel represents the joint performance on Tasks 1 and 2 as people allocate the strategic resource to them in differing amounts. Consider the top left point in the performance operating characteristic. This point represents how well people perform Task 1 (100%) and Task 2 (0%) when they allocate 100% of the strategic resource to Task 1 and 0% to Task 2. The second point from the left represents how well people perform Task 1 (100%) and Task 2 (23%) when they allocate 90% of the strategic resource to Task 1 and 10% to Task 2. Each successive point to the right represents an additional 10% loss of resources for Task 1 and a corresponding 10% gain in resources for Task 2. Thus, the sixth point from the left represents how well people perform Task 1 (93%) and Task 2 (79%) when they allocate 50% of the strategic resource to Task 1 and 50% to Task 2. As the sixth point illustrates, 50% of the strategic resource accomplishes more of Task 1 than of Task 2. In general, a performance operating characteristic represents the trade-offs that occur between two resource-limited tasks performed simultaneously. As one task receives more of the strategic resource, its performance may improve at the expense of the other task (Kahneman, 1973; Navon, 1984; Norman & D.G. Bobrow, 1975).

What is this information processing resource that limits strategic processing? Theorists often assume that it is some kind of limited processing energy, analogous to an electrical source whose fixed wattage limits the number of appliances that can operate at any one time. If too many appliances attempt to use the electrical source, some may fail to function because there is not enough power to go around. In humans, if one strategic task requires all of the available processing energy, no other task can be accomplished simultaneously. If a strategic task requires less than the total processing energy, however, another task can occur simultaneously with the remaining energy.

Alternatively, the limited strategic resource might be a single executive processor that applies and manages executive productions (**4.2.1**). The most important property of this processor is that it can only execute one strategic task at a time but can switch quickly from one strategic task to another. According to this view, the limit on strategic processing arises from the limited ability of the executive processor to switch between tasks. If a strategic task requires extended and uninterrupted use of the executive processor, then no other strategic task can occur simultaneously. Reading a new recipe, for example, may require uninterrupted use of the executive processor to understand the recipe adequately. Resource limitations result because one task requires so much of the processor's time that other strategic processes cannot be pursued. In contrast, if a task only requires short and interruptible use of the executive processor, then switching back and forth between strategic tasks becomes possible, and resource limitations are less likely. Making a recipe, for example, may allow switching to music often enough to follow it (Neumann, 1987; Shiffrin, 1988).

Selectivity.   The process of achieving a goal requires the selection and coordination of various information processing subsystems. *Selectivity* corresponds to what theorists often mean by *attention*. To perform a task, people must select (attend to) different cognitive subsystems at different times and coordinate them. At a given point in a task, one might select the visual system to categorize something, at another point, the memory system to retrieve a script, at yet another point, the motor system to carry out an action. When doing the laundry, for example, one selects the visual system to categorize individual pieces of laundry, the memory system to retrieve information about how to wash each kind of laundry, the motor system to perform the movements that create piles of different laundry types, and so forth. At any given point in the process, executive productions, often under the guidance of scripts, select particular information processing subsystems and specify the operations that they should perform.

The ability to select particular subsystems is extremely flexible in humans. In perception, one can select an entire sensory modality and process the stimuli occurring on it: If audition is selected, the focus is on categorizing auditory stimuli; if vision is selected, the focus is on categorizing visual stimuli. However, selection can be more specific. If one selects a particular ear or eye, stimuli are categorized better on this sensor than on the unselected sensor in the same modality. Selection can be still more specific, focusing on particular sources of information. If one selects the voice of a particular person in a nearby conversation, or a particular person's face on the far side of the room, these sources of information will be processed better than nonselected sources. Selection of motor movements can also be highly specific, given the extent to which people can control their head, trunk, limbs, and fingers.

Researchers have primarily studied selection in audition and vision, with much work addressing people's ability to select one of several competing information sources in these modalities. In audition, researchers have typically used the *shadowing task* to study people's selective ability. In this task, subjects wear headphones that present two messages simultaneously, and their task is to repeat out loud ("shadow") one of the messages as accurately as possible. Subjects' shadowing usually lags behind the presented message by a short duration. When each message is played to a different ear (i.e., *dichotic listening*), subjects show that they can select one ear by only shadowing its message and not mistakenly repeating words from the other message. When both messages are played to both ears simultaneously, subjects can still shadow one message with reasonable accuracy under a wide range of conditions. When different voices speak the messages, subjects can shadow one voice by selecting its acoustic characteristics, focusing on the message having the acoustic characteristics of one person's voice (e.g., a woman's), while tuning out the message having the acoustic characteristics of the other person's voice (e.g., a man's). When the same voice speaks about two different topics, subjects can shadow one topic by selecting its semantic characteristics (**8**.6), focusing on the message whose words are relevant to one topic (e.g., politics), while tuning out the message whose words are relevant to the other topic (e.g., the weather). Even when the same voice speaks about the same topic, subjects can still shadow one message by selecting its syntactic characteristics (**8**.5), focusing on the message whose next word is expected syntactically (e.g., a noun), while tuning out the message whose next word is not expected syntactically (e.g., a verb; J.A. Deutsch & D. Deutsch, 1963; Moray, 1970; Norman, 1968; Treisman, 1969).

Although people can select between different types of information to an impressive degree, they nevertheless make errors when stimuli similar to those in the selected message occur in a non-selected message. Imagine that a person has selected a message about boats to shadow but that "float" occurs in a non-selected message about a parade. This temporary similarity of the non-selected message may cause the person to select it mistakenly as the message to be shadowed. As a result, the person incorrectly says "float" and perhaps a few other words from the competing message as well. Competition between multiple information sources escalates as they become increasingly similar (J.A. Gray & Wedderburn, 1960; Treisman, 1969).

Much research has also addressed people's ability to select information in visual processing. Individuals, for example, can select a specific point in the visual field and process information occurring there more efficiently than information at other points. Imagine that subjects see a letter flashed in front of them in one of eight possible locations positioned around the circumference of a circle. Subjects never know what position will contain the letter, because the position varies from trial to trial. Across trials, however, the letter occurs much more often in some positions than in others, most often at the top and bottom of the circle, and least often at the sides. Once subjects develop expectations about where letters are most likely to occur, they select each position to the extent that letters occur there. As a result, subjects are best at identifying letters in positions that contain a letter most often. If subjects couldn't select positions in the visual field for strategic processing, such differences would not occur, and their ability to categorize letters would be the same for every position (M. Shaw & P. Shaw, 1977).

Do subjects distribute a strategic resource simultaneously over these expected visual positions? Or do they select each position one a time, frequently switching an executive processor from one likely position to another? Subsequent research has generally supported the latter view. Rather than distributing visual processes over multiple locations simultaneously, people focus an attentional "spotlight" on one location at a time. Because they expect letters to occur in some positions more often than others, they focus the executive processor most often on positions that are likely to contain the letter. To the extent that subjects can switch the executive processor between positions efficiently, they can effectively monitor more than one position (Posner, Snyder, & Davidson, 1980).

Not only can people vary the position of the executive processor in the visual field, they can also vary its width, focusing the executive processor on a location the width of a single letter, the width of an entire word, and so forth. In addition, the "light" from this attentional "spotlight" becomes "dimmer" as it spreads out into the area surrounding the current position of the executive processor. When focusing the executive processor on a particular position, people process locations surrounding that position faster than positions further away, although not as fast as at the focal position. Once focused upon a particular position, the executive processor produces a gradient of processing benefit that diminishes with distance (LaBerge & V. Brown, 1989).

People don't have to move their eyes to shift the executive processor within the visual field. Research has shown that subjects can select a new visual position for processing before they move their eyes to it. Consider an experiment by Posner, Nissen, and Ogden (1978). To begin each trial, subjects focused their eyes and attention on a fixation point in the middle of a computer screen. Shortly thereafter, an X flashed very briefly either to the left or the right of the fixation point. Subjects' task was to indicate whether the X occurred on the left or the right as quickly as possible.

On some trials, an arrow appeared at the center of the screen following the fixation point but before the X. The arrow pointed either to the left or the right and usually predicted the position of the X (though occasionally the arrow was misleading). The X then appeared 50 msec after the arrow, on either the left or the right. Thus, if the arrow pointed to the left, the X usually appeared on the left 50 msec later; if the arrow pointed to the right, the X usually appeared on the right 50 msec later. Because the X sometimes occurred opposite the direction of the arrow, subjects couldn't base their final response on the arrow's direction but had to wait until the X appeared.

Of interest was whether subjects could utilize the arrow, when it occurred, and shift their attention to the expected location of the X. If subjects could not shift attention within 50 msec, the presence of the arrow would not help their performance: They would still be focused on the fixation point when the X appeared, and only the X's position would control processing. The arrow would then be irrelevant, because the X is the critical stimulus, and subjects would perform no differently than if the arrow had not appeared at all. If subjects can shift their attention within 50 msec, however, they should already be focused on the expected position of the X when it appeared, and thus be able to process its appearance more rapidly.

Posner found that subjects could indeed use the arrow to shift the executive processor. When an arrow preceded the X, subjects identified the X faster and more accurately than when no arrow preceded it. Subjects were able to shift attention from the fixation point to the expected position within 50 msec. The most critical fact about this experiment is that an eye movement from the fixation point to the expected position could not have been responsible for this shift: Typically, it takes people at least 150 msec to shift their eyes from a fixation point to a nearby position. Because subjects had shifted their attention within 50 msec, an internal shift of the executive processor—not an external shift of the eyes—produced the facilitation (see also Remington, 1980; G.L. Shulman, Remington, & McLean, 1979; Tsal, 1983).

So far, I have focused on people's ability to select particular locations in perceptual fields (e.g., audition, vision). However, people can also select information in memory. As we saw in **2.4** and **2.5**, selecting a category in memory produces substantial top-down effects in categorization. For example, if one selects the category *bread* in memory, a visually perceived loaf of bread can be categorized faster than if this category is not selected. Similarly, the word "bread" could be categorized faster if someone speaks it, and the smell or feel of bread could probably be categorized faster as well. Once people select a category in memory, it facilitates their ability to categorize information on the relevant modalities. Activation can also spread from selected information to related information. When people select *bread*, associates such as *butter* become primed, because of the strong relations between them. Selection can also create inhibition to unrelated categories. Selecting *bread*, for example, is likely to inhibit the categorization of *robins* and *cars*.

In general, selection facilitates the processing of information relevant to the goals of strategic processing and inhibits irrelevant information. To achieve a goal, the cognitive system must be able to select information processing subsystems, locations in perceptual fields, and categories in memory. Without the ability to select, the cognitive system would function chaotically. Because of this ability, people can select subsystems, locations, and categories in myriad but meaningful orders, such that they can achieve a wide variety of acquired goals in a wide variety of manners.

Processing non-selected information. What happens to information that impinges on non-selected perceptual subsystems? To what extent do people process this information? In early work, Cherry (1953; Cherry & W.K. Taylor, 1954) had subjects shadow one message and later asked them about characteristics of the non-shadowed message. Subjects could usually state the sex of the speaker, whether the speaker's voice had ever switched from a man's to a woman's, and whether a pure tone had occurred in the message. However, subjects rarely knew the topic of the non-shadowed message, what language was spoken, or whether the message contained speech played forward or backward. In a similar study, Moray (1959) found that subjects did not know if a particular word, presented 35 times, had ever occurred in the non-shadowed message. These results suggested that people do not categorize the stimuli in non-selected messages but only note some of their salient perceptual characteristics.

Researchers later developed a number of ingenious paradigms to assess more carefully whether people categorize stimuli in non-selected messages. Contrary to Cherry and Moray's findings, some of these studies reported evidence that people do. Consider an experiment by Corteen and Wood (1972). In the first phase of this experiment, subjects saw the names of cities, some of which were paired with a very mild electrical shock (e.g., "Belfast" followed by shock).[1] Corteen and Wood monitored subjects *galvanic skin response* (GSR) throughout the experiment. GSRs result unconsciously when subjects expect an unpleasant stimulus and prepare themselves for it. As subjects learned which city names preceded shock, they produced GSRs to these names unconsciously in anticipation of the mildly unpleasant experience. Learning continued until subjects consistently produced GSRs to the names that predicted shock.

Later in the experiment, subjects performed a shadowing task. Occasionally, a city name, previously associated with shock, occurred on the non-shadowed ear. If subjects were only categorizing information on the shadowed ear, they should not have attended to the city names on the non-shadowed ear, and these names should not have produced GSRs. Corteen and Wood found that subjects were not aware of the city names on the non-shadowed ear. When tested on whether any of the names associated with

---

[1] Do not try this experiment at home! In the United States and many other countries, psychological research with human subjects is carefully monitored by government and university agencies. Psychological experiments cannot be performed unless they satisfy a thorough review process, which only approves experiments that are completely safe both physically and psychologically for subjects. Furthermore, all subjects are advised of their rights and the procedures they are about to undergo, they sign a consent form, they are debriefed following the experiment, and they receive the names of authorities to contact, should they wish to register a complaint. Experimenters must follow these protocols by law for the purpose of ensuring subjects' welfare both during and following experiments.

shock had occurred on this ear, subjects had no memory of them. Nevertheless, the city names on the non-shadowed ear produced GSRs. Moreover, other city names that had not been associated with shock earlier also produced GSRs. Subjects appeared, then, to be processing words on the non-shadowed ear quite deeply, because they unconsciously expected shock every time a city name occurred. Even if a city name had not been associated with shock originally, its conceptual status as a *city* produced a GSR. These findings suggest that people process stimuli in non-selected messages extensively, even though they are not aware of this processing (see also Von Wright, K. Anderson, & Steman, 1975).

Other researchers have found that the meanings of unattended words affect text comprehension, even when subjects are unaware of them. For example, MacKay (1973) had subjects shadow a text that occasionally contained an ambiguous sentence, such as:

They threw stones toward the bank yesterday.

Just prior to the ambiguous word (i.e., *bank*), a disambiguating word occurred on the non-shadowed ear. For example, *river*, which primes one sense of *bank*, occurred on the non-shadowed ear for some subjects, whereas *money*, which primes a different sense of *bank*, occurred on the non-shadowed ear for other subjects. Later, subjects received two sentences and were asked which had occurred on the shadowed ear. For example:

They threw stones toward the side of the river yesterday.
They threw stones toward the savings and loan yesterday.

If subjects had not categorized the dismambiguating word on the non-shadowed ear, they should have been equally likely to pick each sentence (although neither had occurred). However, if subjects had categorized the disambiguating word, it should have biased their understanding of the ambiguous sentence toward one interpretation via top-down priming (2.5, 2.6). Subjects who had received *river* should have understood the ambiguous sentence as referring to a *river bank*, whereas subjects who had received *money* should have understood the ambiguous sentence as referring to a *financial bank*. Subjects did indeed prefer the test sentence that was consistent with the disambiguating word, further suggesting that people categorize non-selected stimuli (see also J.L. Lewis, 1970; Norman, 1969).

Theorists still argue about the interpretation of these findings. Do they really reflect conceptual processing of unattended stimuli? Or do subjects attend illicitly to them? Perhaps subjects switch selection to the non-selected message often enough to make categorizations, even though they aren't supposed to switch. The understanding of learned automatic processes depends critically on the answer to this question. As we have seen, learned automatic processes underlie many categorizations. Because people categorize letters and words so often, they categorize them automatically, as the Stroop effect illustrates. Categorization of physical objects such as clothing, fruit, and animals probably also occurs automatically for familiar exemplars. The issue is whether automatic categorizations only occur for selected perceptual subsystems or whether they also occur for non-selected subsystems. If selection turns out to be necessary for automatic categorization, two possible explanations are: (a) Selection may provide the use of a single-task executive, or it may provide some kind of processing energy, either of which could be necessary for categorizations to occur; (b) categorization mechanisms may generally be inhibited, such that they can only operate when their subsystem is selected and its inhibition lifted. Regardless of whether selection is necessary for categorization, it is clear that processing is much more extensive for selected than for non-selected subsystems (see also Goolkasian, 1981; Kahneman & Henik, 1981).

4.3   SKILL

With increasing practice at an activity, the control of information processing undergoes major changes. As people become skilled at an activity, increasingly large amounts of information processing become automatic. Consider driving. As a novice, much strategic processing is necessary for setting driving goals, for retrieving relevant information from the driving script, and for executing actions. Executive productions that operate on a driving script learned from verbal and written instructions control performance. With experience, though, particular condition-action sequences occur so frequently that these particular parts of the driving script evolve into learned automatic productions. Most importantly, the execution of these productions no longer relies on executive productions. Instead, categorization of relevant stimuli triggers these productions automatically. On seeing a yield sign, a driver no longer has to search the driving script for the perception, decision, and motor operations to perform. Instead, automatic productions execute a perceptual scan for traffic, decide whether to go or wait, and control the car. In other words, the script for driving becomes automated, as relatively static forms of knowledge evolve into more active productions (J.R. Anderson, 1983; T. Winograd, 1975).

Similarly consider the activation of word meanings. If a word's meaning is not activated automatically (e.g., *hyalite*), then executive productions may search memory for past episodes that contain its meaning. With experience, however, a production may develop that automatically triggers *clear colorless opal*, such that strategic search is no longer necessary (LaBerge & Samuels, 1974).

Once automatic productions develop for an activity, executive productions become free to do other things. In driving, executive productions, freed from responding to repetitive traffic situations, can carry out less automated activities, such as planning a vacation or discussing politics with a passenger. Similarly, in reading, executive productions, freed from accessing word meanings, can integrate major points in the text and assess their validity. However, most tasks probably do not become completely automatic. Instead, strategic control may often be necessary for monitoring performance and handling unfamiliar situations that arise. When taking a new route to work, for example, experienced drivers must use strategic processing, because automatic productions that recognize and execute turns along the route do not exist. In their place, drivers might use executive productions to search a newly-formed script for taking the new route, perhaps acquired from reading a map.

The transition to skilled behavior is not a single change from strategic to automatic processing. Instead, skill increases slowly and continuously as more and more stimulus–response subparts of the activity become encoded into automatic productions. In fact, skills never seem to stop becoming automated. As we shall see in **10.6.3**, performance on a wide range of perception, motor, memory, and thinking skills keeps getting better even after many thousands of trials. No evidence has yet been found for an end in improvement. To account for this, theories of skill generally assume that the development of automatic processing continues indefinitely (J.R. Anderson, 1983; Laird, Rosenbloom, & Newell, 1986; Logan, 1988; Newell, 1990; Newell & Rosenbloom, 1981). It is important to note, however, that skill must involve more than simply the automation of performance. Typically, an increased conceptual understanding of the domain develops as well.

4.4 LIMITS TO CURRENT THEORY

As we have seen, cognitive psychologists have tried to banish homunculi from their theories by developing well-defined theories of control. Innate productions control basic aspects of information processing central to survival. Productions learned from the frequent pairing of stimuli and responses extend automatic processing to new stimuli, thereby allowing organisms to adapt to their specific environments. Executive productions operate on goals, scripts, and reminded episodes to select and coordinate information processing subsystems during goal-directed behavior. Repeating particular patterns of strategic processing produces new productions that automate repeated parts of the relevant scripts, freeing executive productions to work on more subtle aspects of the task or to perform multiple tasks simultaneously. Skill develops as increasing amounts of the processing that executive productions perform become automated.

Clearly major gaps exist in this formulation. Where does consciousness fit into automatic and strategic processing (G. Mandler, 1975, 1985; Marcel, 1983a, 1983b)? What role do emotions play (Ortony, Clore, & A.M. Collins, 1988)? Does processing energy, switching, or something else limit strategic processing? What are the executive productions that control strategic processing? To what extent are they innate versus learned? What is the content of scripts and reminded episodes? How do executive productions operate on them during strategic processing to produce the tremendous flexibility and adaptability characteristic of human performance? Much remains to be learned before cognitive psychologists understand the control of human information processing adequately.

Moreover, this formulation may be fundamentally incorrect. Rather than one set of executive productions controlling all strategic processing, multiple sets, each tailored to one general type of cognitive activity may share control (e.g., different sets for vision, movement, thought). Alternatively, there may be no high-level executive control at all, with many activity-specific executives, much like scripts, controlling the cognitive system. Connectionists generally view control as distributed rather than as residing in one or a few central executives (**2.5**).

Several formidable problems face completely distributed views. No one has yet developed a distributed account of control that can rival single-executive accounts. Certainly distributed views may develop, but until they do, cognitive psychologists cannot have much confidence that distributed processing alone will produce strategic processing. Currently, it is not clear how a completely distributed system could produce the complicated and coordinated scheduling that is characteristic of human performance. Moreover, it is not clear how distributed systems explain humans' greater flexibility and computational power in pursuing goals compared to other species. A larger number of distributed processing units and connections alone does not seem sufficient to capture the qualitative ways in which human and non-human information processing differ. Rather, the evolution of a centralized strategic processing mechanism may be responsible.

The single-executive account has many attractive characteristics from a design standpoint. It provides an obvious mechanism for scheduling, monitoring, and trouble-shooting performance. It provides a natural way of explaining humans' advantage over other species in achieving novel goals in novel ways (i.e., the executive system has much greater ability to activate information from diverse scripts and integrate it into new ones). A single executive system is parsimonious: If one mechanism is sufficient to control a wide range of strategic behavior, then why would nature have provided us with many? Nature may have provided many for some other reason, such as to ensure redundancy in case of brain damage, but until we have evidence for every activity having its own executive, theoretical parsimony suggests conservatism. Moreover, modest neuropsychological evidence (Baddeley, 1986, chap. 10; Norman & Shallice, 1986; Shallice, 1988) exists for the single-executive view.

The presence of a single executive by no means implies that it controls the entire cognitive system. Because the executive has little control over many basic processes in perception and movement, many innate productions lie beyond its scope. Similarly, acquired productions control many automated skills such as driving, typing, and reading to a large extent. Instead, the executive may primarily schedule and monitor high-level goals. It may also direct processing when goals are novel, difficult, or dangerous. Consequently, control of information processing is distributed over a variety of control mechanisms, with the executive system providing just one type of control that may be essential for human intelligence.

Finally, what about free will? Doesn't this framework suggest that free will is nonexistant? Doesn't this framework suggest that information processing mechanisms—not a mental being—control a person's behavior? Like behaviorists, most cognitive psychologists believe that the fundamental laws of the physical world determine human behavior completely. Whereas behaviorists view control as only existing in the environment, however, cognitive psychologists view it as also existing in cognitive mechanisms, such as productions. Certainly people believe they experience free will. Yet, most cognitive psychologists believe that physical mechanisms produce an illusion of free will (Fiske & S.E. Taylor, 1991, chap. 6), just as they produce all other cognitive phenomena. The illusion of free will is simply one more remarkable phenomenon in human cognition that cognitive psychologists must explain.

Contrary to this view, many people believe that free will does exist and that mechanistic views excluding it are repugnant characterizations of human nature. Belief in free will, however, revives the homunculus problem: What is free will, if not a homunculus?

5

WORKING MEMORY

Humans exhibit a much greater ability to perform strategic processing than other species. Although other organisms learn, their learning is closely constrained by innately specified goals. A rodent may learn to feed in new places where food is plentiful or to avoid places where predators lurk, but learning, in these cases, primarily modifies innate performance patterns so that organisms can achieve survival-oriented goals more optimally. Rarely do non-human organisms learn to achieve new goals that are not survival-oriented.

In contrast, human learning is much more prolific, because people often achieve new goals in a wide variety of ways. Essential to such creativity is the ability to combine old knowledge into new patterns. Consider cooking, which is an activity that only humans perform. To cook something requires achieving the subgoals of acquiring, preparing, and combining the ingredients and then applying heat. To see that these subgoals are related to one another, as well as to the higher-order goal of eating, requires integrating knowledge about them somewhere in the cognitive system. It is unlikely that an innate control mechanism underlies the integration of cooking subgoals: People are not born knowing how to cook. Instead, such integration probably results from experiences in which these subgoals are processed together. Achievement of many human goals requires the integration of much previously unrelated information.

Language is another area where humans differ dramatically from other organisms. The human ability to communicate relies extensively on the integration of previously unrelated linguistic elements (**8**). People certainly aren't born knowing the combinations of letters and phonemes that compose words in their language. Instead, children spend years establishing these integrations so that they can communicate effectively. Understanding language further requires integrating the words that compose sentences and the sentences that compose texts, where these combinations are typically unique rather than repeated across experiences. Again, the ability to integrate novel combinations of information appears central to human intelligence.

Constructing a novel pattern of information requires representing all of its subparts together so that they can be formed into a single unit, but what cognitive mechanism represents previously unrelated pieces of information while they are being integrated into a new structure? By what means is the activation of diverse information maintained during its integration? This is the central issue that concerns us here.

5.1 SHORT-TERM MEMORY

One of the most central findings in early cognitive psychology was the observation that people are limited in the amount of information they can rehearse at any one time. As we shall see, this limit is central to understanding how people integrate information. To get an intuitive feel for people's limited ability to store information temporarily, read the following string of digits, close your eyes, and rehearse the digits in the correct order to yourself for 10 to 15 seconds:

5   2   7

When you are done, compare the final string you were rehearsing with the string on the page to check your memory. You probably didn't have any trouble rehearsing this string. Now follow the same procedure for each of these strings, starting with the shortest string and proceeding to the longest:

```
8  1  3  9  1
7  3  8  6  9  8  1
2  5  1  9  2  4  7  5  3
9  6  2  8  1  5  8  2  9  3  7  1
```

You probably could rehearse the 5 digit string without error and may have had no difficulty with the 7 digit string. Chances are, though, you had trouble rehearsing the 9 digit string and could not rehearse the 12 digit string.

The backward span task provides another measure of this memory limitation. Imagine that you are listening to a long string of digits being spoken at the rate of one per second. At any given point, the digits can stop, and your task is to recall the digits, beginning with the most recent digit and continuing backward in order to the first. People are extremely limited in how far back they can recall, usually recalling only about five to seven digits back. Again, the amount of information that can be remembered temporarily is limited.

In a classic paper, G.A. Miller (1956) coined the expression, "the magical number seven, plus or minus two," to describe people's limited capacity for storing information temporarily. Most investigators have since concluded that his estimate was high and that the maximum amount is closer to five or less (Crowder, 1976, chap. 6). Regardless of the specific amount, the point is that people have the ability to store a small amount of unrelated information temporarily.

This observation was central to early theories of human information processing, motivating the inclusion of a short–term memory mechanism postulated to play a central role in many cognitive activities. Most importantly, theorists typically assumed that short–term memory was the means by which people integrate unrelated pieces of information to construct new representations. Because people have the ability to store unrelated pieces of information in short–term memory simultaneously, they can form novel patterns of information. The first half of this chapter describes the multi–store model popular during this period and the role of short–term memory in it. The second half presents the more recent construct of working memory that has largely replaced the construct of short–term memory.

5.1.1 The Multi–Store Model

Although theorists proposed many multi–store models during the 1950s and 1960s, Atkinson and Shiffrin (1968) developed the one that is probably the best known and articulated (but see Norman, 1970). They proposed that the cognitive system contains three memory stores: the *sensory store*, the *short–term store*, and the *long–term store*. When a perceptual system detects information initially, it establishes a perceptual representation of the information briefly in its sensory store. For example, the visual system establishes visual images of visual stimuli in its sensory store, the auditory system establishes acoustic images of acoustic stimuli in its sensory store, and so forth. Researchers developed clever experimental paradigms for demonstrating the presence of these sensory stores in the cognitive system. In addition, they demonstrated that these sensory stores can retain relatively unlimited amounts of perceptual information, but that they can retain this information only for a second or so, depending on the modality (Crowder, 1976, chaps. 2 & 3; Sperling, 1960).

Categorization mechanisms attempt to identify perceptual representations that reside in the sensory stores (**2**.3.1, **2**.5). As perceptual representations become categorized, representations of these categories enter the short-term store. For example, a category representation for *chair* might enter the short-term store to represent the image of a chair in the visual sensory store. Because the short-term store is limited in capacity to around five pieces of information, it can only contain about five categorizations of the perceptual representations. Although the sensory stores may contain perceptual representations for dozens of stimuli, the short-term store can only contain category representations for about five of them.

If category representations remain in the short-term store long enough, they may be transferred to the long-term store (**6**.1.1). Because the long-term store is relatively unlimited in capacity, it can contain an indefinitely large number of category representations for entities perceived over the lifetime of an individual (**6**.2.2). In addition, procedures can be retrieved from the long-term store to process category representations in the short-term store. Such procedures could rehearse representations, transform them in various ways (e.g., multiply each digit by 2), or integrate them into new representations (e.g., integrate the letters, *h*, *y*, *a*, *l*, *i*, *t*, *e* into *hyalite*). Consequently, theorists believed that the short-term store was the means by which people integrate diverse information to form new representations.

5.1.2 Characteristics of Short-Term Memory

The primary source of evidence for the multi-store model was that each of its three memory stores seemed to exhibit distinctive performance characteristics. Because people appeared to exhibit three very different types of memory behavior, they appeared to have three distinct memory systems. Much initial work on short-term memory assessed its particular characteristics and, because of their distinctiveness, contributed to the view that short-term memory constituted an autonomous memory system. However, further findings later suggested that short-term memory was not really all that different from sensory memory and long-term memory. Instead, these findings suggested that three different types of memory *states* arise within a single memory system (**5**.1.3). The following subsections review the evidence for an autonomous short-term store within a multi-store system, as well as the evidence that led to the demise of this view (Baddeley, 1986; Craik & Lockhart, 1972; Crowder, 1976, 1982a).

Capacity. Many theorists believed that short-term memory contained a fixed number of slots for storing information. Because both sensory memory and long-term memory had been shown to have unlimited capacity, the limited capacity of short-term memory suggested that it was a unique and autonomous memory system. The problem was that investigators observed the capacity of short-term memory to vary. If a subject's short-term memory is tested on successive trials with different words from the same category, the capacity of short-term memory decreases. For example, subjects might be presented with words for six exemplars of *furniture* on each trial and then recall them immediately. On one trial, they might receive *chair, sofa, rug, painting, lamp,* and *bureau,* and have to recall them. On the next trial, they might receive *desk, bed, bookcase, stool, bench,* and *table,* and have to recall them. Initially, subjects recall most of the words on each trial, but as the trials continue, their ability to recall the words decreases. If short-term memory reflects an autonomous memory system with a fixed number of information slots, then its capacity should not decrease in this manner but should remain constant.

To explain this decrease, theorists suggested that information in long-term memory interferes with information in short-term memory. Words from previous trials maintain a high level of activation in long-term memory and inhibit words on the current trial in short-term memory (D.D. Wickens, 1972; D.D. Wickens, Born, & Allen, 1963). Such *proactive interference* is well-known in long-term memory (**6.2.3**). As the number of words from previous trials increases, the amount of proactive interference increases, and the capacity of short-term memory decreases. Although this explanation accounts for the data, it no longer assumes that short-term memory is an autonomous memory system, but allows long-term memory to have a strong influence on it.

Additional evidence further strengthened this conclusion. When words are drawn from a new category, short-term memory improves dramatically. For example, if subjects are tested on words from *furniture* for several trials but then are switched to words from *clothing,* their recall improves significantly. This *release from proactive interference* indicates that the proactive interference on previous trials was largely coming from exemplars of *furniture* in long-term memory. When the category changes from *furniture* to *clothing,* performance improves because the interference is localized within knowledge of *furniture.* As we shall see, effects such as these have led many theorists to believe that short- and long-term memory reflect different uses of one memory system rather than two autonomous memory stores (**5.1.3**).

It is important to note that people can extend the limited capacity of short-term memory through *chunking.* Try to encode and rehearse the following digit string as you did the earlier ones:

    1 4 9 2 1 7 7 6 1 9 8 4 2 0 0 1

You probably were unable to rehearse this entire string, unless you noted that it contained four famous years (1492, 1776, 1984, 2001). Once you are aware of this, it becomes easy to remember the 16 digits as 4 years. Well-established chunks of knowledge in long-term memory enable you to recode the digits in this manner. As you perceive each set of four related digits, the representation of the corresponding year in long-term memory (i.e., a chunk) becomes active. Then, rather than storing representations of the individual digits in short-term memory, you store representations of the years. Because you have now encoded the digit string as only four representations (i.e., four years), you can store it easily within the limited capacity of short-term memory. Later, when you must recall the original string of digits, you retrieve each representation for a year from short-term memory and report its digits.

As this example illustrates, well-established chunks of knowledge in long-term memory can greatly augment people's ability to recall information from short-term memory. Because chunking enhances short-term memory performance this way, theorists specify the capacity of short-term in terms of chunks. The capacity of short-term memory is not the amount of information that people can reproduce in a short-term memory task (e.g., the number of digits). Rather, it is the number of chunks that people store in short-term memory, which later allows them to reproduce this information. When researchers have assessed the number of chunks that people use to reproduce large amounts of information in a short-term memory task, they typically find that they store around five chunks. As we shall see later in this chapter, chunking plays a central role in many types of skilled performance (5.2.4; Chase & Simon, 1973).

Duration.   Another characteristic of short-term memory that appeared to differentiate it from other types of memory was its duration. To assess the duration of short-term memory, investigators used the *Brown-Peterson task* (J. Brown, 1958; L.R. Peterson & M.J. Peterson, 1959). In this task, subjects receive a small set of words, letters, or digits (the *memory set*) that does not overload short-term memory. Immediately after encoding the memory set, subjects perform a distractor activity, such as saying the alphabet backwards, to prevent rehearsal. Following a variable delay, subjects recall the original information. If the interval is only a few seconds, subjects can still remember much of the information in the memory set. After 20 seconds, however, subjects typically cannot remember the information at all, suggesting that the duration of short-term memory is limited to 20 seconds or less.

Because duration in sensory memory is limited to around a second or so (5.1.1), and because long-term memories can last indefinitely, this intermediate duration for short-term memory again suggested the presence of an autonomous memory system. However, additional findings suggested that the structure of long-term memory affects the duration of information in short-term memory. For example, digits are forgotten faster from short-term memory when the distractor activity is counting backwards in threes from a number than when it is saying the alphabet backwards. Increasing the similarity of the distractor activity to information in the memory set decreases the duration of short-term memory. This kind of interference again suggests that long-term memory affects short-term memory: To the extent that information in the distractor activity and information in the memory set are closely related in long-term memory, the duration of short-term memory suffers from interference (Corman & D.D. Wickens, 1968; Wickelgren, 1965). This finding further called into question the presence of an autonomous short-term memory system.

Regardless of their duration on an particular occasion, short-term memories are short-lived in the cognitive system. However, people do have a way to prevent the loss of these memories, if they wish. Through rehearsal, one can overcome the duration limit of short-term memory and maintain its contents indefinitely until rehearsal ends. Furthermore, the longer that information resides in short-term memory, the better are its chances of becoming established in long-term memory (**6.**1.1).

Forgetting. The duration of short-term memory is tied closely to the factors that cause its contents to be lost or forgotten. The initial view of short-term memory as an autonomous unit with a fixed number of slots suggested that forgetting occurs through *displacement*: As each new chunk is encoded, it displaces a chunk in a short-term memory slot and remains there until displaced itself. An ingenious experiment by Waugh and Norman (1965) suggested that short-term memory for a particular chunk was best predicted by how many chunks had been encoded after it—not by the duration of the test chunk in short-term memory. In other words, forgetting increased as the number of opportunities for displacing the chunk increased, not with how long the chunk had resided in short-term memory.

In contrast, Baddeley and his colleagues have found that duration is central to the forgetting of short-term memories (Baddeley, 1986, chap. 5). In their experiments, the amount of information that subjects retained in short-term memory simply depended on how fast they rehearsed: The faster they rehearsed, the more information they remembered. In general, Baddeley has found that the amount of information subjects rehearse in around 1.5 seconds is the amount they can retain. Because rehearsal *rate* determines forgetting, decay does appear to play some role in the loss of information from short-term memory (see also Reitman, 1971, 1974), and displacement is not the entire story.

Moreover, the displacement view of forgetting does not explain the forgetting that occurs during proactive interference, nor why similar distractor activities cause faster forgetting. Findings such as these suggest that interference from information in long-term memory also contributes to forgetting in short-term memory, at least to some extent. As information in short-term memory becomes increasingly similar to information still active in long-term memory, forgetting in short-term memory increases. Because factors outside short-term memory affect forgetting within it, short-term memory is not an autonomous mechanism. Furthermore, because many theorists now believe that displacement, decay, and interference all contribute to forgetting in short-term memory, and because these factors also contribute to forgetting in long-term memory (**6**.2.2, **6**.2.3), the uniqueness and autonomy of short-term memory again appear dubious.

Coding. Initial studies of short-term memory suggested that its primary purpose was to recode sensory information into language, and more specifically, into verbal (spoken) language. Consider an experiment by R. Conrad (1964). In the preparatory phase of Conrad's study, subjects provided information about the confusability of letters, both visually and acoustically. To assess visual confusability, Conrad presented letters one at a time in brief visual flashes for subjects to categorize. The presentation duration was purposefully brief, so that the letters were barely visible and often miscategorized. The confusions that subjects made between letters during these incorrect categorizations were of primary interest. In general, subjects confused letters that had similar visual properties: When subjects were presented with K, they often confused it with R and X; similarly, the often confused D with O and Q. To assess acoustic confusability, Conrad presented spoken letters in noise for subjects to categorize. The signal-to-noise ratio of the letters to background static was purposefully low, so that subjects made many errors. This time, subjects confused letters that had similar acoustic properties: When subjects were presented with C, they often confused it with V and Z; similarly, they often F confused with S and X.

In the second phase of this study, Conrad presented subjects with visual letter strings in the Brown–Peterson task. Recall that subjects in this task receive a memory set and then perform a distractor activity for a short time before recalling the memory set. Of primary interest here were the confusions that subjects made during recall: For each presented letter recalled incorrectly, Conrad assessed whether the letter recalled in its place was one that had been confused more often with the visual or the acoustic form of that letter in the preparatory phase. Overwhelmingly, subjects intruded letters that had been confused with the acoustic—not the visual—form of the letter: When C was forgotten from short-term memory, V and Z were more likely to replace it than G and O. Although subjects had received the letters visually, their acoustic confusions indicated that they had recoded them verbally. Most importantly, this suggested that short-term memory only contained verbal representations. If short-term memory could contain any type of information, then why did subjects go to all the trouble to recode the letters verbally, when they could have represented them visually? Theorists concluded, therefore, that short-term memory was an autonomous mechanism for storing verbal representations of recently perceived stimuli.

Numerous other findings, however, indicated that people do have short-term memory for visually presented information. R. Conrad (1972) later performed the Brown-Peterson task with congenitally deaf subjects and found that their confusions in the Brown-Peterson task were visual. Because these subjects had never heard language, they could not recode the letters verbally and therefore stored them visually in short-term memory. Other researchers demonstrated visual short-term memory in other paradigms (Posner, Boies, Eichelman, & R.L. Taylor, 1969; Posner & Keele, 1967), and still others demonstrated short-term memory for semantic and lexical information (Baddeley, 1986; H.G. Shulman, 1970, 1971). It would not be surprising if there were also short-term memory for motor movements, given that people often seem to rehearse movements in skilled activities, such as tennis and playing the piano.

Consequently, the verbal coding that seemed to distinguish short-term memory turned out instead to be one of many coding options. People can store many different kinds of information in short-term memory. Because these same coding options also exist for long-term memory, the assumption of an autonomous short-term memory again seemed unjustified.

Retrieval.   Work by S. Sternberg (1966, 1969a, 1969b, 1975) initially suggested that retrieval from short-term memory differed qualitatively from retrieval from long-term memory. On each trial in one experiment, Sternberg asked subjects to rehearse a memory set, whose size varied randomly across trials from one to six digits (e.g, 3, 2 8 5, 9 4 2 6 8 1). At an unpredictable point during the rehearsal of a memory set, subjects received a *probe* digit and had to indicate as quickly as possible whether it was in the memory set or not. If subjects were rehearsing 2 8 5, they responded "true" if the probe was 8 and "false" if the probe was 6.

Sternberg found that the time to make a decision was a linear function of set size, for both true and false trials. For each additional digit added to the memory set, the time to reach a decision increased by a fixed amount, 38 msec, so that response times for memory sets having three digits were 38 msec longer, on average, than response times for memory sets having two digits, and response times for memory sets having four digits were 38 msec longer than response times for memory sets having three digits. This suggested that subjects retrieved the digits *serially* from short-term memory, one after another, to determine if the probe was present. For each additional digit that they had to retrieve sequentially, the time to reach a decision increased by a constant amount. As a result, increases in set size produced linear increases in decision time. Researchers have obtained similar results for many materials besides digits under a wide variety of task conditions.

Results from the Sternberg task convinced many theorists that retrieval from short-term memory is serial, contrary to their belief that retrieval from long-term memory is parallel. When retrieving information from long-term memory, people often appear to access huge amounts of information simultaneously. Consider the ability to retrieve words from long-term memory while listening to a conversation. If the listener retrieved words from long-term memory serially, the time to identify each word could take much time, because individuals typically know at least 50,000 words. Moreover, the time to retrieve words might be expected to increase dramatically with the growth in vocabulary during early childhood, yet, if anything, the ability to retrieve words becomes *more* efficient with age. Upon hearing each string of phonemes that forms a word during a conversation, a listener retrieves the correct word very quickly. Rather than searching through all possible words one after another, the cognitive system appears to examine them simultaneously, retrieving the most appropriate one in the current context (9.2; Marslen-Wilson, 1987; Marslen-Wilson & Tyler, 1980; McClelland & Elman, 1986; but see Forster, 1976, 1979). People's retrieval of many other types of information from long-term memory appears to be parallel as well, and nearly all theories of long-term memory assume parallel search (e.g., J.R. Anderson, 1983; Gillund & Shiffrin, 1984; Hintzman, 1986, 1988; McClelland et al., 1986; Ratcliff, 1978; Rumelhart et al., 1986).

This apparent difference in retrieval between short- and long-term memory contributed to the view that short- and long-term memory constitute autonomous memory systems. Because only short-term memory exhibited serial retrieval, it appeared to be a unique form of memory that arose from a unique memory mechanism. However, theorists later discovered that *limited capacity parallel retrieval models* can account for Sternberg's results. The basic idea behind these models is that people retrieve all items from short-term memory simultaneously (i.e., in parallel). However, the amount of strategic resource available for performing the task is limited and must be divided equally among items in the memory set (4.2.2). If the memory set only contains one item, then it receives all of the strategic resource and is compared quickly to the probe. If the memory set contains two items, then each receives half of the strategic resource and is therefore compared more slowly to the probe. If the memory set contains five items, then each receives one-fifth of the strategic resource and is compared still more slowly to the probe. As the set size increases, each item receives a smaller allocation of the limited strategic resource, and the time to process it increases. As a result, the time to reach a decision increases with set size, even though the items are actually retrieved and examined in parallel. Through judicious choice of mathematical assumptions, these parallel retrieval models can produce a linear increase in decision time as set size increases (J.T. Townsend, 1971, 1990). The success of these models raised further doubts about the existence of an autonomous short-term memory: If both short- and long-term memory exhibit parallel retrieval, then they may not reflect two different memory mechanisms.

Perhaps the presence of set size effects during retrieval from short-term memory and the absence of set size effects during retrieval from long-term memory distinguish these two memory systems. I noted earlier that the retrieval of well-established information from long-term memory does not appear to exhibit set size effects: As people acquire knowledge of new words, objects, and faces over the course of their lives, the time to retrieve a particular one seems, if anything, to decrease. However, researchers have found that set size effects *do* occur during the retrieval of weakly established information in long-term memory. Imagine that subjects study a list of words, presented briefly one after the other. Several minutes later, after performing a distractor activity, subjects receive probe words and have to verify that they occurred in the list. If a probe occurred on the list, subjects respond "old;" if not, they respond "new." Because several minutes elapsed since the list, and because subjects were not allowed to rehearse the words, the words do not remain in short-term memory. Instead, subjects can only retrieve the words from long-term memory to perform their verifications. Under these conditions, the time to verify that a word occurred in a list typically increases with the number of words that the list contained (J.R. Anderson, 1976, 1983; J.R. Anderson & Bower, 1973; Atkinson & Juola, 1974; Gillund & Shiffrin, 1984; S. Sternberg, 1975). Because set size effects can occur for weakly established information in long-term memory, they are thus not unique to short-term memory. Once again, an apparent difference between short- and long-term memory dissolves into a similarity, further questioning their existence as autonomous memory systems.

5.1.3 Short-Term Memory as Highly-Activated Long-Term Memory

In a highly influential paper, Craik and Lockhart (1972) argued against the multi-store model, noting many findings that question the autonomy of short-term memory. They argued further that they could explain short-term memory phenomena more reasonably with a single-store memory model. Because of the frequent interactions between short- and long-term memory, and because of the many similarities between them, Craik and Lockhart concluded that these two types of memory reflect different uses of a single underlying memory system.

Shiffrin and Schneider (1977) later suggested that short-term memory may simply be the most active information in long-term memory. When people rehearse a set of digits, they do not store them in an autonomous short-term memory system independent of the digits' representation in long-term memory. Instead, rehearsal is simply the activation and reactivation of the digits' long-term memory representations, such that this information is more highly activated than other information in long-term memory (2.5). On this view, interference during short-term memory tasks occurs when information *recently* in the short-term memory state of activation competes with information *currently* in the short-term memory state of activation. Similarly, multiple codes are possible in the short-term memory state, because verbal, visual, or any other type of information in long-term memory can be active. In general, short-term and long-term memory exhibit so many similarities simply because they reflect different uses of a single common memory system.

5.1.4 Strategic Processing and Short-Term Memory Load

Baddeley and Hitch (1974) reported findings that further questioned widespread beliefs about an autonomous short-term memory system. According to multi-store models, short-term memory contains the executive processes that perform strategic processing (4.2.1). When the executive carries out rehearsal, learning, language comprehension, reasoning, and other strategic tasks, it purportedly carries them out in short-term memory. To assess this assumption, Baddeley and Hitch had subjects rehearse digit strings of various lengths, as a secondary task, while simultaneously performing one of several primary tasks (e.g., learning word lists, comprehending texts, reasoning about relations between sentences and pictures). Baddeley and Hitch argued that if executive processes operate in short-term memory, then loading it with digits should drastically limit performance on the primary tasks. Because short-term memory is full of digits, executive processes should not have room to operate.

Although Baddeley and Hitch found that primary task performance decreased as digit loads increased from zero to six, these performance decrements were surprisingly small. When subjects rehearsed six digits, their performance generally dropped only slightly on all of the primary tasks. In one reasoning experiment, subjects' performance was approximately 95% accurate regardless of whether they were rehearsing zero or eight digits, and their decision times only increased from 2.2 to 2.9 seconds.

As Baddeley and Hitch concluded, such findings are hard to reconcile with the view that strategic processing takes place in short-term memory. If it does, then how could it occur *at all* when short-term memory is fully loaded with digits? Rather than observing small decrements in primary task performance, Baddeley and Hitch should have seen drastic decrements. Such findings strongly suggest that strategic processing does not occur in short-term memory and instead that strategic processing and short-term memory occur at least somewhat independently (see also Baddeley, 1986).

5.2   WORKING MEMORY

Baddeley and Hitch suggested *working memory* as an alternative to short-term memory, proposing that working memory consists of a set of mechanisms that work together to perform strategic processing. At the center of the working memory system is the executive processor. I will assume that this processor uses executive productions to carry out only one strategic task at a time, although it can switch between multiple tasks rapidly, if none is too demanding (see this interpretation of *limited capacity* in **4**.2.2). Peripheral to the executive processor are temporary memory systems that store information relevant to executive processing. In particular, Baddeley and Hitch suggest that the "articulatory loop" stores verbal information temporarily and that the "visuo-spatial sketch pad" stores visual information temporarily. It would also be reasonable to assume the presence of temporary storage systems for other modalities, especially for movement, within the working memory system.

This view of working memory, through its added complexity, better handles the diversity of short-term memory phenomena than does the short-term store of the multi-store model. By assuming that the executive processor operates independently of the temporary storage systems, this view explains why Baddeley and Hitch's subjects could perform strategic processing while carrying a full short-term memory load. Because separate mechanisms store the digits and perform the primary task, subjects can perform both simultaneously. By assuming that separate storage systems exist for acoustic and spatial information, working memory begins to account for people's ability to store different kinds of information temporarily.

Nevertheless, a major problem still faces this account. Baddeley and Hitch assume that working memory and long-term memory constitute different, autonomous memory systems. As we saw throughout the previous half of this chapter, however, many problems plague the view that the temporary storage system is autonomous (**5**.1.2). Any theory of temporary memory must account for the strong effects of long-term memory on working memory and for the similarities between them.

For the remainder of this chapter, therefore, I adopt a somewhat different view of working memory. Whereas Baddeley and Hitch assumed that working memory is an autonomous memory store, I adopt a unitary memory view of working memory. Following Craik and Lockhart (1972; **5**.1.3), I assume that long-term memory can contain many types of information, including executive productions, auditory information, visual information, motor information, and so forth. At any given point in time, this information can be highly active, lying in the temporary memory state. For each *type* of information, however, a limit exists on how much can be active: Only a limited number of executive productions can be in the temporary memory state, only a limited amount of auditory information can be in the temporary memory state, only a limited amount of visual information can be in the temporary memory state, and so on. Most importantly, these limits are independent of one another, such that the different types of information do not compete for temporary storage. If the maximum number of executive productions are in the temporary memory state, this does not decrease the amount of auditory information that can be in the temporary memory state. Similarly, the amount of auditory information in the temporary memory state does not decrease the amount of visual information that can be in the temporary memory state. Competition exists only within each type of information, as it competes for its specific type of temporary storage. This unitary view of working memory accounts readily for Baddeley and Hitch's experimental results: Their rehearsal task could place the maximum amount of auditory information in the temporary memory state, while their primary task (e.g., reasoning) could still activate whatever number of executive productions it required temporarily.

From here on, my use of the term, "working memory" refers to this unitary view of the construct. When I say "working memory" I mean the information in long-term memory that is currently in the temporary memory state of activation. Similarly, when I say that "information is in working memory," I mean that the information is currently in the *working memory state*, not that the information is in an autonomous working memory store.

As we shall see later in **5.2.4**, another major challenge exists for the working memory view: Much strategic processing appears to occur on information that resides *outside* of working memory in long-term memory. Theorists often assume that the information being manipulated to achieve goals must lie in working memory, but instead, the executive processor may often manipulate information in long-term memory to achieve goals. If so, then theories of working memory need to account for relations between strategic processing and long-term memory, as well as for relations between strategic processing and temporary storage in working memory. Before addressing this issue, I first address several related areas of research.

5.2.1 Modality-Specific Interference

A study by Brooks (1968) suggested that people do in fact store acoustic and spatial information in separate temporary storage systems. In Brooks' spatial task, subjects imagined a block "F" and moved around its circumference mentally from corner to corner, indicating "yes" if a corner was on the extreme top or bottom and "no" otherwise. In his verbal task, subjects moved through a sentence in working memory word by word, indicating "yes" if a word was a noun and "no" otherwise. Subjects used one of two methods to respond: Some subjects uttered "yes" and "no" (vocal response), whereas other subjects pointed to "yes" and "no" on a page (spatial response). Subjects were better at the spatial task when vocalizing their responses but better at the verbal task when pointing to their responses. One interpretation of these findings is that subjects perform best when the task and the response use different temporary storage systems. If there were only one temporary storage system, then the task and the response should not interact in this manner. Because the task and the response do interact, they provide evidence for the independent storage of visual and auditory information in working memory (see also Baddeley & K. Lieberman, 1980; Byrne, 1974; Segal & Fusella, 1970).

5.2.2 Temporary Storage During Language Comprehension

Many theorists, including Baddeley and Hitch, have suggested that working memory stores information relevant to language comprehension. Consider the sentence, "When John bought the violin, he had no idea it would change his life." Upon encountering "he" and "it" in this sentence, how do readers determine that these pronouns refer, respectively, to John and the violin? Clearly, John and the violin must be represented somewhere in the cognitive system for the pronouns to establish reference to them. Moreover, later text could state that the violin contained defense secrets on microfiche, that John's purchase of the violin had been filmed by opposing spies, and so forth. In each case, people must find the original information about John and the violin in memory and integrate it with the new information about them. As we shall see in **8**.7 and **9**.6, language comprehension requires constant integration of new and old information in this manner to construct a coherent account of what a text describes.

Theorists have often suggested that working memory temporarily stores the text just read so that subsequent text can be integrated with it. More specifically, theorists have proposed that a temporary acoustic store within the working memory system (e.g., the articulatory loop) phonologically preserves a small amount of recent linguistic information. To assess this hypothesis, Glanzer, Dorfman, and Kaplan (1981) stopped readers at random points in text and tested their verbatim memory of the previous few sentences. Glanzer et al. found that people generally had good verbatim memory of the previous two sentences but not of sentences further back. Glanzer et al. suggested that, at a given point in time, people store the two most recent sentences phonologically in working memory, thereby facilitating their integration with subsequent sentences. According to this view, working memory is essential to language comprehension because of the role it plays in integrating adjacent sentences (see also Glanzer, Fischer, & Dorfman, 1984;

for an alternative view, see Potter & Lombardi, 1990; Von Eckhardt & Potter, 1985).

Theorists have also suggested that working memory is central to the phonological recoding of written language. When reading "goat," for example, people could access its meaning visually through orthographic information, or they could recode the letters phonologically into internal speech sounds that then access meaning (**9**.2.1). A study by Kleiman (1975) suggested that people use working memory to recode orthographic information phonologically in this manner. To test this, he had subjects perform one of four primary tasks: In the visual task, subjects determined as quickly as possible whether two visually presented words were similar visually (e.g., "bird" and "bind"); in the auditory task, subjects determined whether two visually presented words rhymed (e.g., "plea" and "free"); in the semantic task, subjects determined whether two visually presented words were from the same category (e.g., "daisy" and "tulip"); and in the sentence task, subjects determined whether a visually presented sentence made sense (e.g., "The dog chased the cat" versus "The dot shaped the kit"). Half of the time subjects performed *articulatory suppression* while performing the primary task, and half of the time they did not. To perform articulatory suppression, a subject repeated one word over and over again out loud at a rapid pace (e.g., "the the the the. . . ."). Because articulatory suppression has been found to exhaust the temporary storage of acoustic information, it interferes with any other task that requires temporary acoustic storage, such as the phonological recoding of written words (Baddeley, 1986).

Kleiman found no effect of articulatory suppression on the visual and semantic tasks. Because subjects were able to judge visual similarity and access category information without recoding the words phonologically, the lack of temporary acoustic storage did not interfere, and subjects were able to perform these two tasks using the orthographic information extracted visually. In contrast, articulatory suppression slowed performance on both the acoustic and sentence tasks. Because repeating "the" exhausted the temporary storage of acoustic information, no temporary storage remained for the phonological recoding that these two tasks require. The acoustic task suffered because subjects must compare phonological codes for rhyme judgments, and the sentence task suffered because representing sentences phonologically facilitates the integration of their words. Kleiman concluded that the storage of phonologically recoded text in working memory plays a central role in language comprehension.

Working memory capacity and individual differences in reading. If working memory is central to language comprehension, then good readers might have a higher working memory capacity than poor readers. However, performance on the standard digit span tasks that measure short-term memory capacity (5.1) predict reading performance poorly. Daneman and Carpenter (1980) suggested that working memory capacity might be a better predictor. Perhaps how much processing the executive processor can do—while simultaneously storing information in the temporary acoustic store—better measures the mechanisms that underlie reading ability. In other words, high processing capacity plus high storage capacity might be more essential to good reading than high storage capacity alone.

To test this, Daneman and Carpenter had subjects read text while simultaneously remembering the final word of as many sentences as possible, beginning with the most recently completed sentence and proceeding backwards through sentences toward the text's beginning. If you had performed this task on the previous paragraph, you should have stored "alone, ability, predictor, poorly," and so forth in that order. Note that this task requires both processing (reading) and storage (remembering the last words of sentences). Daneman and Carpenter found that people differed substantially in their *reading spans*, that is, in how many sentence-final words they could remember while reading. Moreover, Daneman and Carpenter found that reading span correlated highly with reading ability. Good readers consistently had higher spans than poor readers, suggesting that *both* the processing capacity and storage capacity of working memory are central to reading ability. Because reading span measures the capacity of working memory and also predicts reading ability, working memory is strongly implicated in reading.

5.2.3 Imagery in Working Memory

So far, I have depicted storage in working memory as a relatively passive process. As information is perceived through the senses, or produced by executive processing, it is stored temporarily in a modality-specific storage mechanism, where it remains accessible to the executive processor for a short time. If certain information is important and needs to be retained, it can be maintained through rehearsal. Otherwise it becomes lost, either as it decays, is displaced by new information, or suffers interference from information in long-term memory. According to this passive view, temporary storage simply serves to provide an historical record of recent perception and processing.

However, the contents of temporary storage mechanisms can be manipulated much more dynamically to simulate events. Imagine walking up a mountain ravine toward a loud waterfall. Imagine walking along a crowded urban sidewalk, looking for a place to have lunch. Not only do such images contain visual information, they may also contain auditory, olfactory, gustatory, tactile, and proprioceptive information. People can repeat the same mental sequence over and over again. They can alter it in a wide variety of ways that may transcend reality. They can freeze and examine it at various points. Numerous options allow people to manipulate temporarily stored information while they imagine events as they might be and as they might have been.

Although a large literature addresses the visual aspect of imagery, little work addresses its auditory, olfactory, gustatory, tactile, and proprioceptive aspects, much less their simultaneous integration. Nevertheless, work on visual imagery has produced important and provocative findings that have had a large impact on cognitive theory.

Operations in visual imagery. An important paper by Shepard and Metzler (1971) strongly suggested that people perform active operations on visual images in working memory. Shepard and Metzler presented subjects with pairs of geometric figures like those on the left of Fig. 5.1. On each trial, subjects determined as quickly as possible whether the two figures represented the same object or different objects, pressing one of two response keys to indicate their decision. In Fig. 5.1, the top pair contains two instances of the same object, where each is a 90° rotation of the other. The bottom pair in Fig. 5.1 contains two different objects. The critical manipulation concerned the *angular disparity* of the two stimuli on the "same" trials, namely, the amount of rotation between them. Sometimes two instances of the same object differed by a 20° rotation, sometimes by a 40° rotation, and so forth, up to a maximum of a 180° rotation. Of primary interest was how these differences in angular disparity affected the time to determine that the two stimuli were instances of the same object. The results are shown on the right of Fig. 5.1. As can be seen, time to make a response for "same" trials increased linearly with angular disparity. With each additional 60° difference in orientation, response time increased by 1 sec.

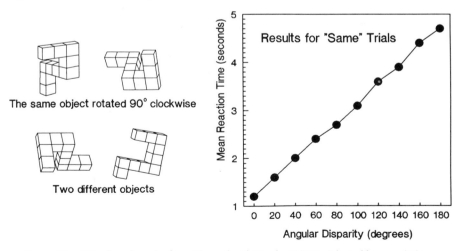

Figure 5.1.   Stimuli and results from Shepard and Metzler (1971). Adapted by permission.

Shepard and Metzler interpreted their results as showing that subjects rotate a visual representation for one of the stimuli continuously until it lines up with the other. The farther subjects must rotate the image, the longer they take to reach a decision. Because subjects rotate the image at a constant rate, decision time increases linearly with angular disparity. Much additional work by Shepard and his colleagues (e.g., L.A. Cooper, 1976; Shepard & L.A. Cooper, 1982) further supported the view that people rotate visual images continuously in working memory. However, recent work by Parsons (1987a, 1987b) indicates that the relation between orientation and decision time is not always linear, with a variety of factors, such as the nature of the object and its axis of rotation, determining the nature of the rotation process.

Upon publication, Shepard's results engendered much controversy. Cognitive psychologists had previously avoided any discussion of imagery, given the heavy criticism it had received from behaviorists after its use by introspectionists around the turn of this century (**1**). Resurrecting the construct of "visual image" made many cognitive psychologists uneasy. Moreover, it challenged the heavy orientation toward symbol processing that had been central to the rebirth of cognitive psychology. For some time, theorists hotly debated whether people had visual images, and if so, whether psychologists could really produce evidence for them (J.R. Anderson, 1978; Palmer, 1978; Pylyshyn, 1973, 1981).

So much additional evidence has accumulated since then that psychologists now widely believe that people construct images in working memory and perform a variety of operations on them. For example, Kosslyn, Ball, and Reiser (1978) explored people's ability to *scan* a visual image. Subjects in one study viewed lines with letters on them, like those on the left of Fig. 5.2. After storing one of these lines in working memory, the physical line was removed, so that subjects only had their memory of it. After being told to focus on one end of the line, they heard the name of a letter on the line and had to determine as quickly as possible whether the letter was in upper or lower case.

As the lines in the upper left of Fig. 5.2 illustrate, the distance from the end point to the target letter varied (i.e., from the left end point to *a*). Of interest was whether this distance affected decision time. If subjects had stored the letters as a verbal list in the temporary acoustic store (e.g., "lower-case *a*, upper-case Q, lower-case *z*"), then distance should not have mattered, because information about spatial distance would be lost, and because *a* is always the first letter on the list. If subjects had stored the line as an image and were scanning across it, however, then decision time should have increased linearly with distance to the *a*. As can be seen from the results on the right of Fig. 5.2, decision time did increase with distance: The farther that subjects had to scan from the end point to the target, the longer their decision time. Subjects, thus, appeared to be scanning visual images to make their decisions.

The lines in the lower right of Fig. 5.2 illustrate a second variable in Kosslyn's study: the number of letters—zero, one, or two—intervening

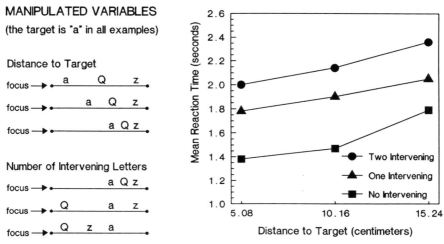

Figure 5.2. Stimuli and results from Kosslyn, Ball, and Reiser (1978). Adapted by permission.

between the end point of a line and a target (i.e., *a*). . As the results at the right of Fig. 5.2 show, each additional intervening letter increased decision time by a constant amount, because subjects stopped at each letter to determine if it was the target. Most importantly, however, the decision time always increased with the distance from the end point to the target, suggesting that subjects were scanning across visual images to perform the task.

In another set of studies, Kosslyn (1975) explored the resolution of visual images. In various task settings, he induced people to imagine the same object in different sizes and then had them verify one of its components. For example, subjects imagined a cat next to an elephant, versus a cat next to a flea. When one imagines a cat next to an elephant, the cat is much smaller in the image than it is when next to a flea, holding the overall size of the image constant. Once subjects had constructed one of these images, they then had to verify whether some component was true of an entity in it. For example, subjects imagining a cat next to an elephant were asked to verify that cats have *ears*. Of interest was whether subjects made these verifications faster when the component was large in the image (next to a flea) than when it was small (next to an elephant). If subjects used a visual image of *cat*, as opposed to some other type of representation, they should have responded faster for a large cat than for a small one, because the resolution of a cat's ears increases as the cat becomes larger. Similar to vision, subjects should "see" large components in an image more clearly than small components and therefore categorize them faster. Kosslyn found that subjects were indeed faster when the critical components of the images were large than when they were small, providing further support for the claim that people process visual images in working memory.

The functional equivalence of imagery and perception. These results, and many others like them, led theorists to an intriguing conclusion: The operations in imagery are functionally equivalent to those in perception (Shepard & Podgorny, 1978). Just as people can perceive a physical object rotating, so can they rotate a visual image. As people can scan a physical scene, so can they scan a visual image. As the ability to verify an aspect of a physical object depends on its resolution, so does the ability to verify an aspect of a visual image. Numerous other results in this literature demonstrate further parallels, so many that theorists believe imagery evolved from visual processes (Finke, 1989; Kosslyn, 1980; Shepard & L.A. Cooper, 1982).

The processes that underlie imagery and perception, however, are not identical. Kerr (1983) found that subjects who are congenitally blind perform visual imagery tasks in much the same way as sighted subjects. When the congenitally blind rotate an imagined object, rotation time increases linearly with the angle of rotation. When they scan an imagined scene, scan time increases with distance. When they verify a property of an imagined object, verification time decreases with size. Although these subjects have never experienced vision in their lives, they nevertheless exhibit many of the imagery effects found for sighted subjects, indicating that the processes underlying vision are not necessary for imagery. Instead, processes that represent space abstractly appear central.

Farah (1988), however, has reported neuropsychological evidence suggesting that visual, as well as spatial, processes underlie imagery (see also Farah, Hammond, Levine, & Calvanio, 1988). When people have both visual and spatial processes available, they use them simultaneously in imagery. Only when people lack vision processes—either because they are congenitally blind, or because they have experienced damage to the vision centers of their brain—do they rely on spatial processes exclusively to perform imagery tasks. Consequently, Farah's results, like Kerr's, indicate that the processes underlying imagery and perception are not always identical. Nevertheless, many compelling results from research on imagery indicate that people manipulate spatial and visual information actively in working memory.

5.2.4 Augmenting Working Memory With Long-Term Memory

Working memory contains an incredibly complex set of mechanisms: It includes the executive processor that implements strategic processing; it represents information from the various modalities temporarily, as well as categorizations of this information activated in long-term memory; and it supports the dynamic manipulation of imagery to simulate events. Moreover, working memory does not operate in isolation of the remaining cognitive system. Rather, working memory interacts continually with the perceptual systems, the motor systems, and long-term memory to coordinate the myriad aspects of cognitive activity. Not only does working memory serve as a means for integrating novel configurations of information (as described earlier), it more generally serves as the staging area for active cognitive processing, temporarily representing partial results from a wide variety of processes for other processes that may need them (Carpenter & Just, 1988).

It is probably wrong, though, to assume that the multiple mechanisms of working memory store all of the information on which the executive processor acts. Findings from many studies strongly indicate otherwise. Consider the subjects of Baddeley and Hitch (1974), who still read competently under a full memory load of six digits (5.1.4). Although performance decreased somewhat with memory load, by no means did a full load completely disrupt language comprehension. Baddeley (1986, chaps. 4 & 8) reports further comprehension studies in which memory loads slowed comprehension but produced little, if any, decrements in comprehension accuracy. If all of the information relevant to language comprehension must be stored in working memory, then how could people continue to comprehend language while carrying a full load of irrelevant digits? No space would be left to store the linguistic information that the executive processor must integrate to produce comprehension. Instead, the executive processor appears to be manipulating information stored somewhere else, outside of working memory, to perform these strategic tasks.

Such results are not limited to Baddeley and Hitch's comprehension experiments. In Baddeley and Hitch's experiments on reasoning and learning, full digit loads had only minor effects on performance. In Kleiman's (1975) experiment, articulatory suppression lengthened latencies during acoustic and comprehension judgments but did not completely prevent subjects from performing these tasks (5.2.2). Although subjects performed these tasks more slowly, they still performed them at a high level of accuracy. Similarly, Daneman and Carpenter (1980) found that people could still comprehend text satisfactorily, while simultaneously loading temporary memory with the final words from previous sentences (5.2.2). Again, the executive processor appears to be manipulating information stored somewhere else, outside of working memory, to integrate information in these strategic tasks.

These observations suggest that temporary storage in working memory is not essential to executive processing. Although temporary storage may make strategic processing easier and more efficient, such storage is not necessary. Nevertheless, the executive processor must be storing relevant information *somewhere* during strategic processing, when irrelevant information exhausts temporary storage. Where might this be? A number of researchers have suggested that the executive processor uses long-term memory to store information that is relevant to strategic processing. Perhaps long-term memory, whose capacity is indefinitely large (**6.2.2**), augments the limited capacity of working memory (Chase & Ericsson, 1981, Waldrop, 1987).

Chunking and expertise. One way that long-term memory can augment working memory is through chunking. As we saw earlier, if several pieces of perceived information form a familiar chunk, people can represent them efficiently in working memory (**5.1.2**). Rather than each piece of information being represented separately, they are stored together as a single unit, thereby using less storage capacity. Long-term memory supports this efficient form of storage by providing a repository for chunks: Without a place to establish and maintain the representations that integrate perceived information, chunking could not occur. As the number of chunks in long-term memory grows, the cognitive system develops more ways to integrate separate pieces of information, and the potential efficiency of temporary storage increases.

A chunk becomes established in long-term memory when its components are encountered together frequently: The more often several pieces of information are processed together in working memory, the better they become integrated as a chunk in long-term memory (**6.1.1**). It follows that people should develop extensive numbers of chunks in their areas of expertise, because being an expert in an area often means being familiar with most possible configurations of information that could occur (**4.3; 10.6.3**).

To see this, imagine a novice chess player looking briefly at a chess board during a game played by two other people. Because the player is a novice, he is not familiar with many configurations of chess pieces that can occur, and therefore views most pieces independently of the others; he does not chunk them together. If the board is removed from the novice's view and he tries to recall the positions of the pieces, he may only recall about five pieces stored independently in working memory. In contrast, consider an expert who has played so much chess that she has chunks in long-term memory for most configurations of pieces that could occur in a game. By using these chunks to represent configurations of pieces on a chess board, rather than storing pieces individually, she can recall many more positions than the novice. Chase and Simon (1973) have demonstrated this phenomenon, showing that chess experts retain much more information about chess boards than novices and that superior chunking is responsible. A large literature on chunking in expertise further documents this finding in other areas of expertise, including running, electronics, music, and the game of *Go* (Chase & Ericsson, 1981; Egan & Schwartz, 1979; Halpern & Bower, 1982; Reitman, 1976).

Does chunking explain how the executive processor can perform strategic processing while working memory carries a full load? No, it does not. When carrying a full load, no room exists for storing the chunks that expand temporary storage capacity. Some other use of long-term memory must provide the executive processor with temporary storage when working memory is full.

Immediate storage in long-term memory. Perhaps the executive processor stores information immediately in long-term memory, completely bypassing working memory. What, then, allows the executive processor to store information so quickly in long-term memory, and what enables the executive processor to find it there later? To a large extent, this is the topic of the next chapter on long-term memory. As we shall see, if people can elaborate incoming information with previously existing knowledge, it is easy to store the information in long-term memory, and it is easy to retrieve it later (**6**.1, **6**.3). Essentially, the previously existing knowledge provides a place to "park" the information in long-term memory and provides a route back to it later during retrieval.

This has important implications for the augmentation of working memory. Much of the information relevant to executive processing may be easily elaborated, so that it becomes stored in long-term memory immediately. This elaboration can later provide pathways back to the information, should it need to be integrated with subsequent information that is also relevant to strategic processing. If the later information activates the same elaborative knowledge, this knowledge may in turn activate the earlier information in long-term memory, such that the executive processor can integrate the new information with the earlier information.

To see this, imagine carrying a full load of digits in working memory while reading a text that introduces a dog initially as "a Chihuahua from Chicago." Although there is no capacity left in working memory to store a representation of this dog, it can be stored in long-term memory with other knowledge about Chicago. If the text states subsequently that "the canine from Chicago devoured a house plant," you can use the information about Chicago to search for relevant information in long-term memory that could be integrated with this statement. Upon discovering *Chihuahua* stored recently with *Chicago*, you can integrate these two parts of the text and infer that it was the Chihuahua who devoured the house plant. To the extent that the executive processor can utilize long-term memory in this manner to integrate information, it may not require the temporary storage of task-relevant information in working memory.

Temporary storage in working memory may certainly enhance strategic processing: When working memory capacity is available, it may allow faster integration than is possible through long-term memory. It may even be necessary for certain strategic tasks, especially for those that construct truly novel configurations of information. However, many of the strategic tasks that researchers have studied thus far do not seem to require temporary storage in working memory. Because subjects can perform strategic tasks such as reading, reasoning, and problem solving under full loads, integration often appears to rely heavily on immediate storage in long-term memory.

6

LONG-TERM MEMORY

What did you have for lunch yesterday? Where were you last Saturday night? What did you do last summer? When was your first date? People can typically answer such questions, indicating that much of their experience becomes stored in memory for the long term. People do not simply process information relevant to the current situation and then expunge it from the cognitive system. Instead, some more permanent effect of processing becomes established.

Not only does long-term memory contain information about personal experience, it also contains extensive information seemingly detached from experience. For example, most people remember that Paris is in France and that the U.S. Bill of Rights grants freedom of speech, even though they no longer remember the particular episodes in which they learned these facts. I focus on people's ability to remember specific events in this chapter; I focus on people's ability to use information detached from experience—knowledge—in the next.

What types of information do people remember about an event? People remember information from every sensory modality, including sights, sounds, smells, tastes, touches, and movements. Although they can remember information from a particular modality in isolation (e.g., the smell of garlic), remembered information is often integrated across modalities into the memory of a complete event (e.g., the smell of garlic while making pesto at a friend's home). People also remember information transmitted through spoken and written language (**8**). Someone might remember a joke heard at lunch, or a story read in the newspaper. As we shall see in **9**.5, people often don't remember much about the particular linguistic expressions used to convey information, even though they remember much about the information conveyed. Finally, people remember their thoughts, as well as their actions, even though they can't always distinguish between them.

Information is remembered in a wide variety of units, from very large to very small. Someone might remember having read a mystery about a deranged golf caddy in Hollywood, where the unit is the story as a whole. On the other hand, the reader might also remember increasingly smaller units of information within the story as well. For example, the reader might remember that the caddy secretly rented a cottage, or the particular condition of the cottage when a detective discovered it. The reader might even remember the particular word the detective used to sum up the situation. Often people remember what generally happened—the gist—and sometimes they also remember specific details.

The large majority of work on long-term memory has studied people's memory for printed or spoken words in lists. Nearly all of the basic memory mechanisms that I review in this chapter were discovered through such means. One might ask whether this approach can produce fundamental insights into the nature of long-term memory. Indeed, this has been a concern of some memory researchers, as I discuss later (**6**.4, **11**.2). For now, I simply note that researchers have discovered many important principles of long-term memory from the study of word lists. As I shall argue, memory mechanisms discovered from this approach are probably central to memory for other types of information in other contexts.

Before proceeding, it is important to note that researchers have addressed memory for other information besides words. Researchers have addressed memory for visual, auditory, and motor information, and to a lesser extent, memory for tactile, olfactory, and gustatory information (Atkinson et al., 1988a, 1988b; Lawrence & Banks, 1973; Rabin & Cain, 1984; Shepard, 1967). A rapidly growing literature addresses people's memory for naturally perceived events (e.g., autobiographical memory, eyewitness testimony; Neisser & E. Winograd, 1988; D.C. Rubin, 1987). A literature also addresses people's memory for thoughts and their ability to distinguish them from actions (e.g., M.K. Johnson & Raye, 1981). Extensive literatures, described in **8**.7, **9**.5, and **9**.6 address memory for linguistic units larger than isolated words (e.g., sentences, texts).

6.1 ENCODING

Theorists often describe the process of memory in three stages: Information enters the cognitive system through *encoding* processes; information then becomes *stored* in memory indefinitely; and information may then be accessed during subsequent *retrievals*. It is probably a mistake to assume that the architecture of the cognitive system divides distinctly into encoding, storage, and retrieval systems. Nevertheless, these stages may characterize cognitive architecture to some extent, and, most importantly for my purposes here, they are useful for organizing what cognitive psychologists have learned about memory (Crowder, 1976, chap. 1; Melton, 1963).

Encoding processes capture information as it impinges on perceptual systems, or as strategic processing produces it in working memory. Categorization, as described in Chapter 2, is certainly central to encoding. As we shall see, the categorization of a stimulus strongly determines its memorability. However, additional factors not discussed in Chapter 2 also have considerable effects on encoding. As recognized by mnemonists for thousands of years, one secret to a skilled memory is the development of sophisticated encoding strategies (Bellezza, 1982; Lorayne & J. Lucas, 1974; Luria, 1968; S.B. Smith, 1983).

6.1.1 Amount of Processing

In general, the more processing information receives, the better it is remembered. A number of specific variables determine amount of processing.

Presentation duration.   The longer that people are exposed to a piece of information, the better they remember it. Consider the effect of presentation duration on the ability to recall and recognize words. On a recall test, people attempt to reproduce the words from an earlier list; on a recognition test, they attempt to discriminate words that occurred in an earlier list from words that did not (**6.3.1**). As Fig. 6.1 illustrates, presentation duration has substantial effects on both recall and recognition. As presentation duration increases from one to three seconds, recall and recognition performance increase as well (Gillund & Shiffrin, 1984). Effects of presentation duration must be assessed with regard to stimulus materials and modality. Although people can categorize a scene from a 100 msec flash (Biederman, 1981; Biederman, Rabinowitz, Glass, & Stacy, 1974), they usually need several seconds to encode a sentence (H.H. Clark & Chase, 1974).

Automatic processes operate during the initial processing of a stimulus, and they may encode considerable information automatically during this period. As we saw earlier (**4.1.1**), people acquire frequency, spatial, and temporal information about a stimulus automatically from a brief exposure to it (Alba, Chromiak, Hasher, & Attig, 1980; Barsalou & B.H. Ross, 1986; Hasher & Zacks, 1979, 1984; M.K. Johnson, M.A. Peterson, Yap, & Rose, 1989). During longer presentations, strategic processes have time to

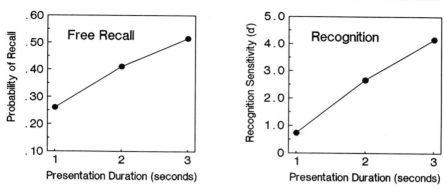

Figure 6.1. Effect of presentation duration on retention from Gillund and Shiffrin (1984). Adapted by permission.

act and produce substantially better encoding (4.2.2). As we shall see shortly, many of the elaboration and organizational strategies that improve memory dramatically occur subsequently, during strategic processing (**6.1.2**, **6.1.3**).

Rehearsal. In assessing presentation duration, it is always important to distinguish between how long a stimulus is present physically versus how much time remains for its subsequent rehearsal (**5.1.2**). Because rehearsal allows people to extend the psychological presence of a stimulus, total presentation time includes the duration of the physical stimulus plus the duration of its subsequent rehearsal. The longer a stimulus is processed—regardless of whether it is physically present—the better it is encoded into memory.

Numerous theorists articulated this assumption in the context of the multi-store model (**5.1.1**): The more rehearsal a piece of information receives, the higher its probability of being transferred from short- to long-term memory, and the higher its probability of being remembered on a later test. To test this hypothesis, Rundus (1971) had subjects rehearse words out loud, in any manner they wished, during presentation of a list. Following presentation, subjects attempted to recall as many of the words as they could remember. Rundus found that the probability of a subject recalling a word increased linearly with the number of times he or she had rehearsed it earlier.

In a different paradigm, Craik and Watkins (1973) presented subjects with a long word list. As subjects received the words, they had to maintain in short-term memory the most recent word beginning with a particular letter. For example, if the experimenter assigned the letter "m," and if the most recent word beginning with "m" were "manic," then subjects would have to maintain "manic" in memory until another word beginning with "m" came along. Upon encountering "moose," for example, subjects would stop rehearsing "manic" and begin rehearsing "moose." By manipulating the number of intervening words not beginning with "m," Craik and Watkins controlled how long subjects rehearsed each word that began with "m." Following this task, subjects were asked to recall the entire list, although they had not been led to expect any subsequent test. Contrary to Rundus' experiment, the amount of rehearsal a word received did not affect its memorability.

To explain this discrepancy, Craik and Watkins suggested that people can perform two different types of rehearsal. In *elaborative rehearsal*, people devote strategic processing to elaborating the information being rehearsed (as in Rundus' experiment). In *maintenance rehearsal*, subjects allocate as little of the strategic resource to rehearsal as possible, allocating just enough to keep information from being lost (as in Craik and Watkins' experiment). Craik and Watkins further proposed that elaborative rehearsal transfers information from short- to long-term memory but that maintenance rehearsal does not. For this reason, increased rehearsal improved recall in Rundus' experiment but not in Craik and Watkins' experiment (see also Craik & Lockhart, 1972). Researchers have since found that even maintenance rehearsal transfers some information to long-term memory. For example, Glenberg, S.M. Smith, and C. Green (1977) found that maintenance rehearsal transfers information that improves recognition but not recall. In general, rehearsal increases memorability, but different types of rehearsal produce different benefits (G. Mandler, 1980).

Number and distribution of presentations. So far, we have only considered the *continuous* processing of a stimulus. However, the total amount of processing that a stimulus receives may be *distributed* over multiple presentations, separated by other information. For example, a word might be presented 5 times in a list, with 10 other items intervening on the average between its repeated presentations. Not surprisingly, the more times that people experience a stimulus, the better they remember it, as Fig. 6.2 illustrates (Tulving, 1962).

Does it matter how the total time spent processing a stimulus is divided over multiple presentations? How do 6 presentations of 4 seconds each compare with 3 presentations of 8 seconds each, where the total time remains constant at 24 seconds? According to the *total time hypothesis*, the distribution of time over presentations should not matter. Instead, retention is proportional to the total time spent processing a stimulus, independent of how that time is distributed. Under certain conditions the total time hypothesis is satisfied, but under others it breaks down, as when subjects attempt to integrate stimuli into higher-order organizations (B.S. Bloom, 1974; E.C. Cooper & Pantle, 1967; Zacks, 1969).

The total time hypothesis also breaks down when the *lag* between presen-

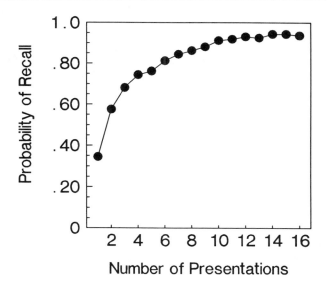

Figure 6.2. Effect of number of presentations on retention from Tulving (1962). Adapted by permission.

tations varies. To see this, imagine an experiment where each item has 4 presentations of 5 sec each, for a total time of 20 sec. Does the number of other items mixed in between the four repetitions of an item affect its memorability? Does it matter whether the repetitions of the item are "massed," with zero items intervening between successive presentations, or whether the repetitions are "distributed," with 20 items intervening? If the total time hypothesis is correct, the lag between repetitions should not matter, because the total presentation time remains constant. As Fig. 6.3 illustrates, however, it does. The longer the lag between repetitions, the more memorable a stimulus becomes.

Of the explanations proposed for the *lag effect* (also known as the *spacing effect*), two have received the most support. According to the *inattention hypothesis*, people pay less attention to repeated presentations that are massed. Because the later repetitions don't seem very novel, people don't pay much attention to them, and memory for the item does not benefit. When repeated presentations are distributed, however, the later repetitions continue to appear novel, people attend to them, and memory for the item benefits. According the *encoding variability hypothesis*, as repetitions become increasingly spaced, the information encoded for them varies increasingly. The conceptual information activated for the item may vary, as may the incidental contextual information associated with it. As the multiple memories for a stimulus become increasingly different, the number of ways to retrieve them increases.

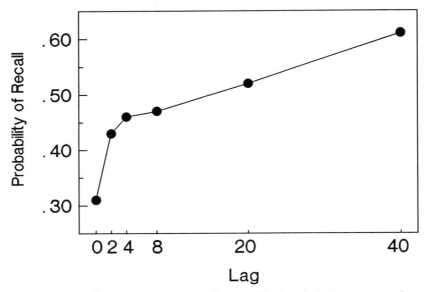

Figure 6.3.   Effect of lag on retention from (Madigan, 1969), where *lag* is the average number of intervening items between two presentations of the same word. Adapted by permission.

Because each piece of information in a memory can be used to retrieve it (**6.3.1**), more total pieces of information stored for an item provide more ways to locate it during the test phase (Crowder, 1976, chap. 9; Hintzman, 1976).

6.1.2 Elaboration

Although amount of processing plays an important role in retention, *type* of processing is at least as important, if not more. As numerous areas of research have shown, how people process a stimulus produces dramatic effects on memory. In this section, I address various kinds of elaborations that people can perform on individual stimulus items. In the next section, I address organizations that people can impose on multiple stimulus items.

Incidental versus intentional learning.   People encode information readily, even when they aren't trying to memorize it intentionally. As we saw in **4.1.1**, people encode information about frequency, location, and time without having the intention to do so. In fact, people rarely try to memorize information, with most of what they remember from their daily activity being encoded through *incidental learning*. Long-term memory results naturally as a by-product of many cognitive activities. As we shall see, the type of processing performed on information is more important than the intention to remember it. When experiments have addressed the role of intention in learning, they have often observed little effect. When intention does help memory, it does so by causing people to perform processing operations they wouldn't perform otherwise. When people are induced to perform similar operations, without having the intention to learn, information is usually learned just as well (Eagle & Leiter, 1964; Hyde & Jenkins, 1969; B. Tversky, 1973).

Depth of processing. One of the most important elaborative variables is depth of processing (Craik & Lockhart, 1972). Although it is difficult to pin down exactly what "depth" means (Baddeley, 1982; T.O. Nelson, 1977), the basic idea concerns the extent to which processing focuses on perceptual versus conceptual aspects of stimuli. Through various *orienting tasks*, an experimenter can induce subjects to focus on different perceptual and conceptual information associated with a stimulus. To orient subjects toward orthographic information in the word "canoe," for example, an experimenter could ask them whether "canoe" contains an "e." To orient subjects toward phonological information, an experimenter could ask them whether "canoe" rhymes with "taboo." To orient subjects toward conceptual information, an experimenter could ask them whether *canoe* is a *vehicle*. Across these three cases, an experimenter induces subjects to process "canoe" increasingly deeply. In the orthographic task, subjects need go no further than the visually presented stimulus. In the rhyming task, subjects must go a step further and focus on phonological information retrieved from long-term memory. In the conceptual task, subjects must go still further and focus on conceptual information retrieved from long-term memory. Following our discussion of automaticity in **4.**1, the presentation of "canoe" probably activates all three kinds of information automatically to some extent. Orienting tasks probably have their effects in focusing subsequent strategic processing on particular information.

Across a wide variety of experimental situations, memory for information typically improves as processing becomes deeper (but see C.D. Morris, Bransford, & Franks, 1977; D.L. Nelson & McEvoy, 1979; D.L. Nelson, Walling, & McEvoy, 1979). As processing focuses more on characteristics not present in the objective stimulus, and as these characteristics become increasingly conceptual, people remember the stimulus better. It does not matter whether they are trying to remember the stimulus intentionally; the critical factor is the depth of processing that the stimulus receives (Hyde & Jenkins, 1969). Moreover, depth of processing is often more important than amount of processing (**6.**1.1). In one study, Craik and Tulving (1975) found that a small amount of conceptual processing produced much better memory than a large amount of perceptual processing.

Generation. Whether people generate an elaboration themselves or have it presented to them has important implications for retention. Imagine that one group of subjects generates the antonyms of words during incidental learning. When given "up," for example, subjects generate "down." Imagine that a second group of subjects receives the complete antonym pairs for intentional learning (e.g., "up-down") and doesn't have to generate anything. When both groups are asked to recall the right-hand word of each pair, the generation group performs better, even though these subjects learned the words incidentally, whereas the other subjects learned them intentionally. In a different paradigm, when subjects are allowed to generate their own continuation to a phrase (e.g., *The frog . . .*), they remember the resulting sentence better than if the experimenter provides them with a continuation (e.g., *The frog gazed dreamily into the eyes of the princess*). In general, people tend to remember information better if they have generated it than if they have been presented with it. The extensive and specific elaboration that occurs during generation improves the chances of later retention (Begg, Snider, Foley, & Goddard, 1989; S.A. Bobrow & Bower, 1969; J.M. Gardiner, Gregg, & Hampton, 1988, Jacoby, 1978; Slamecka & P. Graf, 1978).

Imagery. Imagery (5.2.3) is another form of elaboration that has powerful effects on memory. Across a variety of experiments, subjects asked to visualize the referents of words remember them much better than subjects who simply read them. Even when subjects are not asked to form images, they remember words whose referents are imaged easily (e.g., "robin") better than words whose referents are not (e.g., "truth"). In general, higher imagery produces better memory (Paivio, 1971).

Some investigators have suggested that conceptual elaboration underlies imagery effects in retention. Imagine trying to remember the word pair, "dog-chair." One way to improve your memory of this pair is to construct a sentence that includes both words, such as "The dog slept on his own chair." Experiments have found that this improvement is much like the improvement that would occur after constructing an image of a dog and chair interacting in some way. A common factor that might underlie the advantage of both the sentence and the imaginal orienting tasks is that both produce greater conceptual elaboration of the original material, independent of whether the elaboration is expressly visual. Consequently, it may not be something about visual imagery per se that is responsible, but only the greater amount of conceptual elaboration that it adds to memory. In support of this view, Schwanenflugel, Akin, and Luh (in press) found that memory for abstract words becomes as good as memory for imageable words when both occur in sentential contexts that produce comparable conceptual elaborations (see also S.A. Bobrow & Bower, 1969, Bower, 1972a; Schwanenflugel, 1991; Schwanenflugel, Harnishfeger, & Stowe, 1988; Schwanenflugel & Shoben, 1983; Schwanenflugel & Stowe, 1989).

6.1.3 Organization

As we have seen, elaborating individual stimuli has powerful effects on retention. Another way to improve memory significantly is through the organization of multiple stimuli.

Subjective organization. If subjects receive seemingly unrelated information, such as a random list of words, and if they are asked to learn this information, they typically discover ways to organize it. Under these conditions, subjects often organize the words spontaneously, without being told to do so. As they receive each word, they find ways to link them together. If part of the list contains "magazine," "clock," "executive," and "airplane," a subject might integrate them into the scenario: An *executive*, whose office contains a grandfather *clock*, reads *magazines* about *airplanes*.

These organizations often override the order in which words occur in a list. Tulving (1962, 1964, 1966) presented subjects with the same unrelated words on multiple trials, but each time in a different random order. After each trial, subjects had to recall the words in whatever order they came to mind. Over trials, the order in which a subject recalled the words became increasingly stable and corresponded less and less to the random order of the words in the most recent list. As subjects became increasingly familiar with the list, they developed an increasingly stable organization of its words in long-term memory. These organizations were subjective, because different subjects constructed different organizations for the same words, and different subjects organized the words to different extents, with subjects who organized the list the most remembering it the best.

G. Mandler (1967) extended Tulving's work, providing further evidence for the role of subjective organization in retention (see also G. Mandler & Pearlstone, 1966). Whereas Tulving allowed subjects complete freedom in organizing the list during intentional learning, Mandler manipulated the amount of subjective organization that subjects could establish during incidental learning. Similar to Tulving, Mandler found that the subjects who could impose maximal subjective organization on a list remembered it best during subsequent recall and recognition tests. Even under incidental learning conditions, subjective organization improved memory.

Taxonomic, thematic, and hierarchical organization. Subjective organization of unrelated words demonstrates the lengths to which people will go to organize information, even when no obvious or salient organization exists. Not surprisingly, when organizational schemes are obvious and salient, people will utilize them. For example, if a list contains words from categories such as *birds, fruit, clothing,* and *vehicles,* subjects use these categories to organize the information. Even if the words from each category are distributed randomly throughout the list, and even if the list does not contain the category names, subjects nevertheless cluster the words by category at recall, indicating taxonomic organization. Numerous experiments have shown that taxonomic organization greatly facilitates memory. By using their knowledge of categories to organize information, subjects can dramatically increase their ability to remember. Of course, knowledge of these categories must be well-established in long-term memory to support such organization (Barsalou, 1983, Exp. 3; Bousfield, 1953; Bousfield & B.H. Cohen, 1953; Cofer, 1967; Puff, 1970).

People possess many different kinds of knowledge that they can use to organize information, with taxonomic categories being just one of them. *Frames* (also known as *schemata*) constitute another important kind of organizational knowledge. As we shall see later, frames represent spatial, temporal, causal, and intentional relations between entities and events in familiar situations (**7.2.2, 8.7.4, 9.3.3, 10**.1). Theorists often refer to these relations in frames as *thematic relations*. To see how frames operate during organization, consider the words: *librarian, Minneapolis, jet, island,* and *tan*. To organize these words, one might use the *trip* frame to construct the scenario: A *librarian* from *Minneapolis* takes a *jet* to an *island* to get a *tan*. Within this scenario, various thematic relations integrate particular words: spatial and temporal relations specify that the librarian begins in Minneapolis and then travels to an island; an intentional relation specifies that the librarian takes the trip for the purpose of sunbathing; and a causal relation specifies that lying in the sun on the island produces a tan. When people can use a frame to organize information in this manner, their memory of the information improves substantially (**9**.6.1; Bransford & M.K. Johnson, 1973; Bransford & McCarrell, 1974).

In general, memory for information improves whenever knowledge from memory is available to organize it. The more knowledge available for organization, the better memory becomes. Voss and his colleagues (Chiesi, Spilich, & Voss, 1979; Spilich, Vesonder, Chiesi, & Voss, 1979) have demonstrated this compellingly in the context of expertise. As people develop expertise in a domain, such as baseball, their knowledge of the domain grows. As a result, their ability to organize presented information from that domain increases, which substantially enhances retention. Baseball experts, for example, remember more from watching a particular baseball game than do novices. These effects appear closely related to the benefits of chunking in short-term memory (**5**.2.4).

Finally, hierarchical structure is essential to optimal organization. Imagine receiving 10 exemplars from each of 6 taxonomic categories. If the categories include *birds* and *fruit*, some of the exemplars might be *eagle, hawk, warbler*, and *nightingale*, as well as *lime, grapefruit, mango*, and *papaya*. One way to organize the information would be to construct 6 clusters, 1 per category, but this would mean that each cluster contains 10 pieces of information. An alternative organization would be to subdivide each category into 2 subcategories. As a result, a total of 12 subcategories, each having 5 exemplars, would be nested in the 6 superordinate categories hierarchically. *Birds*, for example, might have subcategories for *predators* and *song birds*, and *fruit* might have subcategories for *citrus* and *tropical*.

A number of studies have found that categories function optimally in retention when they contain about 4 to 5 items (the capacity of short-term memory! **5**.1.2). Consequently, 5 chunks of 5 items each is the maximum amount of information that people should attempt to store without a hierarchical organization. As the number of items to be remembered becomes larger than 25, hierarchical organization becomes increasingly necessary for optimal memory. In support of this conclusion, researchers have found that memory improves dramatically when people apply hierarchical organization to large amounts of information (Bower, M.C. Clark, Lesgold, & Winzenz, 1969; Chase & Ericsson, 1981; G. Mandler, 1967).

6.2 STORAGE

A number of fundamental issues concern the storage of information in long-term memory after the cognitive system encodes it. Where does the cognitive system store newly encoded information? Once stored, does this information decay or become revised? To what extent does this information encounter interference from other information in long-term memory? The following three sections address these issues in turn.

6.2.1 The Episodic-Semantic Distinction

Where does the cognitive system store newly encoded information? Tulving (1972) suggested that long-term memory contains two distinct memory systems: an *episodic* memory system and a *semantic* memory system. According to Tulving's view, the cognitive system stores memories of newly encoded information in the episodic memory system. Each *episodic memory* contains *temporal* and *spatial* information that specifies when and where the cognitive system acquired the new memory (note the relation to Hasher and Zacks', 1979, conclusion that the cognitive system acquires time and location automatically; **4**.1.1). For example, most married people have an episodic memory of their marriage, which contains information about the time and place of this event. Similarly, you may remember when and where you first encountered "hyalite."

In contrast, people could conceivably know that they are married without remembering the time and place of their marriage (of course, people with this problem may not remain married much longer). For these individuals, the knowledge of being married is a *semantic memory*. Rather than existing within an episodic memory, this knowledge has evolved into a semantic memory that describes a particular state of the world. A more plausible example concerns people's semantic memory that Washington, DC is the capital of the United States. Most people cannot remember the actual time and place that they learned this fact, because it has become a semantic memory, detached from the episodic memory of the original learning experience. Note that the term "semantic memory" does not really capture what Tulving had in mind. Because theorists usually reserve "semantic" for the meanings of linguistic forms (**8**.6), using it for referring to other types of knowledge, such as the capital of the United States, is somewhat non-standard. "Conceptual knowledge" is a more appropriate term, because it includes non-episodic knowledge that is related not only to language, but to many other activities as well (e.g., categorization, imagery, reasoning, problem solving).

These intuitive observations about different kinds of memories, along with various findings in the literature, suggest the presence of separate episodic and conceptual memory systems. Certain kinds of amnesia further support this distinction. For example, patients who suffer from retrograde amnesia cannot remember episodes that occurred prior to the point at which the amnesia began, but they can remember conceptual knowledge that they acquired prior to this event. According to the episodic–semantic distinction, damage has occurred to the episodic memory system but not to the conceptual memory system.

Theorists often assume further that different organizations and processing mechanisms operate in these two memory systems: Whereas chronology organizes episodic memories, taxonomic and thematic relations organize conceptual knowledge; although interference operates in episodic memory (**6**.2.3), it does not operate in conceptual knowledge. More recently, Tulving (1983) has proposed a third memory for *proceduralized* information, which contains the learned automatic productions that underlie skilled performance (**4**.1.2, **4**.3, **10**.6.3).

The episodic–semantic distinction has had a profound effect on research, not only in cognitive psychology, but throughout cognitive science. Because researchers often believe that episodic memories and conceptual knowledge constitute separate memory systems, they assume that they can study one type of memory independently of the other. Researchers in episodic memory, therefore, often ignore possible roles of conceptual knowledge, and researchers in conceptual knowledge often ignore possible roles of episodic memory. Increasing numbers of theorists, however, have come to question the episodic-semantic distinction, assuming instead that a single memory system contains both kinds of information.

Consider how a unitary memory view might explain the observations that motivate the episodic-semantic distinction. Soon after learning that Washington, DC is the capital of the United States, one might remember the original learning episode. When this fact is encountered again in later events, the resulting episodic memories become organized together. Rather than being organized chronologically in a separate memory system, these memories become organized around the conceptual fact. In the process, information common to the memories—the fact that Washington, DC is the capital of the United States—becomes strengthened through repetition (Watkins & Kerkar, 1985). In contrast, the individual memories become harder to retrieve, because they compete and interfere with one another's retrieval (6.2.3). As a result, one can remember the common fact but not the individual events in which it occurred. Similarly, for retrograde amnesia, repeated information might acquire sufficient strength in a unitary memory system to withstand the trauma that causes less established information, such as individual episodes, to be forgotten. As these examples illustrate, accounts of a unitary memory system that stores episodic and conceptual knowledge together can usually be constructed to explain the observations that motivate the episodic-semantic distinction.

In general, current evidence is insufficient to determine whether the episodic-semantic view or the unitary memory view is correct. Both can explain the current findings. Moreover, other organizational possibilities exist as well. Given this situation, many theorists prefer to take the more parsimonious course of assuming one memory system instead of several. For further discussion of this issue, see Tulving (1984) and the ensuing peer commentary.

6.2.2 Permanent Memory versus Decay and Revision

Regardless of where a memory is stored, what happens to it over time? Does it remain permanently in the system as originally encoded and never decay? Or does it decay as the brain changes over time? When E.F. Loftus and G.R. Loftus (1980) asked psychologists if they believed that memories remain permanently in the cognitive system, 84% said "yes," as did a similar percentage of non-psychologists. Why do people believe that a memory, once stored, never disintegrates but becomes a permanent fixture of long-term memory? One important influence is Penfield and Perot's (1963) famous report that electrical stimulation of the brain produces vivid childhood memories that had seemingly been long forgotten. Another is that people under hypnosis appear to recover detailed episodic information that also seemed to have been forgotten. Similarly, people sometimes unexpectedly recall an event from long ago that they are surprised to remember. Perhaps everything that people have ever experienced is still in long-term memory, but they simply can't retrieve it.

Loftus and Loftus point out the flaws in these observations. First, there is no way to verify whether the memories of Penfield's patients are valid. Perhaps electrical stimulation causes people to imagine events that seem real but did not occur. Second, under hypnosis, it turns out that the additional information that people "remember" contains fiction as well as fact. In general, people are over-confident that the "memories" they unearth represent actual events.

Currently, it is impossible to conclude anything about this issue. Clearly, people can't remember everything, but this doesn't mean that memories of the forgotten information have decayed: Although they could have decayed such that they no longer exist in memory, they could still be there, waiting for the particular situation that will retrieve them. The fact that people don't remember many past events is consistent with both views. One might be tempted to assume that there isn't enough memory capacity to store everything a person experiences and that memories must therefore decay to make room for new ones. However, no one has ever observed anything to suggest that the capacity of long-term memory is limited in this manner.

A related issue is whether the cognitive system revises memories over time. In research on eyewitness testimony, E.F. Loftus (1975) concluded that the process of remembering a previous episode may cause it to be revised, such that the episodic memory no longer exists in its original form. In her experiments, Loftus found that asking subjects a leading question about an earlier event introduced new information into memory of the event, suggesting that subjects had revised the original memory. In one study, subjects viewed a movie of a car driving through an intersection past a yield sign. Following the movie, subjects were asked, "How fast was the car going when it passed the *stop* sign?" Later, when subjects' memory of the original event in the movie was tested, many believed that the car passed a stop sign rather than a yield sign, suggesting that the leading question had revised the original memory. McCloskey and Zaragoza (1985), however, have since concluded that a leading question does not revise a memory but simply adds a second memory, which later becomes confused with the original.

Regardless of whether memories decay or are revised, long-term memory can be remarkably good. Numerous studies have demonstrated that people remember large amounts of episodic information over long periods of time. In a variety of studies, researchers have presented subjects with hundreds of visual slides for only a few seconds each. When subjects were tested on these slides after a short delay, they often recognized nearly all of them. Even after delays of several days or weeks, subjects still recognized high proportions of the slides (A.G. Goldstein & Chance, 1971; Nickerson, 1965; Shepard, 1967; Standing, Conezio, & Haber, 1970).

In another line of inquiry, H.P. Bahrick tested elderly people's retention of information acquired 50 years earlier during college, including classmates' names and faces, campus geography, and foreign languages (H.P. Bahrick, 1983, 1984; H.P. Bahrick, P.O. Bahrick, & Wittlinger, 1975). In all cases, Bahrick found impressive memory performance, indicating that much of the information had not decayed over time. It is important to note, however, that this excellent retention does not necessarily represent episodic memory, given the large amount of distributed presentation that occurred for each type of learning (6.1.1). Because subjects experienced the names and faces of their friends frequently over their college years, they may have developed conceptual knowledge for them, as well as for campus geography and foreign languages.

One might suppose that the imperfect memory in all of these studies reflects the presence of some decay, but studies by T.O Nelson (1971, 1978) suggest caution in this regard. Several weeks after learning a list of words, Nelson's subjects performed a recognition test on it. Not surprisingly, they failed to remember some of the words. In a subsequent learning phase, though, Nelson presented these "forgotten" words discretely, along with words the subject hadn't seen so far in the experiment. Interestingly, subjects learned the "forgotten" words faster than new ones. If the "forgotten" words had truly decayed, they shouldn't have shown this advantage in learning. As I describe later (6.3.3), work on implicit memory similarly demonstrates that seemingly "forgotten" information can continue to exist in memory and affect processing.

6.2.3 Interference

If memories do not decay, then why do people forget? One widely accepted explanation is that memories interfere with one another in storage. Researchers have found that two important kinds of interference—*proactive* and *retroactive*—can cause substantial forgetting. Figure 6.4 illustrates the basic idea behind these two types of interference. Imagine that three groups of subjects learn the identical information in List 2 to an equal extent. Whereas the control group only learns List 2, the proactive-interference group also learns List 1 (before List 2), and the retroactive-interference group also learns List 3 (after List 2). Following this initial learning phase, subjects in all three groups are tested on List 2. In general, the control group will remember more about List 2 than either the proactive-interference or the retroactive-interference group. The proactive interference group remembers less about List 2, because List 1 interferes proactively with List 2. The retroactive interference group remembers less about List 2, because List 3 interferes retroactively with List 2.

Similarity between lists plays an important role in interference. As Lists 1

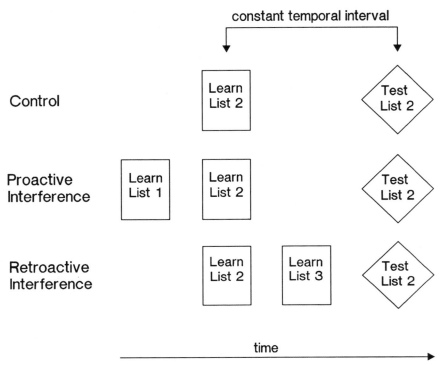

Figure 6.4.   Experimental designs for demonstrating proactive and retroactive interference.

and 2 become more similar, proactive interference from List 1 increasingly depresses memory of List 2. As Lists 2 and 3 become more similar, retroactive interference from List 3 increasingly depresses memory of List 2. Actually, numerous possible relations can exist between lists. Whereas some relations between adjacent lists depress memory, other relations may actually enhance it. Transfer from one list to another, then, can be either negative or positive, with interference representing negative transfer.

Over the years, theorists have proposed numerous mechanisms to explain the wide variety of interference findings. For example, information in Lists 1 and 3 may actively inhibit information in List 2, or information in Lists 1 and 3 may compete with information in List 2 for spreading activation, or for the limited strategic resource (**4.2.2**). Unfortunately, there is little consensus about the nature of interference mechanisms. Nevertheless, interference effects have been amply demonstrated, and they appear to play a central role in making stored information inaccessible (Crowder, 1976, chap. 8; Postman & Underwood, 1973).

A related phenomenon is the *fan effect*, established by J.R. Anderson and Bower (1973; Anderson, 1976, 1981, 1983). During learning, subjects learn multiple facts about a character (e.g., *Brian cooks Indian food, Brian likes to watch basketball, Brian doesn't get enough sleep*). Subjects might learn only one fact about some characters, two facts about other characters, and three facts about other characters. During a subsequent test, subjects receive a statement about a character, which may be true or false (e.g., *Brian cooks Indian food* vs. *Brian likes opera*). The critical result is that the time to determine whether a particular fact is true or false increases with the number of facts known about the character. For example, verification proceeds more slowly for characters associated with two facts than for characters associated with one fact.

Anderson and Bower explain the fan effect in terms of spreading activation (2.5): When subjects receive a statement about a character to verify, a limited amount of spreading activation emanates from the character's representation in memory. If only one fact "fans" off the character, it receives all of the activation and can be retrieved quickly. If two facts fan off the character, each receives half of the activation, so that retrieving the relevant fact takes longer. Three facts take still longer, because each only receives one-third of the activation. As the number of related facts grows, the total amount of interference for a given fact increases. Interference not only prevents information from being retrieved, it also slows the activation of remembered information.

6.3   RETRIEVAL

Once information becomes stored in memory, the key to recovering it is the *retrieval cue*. Information may be available in memory, but many cues may not be effective in retrieving it. The inability of a cue to access a memory is known as *retrieval failure*. As we shall see, retrieval failure can often be overcome by replacing ineffective cues with effective cues. The central issue in retrieval, therefore, concerns why some cues are more effective than others.

6.3.1 Overlap of Cue and Target Information

Retrieval is generally effective to the extent that information in the cue overlaps with information in the target (i.e., the information to be retrieved). The effectiveness of a cue increases as it: (a) shares increasing properties with the target, and (b) contains decreasing properties not in the target. Tulving and Thomson (1973) termed this the *encoding specificity principle*: Retrieval is successful to the extent that the cognitive system reinstates the original encoding context during the retrieval process. If the cognitive system can produce a cue that overlaps with the target, retrieval may succeed; if not, retrieval will probably fail.

Free recall, cued recall, and recognition. Retrieval cues can take a wide variety of forms. Three of the most important occur in free recall, cued recall, and recognition, which differ in how cues overlap with targets. To see how overlap differs, imagine the following experiment: A subject receives 6 words from each of 10 taxonomic categories; the words are not blocked by category but are randomly distributed throughout the list. Assume that the subject stores four pieces of information for each word: perceptual, conceptual, associative, and contextual information. Thus, a memory for the word "parrot" in the list might include: perceptual information about the ink color and type font of the word; conceptual information about the typical body, behavior, and environment of *parrot*, as well as its membership in the category *bird*; associative information linking *parrot* to other birds in the list, such as *robin* and *eagle*; contextual information about the time and place of the experiment, along with what the subject was feeling and thinking at the time. As we shall see, these four types of information play a wide variety of roles in different retrieval contexts.

Consider three possible tests of this list. In *free recall*, the subject must recall as many words from the list as possible, in whatever order they come to mind. In *cued recall*, the subject is given the 10 category names (which did not occur in the list) and must recall as many category members from the list as possible, in whatever order they come to mind. In *recognition*, the 60 words from the list are randomly mixed with 60 distractors not from the list, where the distractors might be 6 additional words from each category. The subject's task is to circle only those words from the original list. In *forced-choice recognition*, the subject receives sets of words, each containing one word from the list plus one or more distractors, and attempts to determine which word was in the list.

Free recall, cued recall, and recognition generally vary in the extent to which retrieval cues overlap with memories of words from the list. In free recall, the retrieval cue is the context of the list: "Recall words that occurred in the list during the experiment." In cued recall, the retrieval cue contains not only contextual information, but also conceptual information: "Recall words from the experiment in the category *bird*." In recognition, the retrieval cue contains not only contextual information, but also the original perceptual information: "Did you see "parrot" in the experiment?" As these examples illustrate, the overlap between cues and targets increases from free recall to cued recall to recognition. In free recall, cues and targets only overlap on contextual information (e.g., the experimental context). In cued recall, cues and targets overlap on conceptual information as well (e.g., *birds* in the experimental context). In recognition, cues and targets overlap further on perceptual information (e.g., "parrot" in the experimental context; note that *bird* is available conceptually, because subjects infer it from reading "parrot" on the recognition test; Barsalou & B.H. Ross, 1986).

Generally speaking, memory is poorest for free recall, better for cued recall, and best for recognition. On an immediate test, free recall subjects in our imaginary experiment might retrieve 30% of the words, cued recall subjects might retrieve 60% of the words, and recognition subjects might circle 95% of the original words (*hits*) and only 5% of the distractors (*false alarms*). In recognition, researchers must assess both hits and false alarms, because of biases that subjects may exhibit in circling words. Sometimes subjects circle words liberally, inflating hits at the expense of increasing false alarms; but sometimes subjects circle words conservatively, minimizing false alarms at the expense of decreasing hits. To remove such bias from a subject's recognition performance, researchers often combine hit and false alarm rates to form the d' measure from signal detection theory, thereby providing a relatively pure estimate of recognition memory (as in Fig. 6.1; see Banks, 1970; Crowder, 1976, pp. 375-376).

Because of the differences between free recall, cued recall, and recognition, researchers must exhibit great caution in concluding that information about a target is not stored in memory (Tulving & Pearlstone, 1966). If researchers base their assessment of the targets in memory on free recall, they would conclude incorrectly that only 30% of them reside in memory. Clearly, this free recall measure underestimates subjects' memory of the list, because when they receive cued recall and recognition cues, they exhibit memory for many additional words. Moreover, researchers must even be cautious when a recognition cue fails to retrieve a word. As we saw earlier for T.O Nelson's (1971, 1978) experiments (**6.2.2**), and as we shall see later for implicit memory (**6.3.3**), memories that are not detectable even on a recognition test may still affect processing, thereby demonstrating their presence. In general, then, a particular memory test only verifies the presence of memories that are accessible with its cues. The failure of a test to retrieve information does not necessarily demonstrate the absence of information in memory.

Further evidence for the importance of overlap. Five intriguing findings further highlight the central role of overlap in retrieval: recognition failure, failure of extra-list cuing, transfer-appropriate processing, context-dependent learning, and state-dependent learning.

In *recognition failure*, cued recall counter-intuitively produces better memory than recognition. During learning, subjects receive word pairs such as "car-light." They then receive the right-hand member of each pair in a recognition test (e.g., "light"). Finally, they receive the left-hand member and have to generate the right-hand member in a cued recall test (e.g., when given "car," try to generate "light"). The surprising result is that subjects sometimes fail to recognize a right-hand member of a pair during recognition but generate it later during cued recall. For example, a subject might say that "light" was not on the list but then generate it when given "car." Counterintuitively, greater cue information in the recognition test produces poorer memory. One interpretation of recognition failure concerns encoding variability (**6**.1.1, **7**.2.3): "Light," when learned initially in the context of "car," might activate information about *light bulbs*; whereas "light," when read in isolation on the recognition test, might activate information about *sunlight*. As a result, "light" on the recognition test does not overlap with the information encoded for "light" during learning. In contrast, "car," when read in isolation on the cued recall test, may overlap with information encoded for "car" during learning and thereby activate the memory that also contains "light." Recognition is not the most sensitive measure of memory, therefore, when a recognition cue activates information that does not overlap with the target (Nilsson, Law, & Tulving, 1988; Tulving & Thomson, 1973).

In *failure of extra-list cuing*, subjects also receive pairs such as "car-light." During a cued recall test, however, some subjects receive a cue that is more strongly associated to the target in everyday experience than the cue associated with the target at learning. For example, subjects might receive "dark" as a cue for "light," which is a stronger associate than "car." Counterintuitively, "car" is a better cue of "light" during the cued recall test than "dark." Similar to recognition failure, the best cue is the one that overlaps most highly with the target information in memory, not the one that is most highly associated. Because subjects did not store "dark" when they encoded "car-light," the highly-associated cue, "dark," does not overlap with the memory that contains "car-light." Instead, a less associated word stored in the memory, "car," provides a stronger cue (Thomson & Tulving, 1970; Tulving & Thomson, 1973).

In *transfer-appropriate processing*, researchers have shown that depth-of-processing effects sometimes reflect poor overlap between cues and targets. Recall that memory after conceptual elaboration of a stimulus is usually better than after perceptual elaboration (**6**.1.2). One problem with the original experiments showing this was that the processing of retrieval cues was not controlled. Imagine subjects are oriented to process "snow" phonologically. When presented with "snow" on a recognition test, however, they spontaneously process it conceptually. As a result, the conceptually oriented retrieval cue does not overlap optimally with the phonologically oriented memory. To correct for this, researchers have oriented subjects the same way at encoding and retrieval. Under these conditions, depth-of-processing effects are significantly smaller and sometimes disappear, providing further evidence for the importance of overlap in retrieval (C.D. Morris et al., 1977; D.L. Nelson & McEvoy, 1979; D.L. Nelson et al., 1979).

In *context-dependent learning*, subjects learn material in one context and then are tested on the material either in the same or a different context. For example, they might learn material in one classroom and then be tested in the same classroom or a different one, or they might learn material under water and then be tested on land or under water. In general, reinstating the original context produces better memory, presumably because it maximizes the overlap between cues and targets (Davies & Thomson, 1988; Eich, 1985; Godden & Baddeley, 1975; S.M. Smith, 1979, 1982, 1986).

Similarly, in *state-dependent learning*, subjects learn material in one mental state and then are tested either in the same or a different state. For example, they might learn material under alcohol intoxication and then be tested either under alcohol intoxication or while sober, or they might learn material while sad and then be tested while either sad or happy. In general, reinstating subjects' original state produces better memory, again because it maximizes the overlap between cues and targets (Bower, 1981; Eich, 1980).

Mechanisms underlying recall and recognition. Theorists generally believe that free recall is difficult because the availability of cue information is low. All that subjects have is information about the context; they have no conceptual or perceptual information about the specific items that occurred in it. The foremost factor in overcoming this problem is *organization*. As we saw earlier, people often use taxonomic and thematic relations to organize information at encoding (**6**.1.3). Such organization greatly improves free recall, because it helps subjects find information at retrieval.

Imagine again the subject who uses the frame for *trip* to integrate *librarian*, *Minneapolis, jet, island*, and *tan* while learning a list (**6**.1.3). Upon recalling one of these words (e.g., *jet*), the subject may be reminded of the frame for *trip*, which then provides cues for the other words integrated into it. Roles associated commonly with the *trip* frame, such as *agent, purpose, departure point*, and *destination*, become active and cue their instantiations, such as *librarian, tan, Minneapolis*, and *island*, respectively. If subjects can organize the information in this way at encoding and then retrieve the organization at recall, they may be able to recover much of the original information. In contrast, if they fail to organize the information at encoding, they have to retrieve each word individually. Recalling one word provides no cues for finding other words, and the entire memory system may have to be searched. As a result, recall is much more difficult and much less likely to succeed. For this reason, materials that lend themselves to organization generally produce much higher free recall than materials that do not. Furthermore, strategies that focus subjects' attention on relations between items produce higher free recall than strategies that focus attention on individual items.

In contrast to free recall, recognition typically does not include the problem of having to decide where to look in memory for targets. Instead, a recognition cue usually directs search to the location in memory where target information is stored (except in phenomena like recognition failure). The problem in recognition is deciding whether the target occurred in the experimental context. For example, the recognition cue "island" directs search to information about *island* in memory, and the goal is finding evidence that "island" occurred during the experiment.

Subjects generally use two strategies to decide if an item occurred in an experimental context: a fast *familiarity strategy*, and a slower *contextual search strategy*. In the fast familiarity strategy, if subjects initially perceive a word as highly familiar, they may infer that it occurred in the experiment, otherwise it wouldn't be so familiar. Words may seem familiar, either because many memories of them become active at test, or because their conceptual representations become highly active. Conversely, if subjects initially perceive a word as being very low in familiarity, they may conclude it couldn't have occurred in the experiment.

When familiarity is not conclusive, or if subjects want to be sure that they don't make a mistake, they may adopt the slower, more conservative strategy of contextual search. In this mode, subjects search for evidence that an item actually occurred in the experimental context. If this search yields associations to items known to have occurred in the experimental context, or if it yields information that describes the experimental context, the subject may conclude that the item occurred. If subjects find no contextual information, they may conclude that the item did not occur. In general, strategies that make targets seem more familiar, or strategies that link targets to other targets and to contextual information, improve recognition.

The relative frequency of the material being remembered interacts with recall and recognition mechanisms in an important way (high-frequency words include "dog" and "chair;" low-frequency words include "sonata" and "mollusk"). In general, recall is better for high-frequency material than for low-frequency material, whereas recognition is better for low-frequency material than for high-frequency material. People recall high-frequency material better, because it is associated to more information in memory. The more often material is encountered, the more likely it is to be organized in different ways. Consequently, there are more "organizational" routes to high-frequency material during recall, making it more likely to be retrieved.

In contrast, the familiarity of high-frequency material makes it difficult to recognize. Subjects have trouble deciding if high-frequency material is familiar because it occurred as a target in the experiment or because it has occurred so often in the past. In contrast, if low-frequency material appears familiar, subjects can be confident it occurred in the experiment; otherwise it would not seem familiar. Low-frequency material is also more recognizable when subjects use the slow, contextual strategy. High-frequency material has so much contextual information associated with it that interference makes it difficult to find contextual information from the experiment (**6.2.3**). In contrast, low frequency material has so little contextual information associated with it that contextual information from the experiment is easy to find. For more on theories of recognition and recall, see J.R. Anderson and Bower

(1972, 1974), Gillund and Shiffrin (1984), Kintsch (1970), G. Mandler (1980), and Tulving (1976).

Exact matches versus plausibility. The standard recognition experiment orients subjects toward exact matches between cues and targets: If subjects can find a target that matches the recognition cue perfectly, and if the target occurred in the experimental context, then subjects should recognize the item. In contrast, partial overlap between a cue and target is often sufficient to perform satisfactorily on certain recognition tasks, as Reder and B.H. Ross (1983) have demonstrated (see also Reder, 1982, 1987). Imagine that some subjects learn the following three facts about Margaret: *Margaret has many friends*; *Margaret is boisterous at basketball games*; *Margaret likes parties*. Imagine that other subjects learn only the first fact. Further imagine that at test, subjects receive the statement: *Margaret is an extrovert*. If subjects' task is to verify that this statement occurred during learning, their decision time becomes slower as the number of statements about Margaret increases, namely, the fan effect we considered earlier (**6.2.3**). If subjects' task, however, is to determine that this statement is a plausible assertion about Margaret, decision time becomes *faster* as the number of statements about Margaret increases (i.e., a *reverse fan effect*).

Differing roles of overlap underlie Reder and Ross' findings of a normal fan effect and a reverse fan effect. When subjects perform verification judgments, they must ensure that information in the cue overlaps exactly with information in the target. Moreover, they must check every known fact, otherwise they might miss a fact that matches the cue. As a result, the more facts they must retrieve and check, the longer it takes to reach a decision. In contrast, when subjects perform plausibility judgments, they simply need to find one fact that is partially consistent with the cue. Because every fact about Margaret is consistent with her being extroverted, only one needs to be retrieved. Moreover, it need not match the cue exactly—it must simply be consistent with it. Although most recognition experiments orient subjects toward exact matches between cues and targets, partial overlaps are often sufficient to perform a task adequately, and they may play many important roles in human cognition.

Priming from retrieval. Ratcliff and McKoon (1978) demonstrated another important property of overlap in retrieval: When a cue activates a target, other information associated with the target becomes activated as well, so that the overlap between a cue and information in memory extends beyond the retrieved target. To show this, Ratcliff and McKoon presented subjects with sentences relating arbitrary words. For example, "The *bird* flew over the *car*" relates *bird* and *car*, which are normally unrelated. At test, subjects received individual words and were asked to verify whether they had occurred in the sentences heard earlier. Some subjects received *bird* to verify on one trial, followed by *car* to verify on the next. Other subjects received *book* to verify on one trial, followed by *car* to verify on the next. Ratcliff and McKoon found that the time to verify *car* was faster when preceded by *bird* than when preceded by *book*. Verifying *bird* activated the sentence memory containing it, thereby priming *car*, which allowed subjects to verify *car* more quickly than they did when *book* preceded it. Cues not only retrieve targets that overlap highly, they also retrieve information associated with the target, thereby expanding the scope of retrieval.

6.3.2 Organization in Retrieval

So far, I have characterized retrieval as a one-step process: A retrieval cue is projected to memory, and information with high overlap becomes activated, as does information associated with it. However, the retrieval process often extends over long periods of time, thereby becoming subject to organizational mechanisms.

Retrieval plans and descriptions.   Because the cues in free recall are so unconstrained, people often adopt retrieval plans for searching memory. Essentially these plans use the organization inherent in conceptual knowledge to suggest possible areas of memory to search. In a study performed by M.D. Williams and Hollan (1981), college students recalled the names of their high school classmates in one-hour sessions for up to a total of 10 sessions. At first, highly memorable names came to mind immediately, but soon thereafter, subjects had to work hard to retrieve additional names. Subjects frequently adopted the strategy of using their conceptual knowledge to suggest where to search, employing knowledge of high school locations (e.g., people usually seen in the library, near the lockers, in the cafeteria, in the principal's office), high school activities (e.g., graduation, football games, proms), and so forth. Williams and Hollan found that such strategies worked impressively. Even after recalling names for 10 sessions, subjects were still discovering additional names.

R.C. Anderson and Pichert (1978) demonstrated the importance of retrieval plans in a somewhat similar way. Subjects adopted the point of view of a home buyer while reading a description of a house and then recalled the description from the same point of view. After completing this first recall, subjects were asked to adopt the point of view of a thief and recall the description of the house again. Interestingly, subjects recalled additional information relevant to robbing the house that they hadn't recalled before (e.g., a faulty lock on the door, a color TV in the den). To assist retrieval, subjects used conceptual knowledge about robbing houses to suggest information that might have been present. Because this knowledge differed from knowledge relevant to buying a home, it suggested different areas of memory to search. This finding qualifies the importance of overlap in retrieval. Subjects probably did not think about robbing the house while reading the description. As a result, they did not encode information about robbery into their original memory. However, knowledge about robbery helped retrieval, indicating that, contrary to the encoding specificity principle, non-encoded information can access encoded information.

When searching memory, people often have only a rough idea of what they want to retrieve. Norman and D.G. Bobrow (1979) proposed that a central activity of many retrieval situations is constructing a specific description for the search object. Consider the cue, "When was the last time you ate popcorn?" This cue may be too general to access specific memories. If it doesn't produce a specific memory, you may construct more specific search descriptions using conceptual knowledge, such as, "eating popcorn while seeing a movie at a theater." If this description doesn't retrieve any memories, it might be refined further by adding additional information, as in "eating popcorn while seeing a movie at the Garden Hills theater with a family member on the weekend." As memories fitting this description become active, they are examined for information about popcorn. Once you have retrieved as many memories of popcorn as possible in this manner, the most recent memory can be selected as the answer. Again, conceptual knowledge is central to organizing the retrieval process.

Reconstruction. If people try to recall a very recent event, they usually have little difficulty remembering its specific details, and they make few mistakes in falsely remembering details that didn't occur. If they try to recall an event further in the past, however, memory is often much poorer. As a result, they may *reconstruct* the event with conceptual knowledge, making plausible inferences about details they don't remember. Most importantly, people often confuse these plausible inferences with what really happened, thereby introducing *intrusions* into their memory of the event. For example, someone on a business trip might have received a ride from a fellow passenger from the airport to the hotel, but several months later, when this event has become difficult to remember, he may recall incorrectly that he took a taxi.

Where do intrusions come from? In classic work, Bartlett (1932) proposed that people use *schemata* to help remember events. Schemata are equivalent to the frames that we considered earlier (**6**.1.3) and that we will consider later in more detail (**7**.2.2). For now, a frame is simply conceptual knowledge that contains general expectations about a kind of event or object. For example, one's frame for *trip* might include the general expectation that people take taxis between airports and hotels. As time passes, the details about a specific trip may become increasingly difficult to retrieve. In their place, one might retrieve general expectations from the frame for *trip*, not realizing that these expectations are intrusions. A person may believe that he took a taxi from the airport to the hotel, because this general expectation provides a plausible replacement of forgotten information. General expectations from frames constitute reasonable guesses of what happened in an event when the original details are no longer accessible.

Numerous experiments have demonstrated the powerful, reconstructive effects of frames on memory. As Alba and Hasher (1983) have noted, reconstruction often reflects vague retrieval cues in free recall. Because recall cues don't overlap much with the specific details of a remembered event, these details are not remembered, and more accessible, general expectations are retrieved instead. Consider the cue, "Recall a trip." All that this cue retrieves directly is the frame for *trip*. It does not cue any details about a particular trip. As a result, details of particular trips may be difficult to remember, and general expectations from the frame may intrude. In contrast, when given *recognition cues* for specific details of a trip, one may be able to access these details because of a much higher overlap. Thus, if asked whether a passenger from the plane provided a ride to the hotel, one might remember this detail correctly. Alba and Hasher conclude that reconstruction only affects recall and not recognition. Owens, Bower, and Black (1979), how-ever, have reported compelling evidence that reconstruction also has pow-erful effects on recognition, as have many researchers in social cognition (Cantor & Mischel, 1977; C.E. Cohen, 1981; Fiske & S.E. Taylor, 1991).

Output interference. What happens to information after people re-trieve it? Once found, does it somehow "get out of the way" of subsequent retrieval attempts so that additional information can be accessed? Unfortu-nately, the opposite occurs. Once retrieved, information enters a much more active state than it was in prior to retrieval. If the same cue is presented to memory over the course of recall, the memory it retrieved previously may keep coming to mind faster than before, because of its increasing activation following each retrieval. As a result, this memory blocks the retrieval of additional memories that may be relevant, at least until its high activation level has had time to decrease. You have probably had the experience of trying to remember a name and retrieving the wrong one, only to find this wrong name coming to mind continually as you search for the correct one. After thinking about something else for a while and allowing the wrong name to decrease in activation, you find that the desired name comes to mind. In general, though, as people retrieve increasing amounts of information over the course of a retrieval period, they experience increasing amounts of output interference from information already retrieved (J. Brown, 1968; Neely, Schmidt, & Roediger, 1983; Roediger & Neely, 1982; Roediger, Neely, & Blaxton, 1983; Rundus, 1973).

6.3.3 Implicit Versus Explicit Memory

In assessing memory so far, we have only considered the intentional retrieval of past events. We have not assessed whether people incidentally retrieve memories when they are not trying to retrieve them. Although we have considered the intentional–incidental distinction at encoding, we have not considered it at retrieval. However, a large and rapidly growing literature demonstrates that people, across a wide variety of tasks, frequently retrieve memories incidentally, without having the intention to do so. Moreover, they often are not aware of these retrievals, nor of their effects on behavior. Theorists refer to this type of incidental retrieval as *implicit memory*, whereas they refer to intentional retrieval as *explicit memory*.

An experiment by Jacoby (1983) demonstrates this distinction. As Fig. 6.5 illustrates, subjects in the generate condition received words and generated antonyms (e.g., given "hot," generate "cold"); subjects in the context condition read a word followed by its antonym (e.g., "hot" followed by "cold"); and subjects in the no-context condition received a row of Xs followed by a word from an antonym pair (e.g., "XXXX" followed by "cold"). The critical words in the experiment were the right-hand members of the antonym pairs (e.g., "cold" in the preceding examples).

Following list presentation, half of the subjects in each learning condition

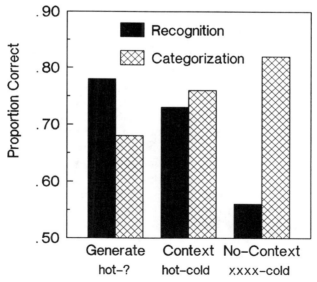

Figure 6.5. Dissociation of recognition and categorization from Jacoby (1983). Adapted by permission.

performed a recognition test, and half performed a categorization test. In the recognition test, subjects received the critical words, mixed with distractors, and had to indicate which had occurred earlier. In the categorization test, subjects received a 33 msec visual flash of a word and had to categorize it. If "cold" were flashed, the task was simply to state that the presented letter string constituted the word "cold," although the brief presentation exposure led to many errors. On some trials, subjects received critical words to categorize; on others, they received words not seen up to that point in the experiment.

As shown in Fig. 6.5, the three learning conditions produced opposite effects on the recognition and categorization tests. For the recognition test, performance was worst in the no–context condition, improved in the context condition, and improved still more in the generate condition. Conversely, performance on the categorization test was best in the no–context condition, deteriorated in the context condition, and deteriorated still more in the generate condition.

These results demonstrate several interesting and important points: First, subjects retrieved memories from the learning phase to perform the categorization test. They must have retrieved these memories, because the learning manipulation affected categorization (see Fig. 6.5). If subjects had not retrieved memories to perform categorization, then categorization should have been identical across learning conditions. Instead, the learning manipulation produced different memories of the critical items in the first phase of the experiment. Later, during the categorization test, subjects retrieved these memories, and because the memories differed among learning conditions, categorization performance differed as well. Although subjects probably didn't have the intention to retrieve these memories, they nevertheless retrieved them implicitly to perform their categorizations.

A second important point concerns the nature of the effect that the learning conditions had on categorization. As we saw earlier (6.1.2), elaboration greatly improves explicit memory: The more extensively people elaborate a stimulus, the better they remember it intentionally. Elaboration is lowest in the no–context condition, because subjects simply read words in isolation. Elaboration increases in the context condition, because subjects organize the two antonyms into a pair, and increases still further in the generate condition, because generation augments the amount and specificity of elaboration. As Fig. 6.5 illustrates, Jacoby's recognition data are consistent with the elaboration principle, because recognition increases with elaboration.

Paradoxically, though, Jacoby's categorization data are entirely inconsistent with the elaboration principle, because categorization decreases with elaboration. Why doesn't categorization increase with elaboration? Jacoby suggests that this is because categorization relies more on perceptual than conceptual information. To see this, consider the perceptual processing of the critical words across learning conditions. In the generate condition, subjects never actually saw the critical words, because they generated them. As a result, they stored little or no perceptual information for these words. In the context condition, subjects saw an antonym followed by the critical word that was its counterpart (e.g., "hot" followed by "cold"). Because the first word so heavily primed the second word, little bottom–up information was necessary for categorizing the second word (2.4, 2.5). Because these subjects actually perceived the critical word, though, they stored more perceptual information for it than did subjects in the generate condition. In the no-context condition, subjects stored the most perceptual information, because they had to rely completely on bottom–up processing to read the word.

Consider, now, the overlap between the memories in these three learning conditions and the perceptual stimuli that subjects had to identify in the subsequent categorization task. Clearly, the memories from the no-context condition overlapped the most with the categorization stimuli, because these memories contained the most perceptual information. When a categorization stimulus appeared, it was therefore more likely to activate one of these memories than were categorization stimuli related to less perceptual memories in the other two learning conditions. Most importantly, activation of the perceptual memories helped categorization, because of people's proclivity to classify by exemplar (2.3): Because the exemplar memories from the no-context condition best matched the categorization stimuli, these memories were most likely to be retrieved implicitly and facilitate categorization (Jacoby & Hayman, 1987).

A third important point about these results concerns the *dissociation* that the three learning conditions produced between recognition and categorization. What does this dissociation tell us about the organization of the cognitive system? Because the learning conditions produced opposite effects on recognition and categorization (Fig. 6.5), these two tasks must utilize different cognitive mechanisms, at least to some extent. What might these mechanisms be? Tulving (1984) suggested that such dissociations reflect different memory systems, with recognition utilizing the episodic memory system, and categorization utilizing the semantic and procedural memory systems (6.2.1). Because these systems contain different mechanisms, they produce different patterns of results.

On the other hand, Jacoby and Brooks (1984) argue that unitary memory theories can explain dissociations as well (6.2.1). As we have seen, different encoding operations store different information for the same stimulus (6.1.2). Because subjects in the different learning conditions of Jacoby's experiment performed different encoding operations on the same stimuli, they stored different information for them. In the no–context condition, for example, subjects stored more perceptual and less conceptual information than subjects in the generate condition. Theorists can often explain dissociations quite readily by simply assuming that encoding different information during learning optimizes different retrieval tasks later: Whereas encoding perceptual information optimizes categorization, encoding conceptual information optimizes recognition. Numerous studies in the literature on implicit memory support this conclusion (e.g., Blaxton, 1989).

Finally, implicit memory demonstrates how difficult it is to draw a clear distinction between episodic memory and knowledge. Supposedly categorization is a knowledge-intensive task, yet episodic memories have a substantial impact on it. Episodic memories appear to be integrated closely with abstract concepts and to play central roles in conceptual processing (**2.3**, **7**.2.2).

6.4 THE GENERALIZABILITY OF LABORATORY RESEARCH

Researchers discovered nearly all of the principles of memory described in this chapter from laboratory research with word lists. What do these principles tell us about more naturalistic memory? Do they explain people's use of memory in everyday situations? In a collection of articles on naturalistic memory, Neisser (1982) concluded that these principles have little if anything to say about people's daily use of memory. The theme of his lead chapter was, "If X is an interesting or socially significant aspect of memory, then psychologists have hardly ever studied X" (p. 4). The remaining articles in his collection reported diverse findings about memory for conversations, oral traditions, historical events, childhood events, and other naturalistic phenomena—but not word lists.

In a review of Neisser's book, Potter (1983) concurred that everyday memory has indeed received little study and that the articles in Neisser's collection represented a useful beginning. However, Potter further noted that no theory is offered to explain these findings and that no such theory appears imminent. Most intriguingly, Potter suggested that principles in the traditional memory literature may provide good accounts of naturalistic memory phenomena. She then provided several compelling examples of how traditional memory principles, such as those in this chapter, readily explain the findings in Neisser's collection.

Clearly, naturalistic memory has received insufficient study, and many important challenges face researchers in this area. Yet, it is not clear that attempts to understand naturalistic memory phenomena cannot benefit significantly from what researchers have already learned from laboratory memory phenomena. Before abandoning current principles of memory, it is first necessary to see how much of naturalistic memory they explain. Perhaps the problem has simply been a failure to extend memory principles outside of the laboratory. Once researchers attempt to do so, they may be surprised at these principles' explanatory power. Perhaps the complexities of naturalistic memory arise through dynamic interactions of relatively simple mechanisms. Most researchers cannot imagine that the basic mechanisms of encoding, storage, and retrieval considered here could have nothing to do with people's daily use of memory. On the other hand, researchers may find that some of these mechanisms operate quite differently in naturalistic memory, and they may discover, as well, the presence of additional mechanisms. Such findings could be of considerable importance in stimulating theoretical development. Until serious attempts to extend current principles are shown to fail, however, the conclusion that they offer no explanation of naturalistic memory is premature. Nevertheless, Neisser's message is important, and much further work will be necessary if we are to understand naturalistic memory.

7

KNOWLEDGE IN MEMORY

A truly impressive characteristic of human intelligence is the ability to acquire, store, and use tremendous amounts of complex knowledge. Because individuals typically know the meanings of over 50,000 words, they know the characteristics for thousands of different kinds of things (e.g., of *birds*, *cars*, *jungles*, *astronauts*, *weddings*, *complements*). These characteristics may include how something looks, how it originates, how it acts, how internal processes control its growth and behavior, and how it serves human needs (e.g., how *dogs* look, originate, act, grow, and serve as companions). For many kinds of things, people have knowledge of specific individuals (e.g., for *friends*, *books*, *cities*), as well as procedures for using and interacting with them (e.g., how to *drive*, *wash*, and *fuel* a car). People are also extremely adept at manipulating knowledge to formulate predictions, make decisions, answer questions, construct new knowledge, and so on. Moreover, people acquire knowledge rapidly, update it easily, and adapt it readily to new situations. As far as we know, there are no limits on how much knowledge a human can acquire. Humans are knowledge–intensive systems *par excellence*.

7.1 BASIC ASSUMPTIONS

In this chapter, I consider only a subset of human knowledge, namely, *general declarative knowledge*. I address other forms of knowledge elsewhere, including episodic knowledge (2.3, **5**, **6**, **8**.7.4, **8**.7.5, **9**.5, **9**.6) and procedural knowledge (**4, 9, 10**). The following six assumptions shape the discussion of knowledge in this chapter:

General knowledge. Much of human knowledge is detached from personal experience, in that people cannot remember the particular circumstances in which it was learned (**6**.2.1). Often such knowledge is quite general and applies to many, many possible entities or events. Most people know that *birds have wings* and that *water-skiing requires a boat*, but cannot remember when they learned these general facts. Instead, these facts represent many specific episodes involving *birds* and *water-skiing* in a detached manner.

Nevertheless, knowledge appears closely related to memories of specific episodes. As we saw in **6**.3.3, specific memories often become active implicitly during the use of knowledge. Moreover, some theorists propose that abstract knowledge can be constructed from episodic memories when needed, rather than being retrieved directly as generalized facts (Hintzman, 1986; Kahneman & D.T. Miller, 1986). For example, the generalization that *birds have wings* could be constructed on the spot by retrieving several memories of particular *birds* and noting that each instance has wings. It is hard to imagine, however, that such a system would not eventually store the generalizations it constructs from episodes. Once a generalization has been constructed from exemplars, basic principles of memory suggest that it should become transferred to long-term memory. As we saw in **6**.1, information that receives extensive processing in working memory through repetition, elaboration, and organization has a high probability of becoming stored permanently. Because generalizations constructed from exemplars are likely to receive extensive processing, they will typically become established in long-term memory, thereby being directly retrievable the next time the category receives processing (Barsalou, 1987, pp. 132-134; 1988, pp. 232-235). In this chapter, I focus primarily on generalized knowledge, although the role of exemplars in category representations (**2**.3.1) becomes relevant at various points.

Declarative knowledge. A person's knowledge varies in how readily he or she can examine it. Consider the procedure for donning an oxygen mask in an airline emergency. As people know from tutorials at the start of airline flights, this procedure involves watching the oxygen mask drop, placing it over one's face, pulling the air hose tight, and tightening the straps on the mask. Because most people have never had to perform this procedure, it has not become automatized (**4**.1.2). Instead, they have simply memorized the steps in a script from having heard it described so often (**4**.2.1, **10**.6.2). If someone asks them to describe the process, they can retrieve the script and describe the steps readily. Theorists often refer to such knowledge as *declarative*.

In contrast, consider the knowledge that underlies tying one's shoes. It is difficult to list the steps in this process. Instead, people can only identify the steps by visualizing or performing the process and then describing what they observe (**5.2.3**). When knowledge becomes automatized, it may become difficult to examine consciously and report. Theorists often refer to such knowledge as *proceduralized*, and we have already encountered examples of it in learned automatic productions (**4.1.2**, **4.3**). We will encounter it again later in skilled problem solving (**10.6.3**).

Declarative and procedural knowledge differ in important ways: Whereas people can readily examine declarative knowledge, they can examine procedural knowledge to a much lesser extent, if at all. Although declarative knowledge can be adapted readily to a wide variety of specific situations, procedural knowledge is much more rigid and tailored to specific contexts. Whereas declarative knowledge requires much time to access and apply, procedural knowledge is found and utilized rapidly. The distinction between declarative and procedural knowledge is closely related to the distinction between strategic and automatic processing (**4.1**, **4.2**): Declarative knowledge is processed strategically by executive productions, whereas procedural knowledge is implemented automatically by learned, automatic productions.

I focus on declarative knowledge in this chapter. However, it is important to remember that declarative knowledge often becomes procedural through practice, and that declarative and proceduralized knowledge are often intertwined in cognitive processes (see also *Computational Intelligence*, 1987, Vol. 3, pp. 149-227; Rumelhart & Norman, 1988; T. Winograd, 1975).

Non-logical knowledge. Traditionally, theories of knowledge have been heavily oriented toward logic (see Johnson-Laird, 1983, for a review). According to these theories, knowledge is a formal propositional system, which may exhibit the logical properties of completeness and consistency (**8.7.4**, **10.5**). When knowledge serves some computational goal, propositions are processed according to the rules of logic, and new propositions are derived from old ones through the application of various operators, connectives, and quantifiers (e.g., *not, or, implies, all*).

In contrast, many psychologists have concluded that human knowledge does not follow logical form closely. This is not to say that human knowledge is illogical, but only that other factors play more significant roles. In other words, human knowledge is generally *non*-logical. Consider a study by Hampton (1982). Subjects were asked questions about category inclusion, such as "Are typewriters office furniture?" In one key comparison, subjects stated that *typewriters* are *office furniture*, that *office furniture* is *furniture*, but that *typewriters* are not *furniture*. This violates the fundamental principle of transitivity in the logic of set membership, which states that if *all X are Y* and *all Y are Z*, then *all X are Z*. Hampton argued that similarity—not logical principles—controlled subjects' decisions about category membership. Subjects perceived *typewriters* as sufficiently similar to *office furniture* to be members; they then judged *office furniture* as sufficiently similar to *furniture* to be members; yet they did not perceive *typewriters* as sufficiently similar to *furniture* to be members (see also Hampton, 1987, 1988; Osherson & E.E. Smith, 1981, 1982; E.E. Smith, Shoben, & Rips, 1974.)

Consider another finding that logical principles don't anticipate. Holyoak and Glass (1975) asked subjects questions about the properties of categories and measured subjects' time to respond (see also Glass & Holyoak, 1975). In one key comparison, Holyoak and Glass found that subjects verified the falsity of *arrows are dull* faster than they verified the falsity of *arrows are wide*. The principles of logic do not predict any difference in the time to answer these two questions, because both are simply false. Holyoak and Glass argued that availability—not logical principles—determines this result. Because *arrow* is more strongly associated with *sharp* than with *narrow*, *sharp* is available sooner in retrieval, thereby enabling subjects to identify *dull* as a contradiction faster than *wide*.

As these two examples suggest, similarity and availability are central to human knowledge. In later sections of this chapter, we shall see many further examples of these factors. Although logical principles may structure knowledge to some extent, the dominant influences of similarity and availability often overshadow them. In chapter 10, we shall see that similarity and availability pervade human thought as well.

Knowledge acquisition. Traditionally, theorists have assumed that people acquire knowledge primarily through experience. Examples of this view include the exemplar and abstraction theories discussed in 2.3.1. According to these theories, information obtained through experience with category exemplars becomes stored in memory and represents the category. In exemplar theories, exemplar memories constitute category knowledge. In abstraction theories, prototypes and definitions are abstracted from exemplars to form more general category representations. For reviews of these theories, see Medin and E.E. Smith (1984), Mervis and Rosch (1981), Oden (1987), and E.E. Smith and Medin (1981).

Many theorists also assume that some knowledge has a biological basis in the cognitive system, requiring only modest experience to become activated and tuned (2.2., 4.1.1). For example, the sensory detectors that identify fundamental perceptual properties, such as color, can be construed as knowledge. Similarly, certain categories essential to survival, such as facial expressions, may have biological bases. Some theorists have even argued that biological determinants shape various kinds of abstract knowledge, including language syntax (Chomsky, 1965, 1968, 1975) and certain conceptual primitives (e.g., *cause*; G.A. Miller & Johnson-Laird, 1976). Not all knowledge is necessarily learned. Biological factors may ensure that people have primitive forms of knowledge at birth to facilitate and shape their later acquisition of knowledge from experience.

Finally, people can also construct knowledge during instruction and inference. During instruction, teachers provide information that students incorporate into existing knowledge. During inference, one applies procedures to existing knowledge to produce new knowledge. As we shall see in **10**.4 and **10**.5, such derivations could proceed according to the formal rules of inductive and deductive logic (DeJong & Mooney, 1986; T.M. Mitchell, Keller, & Kedar-Cabelli, 1986), but are often produced instead through use of less rigorous and more pragmatic procedures for manipulating knowledge (Barsalou, 1991).

Measuring knowledge. Measuring human knowledge is difficult, because researchers cannot observe it directly in an idle form but must view it in use, as various cognitive mechanisms process it. The knowledge that researchers observe is always made available by retrieval processes (**6**.3), which constrain researchers' glimpses of it: Retrieval processes may not produce all of the underlying knowledge for a particular category; they may retrieve knowledge from another category not being studied; and they may transform retrieved knowledge, such that it is summarized, reconstructed, or altered in some other manner (Barsalou, 1990b, pp. 76-77).

For these reasons, cognitive psychologists must be very cautious in drawing conclusions about human knowledge from empirical data. Most theorists believe that human knowledge cannot be modeled independently of modeling the mechanisms that process it. Instead, all theories of knowledge *must* include assumptions about both processing and representation. Experiments cannot test hypotheses about knowledge in isolation but can only test *models* of knowledge use, namely, representation-process pairs (J.R. Anderson, 1978; Barsalou, 1990b; Palmer, 1978).

Knowledge and intelligence. Many people assume that differences in intelligence reflect differences in the ability to *manipulate* knowledge. On this view, high intelligence reflects the ability to draw complex inferences and perform sophisticated computations, such as looking ahead 10 moves in a chess game, or deriving a complex mathematical solution. However, many researchers in artificial intelligence have come to believe that computational power is often not nearly as important as knowledge. Intelligence often reflects the amount and organization of knowledge that is available in an information processing system, not just its ability to manipulate that knowledge.

Consider the expert systems in artificial intelligence that perform tasks like medical diagnosis, financial analysis, and scientific exploration. Typically, these systems use very simple processing mechanisms, much like the productions described in **4**.1 and **4**.2. What makes these systems powerful is the tremendous amount of well-articulated and well-organized knowledge they have about their particular domain, such as detailed facts about diseases, or complex rules for investment.

Knowledge is clearly central to human intelligence as well. Experts at a particular task have much more knowledge than non-experts (e.g., chess masters vs. novices; **5**.2.4). The importance of knowledge in intelligence also underlies an important controversy in intelligence testing: Many people believe that intelligence tests favor cultures that transmit test-relevant knowledge. Individuals from cultures that transmit different knowledge may not have poorer abilities to process information, but may simply not have the optimal knowledge for performing well on these tests.

Both knowledge and processing are essential to intelligence. If knowledge were the whole story, then different animal species would not differ as much in intelligence as they do. Obviously, species differ considerably in their ability to encode, store, retrieve, and transform knowledge. However, these processes alone are insufficient for intelligence. Ultimately, an organism's ability to adapt intelligently to its ecological niche also depends on the knowledge that these processes produce and manipulate.

7.2 CONCEPTS

Concepts constitute the fundamental units of knowledge, and the remainder of this chapter revolves around them. In this section, I first address the uses of concepts and attempt to define what concepts are. I then address conceptual structure, the construction of conceptualizations, and conceptual combination. In the final sections of this chapter, I discuss the categories that accompany concepts and the systems of concepts that they form.

7.2.1 Uses of Concepts

Concepts serve two fundamental cognitive activities: *categorization* and *conceptualization*. In the following sections, I describe these two activities and their implications for the concept of *concept*.

The concept of *concept* is notoriously difficult to define. Perhaps the most widespread definition is related to categorization: A concept is information that allows people to discriminate members of a category from non-members (**2**.3). Consider the category of *odd numbers*. The concept for this category is:

An odd number is any whole number that yields a remainder of one when divided by two.

Or consider the concept for *bachelor*:

A bachelor is any adult male human who is unmarried.

Specifying concepts becomes more slippery, of course, for categories for which no clear rule is known (**2**.1). For example, it is difficult if not impossible to find precise concepts for categories such as *games, furniture, tools*, and *clothing*. As we saw in **2**.3.1, one way to represent the concept for a fuzzy category is with a prototype. Thus, if something is sufficiently similar to the prototype for *game*, it belongs to the category. As we also saw in **2**.3.1, one may also represent a fuzzy category with exemplar representations. If something is sufficiently similar to known exemplars of *furniture*, it belongs to the category. Regardless of the particular information used to determine category membership, standard views assume that concepts contain this information.

A second way of viewing concepts has to do with how people conceive of a category at a particular point in time, namely, their *conceptualization* of it. Consider the ideal *car* one might imagine while visiting automobile dealerships. This conceptualization does not discriminate *cars* from *non-cars*: Whereas the ideal car might produce no pollution and produce superb stereo sound, these characteristics do not define *cars*; they are also true of high fidelity headphones. Conceptualizations of categories typically fail to provide categorization rules, because they serve goals other than determining category membership, such as minimizing pollution or enjoying music. Although many theorists reserve "concept" for information used to determine membership, I will also use it for people's conceptualizations of categories under a much wider variety of circumstances.

Figure 2.4 in section **2**.3.1 illustrates one way to integrate these two views. According to this figure, the categorization of an entity provides access to information useful for interacting with it. Concepts—as exemplars, prototypes, and rules—are essential to this categorization process. The purpose of categorization, though, is not simply to identify what something is. Categorization also provides access to a tremendous amount of knowledge that is relevant to interacting with category members. Once people categorize an entity, they must construct conceptualizations of it that optimize their ability to achieve whatever goals are currently relevant. As we shall see, other knowledge besides exemplars, prototypes, and rules is often central to this process.

Conceptualizing categories is central to three fundamental tasks: comprehension, prediction, and action. Once people have categorized something, they may want to comprehend its origins and behaviors, to predict its future behaviors, or to interact appropriately with it. Imagine that you discover fleas in your living room. Whereas exemplars, prototypes, and rules may have enabled you to categorize the fleas as *fleas*, fairly different knowledge enables you to comprehend where they came from and what they are doing. Such knowledge might produce the inference that a pet brought fleas into the house and that they remain because the house provides an ideal environment for reproduction. To the extent that you understand how fleas function, you can comprehend their presence and behavior.

Knowledge of categories also allows people to predict future events. For example, if you observe a few fleas in your home, knowledge of flea reproduction may allow you to predict that the number of fleas will grow dramatically over time. You can predict further that your pet will suffer increasingly and that family members will suffer in its extended absence.

Knowledge of categories further allows people to interact with category members appropriately. If you understand the flea reproductive cycle, you know that simply killing the adult fleas will not solve the problem, because existing flea eggs will hatch to produce a new generation; you also need to control the larvae that will hatch from these eggs and develop into adult fleas at a later time.

The knowledge that allows people to comprehend category members, to predict their behavior, and to interact with them is extremely important. In some sense, it is more important than the exemplars, prototypes, and rules that underlie categorization. Clearly, people must know what something is before they can understand, predict, and interact with it, but without the knowledge that underlies these later processes, people would be relatively helpless in their interactions with the world. They would simply know what things are and nothing more. For this reason, I propose a fairly complex definition of *concept*: Concepts include, not only the exemplars, prototypes, and rules that determine category membership, but also the conceptualizations of categories that underlie comprehension, prediction, and action. As we shall see (**7.2.3**), the conceptualization of a category on a particular occasion includes a very small subset of the total knowledge for a category in long-term memory, with the active subset varying widely from occasion to occasion.

The remainder of this chapter focuses primarily on aspects of concepts that underlie conceptualization. For discussion of aspects that underlie categorization, see chapter 2. Concepts receive further discussion in later sections on meaning (**8.6**, **9.2**), propositions (**8.7.4**, **9.3**), and induction (**10.4**).

7.2.2 Structure of Concepts

In this section, I sketch three different approaches to representing the structure of concepts: feature lists, frames, and mental models. As we shall

CAR			BUY	
Feature	Type		Feature	Type
engine	part		customer	primary agent
wheels	part		salesperson	secondary agent
made of metal	composition		credit card	instrument
motor vehicle	superordinate		cash	instrument
sedan	subordinate		merchandise	object
made in a factory	origin		groceries	object
expensive	evaluation		pay	action
uses gas	related object		mall	location
pollutes the atmosphere	action		shopping bag	instrument
you drive it	operation		need the item	goal
takes the kids to school	function		like the item	preference
kept in the garage	location		drive to the store	precondition
necessary for modern life	belief		shop for the best item	action
used daily	frequency		check the return policy	request

Figure 7.1. Examples of feature lists for *car* and *buy*.

see, these representational forms build upon each other, such that frames subsume feature lists, and mental models subsume frames. To show the wide applicability of these representational forms, I discuss how each represents a physical entity (*car*) and an event (*buy*).

Feature lists. To assess the contents of a concept, researchers often ask subjects simply to list what they know about it. Figure 7.1 illustrates the kinds of features that people might list for *car* and *buy*.[1] As this figure shows, people produce a tremendous variety of features. For *car*, they list physical parts, compositions, superordinates, subordinates, origins, and so forth. If one restricts *feature* to mean any aspect of a category's members, then many of the items that subjects list are not features. For example, superordinates (e.g., *motor vehicle*) and subordinates (e.g., *sedan*) are not really aspects of cars but instead are associated concepts from the taxonomy for *vehicle* (7.4.1). Also note that features are often only partly true. For example, *made of metal* doesn't completely describe *car*, because other parts are made of *glass*, *cloth*, and *plastic*. Similarly, many features are not defining: *Kept in the garage* is not true of all cars. Finally, many features concern human interaction, including functions, operations, and evaluations.

---

[1] In all previous sections of this book, I have used "property" to mean any piece of information in a concept. In this section, however, I use "feature" to mean an *independent* property in a concept, in contrast to the *structural* properties of concepts described shortly (attributes, values, relations). Following this section, I continue using "property" generically to mean any piece of information in a concept, including features, attributes, values, relations, and so forth.

When one collects extensive feature listings from a large population of subjects for a single concept, the number and variety of features is overwhelming. Such lists are much longer than those in Fig. 7.1 and contain an even larger variety of feature types. People clearly have substantial amounts of complex knowledge for familiar concepts. Moreover, it is often difficult to determine where the knowledge for a concept begins and ends. Consider the feature, *takes the kids to school*, for car. Is this a feature of *car, children*, and/or *school?*

Many theorists, especially in philosophy and linguistics, attempt to extract the defining features of concepts from lists like those in Fig. 7.1. In general, they seek to identify the rule that produces correct categorization (2.3.1, **7**.2.1). Thus, *buy* might be defined as *exchanging some form of money for goods.* The problem with such rules is that they fail to capture the rich knowledge that allows people to understand, predict, and interact with the instances of a concept: Knowing the definition for *buy* is of little use in understanding why someone wants to buy your house, in predicting how much they will offer, and in knowing how best to counter their offer. To develop a satisfactory account of human knowledge, cognitive psychologists must develop theories of the more encyclopedic and experiential knowledge that accompanies definitions.

As we shall see shortly, feature lists also fail to capture important structural properties in human knowledge. Nevertheless, these representations often provide a sufficient account of knowledge to support acceptable levels of prediction in various tasks. One way to view feature lists is as bits and pieces of a much richer and structurally integrated underlying representation. The next two accounts of representation—frames and mental models—attempt to recover greater amounts of this underlying structure.

Frames. Frames solve two significant problems of feature lists: First, feature lists fail to capture *attribute-value relationships*. Consider a feature that people might list for car: *standard transmission*. This feature is actually a value of a more general attribute, *transmission*, which also has other values, such as *automatic transmission* and *four-wheel drive*. Feature lists generally obscure the distinction between attributes and values, in that some features may be attributes (e.g., *engine*), whereas others may be values (e.g., *four-cylinder engine*). Feature lists treat attributes and values as a single, uniform type of representational entity.

A second problem with feature lists is that they typically fail to specify *thematic relations* between features (**6**.1.3). Certainly features are not unrelated. Numerous kinds of relations integrate features in human knowledge, including spatial relations, temporal relations, causal relations, and intentional relations. For *car*, the feature of *uses gas* is clearly related *to engine*, both of which are clearly related to *pollutes the atmosphere*.

Although features for relations could be added to feature lists (e.g., *engines combust gas*), this is a rather ad hoc and inelegant way of handling them. The problem with this solution is that it fails to capture the *productive* nature of relations. Consider the spatial relation *above*. This relation applies to a wide variety of instances, including *ABOVE (head, neck)* in the concept for *human*, *ABOVE (roof, walls)* in the concept for *house*, and *ABOVE (trunk, roots)* in the concept for *tree*. *Above* is productive because a single relation can apply to a large variety of instances, many of which have never been seen before (e.g., seeing *ABOVE (tractor, barn)* for the first time). Features for relations fail to capture the productive nature of *above* for several reasons: First, they fail to capture the commonalty of *above's* instances, treating each instance as a separate and unrelated feature. Second, they require that a feature for every recognizable instance of *above* exist a priori in memory, no matter how implausible and no matter how many might be required (e.g., *ABOVE (tractor, barn)*, *ABOVE (tractor, airplane)*, *ABOVE (barn, airplane)*, and the infinite number of other such instances). Third, they fail to provide a means of extending *above* to any instance not represented by an a priori feature in memory. Although people can readily extend *above* to an infinite number of novel instances whose commonalty is obvious, feature lists cannot.

Frames, which theorists also refer to as *schemas* or *schemata*, handle these two problems of feature lists. Although little work in psychology has addressed the structure of frames, much work in linguistics and artificial intelligence has (in linguistics, see Fillmore, 1968, 1977, 1985; Jackendoff, 1983, 1987; in artificial intelligence, see D.G. Bobrow & T. Winograd, 1977; Charniak & McDermott, 1985; Minsky, 1977, 1985; Schank, 1975, 1982; Schank & Abelson, 1977). In addition, the concept of *frame* is related to the concept of *predicate* in logic (P.J. Hayes, 1979). My treatment of *frames* (Barsalou, 1991, 1992; Barsalou & Billman, 1989) borrows heavily from the work of Norman, Rumelhart, and their colleagues (Norman, Rumelhart, and the LNR Research Group, 1975; Rumelhart & Norman, 1978, 1988; Rumelhart & Ortony, 1977; see also G.L. Murphy, 1988; E.E. Smith, Osherson, Rips, & Keane, 1988).

Frames handle the first problem of feature lists by distinguishing between attributes and values. Consider the partial frames for *car* and *buy* in Fig. 7.2, which, for simplicity, omit tremendous amounts of knowledge. The frame for *car* includes attributes for *driver, fuel tank, engine, transmission,* and *wheels*. The frame for *buy* includes attributes for *buyer, seller, merchandise,* and *payment*. Note that the attributes in a frame may be incomplete, unsystematic, and even incorrect when people have only partial knowledge of a concept (e.g., as is often the case for non–mechanics with respect to *car*). In addition, people may differ considerably in the attributes they know (e.g., not everyone may know that *transmission* is an attribute of *car*).

Figure 7.2 further illustrates values of *car* attributes. In the frame for *car*,

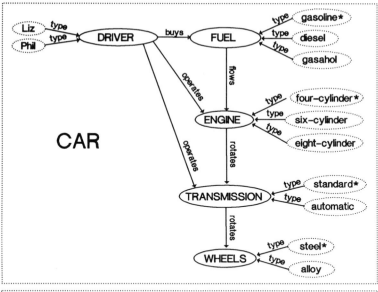

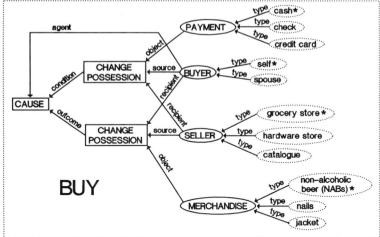

Figure 7.2. Partial frames for *car* and *buy*.

values of *engine* may include *four-cylinder, six-cylinder*, and *eight-cylinder*. In the frame for *buy*, the values of *payment* may include *cash, check*, and *credit card*. Note that values can operate simultaneously as attributes. Whereas *six-cylinder* is a value of *engine, six-cylinder* is simultaneously an attribute for the value *slant six*, which is a type of six cylinder engine. Like attributes, people's knowledge of values may be incomplete and may vary widely (e.g., not everyone may know that *six-cylinder* is a value of *engine*).

On encountering an exemplar of a category, people retrieve the frame for the category and assign features of the exemplar as values of frame attributes. On seeing a particular car, for example, one might assign *Liz* as the value of *driver, four-cylinder* as the value of *engine, standard* as the value of *transmission,* and so forth. On seeing a different car, one might assign *Phil* as the value of *driver, gasoline* as the value of *fuel,* and *alloy* as the value of *wheels.* As people encounter different exemplars of the category, they bind its values to the frame's attributes. By doing so, they relate the exemplar's specific features to the more general characteristics of the category.

Often, however, people do not know an exemplar's values for certain attributes. Imagine that one's spouse says over the phone,

> The shop lent us a car while they're fixing ours.

This statement provides no information about the attribute values of this unfamiliar car. Under such circumstances, *default values* provide the best guess as to what the values might be. The default value assigned is often the value of an attribute that has occurred most frequently across previous exemplars. If *four-cylinder* and *standard* have been the most frequent values for *engine* and *transmission* in someone's experience, then the assumption may be made that the unfamiliar car from the shop has a four-cylinder engine and a standard transmission. Examples of default values in Fig. 7.2 have an asterisk (*) next to them. Default values are more likely to become active than other values, because their pathways to the attribute are stronger and transmit spreading activation more rapidly (**2.5**). Default values play a central role in the process of reconstruction, which we considered earlier (**6.3.2**).

Frames solve the second problem of feature lists by specifying relations between attributes and between values. Consider the relations between attributes in Fig. 7.2. In the frame for *car,* a relation for *operates* indicates that the *driver* controls the *engine.* Similarly, a relation for *rotates* indicates that the *engine* turns the *transmission.* In the frame for *buy,* a relation for *cause* indicates that changing the possession of the *payment* leads to changing the possession of the *merchandise.* Similarly, a relation for *agent* indicates that the *seller* instigated the *causal* event. Again, relations may be incomplete, unsystematic, and incorrect, to the extent that someone is not an expert, and may differ considerably across individuals (e.g., not everyone may know that *transmissions rotate wheels*).

Constraints or correlations between values constitute a second important form of relations in frames. Imagine that *racing engine* is the value for *engine.* By knowing this value, you can predict other values. For example, you might predict that *standard* is the value for *transmission* and that *alloy* is the value for *wheels.* In the frame for *buy,* the values of *seller* constrain the values of *merchandise,* because certain stores only sell certain products. Similarly, the values of *merchandise* constrain the values of *payment*, because certain forms of payment are more appropriate for some products than for others. In general, the values of attributes are not independent but are often correlated and sometimes require one another. As a result, people's knowledge of default values often includes typical patterns of values that are likely to cooccur.

Frames provide a natural way to represent exemplars (**2.3.1**; Barsalou, 1988, 1992; Barsalou & Billman, 1989). Consider Fig. 7.3, which shows a very small subset of the attributes and values that a person might represent for *bird*. Each exemplar of *bird* is a cooccurring set of values for the frame's attributes. Bird–1 has the values of *small*, *brown*, and *straight* for the attributes of *size*, *color*, and *beak*, whereas bird–2 has the values of *small*, *red*, and *straight*. As the number of exemplars integrated into the frame increases, the values that fan off of each attribute increase as well. As a result, values increasingly interfere with each other, such that particular exemplars become harder to remember (see interference and the fan effect in **6.2.3**; Thorndyke & B. Hayes-Roth, 1979; Watkins & Kerkar, 1985). One advantage of this type of exemplar representation is that exemplars are stored together and integrated into shared, higher order knowledge (i.e., the frame). In contrast, most exemplar models assume that exemplars are stored independently of one another as autonomous and unattached memories (Brooks, 1978; Estes, 1986; Hintzman, 1986; Medin & Schaffer, 1978; Nosofsky, 1984). Integrating exemplars and frames in this way also contrasts with Tulving's episodic-semantic distinction, which proposes that exemplars and frames reside in separate memory systems (**6.2.1**).

Frames provide a natural way to represent prototypes, utilizing the *default values* just described. Consider the values for the prototype in Fig. 7.3 (i.e., *small*, *brown*, and *straight*). These are default values because they are the most frequent values across exemplars. Together these default values constitute the prototype for *bird*. Imagine someone saying,

When I came home, a <u>bird</u> was sitting on the porch.

Although the speaker has provided no information about the characteristics of this bird, default values in the *bird* frame become activate and provide prototypical information about what it might have been like. To appreciate this, imagine how surprising it would be if the bird turned out to be a turkey.

Frames further allow for the representation of multiple prototypes (Barsalou & Billman, 1989). If people frequently encounter several different kinds of birds, they may develop a prototype for each. For example, if they frequently encounter exemplars of *poultry* with the values *large*, *white*, and *curved*, they may establish a prototype for this subset of *birds*, as Fig. 7.3 illustrates. Imagine that someone who has this prototype for *poultry* hears the following sentence:

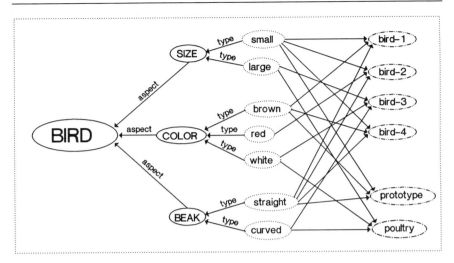

Figure 7.3.   Examples of how a frame can represent exemplars and prototypes.

When I came home, a <u>white bird</u> was sitting on the porch.

White and *bird* in this sentence activate the prototype for *poultry*, rather than the overall prototype for *bird*. Because more activation spreads to *poultry* than to the overall prototype, the values for *poultry* become the defaults (**2.5**), such that *large* becomes the value for *size,* and *curved* becomes the value for *beak*. Prototypes for other types of birds (e.g., *songbirds*) and for various subordinates of *bird* (e.g., *robin, eagle*) could be represented similarly.

For the remainder of this book, my use of "exemplar" and "prototype" assumes these frame-based accounts. Exemplars will be collections of attribute values, and prototypes will be the most frequent sets of values across exemplars (i.e., defaults). In **8.7.4**, I further describe how frames can represent *propositions,* namely, units of knowledge that can be either true or false.

A final feature of frames is that they embed recursively within one another (Norman et al., 1975; Rumelhart & Ortony, 1978). Consider the frame for *car* in Fig. 7.2. Each of its attributes is actually a more specific frame: *Engine* is a frame with attributes for *ignition system, fuel system, lubrication system,* and *cooling system*; in turn, *ignition system* is a frame with attributes for *battery, starter,* and *distributor*; in turn, each of these attributes is a frame, and so forth. In general, a concept is a complex organization of embedded frames, not a single flat level of unrelated features. Figure 7.2 illustrates such embedded frames, with two frames for *change possession* embedded in the frame for *cause,* which in turn is embedded in the frame for *buy*.

Before leaving the topic of frames, it is important to note that little work in psychology has explicitly addressed their structure, although extensive work has demonstrated their presence. All of the top-down, expectation effects discussed in **2**.4, **4**.2.2, and **9**.4 can be attributed to frames. Similarly, the organization of chunking (**5**.1.2, **5**.2.4) and of encoding and retrieval (**6**.1.3, **6**.3.2) can be attributed to frames. When we come to thought further on, we shall see pervasive effects of *framing* (**10**.1). Cognitive psychologists have shown that knowledge of this form has powerful effects in virtually every cognitive task (Alba & Hasher, 1983; Fiske & S.E. Taylor, 1991; McClelland & Rumelhart, 1981; Kahneman et al., 1982; Marslen-Wilson, 1987; Palmer, 1975a). Literally hundreds of experiments have demonstrated such effects, and it is hard to think of an effect that has been demonstrated more often across the cognitive literatures. Virtually everywhere cognitive psychologists look, they see the effects of frames in performance. Despite this, we know very little about the structural characteristics of this knowledge.

Several factors underlie cognitive psychologists' relative ignorance about frame structure. First, little research has attempted to verify the presence of such structure directly. Researchers often make assumptions about the representations that underlie the phenomena they study, yet test few of these assumptions as hypotheses. Moreover, researchers often adopt fairly simple representations, such as feature lists, because more complex frame representations are not necessary for their research goals, and because more complex representations generally make formal analysis less tractable. Second, as mentioned earlier, researchers cannot observe knowledge directly, but can only measure it subject to retrieval and constructive processes (**7**.1). For this reason, researchers have often been rightfully cautious and unsure in their assessments of knowledge. With a more sophisticated methodology, we might be able to justify more fine-grained distinctions about structure empirically. Third, theoretical frameworks for representing knowledge in cognitive psychology have not been developed sufficiently to make sense of the kinds of information that people produce for concepts, such as the features for *car* and *buy* in Fig. 7.1. Instead, cognitive psychologists have primarily developed various forms of feature list and very simple frame representations, failing to incorporate the more complex frame representations developed in artificial intelligence and linguistics. As all of these limitations illustrate, we must develop major new methodological tools before we will see significant progress in measuring the structure of human concepts.

Mental models. A limitation of frames is that they are relatively static and non-dynamic. Frames don't provide much of an account of how events unfold over space and time. Consider the frame for *buy* in Fig. 7.2. Although this frame captures the relevant attributes for *buy* and how they relate, it fails to capture the detailed sequence of events that constitutes the overall event.

Mental models, similar to scripts (**4.2.1, 10.**6.2), reflect an attempt to develop representations that capture the dynamic, changing character of events over space and time.

Before proceeding further, it is important to note that theorists use the term "mental model" in many different ways (J.H. Holland et al., 1986; Gentner & A.L. Stevens, 1983; Johnson-Laird, 1983; Rips, 1986). To some, a mental model is any kind of human knowledge about the world. To others, mental models are perceptual representations of objects and events. My discussion of mental models follows neither of these usages. Instead, I adopt a view of mental models that makes the following two assumptions: First, a mental model is a frame whose attributes and relations are analogous to the physical parts and relations of category members. For example, if cars contain certain components and relations between those components (e.g., *engine, transmission, engine rotates transmission*), then a mental model should contain attributes and relations that represent them. A mental model need not be complete, correct, or consistent. The representation must simply be an attempt to construct an analogous representation of physical structure. Second, a mental model must produce quasi-continuous simulations of events. So, a mental model for *car* should enable simulating its successive states of operation over space and time. This might involve making predictions about how the engine would run under certain circumstances, or how it would operate non-optimally if certain parts were broken. Similarly for *buy*, a mental model should enable simulating the successive states of an imagined purchase. Again, such simulations need not be complete, correct, or consistent, but need merely attempt to provide some degree of simulation.

Mental models are not necessarily perceptual. Rather, they are a form of abstract knowledge that may sometimes produce perceptual representations. For example, the mental model for *buy* may produce visual images of the specific events in an imagined purchase (**5.**2.3). To produce a meaningful sequence of images, however, a mental model must also contain conceptual principles that explain the content of the images and the sequence in which they occur: The mental model for *buy* must explain why one person possesses money in an early image of a purchase sequence but not in a later image. In addition, a mental model must be able to explain unexpected events and to produce predictions about what may follow. For example, the mental model for *buy* must be able to explain sales that fall through and predict what the buyer and seller will do next. In summary, mental models contain knowledge that can produce event sequences dynamically and explain how they occurred. Sometimes the operation of these models may produce images, but frames and explanatory principles—not images—constitute the core of mental models.

Presently, we understand little about how people's knowledge enables them to construct such simulations, yet clearly, people simulate events frequently. One possibility is that various kinds of procedures manipulate frames to produce the successive states of an event sequence. While the frame's attributes and relations remain constant, procedures change the attributes' values, with the current set of values at each point representing the current state of the mental model.

Figure 7.4 illustrates how frames can be extended in this manner to represent a person's intuitive mental model for engine performance (Barsalou, 1992). As can be seen, the frame for *engine* contains a variety of attributes, including *carburetor, ignition system, intake valve,* and so forth. The values of each attribute are its possible states, so, for example, the *intake valve* can be either *open* or *closed.* Each vertical line represents one event in the engine cycle (a *stroke*). The state of each engine component on a given stroke is the attribute value connected to the stroke line by a solid circle. On the first stroke, the *carburetor* is *forming fuel vapor,* the *ignition system* is *charging,* the *intake valve* is *open,* the *exhaust valve* is *closed,* the *piston* is *decompressing,* and the *action* is *suctioning fuel vapor.* Over time, procedures change the values of these attributes to produce the next stroke. In some cases, explanatory principles may explain these transitions (e.g., the principles of combustion). In other cases, one may simply know the nature of a transition but not have any idea of what causes it. In any event, transitions in the values of the frame represent the system over time, thereby simulating its performance.

A modest amount of empirical work on mental models has accrued in cognitive psychology and related areas (Gentner & A.L. Stevens, 1983; Johnson-Laird, 1983; Kieras & Bovair, 1984; Rasmussen, 1986; Rouse & N.M. Morris, 1986). Much of the theoretical development on mental models has proceeded outside psychology, primarily in the area of qualitative reasoning in artificial intelligence (de Kleer & J.S. Brown, 1984; Forbus, 1984). One lesson from computer simulations of qualitative reasoning is that people's mental models are probably incomplete. Complete qualitative systems are so complex—even for very simple physical systems—that people could not represent all of their possible transitions. Instead, people probably use a variety of short-cuts and heuristic strategies for simulating physical systems and events. Cognitive psychologists have much to learn about these important topics.

7.2.3 Constructing Conceptualizations of Categories

As we saw earlier, people have a tremendous amount of knowledge for familiar categories. Upon conceptualizing one of these categories on a particular occasion, do people activate all of its associated knowledge simultaneously? Or do they only activate a subset? If they only activate a subset, how much does this subset vary from context to context? A variety of evidence

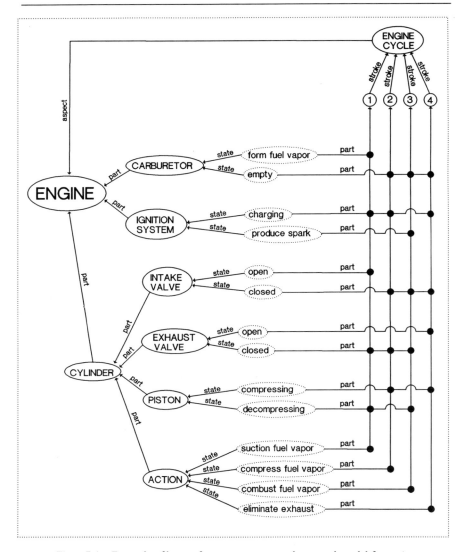

Figure 7.4.   Example of how a frame can represent the mental model for *engine.*

suggests that the conceptualizations constructed for a category vary substantially across contexts. This further implies that people don't activate everything they know about a category, because there would be no variability if
they did.

One source of evidence for variability comes from the memory literature.
In **6**.1.1, we saw that increasing the lag between presentations of the same
word improves subsequent memory for it. According to the encoding vari-

ability explanation of the lag effect, the information activated for a word on different occasions varies increasingly with lag. If the lag is short, the information activated for *bird* might be highly similar from presentation to presentation, (e.g., information describing *robin*). As the lag becomes longer, however, the information representing *bird* on each presentation becomes increasingly different. For example, the information might describe a *robin* on the first presentation, a *blue jay* on the second, and a *cardinal* on the third. The evidence that has accrued for this account of the lag effect supports the conclusion that the information activated for a category varies from occasion to occasion.

Other findings concerning overlap in retrieval further support this conclusion (**6**.3.1). In recognition failure, a word such as "light" activates one set of properties as a recognition cue (e.g., the properties of *sunlight*) but activates a different set of properties from a recall cue (e.g., the properties of *light bulb* from the cue "head"). In general, the memory literature provides substantial evidence that the information activated for a category varies widely (R.C. Anderson & Ortony, 1975; R.C. Anderson, Pichert, Goetz, Schallert, K.V. Stevens, & Trollip, 1976; Barclay, Bransford, Franks, McCarrell, & Nitsch, 1974; Bower, 1972b; Greenspan, 1986; Thomson & Tulving, 1970; Tulving & Thomson, 1973).

A second source of evidence for variability comes from measuring the information retrieved following *lexical access* (i.e., the categorization of a spoken or written word; **4**.1.2, **9**.2, **9**.4). A number of investigators have shown that manipulating the context in which subjects read a word activates different properties for it (Barnes, 1987; Barsalou, 1982; C. Conrad, 1978). For example, the sentence, "To clean up the spilled paint, Marsha got a newspaper," activates *absorbent* for *newspaper*. In contrast, the sentence, "To start a fire, Marsha got a newspaper," activates *flammable* for *newspaper*. *Absorbent* would probably not be active for *newspaper* in the sentence about a fire, whereas *flammable* would probably not be active for *newspaper* in the sentence about spilled paint. Consequently, the properties activated to form a conceptualization are context-dependent, at least to some extent.

Does the information included in a conceptualization depend completely on context? Several investigators have found that some properties are included across all contexts, regardless of whether they are relevant (Barnes, 1987; Barsalou, 1982; C. Conrad, 1978; Greenspan, 1986; Whitney, McKay, & Kellas, 1985). For example, *black and white, square*, and *reading material* might all be active for *newspaper* in both of the sentences just mentioned, at least initially, even though these properties are not relevant to the topic of either. Consequently, some properties appear to provide stability across contexts, occurring in all conceptualizations of a category.

It is not clear at this time why some properties become stable, whereas others vary. One possibility reflects learned automatic processing (**4**.1.2).

Recall the Stroop phenomenon, where subjects have to name the ink color of color words (e.g., the word "orange" written in purple ink). As we saw, the meaning for *orange* is activated obligatorily, thereby interfering with naming purple as the ink color. This activation is similar to the activation of context-independent properties, such as *black and white, square*, and *reading material* for *newspaper*. In both cases, the underlying mechanisms may be frequency of association and consistent mapping: To the extent that a particular property is associated with a word consistently across many contexts, its activation becomes obligatory, regardless of whether it is relevant in the current context (**4.1.2**). Properties that occur less frequently for a category don't become obligatory and instead are activated only by relevant contexts.

A third source of evidence for variability comes from assessing how different people conceptualize the same category, and how the same person conceptualizes it differently over time (**7.3.2**). McCloskey and Glucksberg (1978) presented subjects with various entities and asked them whether they belonged to a particular category (e.g., whether *apple, banana, avocado, olive, acorn, pumpkin, onion*, and *carrot* belong to *fruit*). Subjects differed substantially in the entities they assigned to each category, indicating they constructed different categorization rules. A month later, McCloskey and Glucksberg asked the same subjects to make the category assignments again. Surprisingly, a given subject often changed his or her mind about whether a particular entity belonged to a category, indicating that the same person constructed different categorization rules on different occasions.

Other work has measured the stability of word definitions, prototype descriptions, and typicality judgments among individuals and within the same individual over time (Barsalou, 1987, 1989; Barsalou & Billman, 1989; Barsalou, Sewell, & Ballato, 1986; Barsalou, Spindler, Sewell, Ballato, & Gendel, 1987; Bellezza, 1984a, 1984b, 1984c). The same pattern of results has emerged in all cases: The conceptualization constructed for a category varies substantially both between and within individuals. Much remains to be learned about people's ability to construct conceptualizations in such a flexible manner.

7.2.4 Conceptual Combination

People's stock of established concepts in memory is not sufficient for their representational needs. As a result, new concepts are often constructed from existing concepts, a process known as *conceptual combination*. Examples of conceptual combination include *orange dog, wooden spoon, pet fish, plastic lemon, sports that are games*, and *activities to do with one's grandmother in Tokyo*.

One way concepts can be combined is through Boolean operations for combining sets, such as intersection, union, and complementation. When combining *pet* and *fish*, for example, the category of *pet fish* could contain everything that is both a *pet* and a *fish* (i.e., their intersection). However, this account runs into problems. According to the intersection rule, an entity should only belong to a conceptual combination if it belongs to each of the constituent categories. Thus, an entity should belong to *sports that are games* only if it is both a *sport* and a *game*. However, Hampton (1987, 1988) has shown that people violate this requirement, assigning *wrestling, rowing,* and *trampoline* to *sports that are games*, even though they do not consider them to be *games*.

Osherson and E.E. Smith (1981, 1982) note a related problem with a somewhat different Boolean view of conceptual combination: *fuzzy set theory*. According to fuzzy set theory (Zadeh, 1965, 1982), exemplars in categories have varying degrees of membership. For example, typical *fish* have higher membership strength than atypical *fish* (e.g., *trout* vs. *sturgeon*). Also according to fuzzy set theory, membership in a conceptual combination should follow the *min rule*: An exemplar's membership strength in a conceptual combination is the minimum of its membership strengths in the constituent categories. Thus, if *guppy's* membership strength in *fish* is moderate, and if *guppy's* membership strength in *pet* is low, then its membership strength in *pet fish* should be low, because *low* is the minimum of the two membership strengths. Contrary to this theory, however, most people perceive *guppy* as having high membership strength in *pet fish*. Osherson and Smith demonstrate this and several other problems for fuzzy set theory as an account of conceptual combination.

Rather than performing operations on sets to perform conceptual combination, people could manipulate concepts directly. Consider the conceptual operations that might underlie the conceptual combination for *orange dog*. E.E. Smith et al. (1988) suggest that people construct the concept for *orange dog* by selectively modifying the *color* attribute in the frame for *dog* (7.2.2), replacing the default value for *color* (*brown*) with the value *orange*. In addition, the attribute for *color* is weighted more heavily than normal, such that *color* becomes more important in thinking about *orange dog* than it would be in thinking about *dog*.

This process of selective modification is complicated by the fact that the values of attributes constrain one another (7.2.2). Consider *wooden spoon*. According to Smith and Osherson's selective modification model, *wooden* should only modify the attribute for *composition*; it should not modify any other attribute. Medin and Shoben (1988), however, found that *wooden* modifies other attributes as well: When *wooden* modifies *composition*, it also modifies *size*, replacing the default (*small*) with *large*. Knowledge of the correlation between *composition* and *size* in *spoons* leads people to override the default for *size* with the value most likely to be true, even though it is not stated explicitly. Because correlations between attribute values pervade human knowledge, the explicit modification of one attribute often produces implicit modification of correlated attributes in this manner.

Conceptual combinations can also reflect complicated uses of background knowledge (G.L. Murphy, 1988). Consider *apartment dog*. In no sense does this combination involve Boolean operations (*apartment dogs* are not the intersection of *apartments* and *dogs*). To interpret this combination, one must integrate knowledge about *apartments* and *dogs* in a complex manner. For *apartments*, one might access properties for *limited space, contain many residents in close proximity, do not have fenced yards*, and *have regulations about pets*. For *dogs*, properties for *bark, bite*, and *need room to run* might be accessed. From somehow combining all of these properties, one then constructs a conceptualization of what an *apartment dog* might be like.

People also construct conceptual combinations during planning (Barsalou, 1983, 1991). Imagine a young man planning a vacation with his grandmother to Tokyo in December. To plan this vacation, he must find acceptable values for various attributes in the frame for *vacation*, such as values for the *activities* attribute (e.g., *sightseeing, museum visits, dining*). To find acceptable values for *activities*, he must consider the attributes for *companion, location*, and *time*, which have already received the values of *grandmother, Tokyo*, and *December*, respectively. He cannot ignore these attributes and their values, or he might select activities that are inappropriate for his grandmother, Tokyo, or December (e.g., *visits to singles bars, surfing*). Instead, he must combine *activities* with the constraining values of other attributes to form the conceptual combination: *activities to do on a vacation with one's grandmother in Tokyo during December*. By combining concepts within the frame, the planner contextualizes *activities* to reflect the current constraints on planning.

Much remains to be learned about conceptual combination. Understanding this important ability will provide fundamental insights into the dynamic and creative character of human intelligence. We shall encounter conceptual combination again frequently in discussions of language structure processing (**8**.4, **8**.6.2, **8**.7.4, **8**.7.5, **9**.3.3; see also H.H. Clark & E.V. Clark, 1978; P. Downing, 1977; Levi, 1978).

7.3 CATEGORIES

In **7**.2.1, the definition of *concept* rested heavily on the notion of categories: Concepts include the rules that determine *category* membership, as well as the conceptualizations of *categories* on particular occasions that underlie comprehension, prediction, and action. *Category* is actually a fairly ambiguous term, in that different theorists use it in different ways. Although some theorists use *concept* and *category* interchangeably to mean what I have referred to as *concept*, many theorists view *concept* and *category* as separate theoretical constructs. According to traditional usage, *category* refers to the physical exemplars of a concept. For example, the category associated with the concept for *clock* is simply all of the physical clocks in existence, or the relevant subset on a particular occasion. This use of *category* is similar to the terms *extension* and *denotation* in formal semantics (**8**.6.2, **8**.6.3; Lyons, 1977a, 1977b). According to a second usage more common among psychologists, *category* refers to representations of a concept's exemplars in memory (as Fig. 7.3 illustrates; see also **2**.3.1). For *clock*, this sense of category refers to memories of particular clocks. According to a third usage also common among psychologists, *category* refers to concepts for the kinds of exemplars in a category. Thus, the category associated with *clock* includes the concepts for *alarm clock, grandfather clock, time-card clock,* and so forth. Note that these exemplar concepts are not memories of particular exemplars but are abstractions over them (**2**.3.1). Clearly, each sense of *category* is important, describing an important aspect of a concept's exemplars or people's knowledge of them. In the sections to follow, however, most of the discussion concerns categories as sets of exemplar concepts.

7.3.1 Dividing the World into Categories

Why do people divide the world into some categories and not others?

Similarity. One possibility is that people group things according to similarity (**10**.2). More specifically, people form groups whose members are highly similar to one another but highly different from the members of other groups. For example, members of *bird* are highly similar to one another, sharing many common properties such as *wings, feathers,* and *beak*. Simultaneously, *birds* are quite different from the members of other categories, such as those in *fish, mammals,* and *trees*.

Why is it important to maximize within–category similarity and minimize between–category similarity? One reason is to optimize the ease of categorizing specific entities (**2**.3). As the exemplars within a category become increasingly similar to each other, and as the differences between categories become increasingly large, it becomes easier to assign an entity to its correct category: Maximizing within-category similarity and minimizing between-category similarity optimizes the *discriminability* of categories. For example, categorizing people at a party as *males* and *females* is much easier than categorizing them as *Democrats* and *Republicans* (assuming they do not state their party affiliation explicitly). Because within–category similarity is higher for the first pair of categories, and because between–category similarity is lower, the first pair of categories is more discriminable, and categorization is easier.

A second reason for optimizing within- and between-category similarity is to optimize *category-based induction* (**10**.4.4). If all members of a category are highly similar to one another and very different from other categories, then it is reasonable to assume that a new member will have all of the properties of most category members and few properties of other categories. For example, if a new entity is believed to be a *bird*, then it is reasonable to assume that it will have *wings* and *feathers*, because the within-category similarity of *birds* is high. In addition, this new entity is unlikely to have *gills*, because the between-category similarity of *birds* and *fish* is low. In contrast, if within-category similarity is low and between-category similarity is high, drawing confident inferences about the properties of a new category member is difficult. Imagine drawing inferences for *Democrats* versus *Republicans*. If we discover that someone is a Democrat, we can't draw many confident inferences about her, because within-category similarity is low, and between-category similarity is high. As categories become less discriminable, inductive inferences become less reliable and informative.

Rosch, Mervis, W.D. Gray, D.M. Johnson, and Boyes-Braem (1976) suggested that people's delineation of natural categories follows the *correlational structure of the environment*, in order to maximize within-category similarity and minimize between-category similarity. On this view, properties do not occur independently of one another in the environment, but form clusters of correlated properties. Thus, *wings, feathers*, and *beak* cooccur frequently but never cooccur with *gills, fur*, or *antennae*. Most importantly, the categories that people form circumscribe these clusters of correlated properties. *Bird* circumscribes those entities in the world sharing one cluster of correlated properties, whereas *fish* circumscribes other entities that share a different cluster of correlated properties.

Because the environment contains correlational structure, forming categories around it maximizes within-category similarity and minimizes between-category similarity. If a category circumscribes a cluster of correlated properties, then within-category similarity is high, because most members share the same correlated properties. In contrast, if a category straddles two clusters of correlated properties, within-category similarity is lower, because some members have properties from one cluster, and some have properties from the other. For example, if the category of *tragles* contains all *trout* and all *eagles*, then some *tragles* have the correlated properties for *fish*, whereas other *tragles* have the correlated properties for *bird*. Within-category similarity is low because entities within *tragles* differ considerably from each other.

Failing to align categories with correlational structure also has non-optimal effects on between-category similarity. Consider the between-category similarity of *tragles* and another such category *shobins*, the category of *sharks* and *robins*. Between-category similarity is high, because each category contains some members having the correlated properties for *fish*, and some having the correlated properties for *bird*. As a result, *tragles* are highly similar to *shobins*. In contrast, as categories align themselves increasingly with correlational structure, between–category similarity decreases, because different correlated properties occur in each category (e.g., *fish* vs. *bird*). As these examples illustrate, within– and between–category similarity are optimal when categories circumscribe different clusters of correlated properties (Barsalou & Billman, 1989; Billman & Heit, 1988; G.V. Jones, 1983; Malt & E.E. Smith, 1984; J.D. Martin & Billman, 1991; Medin, 1983; Medin, Wattenmaker, & Hampson, 1987; Medin, Wattenmaker, & Michalski, 1987; G.L. Murphy, 1982).

Intuitive theories.   Theorists often note an extremely serious problem with similarity–based approaches to category formation: These approaches will not work unless constraints specify the properties relevant to similarity (**10**.2.3, **10**.4.1). The philosopher Goodman (1955, 1972) has noted that an infinite number of properties are potentially relevant to a similarity judgment. Not only are *robins* and *sparrows* similar in having *wings* and *feathers*, they are also similar in being *less than a foot tall, non-metallic, less than a foot tall or metallic*, and so forth. Upon considering the infinite number of ways that *robins* and *sparrows* are similar, it becomes apparent that any two things can be just as similar as any two other things: *Apples* and *toothpicks* are also *less than a foot tall, non-metallic, less than a foot tall or metallic*, and so forth. Counterintuitively, *apples* and *toothpicks* become highly similar to each other, as well as to *robins* and *sparrows*, when similarity is free to range over the infinity of possible properties. Unless constraints specify some properties as relevant and others as irrelevant, similarity becomes a meaningless construct.

Why do people generally consider some properties and ignore others, such that similarity becomes useful in forming categories (**10**.2.3, **10**.4.1)? Why do people focus on *temperature regulation, locomotion*, and *outer covering* when distinguishing *reptiles* from *birds* while ignoring *color* and *size*? What determines the properties relevant to similarity comparisons? G.L. Murphy and Medin (1985) proposed that people's intuitive theories about the world play important roles in category formation. First, intuitive theories inform the selection of relevant properties. Thus, cultures sometimes place *whale* in *fish* (not *mammal*), because their intuitive theories state that *shape, habitat*, and *locomotion* (not physiological and genetic properties) are important to forming categories. Second, intuitive theories guide the interpretation of properties. For example, if one adopts an evolutionary theory of biology, a species' color might be interpreted as a camouflage that evolved to hide it from predators, thereby aiding survival. Third, intuitive theories provide relations between attributes. An intuitive theory of temperature regulation might explain why dogs that have evolved in colder climates have longer hair. In general, then, intuitive theories constrain similarity by selecting, interpreting, and integrating the properties of category members (Carey, 1985; Keil, 1989; Lakoff, 1987; Markman, 1989; Schank, G.C. Collins, & Hunter, 1986; Wellman & Gelman, 1988).

Intuitive theories are often linked to scientific theories. For example, theories of physics, chemistry, and geology influence people's naive beliefs about *carbon, water,* and *diamonds.* Similarly, theories of botany, zoology, and biology influence people's beliefs about *corn, trout,* and *apes.* Although people often view categories more mundanely, they may on occasion view them in the context of scientific theories. Thus, people might typically distinguish *salt* and *water* primarily in terms of perceptual and functional properties, but if asked to describe the fundamental difference between them, might invoke their respective molecular structures. Similarly, people might typically distinguish *dog* and *cat* primarily in terms of perceptual and functional properties, but if asked to describe the fundamental difference between them, might invoke their respective genetic structures. Much current work aims to explain people's understanding of the scientific bases of categories and its relations to perceptible properties and behaviors (Carey, 1985; Keil, 1989; Kripke, 1972; Ortony & Medin, 1989; Putnam, 1970, 1973, 1975; G. Rey, 1983; Rips, 1989; E.E. Smith, Medin, & Rips, 1984).

Intuitive and scientific theories clearly play central roles in category formation. People do not divide the world into categories according to raw similarity, relying only on information obtained from bottom-up processing to determine clusters of entities that are perceptually similar. Rather, top-down processing that projects theories of nature and human activity onto the world greatly constrain similarity.

Goals.   People also divide things in the world according to goals. For someone on a diet, *food* is divided into *food to eat on a diet* versus *food not to eat on diet.* Similarly, someone about to take a vacation divides *clothing* into *clothing to take on a vacation* versus *clothing not to take on a vacation.* Goal-relevant properties specify these categories (7.2.4, 7.3.2): *Low caloric value* specifies *food to eat on a diet,* and values for the attributes of *activity, location,* and *time of year* specify *clothing to take on a vacation.*

Typically, categories derived from goals are temporary and secondary categorizations of entities. Consider the goal-derived category, *food to eat on a diet.* The exemplars of this category have primary categorizations such as *celery, tofu,* and *rice cakes.* People do not think of each exemplar of *celery* initially as *a food to eat on a diet;* they think of it initially as *celery. Food to eat on a diet* is a subsequent and temporary cross-classification of *celery* that happens to be relevant because of the current goal. Our ability to cross-classify primary categories in secondary ways further reflects the flexibility of the human conceptual system (Barsalou, 1983, 1991).

7.3.2 Graded Structure

Perhaps the most central characteristic of categories is their graded structure (also known as *typicality* and *goodness of exemplar*; 2.3.2). Consider the category of *birds*. People generally view some *birds* as being better examples of the category than others. For example, Americans tend to perceive *robin* as more typical than *dove*, and *dove* as more typical than *ostrich*. This graded structure even extends beyond the category boundary, with *butterfly* being a poorer example of *non-birds* than *helicopter*, which is a poorer example than *chair*.

Graded structure is ubiquitous: Every category that researchers have ever examined has it. One might think that graded structure is an epiphenomenon having little to do with category use. However, if one peruses reviews of work on categorization, no other variable accounts for as much data as graded structure (Mervis & Rosch, 1981; Medin & E.E. Smith, 1984; Oden, 1987; E.E. Smith & Medin, 1981): It predicts categorization time, with typical exemplars being categorized more efficiently than atypical exemplars (2.3.2); it predicts exemplar generation, with typical exemplars being produced more often than atypical exemplars; it predicts exemplar acquisition, with typical exemplars being acquired before atypical exemplars; and it predicts inductive property inferences, with typical exemplars producing stronger inductions than atypical exemplars (10.4.4). Typicality clearly reflects something central about how people represent and process categories.

Does typicality reflect degree of category membership? According to fuzzy set theory (7.2.4), typicality and membership are one and the same thing: As an exemplar's membership strength increases, its typicality increases as well. Consider, though, the category of *odd number*, which has the membership rule, *any whole number that produces a remainder of one when divided by two*. All members of *odd number* have equivalent membership strength, because they all satisfy the rule equally. Yet, as Armstrong, L.R. Gleitman, and H. Gleitman (1983) have found, *odd number* has a graded structure: Some odd numbers are better examples than others (e.g., 3 is more typical than 57, which is more typical than 501). Armstrong et al. similarly found that other categories with clear membership rules, such as *female* and *plane geometry figure*, exhibit graded structure. For each of these categories, then, knowledge beyond its membership rule must be responsible for graded structure: Whereas the rule produces all-or-none membership, other knowledge of some sort produces differences in typicality. Consequently, membership and typicality are unrelated in some categories.

Nevertheless, typicality and membership are related in many other categories. Consider the goal-derived category, *foods to eat on a diet*. In this category, an exemplar's number of calories determines its membership strength: As an exemplar's number of calories decreases, it becomes an increasingly clear category member. However, number of calories also determines an exemplar's typicality: As an exemplar's number of calories decreases, it becomes increasingly typical. Membership strength and typicality covary for the exemplars of *foods to eat on a diet*, with number of calories determining both. Although membership and typicality are unrelated in some categories, they are closely related in many others (Barsalou, 1991; Chater, Lyon, & Myers, 1990; Fehr & Russell, 1984, Exp. 5; Hampton, 1979, 1988; McCloskey & Glucksberg, 1978).

Why are some exemplars more typical of a category than others? A number of factors are responsible. First, typicality reflects how closely an exemplar approximates its category's central tendency, where central tendency might be a prototype averaged across exemplars (2.3.1). In *fruit*, exemplars are typical to the extent that they approximate the average physical and functional characteristics of the category. *Apple* is typical because it is close to the average *fruit*, whereas *watermelon* is atypical because it's far. Second, typicality reflects how frequently people perceive an exemplar as a category member. In *fruit, cantaloupe* occurs more often than *Crenshaw melon* and is therefore more typical. Third, typicality reflects how closely an exemplar approximates ideal characteristics relevant to a goal the category serves. In *fruit, orange* is more typical than *lemon* because it is sweeter, where *sweetness* serves the goal of culinary enjoyment. Researchers have found that all three of these determinants can contribute to a category's graded structure (Barsalou, 1985, 1991; Borkenau, 1990; Chaplin, John, & Goldberg, 1988; Hampton & M.M. Gardiner, 1983; Lakoff, 1987; Lehrer, 1992; Loken & Ward, 1990; Read, D.K. Jones, & L.C. Miller, 1990; Rosch & Mervis, 1975).

A category's graded structure is extremely labile. Imagine that Americans judge the typicality of a category either from their own point of view or from the point of view of the average Chinese citizen. For many categories, graded structure inverts, with the typical exemplars from one point of view being atypical from the other point of view. For *birds*, Americans perceive *robin* as typical and *swan* as atypical from their own point of view but perceive *robin* as atypical and *swan* as typical from the Chinese point of view.

Such inversions do not reflect random responding, because agreement among subjects is relatively high for the Chinese point of view. Although these individuals are probably *not* constructing accurate points of view for Chinese citizens, they are at least consistent in the conceptualizations they construct. Regardless, the inversions that subjects produce illustrate that people can restructure their knowledge of a category easily and rapidly, making it relevant to the current context. Rather than being a rigid structural property, the graded structure of a category simply reflects one's current conceptualization of the category (7.2.3). Depending on the information retrieved for a category, and depending on the information perceived as important, different conceptualizations are constructed, which in turn produce different graded structures (Barsalou, 1987; Barsalou & Medin, 1986; Barsalou & Sewell, 1984; Roth & Shoben, 1983; Schwanenflugel & M. Rey, 1986).

Within a particular context, the graded structure of a category varies considerably both between individuals and within individuals. What one person perceives as typical for a category may appear atypical for someone else. What an individual perceives as typical for a category on one occasion may appear atypical on another, even though the context has not changed significantly. These results further illustrate the flexibility of graded structure: Because different individuals conceptualize a category differently, and because the same individual conceptualizes a category differently over time, they construct different graded structures for it (Barsalou, 1987, 1989; Barsalou & Billman, 1989).

7.4 SYSTEMS OF CONCEPTS

Concepts do not exist independently of one another in memory; they form conceptual systems. As we saw earlier, concepts are often associated together in categories. Exemplar concepts *alarm clock* and *grandfather clock*, for example, are interrelated in the category for *clocks*. As we also saw earlier, concepts are often associated together in frames. Attribute concepts for *wheels*, *engine*, and *fuel tank*, for example, are interrelated in the frame for *car*.

7.4.1 Taxonomies and Partonomies

These examples for *clock* and *car* illustrate two fundamentally different kinds of conceptual systems: taxonomies and partonomies. The primary difference between them reflects different organizing relations. In *taxonomies*, concepts are organized by the *type* relation, which specifies that one concept is a type, instance, or subset of another. Thus, *travel alarm clock* is a type of *alarm clock*, which is a type of *clock*. In contrast, concepts in *partonomies* are organized by the *part* relation, which specifies that one concept represents a part of another. Thus, *carburetor* is a part of *engine*, which is a part of *car*. A partonomy is actually a type of frame, because the attributes of a frame often represent the parts of a category's members (see Figs. 7.2, 7.3, 7.4). As we saw earlier, however, various other relations and constraints interrelate part attributes in frames as well (e.g., the *engine rotates* the *drive train*; *racing engines cooccur* with *standard transmissions*). Consequently, frames are more complex than simple partonomies, which only represent the part–whole relations of a system (Barsalou, 1992; Chaffin, 1992; A.M. Collins & Michalski, 1989;

G.A. Miller & Johnson-Laird, 1976; Rips & F.G. Conrad, 1989; M.E. Winston, Chaffin, Herrmann, 1987).

Although taxonomies and partonomies differ in their fundamental organizing relations, they both exhibit *hierarchical structure*. In a hierarchical system, each concept decomposes into more specific concepts, which in turn decompose into still more specific concepts, and so forth, until the most specific concepts can decompose no further. Consider the hierarchical taxonomy for *animal*. At the root of this taxonomy, *animal* decomposes into *mammal, bird, fish*, and so forth. *Mammal*, in turn, decomposes into *cat, dog, horse*, et cetera; *bird* decomposes into *eagle, robin, dove*, et cetera; and so on. *Cat*, in turn, decomposes into *Abyssinian, Burmese, Maine Coon*, et cetera; *eagle* decomposes into *Golden Eagle, Bald Eagle*, et cetera; and so forth. People know many taxonomies in ontological domains as diverse as *animals, artifacts, locations, times, activities, thoughts*, and *emotions*.

People also know many hierarchical partonomies for numerous kinds of physical entities in the world. Consider the partonomy for the *human body*. At the root of this partonomy, *human* decomposes into *head, arms, legs*, and so forth. *Head*, in turn, decomposes into *eyes, ears, brain*, et cetera; *arm* decomposes into *hand, wrist, elbow*, et cetera; and so on. *Eye*, in turn, decomposes into *cornea, retina, iris*, et cetera; *hand* decomposes into *thumb, finger, palm*, et cetera; and so forth. Hierarchical taxonomies and partonomies organize human concepts extensively. As we shall see shortly, however, violations of strict hierarchical structure often occur in these conceptual systems.

7.4.2 Cognitive Economy and Inheritance

How elegantly and parsimoniously do humans represent systems of concepts? Research on *cognitive economy* has addressed this issue. Consider the partial taxonomy for *animal* in Panel A of Fig. 7.5. As can be seen, the property *eats* is only associated with the concept for *animal*. Clearly, however, *eats* is also a property of *bird, mammal, robin*, and *dog*, even though it is not associated explicitly with them. Similarly, *fur* is a property of *dog*, even though it is only associated with *mammal*. The taxonomy in Panel A represents cognitive economy for properties: Each property is only represented once at the highest level for which it is generally true, yet it is *inherited* by all concepts along any descending chain of *type* relations. Thus, *eats* is true of every subordinate concept that descends through *type* relations from *animal*. Consequently, the properties true of *dog* include *barks* (directly associated), *fur* (inherited from *mammal*), and *eats* (inherited from *animal*).

Panel A also illustrates cognitive economy for *categories*: *Dog* is only shown as a type of *mammal*; it is not shown as a type of *animal*. Each category is only represented once at the highest level for which it is generally true, but is inherited by all concepts along any descending chain of *type* relations. As a

Panel A

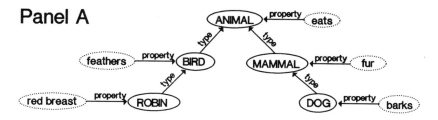

Panel B

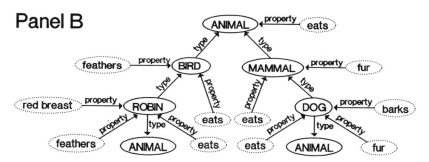

Figure 7.5. Examples of a taxonomy with cognitive economy (Panel A) and without cognitive economy (Panel B).

result, *dog* inherits being an *animal*, even though it is not directly associated with it.

Panel B, in contrast, shows a taxonomy that violates cognitive economy. It violates cognitive economy for properties, because each property is explicitly related to every category for which it is true: Thus, *eat* is stored with *bird*, *mammal*, *robin*, and *dog*, not just with *animal*. This taxonomy also violates cognitive economy for categories, because each category is explicitly related to all of its subordinates: *Animal* is stored with *robin* and *dog*, not just with *bird* and *mammal*.

In seminal work that played a central role in initiating the study of human knowledge, A.M. Collins and Quillian (1969) assessed whether human taxonomies exhibit cognitive economy (see also Quillian, 1968). In a property verification task, subjects received sentences such as "Dogs bark" and "Dogs have feathers." Their task was to determine, as quickly as possible, if each statement was true or false. Collins and Quillian predicted that if human taxonomies exhibit cognitive economy, then sentences requiring longer inheritance chains should take longer to verify, because people have to search further in the taxonomy to find the connection between the concept and the property. For example, the taxonomy in Panel A predicts that "Dogs eat" should take longer to verify than "Dogs have fur," which should take longer than "Dogs bark" (unlike these examples, sentence length is controlled in studies of this sort). Similarly, "Dogs are animals" should take longer to verify than "Dogs are mammals." Collins and Quillian reported that verification times indeed followed these patterns, suggesting that human taxonomies exhibit cognitive economy.

Subsequent work, however, has converged definitively on the opposite conclusion: Cognitive economy does *not* constrain human knowledge. Various investigators discovered that factors such as associative strength, similarity, and familiarity explained Collins and Quillian's distance effects. When researchers controlled these other variables, they found that logical distance in an inheritance tree (i.e., Panel A of Fig. 7.5) had no consistent effect on verification time. Moreover, sometimes people verified long inheritance chains quickly (*a cantaloupe is fruit*), and sometimes they verified short inheritance chains more slowly (*a cantaloupe is a melon*; C. Conrad, 1972; E.E. Smith et al., 1974; see also A.M. Collins & E.F. Loftus, 1975; McCloskey 1980; McCloskey & Glucksberg, 1979; Meyer, 1970; E.E. Smith, 1978).

These findings suggest that human knowledge looks much like Panel B of Fig. 7.5: Concepts and properties in human knowledge are organized with little concern for elegance and parsimony. Rather, they become associated after being processed together on a regular basis in working memory, regardless of their distance in a logical inheritance tree. If people frequently perceive cantaloupes as fruit and not as melons, then *cantaloupe* becomes more strongly associated with *fruit* than with *melon*, thereby violating cognitive economy. Similarly, if people frequently perceive dogs as having fur and not as chasing cars, then *dog* becomes more strongly associated with *fur* than with *chasing cars*.

The lack of cognitive economy in human knowledge demonstrates an important trade-off between storage and processing. Cognitive economy in representation optimizes storage, because categories and properties are not stored redundantly. Optimizing storage in this manner, however, incurs high processing demands: To find all of the concepts and properties true of a concept, it would be necessary to search up its type chain and accumulate inherited information. In Panel A, for example, the concepts and properties for *dog* must be accumulated by searching up the type chain to *mammal* and then to *animal*.

In contrast, the taxonomy in Panel B optimizes processing at the expense of storage. Although space is wasted storing concepts and properties redundantly, the retrieval of concepts and properties occurs quickly without searching beyond the concept of interest. In retrieving information about *dog*, much of what one might want to know is stored directly with the concept, so that little search is necessary. Inheritance could still play a role in inference: *Lungs* and *warm-blooded* might not be stored directly with *dog* because they have never been relevant to processing this category, yet one can still infer them through inheritance from knowledge of *mammal*. Nevertheless, much information appears to be stored redundantly. As we saw in **6.2.2**, the capacity of human memory is indefinitely large. The cognitive system, in storing knowledge redundantly, often capitalizes on this abundant resource to optimize processing time, a choice that has clear payoffs for survival.

7.4.3 The Basic Level

The existence of taxonomies raises an important problem about categorization. Imagine going through your attic and discovering an old Phillips head screwdriver that you lost several years ago. How do you categorize it? To see the problem, consider the taxonomy for *tools* in Fig. 7.6: This rediscovered screwdriver could be categorized as a *Phillips head screwdriver*, a *screwdriver*, or a *tool*.

Rosch et al. (1976) suggested that two contrasting principles control the taxonomic level at which people prefer to categorize (see also Rosch, 1978). First, people prefer to minimize the number of categories they must consider in making a categorization. According to this *efficiency principle*, categorizations should be easiest at the highest levels of taxonomies, where the number of categories is smallest. For example, one might use *tool* to categorize the lost screwdriver, because the number of contrasting categories at this level (e.g., *tool, clothing, furniture, fruit*) is much less than at the next level down (e.g., *screwdriver, hammer, wrench, shirt, pants, socks, chair, table, bed, apple, banana, pear*). The second principle is that people prefer to maximize the informativeness of their categorizations. According to this *informativeness principle*, categorizations are optimal at the most specific levels of taxonomies, where informativeness is highest: One would use *Phillips head screwdriver* to categorize the lost screwdriver, because it provides more information than *screwdriver*.

Rosch et al. argued that people prefer to use intermediate taxonomic levels in categorization to optimize both efficiency and informativeness. Their analysis addressed three levels of taxonomies, which they called the *superor-*

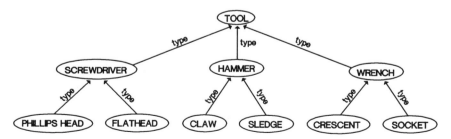

Figure 7.6. A partial taxonomy of *tools*.

dinate, basic, and *subordinate* levels. Examples of superordinate level categories include *tool, clothing, furniture, fruit,* and *vegetable.* Examples of basic level categories include *screwdriver* and *hammer, shirt* and *pants, chair* and *table, apple* and *banana, carrot* and *onion.* Examples of subordinate level categories include *Phillips head screwdriver* and *flat head screwdriver, jeans* and *slacks, kitchen chair* and *rocking chair, McIntosh apple* and *Granny Smith apple, Bermuda onion* and *Vidalia onion.*

To assess the hypothesis that people prefer intermediate level categories, Rosch and Mervis had subjects produce properties for categories at different taxonomic levels, such as *tool* versus *screwdriver* versus *Phillips head screwdriver.* Following the informativeness principle, fewer properties should generally be true of *tool* than *screwdriver,* and fewer properties should generally be true of *screwdriver* than *Phillips head screwdriver.* Of particular interest, however, is the *rate of gain* in informativeness: As categories become increasingly specific, how much new information is added over the previous level? For example, how much new information does *screwdriver* add to *tool,* and how much new information does *Phillips head screwdriver* add to *screwdriver?*

Across different taxonomies, Rosch et al. found that basic level categories provided substantial gains in informativeness over superordinate categories (e.g., *screwdriver* added much information over *tool*), but that subordinate level categories provided very little gain in informativeness over basic level categories (e.g., *Phillips head screwdriver* added little information over *screwdriver*). On the basis of these results, Rosch et al. concluded that intermediate levels of taxonomies constitute the basic level. Because intermediate level categories are substantially more informative than the superordinate categories, the gain in information that they provide is worth the cost of having to process more categories. Conversely, because subordinate categories don't increase informativeness by much, the small gain in information that they provide is not worth the increased processing costs. Rather than using the most informative categories available, people use intermediate categories, because they are sufficiently informative and do not demand too much processing. Other researchers have obtained similar results in other ontological domains, including *people, events,* and *locations* (Cantor & Mischel, 1979; Rifken, 1985; B. Tversky & Hemenway, 1983).

Several other findings indicate further that people prefer intermediate taxonomic levels in categorization. First, developmental psychologists have found that children generally learn intermediate level categories before they learn categories at other levels (Anglin, 1983; Mervis, 1987; Rosch et al., 1976). Second, people are more likely to name pictures of objects spontaneously with intermediate level categories than with superordinate or subordinate categories (Rosch et al., 1976). Third, people verify that a pictured object belongs to an intermediate level category faster than they verify that it belongs to a category at another level (Joliceur, Gluck, & Kosslyn, 1984; G.L.

Murphy & Brownell, 1985; G.L. Murphy & E.E. Smith, 1982; Rosch et al., 1976). Fourth, anthropological linguists have found that the names of categories at intermediate levels are consistently shorter than the names of superordinate and subordinate categories (e.g., "chair" versus "furniture" and "kitchen chair"). Because increased frequency of use decreases word length over the history of a language, the shortest labels at intermediate levels suggest that these categories are indeed the ones that people prefer most (Berlin, Breedlove, & Raven, 1974; Berlin & Kay, 1969).

Rosch et al. further found that exemplars of basic level categories often share a common shape. Consider the shape common to exemplars within *screwdriver*, within *hammer*, within *shirt*, and within *sock*. In contrast, exemplars of superordinate categories do not share a common shape (e.g., no common shape occurs within *tool* or within *clothing*). Although exemplars of subordinate categories also share a common shape (e.g., within *Phillips head screwdriver*, within *shirt*), Rosch et al. argued that the gain in informativeness for shape is so small when going from the basic to the subordinate level that the basic level is again preferred.

Recent theorists have suggested that shape may be much more important to the basic level than even Rosch et al. suspected (Barsalou, 1991; Barsalou & Billman, 1989; Biederman, 1987; B. Tversky & Hemenway, 1985) . In fact, these theorists have suggested that shape alone—not a compromise between efficiency and informativeness—determines the basic level. The key assumption underlying this view is that the shape of an object is extracted more rapidly during visual perception than any other visual information. As a result, categories based on shape are assigned to an object more rapidly than categories based on other kinds of information that are extracted after shape. Thus, *screwdriver* is the first category assigned to the rediscovered screwdriver in the attic, because the shape common to screwdriver is the first information extracted visually. *Phillips head screwdriver* is not assigned, because it requires visual information that is more detailed than that provided by general shape. *Tool* is not assigned, because the shape of a screwdriver is not true of all tools and therefore is not highly associated with *tool*.

This perceptual account of the basic level makes an interesting prediction: Members of a basic level category whose shape differs from the shape common to most category members should be classified at the subordinate level. To see this, consider the basic level category of *bird*. Most exemplars in this category share a common shape, namely, the shape common to *robin*, *dove*, *blue jay*, and *cardinal*. However, a few atypical exemplars, such as *chicken*, have a different shape. If the perceptual account of the basic level is correct, then a chicken should not be classified initially as *bird*, because its shape does not activate the common shape for *bird*. Instead, a chicken should activate the category for which its shape is common, namely, *chicken*. As a result, people should classify chickens faster as *chicken* than as *bird*. In support of this prediction, investigators have indeed found that people classify atypical members of basic level categories fastest at the subordinate level (Joliceur et al., 1984; G.L. Murphy & Brownell, 1985).

We have considered two possible determinants of the basic level: informativeness and shape. Which account is correct? Perhaps both, with different determinants producing different basic levels on different tasks. During perceptual processing, a common shape may control initial categorizations, such that shape-based categories constitute the perceptual basic level. In other situations, such as linguistic interaction, informativeness may determine a different basic level. Consider an example from Cruse (1977). Someone who owns two dogs, a Spaniel and an Alsatian, says, "I'll have to take the dog to the vet tomorrow." Although *dog* is the basic level category whose shape is common to the two dogs, it is an inappropriate categorization. Clearly a categorization at the subordinate level (*Spaniel, Alsatian*) is required. Consider another example from Cruse. Someone arriving at a British port with a dog is told by a customs agent, "I'm sorry, sir, but all dogs coming from abroad must be put into quarantine for six months." Because British law actually states that all *animals* coming from abroad are subject to quarantine, the basic level category, *dog*, is inappropriate. Instead, the customs agent must communicate the scope of the law fully, by using *animal*, lest the traveller return with a cat, thinking that the quarantine applies only to dogs. In general, once an entity is categorized initially at the perceptual basic level, it may later be recategorized to optimize informativeness in the current context (Barsalou & Billman, 1989, pp. 175–181).

CONCLUSION

People's use of knowledge is impressive. One recurrent theme is their remarkable ability to adapt knowledge to new situations: People divide the world into categories in ways that serve their intuitive theories and goals. People use conceptual combination to construct new concepts from existing concepts. People conceptualize categories differently depending on what is relevant in the current context. People reorganize the graded structure of a category to reflect goals and constraints. People adjust the basic level to reflect what is informative in the current context. People simulate events over space and time with mental models. Clearly, we have an impressive ability to manipulate knowledge in myriad ways.

Another recurrent theme is the importance of similarity and availability in human knowledge, in contrast to the much less apparent role of logic (**10**.1): Rather than using definitions to perform categorization, people rely more on similarity to prototypes and exemplars. Rather than representing concepts with information that is derived through logical operations, people represent concepts with information that is highly available. Rather than performing conceptual combination according to the rules of set theory, people rely on procedures for manipulating frames. Rather than using transitivity to determine chains of categorical inferences, people use similarity. Rather than representing taxonomies elegantly and parsimoniously according to cognitive economy, people organize them to optimize speed of access.

Clearly, there is more to the human conceptual ability than similarity and availability. The importance of intuitive theories, scientific theories, and goals indicates that reasoning of some sort is also important in people's use of knowledge. As we shall see in **10**.4 and **10**.5, however, cognitive psychologists are only beginning to understand the nature of the reasoning abilities that interact with similarity and availability.

Numerous important and difficult issues continue to challenge research on human knowledge. One extremely pressing issue, raised earlier, concerns researchers' ability to measure knowledge (**7.2.2**). Researchers need to develop more sophisticated methods for eliciting knowledge, as well as more sophisticated theories for making sense of the complex data they obtain. Without significant progress in these important areas, cognitive psychologists will remain fairly ignorant about the content and organization of human knowledge. Cognitive psychologists also have much to learn about various types of knowledge that have previously received little attention, including knowledge of time (G.A. Miller & Johnson-Laird, 1976), locations (B. Tversky & Hemenway, 1983), mental activities (Rips & F.G. Conrad, 1989; Wellman & Gelman, 1988), physical activities (Schank & Abelson, 1977), and emotions (Ortony et al., 1988).

Finally, cognitive psychologists have little, if any, understanding of how people represent the current state of the world. Everyone appears to have a *world model* that represents his or her current knowledge of where specific people, objects, and activities exist currently in the environment (Barsalou, 1991; for relevant work in artificial intelligence, see F.M. Brown, 1987; P.J. Hayes, 1985; McCarthy & P.J. Hayes, 1969). As I write this, I know that my wife is at work, my car is in a parking lot outside my office, and students are demonstrating for democracy in China. People constantly update world models as their environment changes, and they reference events and changes that will occur in the future. In a sense, world models reflect the continual updating of general knowledge with episodic memories: As we encode changes in the environment, the resultant memories update the relevant general knowledge. Although this coordinated use of knowledge and memory has received virtually no study in cognitive psychology, it must be central to human cognition.

8

LANGUAGE STRUCTURE

Language is one of the most unique and amazing human abilities. People rapidly string together long, complex sequences of sounds to represent an infinitely large number of meaningful states of affairs. Not only can we describe the current situation, we can also describe the past and the future, alternatives to reality, and false states of affairs. Other organisms besides humans communicate. Birds communicate a simple and fixed set of messages about important life events (Marler & Mundinger, 1971). Bees, using a somewhat more flexible and productive set of signs, communicate messages about the location, quality, and amount of pollen available (von Frisch, 1974). Apes and other non-human primates use signals to indicate social relations, territorial claims, and threats (Snowdon, C.H. Brown, & M.R. Peterson, 1982). Clearly, organisms communicate in a large variety of ways, but how similar are these other communication systems to human language? As far as researchers can tell, no other natural communication system bears much similarity to human language, nor is any as expressive. A large amount of work has addressed whether non-human primates, such as apes, chimpanzees, and dolphins, can be trained to communicate like humans. Although non-human primates appear to develop some human-like communication skills, the growing consensus is that these acquired skills are limited, falling short of human language in important ways (Premack, 1976; Premack & Woodruff, 1978; Terrace, Petitto, Sanders, & Bever, 1979; but see Savage-Rumbaugh, Rumbaugh, & Boysen, 1980).

Many theorists believe that biological factors make human language possible and underlie its unique characteristics. Biological factors appear to prepare humans for language in at least three ways: First, humans have a unique vocal tract and facial musculature that allows for sophisticated control over the production of sounds, giving us the ability to produce the extremely rapid sound sequences that characterize human speech production (MacNeilage, 1983; MacNeilage & Ladefoged, 1976; G.A. Miller, 1981). Second, the human brain contains two hemispheres, one of which appears to become specialized for language through lateralization. This specialization may underpin the abilities to translate rapid sound sequences into meaning and to represent a wide range of meanings in a flexible manner (Geschwind, 1972; Lenneberg, 1967; P. Lieberman, 1975; Segalowitz, 1983). Third, all children go through the same stages of language acquisition, suggesting that specific maturational changes in the brain are important (Ingram, 1989; Slobin, 1985). Moreover, children do not need formal instruction in language, nor do they rely heavily on feedback from adults. Some theorists have even argued further that people's knowledge of language syntax has a biological basis (Chomsky, 1957, 1965, 1968, 1975), although others disagree with this claim.

8.1 LINGUISTIC UNIVERSALS

Linguistic universals provide further evidence for a biological basis of human language (Greenberg, 1966a,b; Hockett, 1966). Consider the following observations from cross-cultural research in linguistics:

Universality.   All humans use language, with the exception of those having severe neurological disabilities and perhaps those excluded from human interaction during childhood (Curtiss, 1977; Goldin-Meadow, 1982; Lane, 1979).

Complexity.   All human languages appear to be equally complex and to possess equal expressive power. Many years ago, theorists believed that languages of technological societies were more complex and more expressive than languages of non-technological societies, but subsequent, more careful, work has found no important differences. In addition, sign languages used by the deaf are just as complex and expressive as spoken languages (Greenberg, 1966a; Salmon, 1969).

Arbitrary mapping from signs to meanings.   All human languages include perceptual signs that bear arbitrary relations to their meanings. Consider "dog," "chien", and "perro," which mean *dog* in English, French, and Spanish, respectively. No similarity exists between these three words acoustically or visually. More importantly, nothing in their acoustic or visual form provides a clue about their meaning to people who don't know the language. Only onomatopoetic words, such as "woof" and "boom," signal their meanings, but such words are extremely rare. Words, in general, are arbitrary symbols whose meanings must be learned.

Discrete, specialized signs. Variability in the production of a sign typically doesn't indicate corresponding variability in meaning. As the pronunciation of "dog" varies across dialects, for example, it functions discretely, generally referring to the same kind of thing. Additionally, signs are specialized, being used only for language and serving no other human purpose. In contrast, the knowledge that underlies meaning is not specialized, and enters into many other processes besides language (e.g., categorization, memory, imagery, thought).

Infinite meanings from finite signs. Most languages start with a finite number of sounds (about 50). From this finite number of sounds can be produced an infinitely large number of words, even though the total number in a language is usually less than 100,000. From the relatively finite number of words in a language, people can produce an infinitely large number of sentences. As we shall see shortly, knowledge of syntax and semantics allows us to combine these words productively to convey an endless variety of meanings.

Common structural characteristics. All languages share common structural characteristics that may be phonological (e.g., consonants and vowels), morphological (e.g., singular and plural), syntactic (e.g., nouns and verbs), semantic (e.g., negation and agency), and pragmatic (e.g., questions and commands).

In sum, language is universal and equally expressive across cultures, always using a finite number of arbitrary, discrete, and specialized signs to convey an infinite number of meanings. These similarities across languages, along with a universal progression in language development, strongly suggest that human language has a biological basis. Certainly language acquisition depends on experience in important ways, but it can't result from experience completely: It it did, researchers would observe many more cases of people not using language, large differences in complexity and expressiveness across cultures, fundamentally different relations between signs and meanings, and developmental progressions that depend much more on experience.

How does one characterize and assess human language? Of all the topics discussed in this book, language has received attention from more disciplines than any other. Central contributions to the study of language have come not only from linguistics, but also from philosophy, cognitive psychology, developmental psychology, artificial intelligence, engineering, biology, ethology, and neuroscience. As we shall see, the study of language is truly interdisciplinary.

In this chapter, I address the structural patterns of language. By *structural patterns*, I mean the basic characteristics of *linguistic utterances* and *language behavior*. For example, certain patterns of phonological and syntactic information, but not others, structure linguistic utterances. Similarly, certain patterns of behavior, but not others, structure people's attempts to communicate cooperatively with other speakers. Whereas this chapter describes the structural patterns that characterize language, the next chapter addresses the underlying cognitive mechanisms that produce them. Because language is so multifaceted, many kinds of structural patterns exist. I begin by describing some of the structural patterns in language sounds, documented in the linguistic literatures on phonetics and phonology. I then describe some of the structural patterns in words and sentences from the morphology and syntax literatures in linguistics. Finally, I describe some of the structural patterns in the meanings of linguistic expressions and in the use of them to achieve communicative goals, documented in the linguistic, philosophical, and psychological literatures on semantics and pragmatics. In each area, I describe only the most fundamental structural patterns, ignoring many important distinctions and glossing over others. The primary purpose of this chapter is to acquaint readers with some of the basic properties of linguistic utterances and language behavior. The following chapter then considers the underlying cognitive mechanisms that produce these structural patterns.

8.2 PHONETICS

Analyses of linguistic structure typically begin at the level of *phones*, the sounds produced by the human articulatory system. Properties of the articulatory system constrain production of phones. Although all humans can (with practice) produce the same phones, languages differ somewhat in the phones they include. Although many phones occur in most languages, other phones only occur in a few (MacNeilage, 1983; MacNeilage & Ladefoged, 1976; G.A. Miller, 1981).

Consonants and *vowels* constitute two fundamentally different kinds of phones. Theories of *phonetics* distinguish consonants and vowels according to differences in how they are articulated. The production of consonants obstructs air as it passes through the articulatory system, whereas the production of vowels allows air to pass unobstructed.

English consonants vary on three primary attributes. Consonants vary first in *place of articulation*: where the vocal tract obstructs air. When producing the phone for the letter b, notated as [b], you obstruct air by closing your lips (*bilabial*); to produce [s], you obstruct air by pressing the tip of your tongue against the roof of your mouth (*alveolar*). Consonants also vary in *manner of articulation*: how the vocal tract obstructs air. To produce [b], you close your lips completely, thereby temporarily stopping air flow (a *stop*); to produce [s], you force air between your tongue and the roof of your mouth, thereby producing continuous turbulence as air passes between them (a *fricative*). Finally, consonants vary in *voicing*: whether or not the vocal chords vibrate as air passes through the vocal tract. For example, the vocal chords vibrate during the production of [b] (*voiced*) but not during the production of [s] (*voiceless*). By combining attribute values, linguists characterize [b] as a *voiced bilabial stop* and [p] as a *voiceless bilabial stop*, [z] as a *voiced alveolar fricative* and [s] as a *voiceless alveolar fricative*.

Tongue height (how close the tongue is to the roof of the mouth) and *tongue position* (the highest part of the tongue) provide the primary differences among English vowels. For example, the "ee" sound in "wheat"—notated as [i]—is a *high front* vowel, because the tongue is high, and the front of the tongue is highest. In contrast, the [a] in "star" is a *low central* vowel, and the [o] in "float" is a *middle back* vowel. In general, linguists have been quite successful in characterizing structural patterns among phones by using articulatory distinctions like these (Ladefoged, 1981).

8.3   PHONOLOGY

Whereas phonetics characterizes the sounds of a language, *phonology* specifies how sounds distinguish one word from another. The fundamental unit of phonology is the *phoneme*, which represents a set of phones that are equivalent in their determination of meaning (*allophones*). To see the difference between phones and phonemes, consider the words "tap" and "tape." The phone [p] in "tap" is *unaspirated*, which means that you do not release air following the bilabial stop. In contrast, the phone [pʰ] in "tape" is *aspirated*, which means that you do release air following the bilabial stop. Note, however, that you can end "tap" with either [p] or [pʰ], just as you can end "tape" with either [p] or [pʰ]. People categorize "tap" as *tap*, regardless of whether the "p" is aspirated or unaspirated, and the same is true for "tape." Because [p] and [pʰ] are equivalent in their determination of meaning, they are allophones of the phoneme /p/. Note that [p] and [pʰ] signal different meanings in other languages, thereby constituting two different phonemes, /p/ and /pʰ/, although they constitute a single phoneme, /p/, in English. Similarly, the unaspirated and aspirated phones for "t" in "stop" and "top"— [t] and [tʰ], respectively—are allophones of the phoneme /t/.

A wide variety of structural relations coordinate adjacent phonemes in the speech stream. Consider the formation of plurals: To form the plural of "bat" you add /s/; but to form the plural of "bag" you add /z/. Similarly, to form the past tense of "botch" you add /t/, but to form the past tense of "bog" you add /d/. Why doesn't formation of the plural only use one ending (e.g., /s/)? And why doesn't formation of the past tense only use one ending (e.g., /d/)? Why is one ending voiceless and the other voiced in formation of the plural (/s/ vs. /z/), and in formation of the past tense (/t/ vs. /d/)? The regularity underlying these structural patterns is that the voicing of the final phoneme in a word determines the voicing of the suffix: Because the /t/ in "bat" is voiceless, you add the voiceless form of the plural, /s/; because the /g/ in "bag" is voiced, you add the voiced form of the plural, /z/. An analogous rule determines the voicing of the past tense. In every case, the suffix takes the form that is easiest to produce following the end of the word. As the examples in this section illustrate, phonemes and phoneme relations exhibit a wide variety of systematic structural relationships (S.R. Anderson, 1974; Hyman, 1975).

8.4 MORPHOLOGY

Morphology specifies the fundamental units of meaning in a language (Mathews, 1976). The fundamental unit of morphology is the *morpheme*, namely, any meaningful unit of speech that cannot be broken down into smaller units of speech that still have meaning. *Free morphemes*, such as "dog" and "saddle" are words that can stand on their own. *Bound morphemes*, such as "anti-" and "-ment" cannot stand alone, but must be affixed to a free morpheme. Bound morphemes include *prefixes*, such as "anti-," "pre-," and "un-," and suffixes, such as "-ment," "-s," and "-ed." There are *derivational morphemes*, which change a word's grammatical class, and *inflectional morphemes*, which do not. For example, "-ment" is derivational because it changes verbs to nouns (e.g., "enjoy" to "enjoyment"), whereas, "-ed" is inflectional because its addition to verbs does not change their grammatical class (e.g., "thrive" and "thrived"). Finally, words can contain almost any number of morphemes, as in "demographics" and "professionalized."

People's knowledge of morphemic structure includes not only knowledge of well established morphemes, but also knowledge of how to combine morphemes productively. They know that they can add "-s" to some nouns and verbs but not to adjectives and adverbs. Furthermore, they know that adding "-s" to a noun forms a plural, but adding "-s" to a verb indicates a third-person singular subject (e.g., "I walk" vs. "He walks"), and that adding "non-" to a word means its opposite, whereas adding "-ment" to a verb indicates a state rather than a process. People's ability to combine morphemes productively is a form of conceptual combination that greatly increases their expressional power (see **7.2.4** for additional discussion of conceptual combination).

8.5 SYNTAX

Syntax specifies the grammatical sentences in a language (Culicover, 1976). Whereas some sequences of words form grammatical sentences, others do not. For example, "The mule ate grass" is grammatical, but "Grass mule ate the" is not. *Grammatical class* constitutes one important aspect of syntax. The grammatical classes in a language may include *noun, verb, adjective, adverb, determiner, preposition*, and so forth. People know at least one or more grammatical class for every word, knowing, for example, that "window" is a noun, "give" is a verb, and "spring" is an adjective, noun, and verb. As we shall see, words in the same grammatical class play similar syntactic roles across sentences.

Rules of order constitute another important aspect of syntax. Order generally takes three forms in sentences: *constituent structure, hierarchical organization*, and *thematic roles*. A constituent is a string of words that form a natural subgroup within a sentence. Figure 8.1 provides eight examples of constituents, including "the farmer," "on the train," "the farmer on the train," and so forth. Rules of order specify how grammatical classes can combine to form constituents. Thus, in English, a constituent can contain a determiner followed by a noun, but not a noun followed by a preposition. Whereas "the farmer" is a grammatical constituent, "farmer on" is not.

Rules of order further specify the hierarchical organization of constituents. For example, a noun phrase and a prepositional phrase can combine to form a larger constituent, as "the cider / from Quebec" in Fig. 8.1 illustrates. This figure further demonstrates that constituents combine hierarchically to form increasingly large constituents until they form an entire sentence.

Rules of order also specify the positions of thematic roles in a sentence. Consider how the verb, *eat*, assigns the thematic roles, *agent* and *theme*. For *eat*, the agent is the entity that does the eating, and the theme is the entity that the agent eats. As the following two sentences illustrate, the agent and the theme

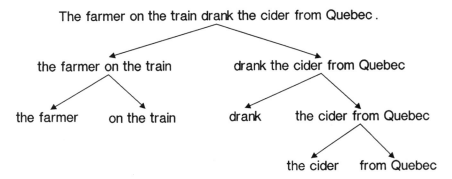

Figure 8.1. An example of hierarchical constituent structure.

occur in different sentence positions, depending on whether *eat* is in the active or passive voice:

> The lion ate the tiger.
> The lion was eaten by the tiger.

When *eat* is active in the first sentence, the subject of the verb (*lion*) is the agent, and the direct argument of the verb (*tiger*) is the theme. When *eat* is passive in the second sentence, however, the subject (*lion*) is the theme, and the oblique argument (*tiger*) is the agent. As these examples illustrate, different rules of order associated with the active and passive forms of *eat* assign different thematic roles to different sentence positions.

Not all languages specify thematic roles through sentence position. Some languages, such as Mandarin Chinese and Dyirbal, affix morphemes to nouns to specify the thematic role that each noun plays. In these languages, position is less important, and words can occur in a wider variety of sequences.

8.5.1 Phrase Structure Grammars

One general approach to syntax has been to develop grammars that produce the hierarchical constituent structures of sentences (Chomsky, 1957, 1965; Gazdar, Klein, Pullum, & Sag, 1985). Consider the fragment of a grammar in Fig. 8.2, which contains four *phrase structure rules*. Note that this example greatly underestimates the number and complexity of the phrase structure rules needed to account for English syntax. Nevertheless, it provides a sense of how these rules work. The first rule simply states that every sentence must contain a noun phrase and a verb phrase. The second rule states that a noun phrase contains an optional determiner, an optional string of adjectives, an obligatory noun, and an optional string of prepositional phrases

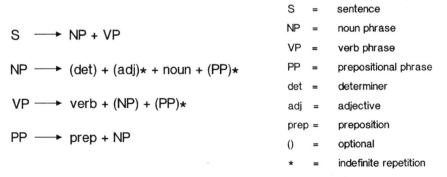

S	=	sentence
NP	=	noun phrase
VP	=	verb phrase
PP	=	prepositional phrase
det	=	determiner
adj	=	adjective
prep	=	preposition
()	=	optional
*	=	indefinite repetition

S ⟶ NP + VP

NP ⟶ (det) + (adj)* + noun + (PP)*

VP ⟶ verb + (NP) + (PP)*

PP ⟶ prep + NP

Figure 8.2. Four examples of simplified phrase structure rules.

(parentheses represent optionality, and asterisks represent possible repetition). Examples of noun phrases that this rule produces include:

    Douglas
    the large, friendly, golden dog
    the tennis ball under the edge of the patio

The third rule states that every verb phrase must contain a verb and may contain an optional noun phrase and an optional string of prepositional phrases. Examples of verb phrases that this rule produces include:

    smiled
    chased the frisbee
    fell into a hole onto a gopher in a deep sleep

The fourth rule states that every prepositional phrase must contain a preposition and a noun phrase. Examples of prepositional phrases that this rule produces include:

    by the window
    into the overgrown field by the gently flowing river

Figure 8.3 illustrates how phrase structure rules produce *phrase markers*, the hierarchical constituent structures of sentences. Consider the phrase marker for the sentence, "The dog chased the cat," in Fig. 8.3. As can be seen, the sentence (S) decomposes into a noun phrase (NP) and a verb phrase (VP), following the first phrase structure rule in Fig. 8.2. In turn, the noun phrase

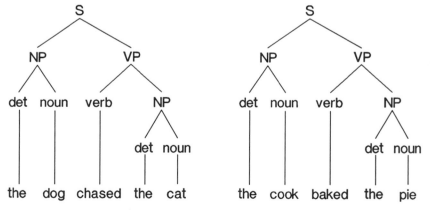

Figure 8.3.   An example of two sentences that share the same phrase marker but that have different meanings.

decomposes into a determiner and a noun, following the second phrase structure rule in Fig. 8.2. Analogously, the verb phrase decomposes into a verb and a noun phrase, following the third phrase structure rule, and the noun phrase in the verb phrase decomposes into a determiner and a noun, following the second phrase structure rule. As this example illustrates, phrase structure rules produce the hierarchical constituent structure that constitutes a phrase marker.

It is essential to note that the phrase marker for a sentence is not its meaning, even though the two are sometimes equated mistakenly. To see the distinction, consider the phrase marker on the right of Fig. 8.3 for the sentence, "The cook baked the pie." This phrase marker is identical to the phrase marker on the left for "The dog chased the cat." Each phrase marker contains the same hierarchical organization of constituents and grammatical classes. Because the meanings of these two sentences clearly have nothing in common, their identical phrase markers have little to do with meaning.

One important property of phrase structure rules is *recursion*. As the NP rule in Fig. 8.2 specifies, a noun phrase can contain a prepositional phrase, which in turn can contain a noun phrase, which in turn can contain a prepositional phrase, which in turn can contain a noun phrase, and so forth, as in:

the large cage on the lonely dock at the airport terminal in the sun . . .

In other words, phrase structure rules allow the same rule to embed within itself endlessly. This powerful form of structure allows tremendous expressional power and flexibility. Because each new application of a rule produces a new phrase structure, applying a rule recursively an infinite number of times produces an infinite number of phrase markers.

More generally, phrase structure rules are *productive* or *generative*. Imagine applying the four simple rules in Fig. 8.2 to all of the determiners, adjectives, nouns, verbs, and prepositions in English. Through repetition (*) and recursion, these rules can generate an infinite number of sentences. A more complete set of phrase structure rules would be still more powerful. This productive property of phrase structure grammars is important, because it captures the *linguistic creativity* of humans. People rarely utter the same sentence twice. Instead, they produce a tremendous variety of sentences, depending on their current situation and communicative goals. The ability of phrase structure grammars to describe this type of linguistic creativity is one of their most impressive properties.

8.5.2 Verb Frames and Thematic Roles

One limitation of phrase structure grammars is that they don't readily account for thematic roles. Consider the sentences:

Greg obtained the sailboat with compliments.
The sailboat was obtained with compliments.
Compliments obtained the sailboat.

In all three sentences, *Greg* is the *agent*, *sailboat* is the *theme*, and *compliments* is the *instrument* that Greg uses to achieve his goal of obtaining the sailboat, yet phrase markers don't capture these constant roles of *Greg*, *sailboat*, and *compliments*. Instead, they only represent these nouns as parts of noun phrases.

To remedy this problem, the linguist Fillmore (1968, 1977, 1985) proposed that frames for verbs organize syntactic information around *thematic roles* (see **7**.2.2 for further discussion of frames; see also Jackendoff, 1983, 1987; Wilkins, 1988). The frame associated with a verb specifies the thematic roles it can take and where they can occur in a sentence.[1] Consider the frames associated with *walk*, *buy*, and *put*. The frame for the active voice of *walk* specifies that it takes an agent as its subject. An *agent* is typically an animate entity that causes an action to occur, and a *subject* is typically the noun phrase that precedes a verb, as in:

The young infant walked.[2]

The frame for the active voice of *buy* specifies that it takes an agent as its subject and a theme as its direct argument. A *theme* is typically an entity that an agent acts upon, and a *direct argument* is typically a noun phrase that immediately follows a verb, as in:

Debbie bought *a blue dress*.

The frame for the active voice of *put* specifies that it takes an agent as its subject, a theme as a direct argument, and a goal as an indirect argument. A *goal* is typically an end point in an event, and an *indirect argument* is typically a prepositional phrase that follows a verb, as in:

Marjorie put her coat *on the hook*.

Conversely, a *source* is a starting point in an event, as in:

Susan drank juice *from the bottle*.

---

[1] Many linguists currently use *thematic grid* to mean roughly the same thing as *frame*.

[2] In this example and later ones, the thematic role of interest is underlined (i.e., the agent, theme, goal, or source) and the sentential role of interest is italicized (i.e., the subject, direct argument, indirect argument, or oblique argument). Italicized sentential roles are omitted in sentences where only thematic roles are of interest.

As we saw earlier, the frames for the active and passive voices of a verb, when both exist, assign different sentential roles to the same thematic roles: Thus, the active voice of the verb, *clear*, assigns the sentential role of subject to the thematic role of agent, and the sentential role of direct argument to the thematic role of theme, as in:

> The <u>ranger</u> cleared *the trail*.

In contrast, the passive voice of *clear* assigns the sentential role of subject to the thematic role of theme, and the sentential role of oblique argument to the thematic role of agent, as in:

> The *trail* was cleared *by the ranger*.

The thematic roles in a frame vary in status. Some thematic roles are *obligatory* for a verb and must occur in every sentence that contains it. Consider the frame for the verb, *stuff*. Any sentence containing this verb must contain an agent and a goal, as in:

> The <u>chef</u> stuffed the <u>eggplant</u>.

Any sentence that contains only an agent or only a goal for the verb *stuff* is ungrammatical. Other thematic roles are *optional* for a verb and may or may not occur in sentences containing it. Again, consider *stuff*. Any sentence containing this verb can optionally contain a theme, as in:

> The chef stuffed <u>peppers</u> into the eggplant.
> The chef stuffed the eggplant with <u>peppers</u>.

Note that the optional theme can occur as either a direct or indirect argument of the verb, indicating that a frame may sometimes permit flexibility in the positioning of thematic roles within a sentence.

Both phrase markers and verb frames capture essential aspects of syntax. Whereas phrase markers represent constituent structure, verb frames represent thematic roles. Because both types of structure are indispensable to syntax, the syntactic representation of a sentence must contain both. Figure 8.4 illustrates one approach to representing both types of structure for the sentence:

> The chef stuffed peppers into the eggplant.

At the top right, the verb frame for *stuff* specifies three thematic roles for agent, goal, and theme. The frame also specifies the *voice* and *tense* of the verb.

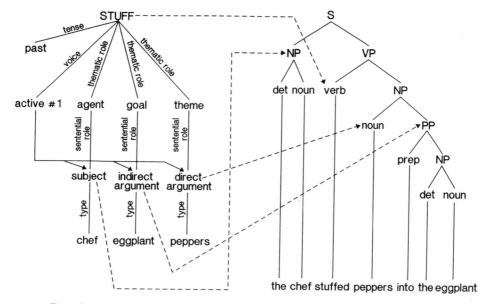

Figure 8.4. An example of a frame that integrates thematic roles and phrase markers.

Because the *voice* of the verb is *active #1*, the verb assigns sentential roles to thematic roles in one particular way: the subject of the verb is the agent, the indirect argument of the verb is the goal, and the direct argument of the verb is the theme. In a moment, we will consider the alternative assignments for *active #2* and a variety of passive voices.

The right side of Fig. 8.4 contains the phrase marker for the sentence, as derived from the phrase structure rules in Fig. 8.2. This phrase marker represents the constituent structure of the sentence, parsing it into noun phrases, a verb phrase, and a prepositional phrase. The dashed lines between the verb frame and the phrase marker represent the key mappings between them. The subject, containing the agent, maps to the first noun phrase of the sentence. The direct argument, containing the theme, maps to the head noun of the noun phrase embedded in the verb phrase. The indirect argument, containing the goal, maps to the prepositional phrase embedded in the verb phrase.

Consider now what the mappings would be if the voice of the verb were *active #2*. As we saw earlier, the assignments of direct and indirect argument reverse: The indirect argument is assigned to the theme, and the direct argument is assigned to the goal, as in:

The chef stuffed *the eggplant* with *peppers*.

Examining Fig. 8.4, you can see that the phrase marker for *active #2* would be no different than the phrase marker for *active #1*. Although the same arrangement of constituents would occur for both active voices, the mappings from the verb frame to the phrase marker would differ, because the assignments of sentential roles to thematic roles in the verb frame have changed. For *active #2*, the goal now maps to the head noun of the noun phrase embedded in the verb phrase, and the theme maps to the prepositional phrase embedded in the verb phrase.

For further examples of how verb frames and phrase markers can combine to represent syntax, consider some of the passive forms of *stuff*, as in:

The eggplant was stuffed with peppers by the chef.
The eggplant was stuffed by the chef with peppers.
The peppers were stuffed into the eggplant by the chef.
The peppers were stuffed by the chef into the eggplant.

Because two prepositional phrases now follow the verb (instead of a noun phrase), the phrase markers for these sentences differ from the one in Fig. 8.4. Because the assignments of sentential roles to thematic roles differ as well, so does the verb frame: For the first of these passives, the subject is assigned to the goal, the indirect argument is assigned to the theme, and the oblique argument is assigned to the agent. Finally, mappings from the verb frame to the phrase marker differ across the various passive voices. As these examples illustrate, using verb frames and phrase markers jointly to represent syntax captures important syntactic similarities and differences among sentences (see also Bresnan, 1978, 1982; Chomsky, 1981; Schieber, 1986).

8.6 SEMANTICS

Semantics specifies the meanings of words, sentences, and texts. Psychologists often use the term "semantics" more broadly, extending it to include any kind of general knowledge (see the discussion of semantic memory in 6.2.1). However, I will follow conventional usage in reserving "semantics" for the meaning of language.

8.6.1 Reference and Image Theories

The meaning of "meaning" is one of the hardest concepts in cognitive science to define. One simple account is *reference theory*: The meaning of a word is simply what it refers to in the world. Thus, "sand" refers to small, loose, granular particles of disintegrated rock. Similarly, "bachelor" refers to those humans who happen to be male, adult, and single. However, this approach has significant problems. What is the meaning of "unicorn" and other expressions that don't have physical referents? Further, what is the meaning of "tiger" in the sentence:

Jerry hunted a tiger.

How can the meaning of "tiger" be its referent, when the referent is not yet known (i.e., the indefinite article "a" in the sentence implies that no particular tiger is being hunted; J.A. Fodor, 1975). Still another problem concerns the meaning of abstract words such as "abstract" and the meaning of function words such as "the." What are the referents of these words? Finally, reference theory has no way of accounting for the meaning of different expressions that have the same referent. For example, "morning star" and "evening star" clearly don't have the same meaning, even though the planet Venus is the referent of both.

Another simple account of meaning is *image theory*: The meaning of a word is an image (5.2.3). Rather than the meaning of a word being its physical referent, the meaning of a word is an image of its referent. For example, the meaning of "sand" might be a visual image of some sand, and the meaning of "bachelor" might be a visual image of a specific bachelor. Like reference theory, image theory has trouble accounting for the meanings of abstract words such as "abstract" and "the." Furthermore, how can image theory account for the generic senses of words, given that images tend to represent specific individuals? Do many different particular images represent the generic concept of *bachelor* simultaneously? Or are these different images somehow amalgamated into a single generic image? For further discussion of reference and image theories, see H.H. Clark and E.V. Clark (1977, chap. 11) and Foss and Hakes (1978, chap. 2).

8.6.2 Truth Conditional Semantics

Formal semantics, the dominant approach to semantics in philosophy and linguistics, assumes that meaning is *truth conditional*. According to this view, the conditions that must hold for a word to be true constitute its meaning (Dowty, Wall, & Peters, 1981). The truth conditions of a word are roughly equivalent to the notion of a concept as a categorization rule. As we saw in 7.2.1, theorists often view a concept as a categorization rule that allows people to discriminate members of a category from non-members. This is essentially the idea behind truth conditional semantics: The concept that identifies the members of a category constitutes the truth conditions for the *word* that refers to the category. For example, the concept, *unmarried adult male human*, constitutes the truth conditions for the word "bachelor." According to truth conditional semantics, the concept that identifies a word's possible referents constitutes its meaning.

Similarly, the meaning of a sentence is the set of conditions that must hold for it to be true. For example, the sentence "The empty cup is in the center of the wooden table" is true under certain conditions and false under others. *Truth functional semantics* assumes that the truth conditions for a sentence are a function of the truth conditions for its individual words. Once the truth conditions for the individual words are known, the truth conditions for the sentence's constituents can be derived, as can the truth conditions for the sentence itself, according to rules of logic. In other words, the truth conditions for a sentence can be viewed as a complex categorization rule, much like those discussed for conceptual combination in **7.2.4**. As we saw in **7.2.4**, however, establishing the truth conditions for a conceptual combination does not always follow the rules of formal logic: People often fail to perform the Boolean operations that logics prescribe for combining conceptual information. Instead, people manipulate frames in ways that theorists are only beginning to understand. Thus, we are far from having a satisfactory account of how to form the truth conditions for the wide variety of conceptual combinations that can occur in sentences (Johnson-Laird, 1983, chap. 8; Osherson & E.E. Smith, 1981, 1982).

In addressing meaning, most cognitive psychologists adopt what might be viewed as a "looser" view of truth conditional semantics. Rather than requiring that the truth conditions of a word be a strict categorization rule, cognitive psychologists often assume that truth conditions revolve more around other kinds of information that are less formal and less definitional. For example, cognitive psychologists often assume that prototypes and exemplars constitute the truth conditions of a word (**2.3.1**, **7.2.2**). As we saw earlier, people use prototypes and exemplars to identify the members of many categories. Because prototypes and exemplars similarly allow us to establish the referents of words, they can constitute the truth conditions of words and therefore constitute their meanings.

Cognitive psychologists often view the truth conditions of sentences in a similar manner: When establishing the truth conditions of a sentence, people use verb frames and other forms of knowledge to integrate prototypes and exemplars for the sentence's words (**7.2.4**, **8.7.4**, **8.7.5**). In section **9.3.3.**, I present examples of how semantic strategies for processing sentences manipulate frames to produce conceptual combinations. In general, cognitive psychologists tend to equate truth conditions and meaning more with knowledge of prototypes, exemplars, and frames than with strict definitional rules and truth functional semantics. This is not surprising, given that psychologists typically assume that prototypes and exemplars—not rules—determine category membership (**2.3.1**).

8.6.3 Sense and Reference

We have gone from one extreme of viewing meaning as reference, to another of viewing meaning as knowledge. Actually, both reference and knowledge are central to meaning. Frege (1892/1952) was the first to have this insight, drawing an important distinction between *sense* and *reference*. According to his view, each word is associated with a sense, which specifies its truth conditions, or in the terms of **7.2.1**, a categorization rule. Frege viewed sense as an abstract, non-psychological description of a referent that human minds may grasp on occasion. However, sense is also quite useful as a psychological construct, and theorists frequently confer this alternative status upon it. According to this view, a word's sense is a cognitively represented rule that allows people to identify its referent, analogous to how a categorization rule allows people to identify a category's members. For example, if someone says "Can you hand me the apple?", the sense for "apple" specifies a rule that enables the listener to identify the entity being requested. Note that formal semanticists often use *intension* and *extension* to mean the same thing as sense and reference (Bechtel, 1988a; Johnson-Laird, 1983; Lyons, 1977a, 1977b).

The distinction between sense and reference solves many of our earlier problems. "Morning star" and "evening star" can have the same referent but differ in meaning, because they have different senses. One sense describes Venus in the morning sky, whereas the other describes Venus in the evening sky. Certain terms, such as "unicorn," may not have referents but still have a sense. In "Jerry hunted a tiger," "tiger" has a sense but not a known referent. Substantial flexibility in meaning can be achieved through the interaction of sense and reference.

The notion of sense, however, must be loosened to accommodate modern psychological theory. Philosophers and linguists typically assume that senses contain definitional information that is necessary and sufficient for category membership (i.e., a rule). As we have seen in **2.3.1**, **7.2.2**, and **8.6.2**, cognitive psychologists believe instead that categorization rules are more likely to contain prototypes and exemplars than rules. Consequently, a more psychological view of sense and reference is that many kinds of knowledge associated with a word—including prototypes, exemplars, and rules—allow people to establish reference.

Another important consideration concerns whether the sense of a term only contains information relevant to establishing reference. As we saw in **7.2.1**, people often conceptualize a category in ways that are not relevant to categorization, using information that is relevant to comprehension, prediction, and action. Imagine that someone says, "Look at that flea crawling across my dog's stomach." The listener may represent the meaning of *flea* with information about where it came from and what it is likely to do, even though this information was not used to establish the referent of "flea" in the speaker's utterance. Moreover, someone may not know how to identify a flea or be able to establish a referent, yet may still understand the main point that the utterance conveys, namely, that an insect having certain origins and dispositions is crawling across the dog's stomach. The psychological senses of words during normal language usage often go far beyond categorization rules.

8.7 PRAGMATICS

Roughly speaking, pragmatics concerns the practical aspects of language that lie beyond its linguistic elements (i.e., its phones, morphemes, sentences, etc.). For example, pragmatics addresses the integration of sentences in texts, the coordination of conversations, and the use of language to achieve goals. As we shall see, pragmatics captures a wide variety of structural patterns at the textual and social levels of linguistic analysis.

8.7.1 The Cooperative Principle

When people communicate with each other, they typically try to be cooperative, unless they are trying to be deceitful or don't care about the success of the interaction. The philosopher Grice (1975) summarized the nature of this cooperation with four maxims:

Quality: Utterances should be true and based on sound evidence.   If I were now to state that the cooperative principle has a biological basis in the brain, I would violate the maxim of quality, because I have no evidence for this claim.

Quantity: Utterances should be as informative as possible but not more informative than required.   If I were now to describe everything ever written about the maxim of quantity, I would violate it, because I am conveying more information than the reader probably wants to know.

Relation: Utterances should be relevant to the goals of the current conversation.   If I were now to describe a time I once went surfing in La Jolla, I would violate the maxim of relation, because surfing has nothing to do with the topic of this chapter.

Manner: Utterances should be clear, unambiguous, and orderly.   If I were now to state, "Conversational implicatures around the corner," I would violate the maxim of manner, because I am not stating clearly that the next topic is conversational implicatures.

In normal cooperative communication, people typically follow Grice's maxims. However, they also cooperate frequently in *violating* these maxims. Sometimes a speaker violates a maxim obviously, thereby signaling to the listener that the literal meaning of the utterance is false. The listener then assesses the nature of the violation in the current context to draw a *conversational implicature* and thereby establish the speaker's intended meaning.

Imagine that you hear a great review of a movie, claiming it to be the best of the year. You convince a reluctant friend, who has heard the opposite, to go. Half an hour into the movie, you both leave because the movie is terrible. On the way out your friend says, "That was indeed the best movie of the year." Obviously, your friend is not trying to deceive you. Instead, this blatant violation of the maxim of quality authorizes you to draw certain implicatures. In particular, your friend has authorized you to infer that the movie was lousy, that you are responsible for his going to see it, and that your opinion may receive less credence in the future.

Consider some further examples. After a disappointing date, a friend might state in response to your request for information, "He had neatly polished shoes." By obviously violating the maxim of quantity, your friend has authorized inferring that her date didn't have much going for him. After a much more enjoyable date, your friend might say instead, "Wonderful day, isn't it?" Here, obviously violating the maxim of relation, your friend has now authorized you to infer that her date was splendid and that she'd rather not talk about it. As these examples demonstrate, cooperative violations of pragmatic conventions endow people's utterances with subtlety and playfulness (see also Gibbs, 1984, 1986, 1989.)

8.7.2 Common Ground

As we saw earlier, people use word senses to establish reference. Cooperation is also essential to this process. Imagine that a friend utters the following sentence:

Consider the stallion.

If the two of you are in a pasture with a horse, you infer that "stallion" refers to the horse, but if the two of you are in an art gallery near a painting of a horse, you infer that "stallion" refers to the painting, or if the two of you are in a veterinary laboratory that contains blood samples from different animals, you infer that "stallion" refers to a blood sample.

"Stallion" has very different referents in these three examples, including a live stallion, a painting of a stallion, and a blood sample of a stallion. Such examples are impossible to reconcile with a standard psychological assumption that meaning is equivalent to knowledge. The meaning of "stallion" in these examples cannot be equated with a prototype, definition, or previous exemplars. Instead, the meaning of "stallion" depends critically on whether the speaker and the listener can coordinate what "stallion" refers to in their *common ground*. If the speaker and listener are both aware of a blood sample of a stallion, then the blood sample lies in their common ground, and the listener can probably establish reference to it. However, if the listener is not aware of a blood sample from a stallion, he may establish reference incorrectly, perhaps inferring that "stallion" refers to a live stallion. Communication fails because the blood sample was not in common ground.

Speakers and listeners constantly assess and update their common ground so that reference can succeed. According to H.H. Clark and Marshall (1981), one way that referents enter common ground is through *physical co-presence*. If a speaker and listener have just been analyzing a blood sample from a stallion together, then it is an obvious referent for "stallion." Because the two conversationalists know that each has perceived the referent recently, they can assume that it will be considered as a possible referent of referring terms.

Entities can also enter common ground through *linguistic co-presence*. If I say, "The clown was outrageous last night," you cannot establish the referent of "clown," because it is not physically co-present. If, however, I had told you previously that my friend George went to a costume party last night as a clown, you can easily establish that the outrageous clown is my friend George. In other words, entities that have been mentioned in the conversation previously enter common ground and become likely referents for later utterances. As we shall see in **9**.6.1, linguistically co-present information becomes increasingly less active in memory with the passage of time, such that references to it become increasingly difficult.

Finally, entities can enter common ground through *cultural co-presence*. If I say, "Peachtree goes on forever," you may have trouble establishing the referent of "Peachtree," unless you know the city of Atlanta, where Peachtree Street extends through much of the metropolitan area. A speaker can assume that such entities are in common ground if the listener shares a similar cultural background. Without such background, a speaker must fall back on linguistic co-presence, stating first that Peachtree is Atlanta's preeminent thoroughfare.

Conversationalists constantly use physical, linguistic, and cultural co-presence to assess and update common ground. To the extent that such attempts are successful, speakers can design utterances that optimize their listeners' ability to identify intended referents. Figure 8.5 summarizes how conversationalists coordinate word senses and common ground to establish meaning.

8.7.3 Speech Acts

Unlike the examples we have considered thus far, utterances do not always describe a state of affairs. People also use language to achieve other goals,

Coordinating Word Senses and Common Ground to Establish Meaning

---

(1) **Conversationalists enter a communicative setting with word senses that include definitions, prototypes, and exemplars.**

(2) **To establish initial common ground, conversationalists identify referents that are culturally co-present.**

(3) **Additional common ground becomes established through physical and linguistic co-presence over the course of the conversation.**

(4) **When a speaker intends to refer to something, he or she selects a linguistic expression that optimizes the listener's chances of correctly identifying the intended referent in the common ground.**

(5) **Upon hearing the expression, the listener activates the relevant word senses associated with it as part of its meaning.**

(6) **The listener compares potential referents in common ground with the sense of the expression.**

(7) **The listener selects the potential referent that is most similar to the sense of the expression and adds it to the expression's meaning.**

(8) **If the listener is not confident that the referent is what the speaker intended, the listener may request additional sense information about the referent from the speaker.**

Figure 8.5.   The pragmatics of establishing meaning.

such as getting a listener to do something. Listeners must not only establish what an utterance means literally (its *locutionary force*), they must also establish the speaker's goal in stating it (*illocutionary force*), and they may act on their interpretation of the utterance (*perlocutionary force*). Speech act theory, developed initially by philosophers J.L. Austin (1962) and Searle (1969), attempts to account for the very general types of goals that people attempt to achieve with language. Five important types of speech acts are:

Representatives: Utterances that convey the belief a proposition is true.   These are essentially descriptions of the world (e.g., "My desk has disappeared").

Directives: Utterances that attempt to get a listener to do something.   These include commanding, requesting, pleading, and begging, which vary in the relative status of the speaker and listener (e.g., "Stop putting things on my desk" vs. "I beg you to stop putting things on my desk").

Commissives: Utterances that commit the speaker to some future course of action. These include promises and threats (e.g., "I'll throw into the trash anything more that you put on my desk").

Expressives: Utterances that assert something about the speaker's psychological state. These include descriptions of how one feels (e.g., "I feel overwhelmed with everything I have to do") and evaluations of external states (e.g., "I'm glad it's raining outside").

Declarations: Utterances that bring about a new state of affairs in the world. These include utterances that hire someone, fire someone, and pronounce a couple to be husband and wife (e.g., "You're hired").

Establishing the intended speech act of an utterance is not always straightforward. Whereas some speech acts can be determined from the literal meaning of an utterance, *indirect speech acts* cannot. Consider the following utterances:

What is your name?
What is the world coming to?

If literal meaning always signaled speech acts, both of these utterances would be directives, because both are literally questions. Although the first utterance is indeed a directive, the second is actually an expressive, with the speaker revealing angst about current events. Indirect speech acts can become quite complex, as in:

You are standing on my shoes.

Although this utterance is literally a declarative, it is also a directive (get off my shoes), an expressive (you are hurting my feet), and possibly a commissive (if you don't get off my shoes, I will remove you myself). Inferring a speaker's intended speech act is often a complex process requiring a careful assessment of context (Gibbs, 1984, 1986, 1989).

8.7.4 Discourse Propositions

Rarely does a conversation consist of a single sentence. Instead, a speaker often strings together many sentences to form a *discourse*, and the listener must integrate these sentences to form a coherent discourse representation.

Theorists generally believe that *propositions* underlie the structure of a discourse (J.R. Anderson, 1976, 1983; J.R. Anderson & Bower, 1973; H.H. Clark & E.V. Clark, 1977; Just & Carpenter, 1987; Kintsch & van Dijk, 1978; van Dijk & Kintsch, 1983). One way to view a proposition is as an instantiated frame that corresponds to an exemplar (P.J. Hayes, 1979). As we saw in

7.2.2, frames are category representations that contain attributes integrated by relations. For example, the frame for *car* contains attributes for *engine*, *transmission*, *wheels*, and so forth, integrated by relations such as *operates* and *rotates* (see Fig. 7.2). To represent a category exemplar, specific aspects of the exemplar instantiate the frame's attributes as values (Fig. 7.3). For example, if Liz's car has a four-cylinder engine and a standard transmission, then applying the frame for *car* to this exemplar produces the following proposition:

CAR
(OWNER = Liz)
(ENGINE = four-cylinder)
(TRANSMISSION = standard)

Note that a complete propositional analysis would require that frames include further information, such as information about quantifiers (e.g., there is *one* car that the frame represents). All of the examples of frames here and in later chapters are greatly simplified for the sake of brevity and clarity.

More technically, a proposition is a unit of knowledge that can be either true or false. If the proposition just mentioned about Liz is true, then the following proposition about her is false, assuming that she only owns one car:

CAR
(OWNER = Liz)
(ENGINE = eight-cylinder)
(TRANSMISSION = standard)

This proposition is false, because the engine of Liz's car is has four cylinders. Note that an instantiated frame is not a proposition if it does not purport to be about the world. Because discourses are typically about the world, however, the exemplars they describe constitute propositions that can potentially be true or false.

A sentence in a discourse may contain multiple propositions. Consider the sentence:

Fred, the incompetent sales representative, lost my new skis.

This sentence contains three interrelated propositions:

SALES REPRESENTATIVE   **LOST**   **SKIS**
(NAME = Fred)   (AGENT = ↑)   (OWNER = me)
(COMPETENCE = low)   (OBJECT = ↓)   (AGE = new)

Constructing these propositions and integrating them is a complicated matter. As we have seen, logical approaches, such as fuzzy set theory and truth functional semantics, fail to account for the tremendous variety of conceptual combinations possible (**7**.2.4, **8**.6.2). Instead, people appear to use less formal procedures that manipulate frames to construct propositional representations. For example, the meaning of "incompetent sales representative" is not the simple intersection of the categories for *incompetent*, *sales*, and *representative*. Nor is it the union of their conceptual properties. Instead, people somehow manipulate frames to construct a coherent combination of these three concepts. Section **9**.3.3 provides examples of semantic strategies for processing sentences that integrate frames to produce conceptual combinations. Again, theorists have much to learn about conceptual combination. Moreover, theories of conceptual combination need to account not only for the combination of word senses in sentences, but also for the ultimate establishment of reference.

Another difficult issue concerns which attributes of a frame to modify in forming a proposition. In the last example, frame attributes were only instantiated if the sentence mentioned them. For example, the only attributes instantiated for *sales representative* were *name* and *competence*, because the sentence mentioned "Fred" and "incompetent." Following our discussions of constraints (**7**.2.2, **7**.2.4), however, we know that people may also instantiate additional attributes with default values: Thus, they might assume that Fred's *age* is *young* and that his *athleticism* is *high*, given that young skiers often work in ski shops (Medin & Shoben, 1988). Consequently, a complete propositional representation of a sentence must include all activated information, regardless of whether a text mentions it explicitly (Schank, 1975; Schank & Abelson, 1977).

8.7.5 Referent Models

The purpose of communication is to describe, evaluate, and/or control a particular state of affairs. People use representatives to describe a state of affairs; they use expressives to evaluate it; and they use directives, commissives, and declarations to control it (**8**.7.3). At most points during a linguistic interaction, conversationalists attempt to coordinate common ground (**8**.7.2), such that they can construct a shared propositional representation of the topic, namely, a *referent model*. As a conversation progresses, the referent model evolves as the conversationalists add, delete, and transform its propositions. Note that a referent model is only a subset of common ground, which can contain other information as well (e.g., culturally shared knowledge, beliefs, and assumptions not currently under discussion). Referent models are similar to what theorists often call *mental models* and *situation models*

(7.2.2; Johnson-Laird, 1983; Just & Carpenter, 1987; Kintsch & van Dijk, 1978; van Dijk & Kintsch, 1983).

As a reader or listener comprehends a text, how are its propositions integrated into an evolving referent model? This is the problem of conceptual combination at the discourse level and is arguably the most central issue in discourse theory. If people cannot integrate the propositions in a text, then they cannot construct a coherent referent model for it. Imagine that the following sentence begins a discourse:

Rick, feeling festive, rented a house near a tropical reef.   (1)

Upon reading this sentence, one activates frames for *Rick, rent, house,* and *reef* to represent its propositions in an initial referent model (see Fig. 8.6). The number following each frame in Fig. 8.6 indicates the sentence that first mentioned it (e.g., Rick[1] indicates that Sentence 1 was the first to mention Rick).

Imagine that the following sentence continues the discourse:

Rick had recently built a house worth three million dollars.   (2)

How does one integrate the propositions from this sentence with those from Sentence 1? The central strategy is to determine which linguistic expressions in the current sentence refer back to propositions from previous sentences, or more technically, *anaphora.* One anaphoric device is *repetition* of the same linguistic expression. Upon encountering "Rick" in Sentence 2, one assumes that it refers to the *Rick* mentioned in Sentence 1. Figure 8.6 indicates this *co-reference* by representing *Rick* as the agent of both the *RENT* and *BUILD* propositions. However, repetition does not always signal co-reference. Although "a house" occurs in both Sentences 1 and 2, these two expressions represent different category exemplars. As a result, *house #1* is the object of *RENT,* whereas *house #2* is the object of *BUILD.*

The next sentence continues:

He had visited the reef long ago.   (3)

This sentence illustrates two more anaphoric devices. First, *pronouns,* such as "he," signal anaphoric reference. As a result, the agent of *VISIT* is assumed to be "Rick" in Fig. 8.6, because "he" refers to a male organism, and no other male organism has been mentioned thus far in the discourse. Second, *definite reference,* such as "the reef," may also signal anaphoric reference. If Sentence 3 had contained an *indefinite reference* to "*a* reef" instead of a definite reference to "*the* reef," it would imply that Rick had visited a reef long ago that differs from the one near the house he has rented. Instead, "reef" in this sentence

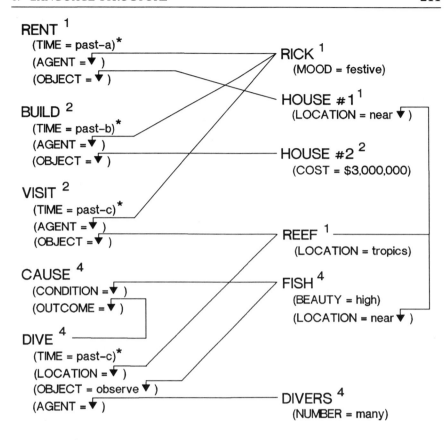

RENT [1]
   (TIME = past-a)*
   (AGENT = ▼)
   (OBJECT = ▼)

BUILD [2]
   (TIME = past-b)*
   (AGENT = ▼)
   (OBJECT = ▼)

VISIT [2]
   (TIME = past-c)*
   (AGENT = ▼)
   (OBJECT = ▼)

CAUSE [4]
   (CONDITION = ▼)
   (OUTCOME = ▼)

DIVE [4]
   (TIME = past-c)*
   (LOCATION = ▼)
   (OBJECT = observe ▼)
   (AGENT = ▼)

RICK [1]
   (MOOD = festive)

HOUSE #1 [1]
   (LOCATION = near ▼)

HOUSE #2 [2]
   (COST = $3,000,000)

REEF [1]
   (LOCATION = tropics)

FISH [4]
   (BEAUTY = high)
   (LOCATION = near ▼)

DIVERS [4]
   (NUMBER = many)

* time-c ‹ time-b ‹ time-a

Figure 8.6.   An example of a developing referent model.

refers back to the reef introduced in Sentence 1 (see Fig. 8.6). Conversely, the indefinite reference to "a house" in Sentence 2 signals that this house is not the same as the house in Sentence 1.

Definite reference does not always signal co-reference, as the final sentence of the discourse illustrates:

The fish had been beautiful, and many divers were present.   (4)

"The fish" does not refer to anything mentioned previously in the discourse, but this definite reference does refer to something *associated* with a referent mentioned earlier, namely, *reef*: Because fish often accompany reefs, one may infer that "The fish" in Sentence 4 are near the reef in the referent model (as Fig. 8.6 illustrates). General knowledge about the world often enables anaphoric inference in this manner. If one did not know that reefs have fish swimming around them, reference could not be established.

The second half of Sentence 4 provides a still more complex example of how general knowledge supports the integration of discourse propositions: One must infer that the beautiful fish *caused* many divers to be present. Without general knowledge about the reasons people dive, this inference would be impossible, and one would be unable to connect the two halves of the sentence. Note that this use of general knowledge has inserted a proposition into the referent model that the discourse does not mention explicitly, namely, the causal relation between diving and fish (see Fig. 8.6). As numerous theorists have proposed, readers and listeners constantly add inferred propositions to a referent model in order to make it coherent (Just & Carpenter, 1987, chaps. 7 & 8; Schank & Abelson, 1977; van Dijk & Kintsch, 1983). Rarely does a writer or speaker provide all of the necessary information explicitly.

As we have seen from this example, integrating discourse propositions is extremely complicated: Sometimes a repeated word indicates co-reference and sometimes not. Usually a new word does not indicate co-reference, but sometimes it does. Comprehension often requires the inferring of new referents that the text does not mention explicitly, as well as implicit relations between propositions. A wide variety of linguistic devices, accompanied by general knowledge, allow us to manage the spectrum of conceptual combinations that arise during the construction of a referent model (**9**.6.1).

CONCLUSION

The structure of language is complex yet elegant. As we have seen, linguistic utterances and language behavior exhibit systematic patterns at many levels of analysis. From phonetics to pragmatics, structural patterns emerge. Remarkably, all of these patterns coordinate smoothly to enable communication. Rarely do people struggle to comprehend or produce language. Still more rarely are people aware of the processes that underlie these abilities. Whatever mechanisms are responsible must be truly remarkable.

9

LANGUAGE PROCESSES

In the previous chapter, I reviewed structural characteristics of linguistic utterances and language behavior. In this chapter, I address the cognitive processes that produce this structure. I begin with speech perception, examining the cognitive mechanisms that underlie the processing of phones and phonemes. I then address lexical access and the processing of sentences, examining the cognitive mechanisms that underlie morphology, syntax, and semantics. In the section on immediacy of interpretation, I review the important role that top-down processing plays in language. Two final sections address sentence memory and discourse processing, focusing on the mechanisms that extract propositions from text and integrate them into referent models. Although most of this chapter focuses on language comprehension, a final section reviews language production.

9.1 SPEECH PERCEPTION

People's ability to recognize phoneme sequences is impressive. Consider four properties of the normal speech signal:

Rapid rate.   Given that normal speech contains an average of 15 phonemes per second, people categorize about 1 phoneme every 67 msec. If pushed, they can even categorize normal speech that has been speeded up to a rate of 50 phonemes per second, or about 1 phoneme every 20 msec (Foulke &

Sticht, 1969; Liberman, F.S. Cooper, Shankweiler, & Studdert-Kennedy, 1967).

Absence of clear boundaries.   One might expect brief periods of silence to lie between adjacent phonemes, isolating the information critical to each phoneme in a sequence. However, acoustic analysis of speech shows that phonemes typically blend into one another, with periods of silence occasionally occurring for stop consonants and pauses in speaking. Speakers do not mark phoneme boundaries clearly. Worse yet, segments of speech often carry information about more than one phoneme, namely, *parallel transmission* or *co-articulation.* As one phoneme blends into another, the speech segment in which the blending occurs simultaneously provides information about both (Liberman et al., 1967).

Variability.   The information that specifies a given phoneme varies widely (2.1). For example, the acoustic information produced for /d/ varies across different words that contain this phoneme (e.g., *d*elight, *d*apper, *d*ubious). Moreover, the acoustic information for /d/ within the same word varies across different registers (e.g., yelling, whispering, singing) and across different speakers (e.g., males vs. females, children vs. adults, Katharine Hepburn vs. Meryl Streep; Liberman, 1970).

Low quality information.   The quality of information in the speech stream is typically quite poor. Only about 50% of the words uttered in normal speech are intelligible when presented in isolation. The remaining words are unintelligible unless presented in the context of the words that surround them (Pollack & Pickett, 1964).

How, then, are people able to categorize low quality phonemes whose characteristics vary widely as they blend into one another at a rate of 15 phonemes per second? The following sections address various cognitive mechanisms that underlie this impressive ability. As of yet, cognitive psychologists have no complete theory. If they did, they would be closer to building a speech recognition device that could understand any speaker of a language, just as all of its speakers can.

9.1.1 Processing Phonetic Features

As we saw in **8**.2, linguists have characterized the structure of phones according to their articulatory features, describing [b] as a voiced bilabial stop, and so on. What evidence exists that people use these features to categorize phones?

In a classic study, G.A. Miller and Nicely (1955) presented consonant-vowel syllables such as [pa], [ba], [sa], and [za] to subjects, where the vowel in every syllable was [a], and only the preceding phone for the consonant varied.

The syllables occurred in loud background noise so that they were difficult to categorize. The data of interest were the confusions that subjects made when they erred in categorizing these syllables. When subjects miscategorized [ba], for example, which syllables were they most likely to confuse with it? Miller and Nicely found that subjects were more likely to confuse a presented syllable with a non-presented syllable to the extent that their respective consonants shared articulatory features. So, subjects frequently confused [ba] with [da], because the consonants in both are voiced stops and only differ in place of articulation. In contrast, subjects rarely confused [ba] with [sa], because the consonants in these two syllables share no articulatory features. Researchers using other methodologies have obtained similar results (Greenberg & Jenkins, 1964; Mohr & Wang, 1968; Pisoni, 1975; Pisoni & P.A. Luce, 1987; Shepard, 1972; Wish & Carroll, 1974). For example, subjects judge two phones as subjectively similar if their articulatory features overlap and subjectively dissimilar if they do not (**10**.2). Together, these findings strongly suggest that people use articulatory features to categorize phones.

9.1.2 Processing Acoustic Cues

The ability to identify phones utilizes information about articulatory features, but how do people first identify these articulatory features? What acoustic cues allow one to identify the stop in [p], the voicing in [b]?

Researchers often use *speech spectrograms* to address this issue. For a given speech sound, a speech spectrogram plots its pitch (i.e., frequency) and loudness as a function of time. Consider Fig. 9.1, which shows spectrograms for [bab], [dad], and [gag] uttered in sequence. Each spectrogram plots time on the *x*-axis and pitch on the *y*-axis. Darkness represents loudness, with greater darkness corresponding to greater loudness. Wherever a spectrogram is blank, no sound exists. Wherever a spectrogram is gray or black, there is sound at that pitch at some loudness. Figure 9.1 further illustrates how several bands of sound typically occur over the time course of a syllable. In [bab], for example, the lowest band of sound occurs between 300 and 700 hertz (Hz, or cycles per second), another occurs between 1200 and 1600 Hz, and another occurs between 2000 and 2400 Hz. These bands of sound are called *formants*, with the lowest formant being the *first formant*, the one above it being the *second formant*, and so on. Typically, the first two or three formants are sufficient to categorize a phone. Although formants at higher frequencies exist, they don't appear as relevant to identifying a phone as lower formants (Ladefoged, 1981).

Researchers have identified patterns in spectrograms that signal articulatory features (Painter, 1979; Tartter, 1986, chap. 7). In Fig. 9.1, consider how all of the formants rise from 0 to 30 msec for [bab] and how three of the formants fall for [gag]. *Transitions* such as these typically indicate the presence

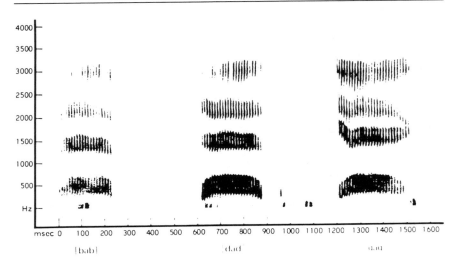

Figure 9.1. Examples of speech spectrograms from Ladefoged (1975). Reproduced by permission.

of the *stop* feature, which occurs for [b] and [g]. In contrast, consider how the internal parts of the syllables are flat (e.g., from 30 to 200 msec in [bab]). *Steady states* such as these typically indicate the presence of a vowel, such as [a]. Many other acoustic cues, including the pitch of a transition, the slope of a transition, and the relative loudness of two formants, similarly signal other articulatory features, such as *bilabial* and *voiced*.

Spectrograms allow researchers to address the issue of parallel transmission. Imagine what might happen if researchers tried to separate the initial consonant from the subsequent vowel in one of the syllables in Fig. 9.1. Using a speech synthesizer, an experimenter could construct the initial transitions in [bab] from 0 to 30 msec and nothing else. On hearing these transitions, would listeners hear [b]? No, they would simply hear a chirp, indicating that [b] is distributed into the steady states that also represent [a].

Spectrograms allow researchers to address the issue of variability. How stable is the acoustic information that specifies an articulatory feature? Do the same acoustic cues always specify an articulatory feature across utterances? Consider the transitions that begin [dad] in Fig. 9.1. To what extent do these particular transitions specify a stop for different instances of [d], such as the [d] in [dad], [did], and [dud]? Do the same transitions occur for [d] in every syllable, or do different transitions occur for [d] in different phonetic contexts?

Analyses of spectrograms have provided a clear and sobering answer to this question. Consider Fig. 9.2. Each panel shows the first two formants for the same consonant in different vowel contexts. For example, the top panel shows the first two formants for [b] when followed by [i], [e], and so forth.

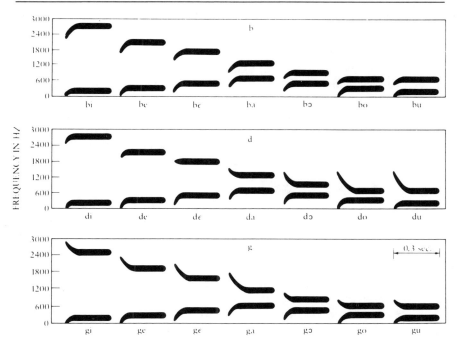

Figure 9.2. Examples of how the first and second formants for a consonant vary in different vowel contexts. From Delattre, Liberman, and F.S. Cooper (1955), reproduced by permission.

Note how different the transitions are for the same consonant when different vowels follow it, especially in *pitch*: For [d], the first and second formant transitions start at around 0 Hz and 2400 Hz prior to [i] but start at around 400 Hz and 1600 Hz prior to [a]. Moreover, the *direction* of the transitions can vary as well: Whereas the second formant for [d] rises prior to [i], it falls prior to [u] (Delattre et al., 1955).

These examples illustrate the formidable variety of acoustic forms that the same phone can take. Given this variability, what allows people to categorize different acoustic signals as instances of the same phone? What acoustic invariants, if any, define a phone category? In general, it is hard to find a single acoustic characteristic that remains constant across all instances of a phone. Instead, the characteristics that define a phone depend on the phones that surround it and on its position in a syllable. In other words, different combinations of acoustic cues specify the same phone in different phonetic contexts. Although these different combinations are often systematically related to one another, they typically exhibit few, if any, simple commonalities. Whatever mechanism performs phone categorization is obviously quite complex and dynamic, being able to utilize many sources of interacting information (Repp & Liberman, 1987; Tartter, 1986, chap. 7).

9.1.3 Categorical Perception

Given the tremendous variability in acoustic cues, one might think that subjective perception of the same phone would vary widely, but do all of the different acoustic forms of [d] actually sound different? Perhaps the cognitive system produces the same subjective experience for all of them, discarding their idiosyncrasies. To study this issue, researchers use speech synthesizers to construct artificial phones that sound much like human language. Imagine that researchers construct different versions of the same phone. Upon hearing these different versions, can people tell them apart, or do they perceive them as identical?

Consider [b], which is a voiced bilabial stop. Different instances of [b] vary in *voice onset time* (VOT), which is an acoustic cue that specifies voicing. In most instances of [b], the vocal chords begin vibrating *before* air is released for the bilabial stop. VOT is simply how much time elapses between the onset of vocal chord vibration and air release. For example, a VOT of -100 means that voicing begins 100 msec before air release. As we have seen, [p] is also a bilabial stop, differing only from [b] in the absence of voicing. For [p], the vocal chords begin vibrating *after* air is released for the bilabial stop. Whereas the values of VOT are typically negative for [b], they are usually positive for [p]. For example, a [p] might have a VOT of 100, which means that voicing begins 100 msec after air release.

Using a speech synthesizer, researchers can construct bilabial stops that vary continuously in VOT, with all other acoustic cues held constant. What happens as VOT varies from -150 to 150? Which of these stimuli sound like [b], which sound like [p], and which, if any, are indeterminate? The left panel of Fig. 9.3 illustrates two possibilities. According to many prototype and exemplar models, phone categorization should show the standard graded structure effect (2.3.2, 7.3.2). To see this, assume that the prototypical VOT for [b] is -150, whereas the prototypical VOT for [p] is 150. Categorization should be best for VOTs near these prototypes. As VOTs move away from a prototype, they become less similar to the correct prototype and more similar to the competing prototype. For example, a VOT of 50 is less similar to the prototype for [p] than a VOT of 75, while simultaneously being more similar to the prototype for [b]. As a result, the ability to categorize a VOT of 50 as a [p] should be worse than the ability to categorize a VOT of 75.

Alternatively, the mechanisms that categorize phones may function *categorically*, such that people categorize a wide variety of acoustic cues equally well as members of the same phonetic category. The left panel of Fig. 9.3 illustrates this prediction for *categorical perception*. As can be seen, people should categorize all stimuli with a VOT less than some critical value perfectly as [b], but categorize all stimuli with a VOT greater than this critical value perfectly as [p]. In other words, they should treat the stimuli within a phonetic category as equivalent, regardless of VOT differences between them.

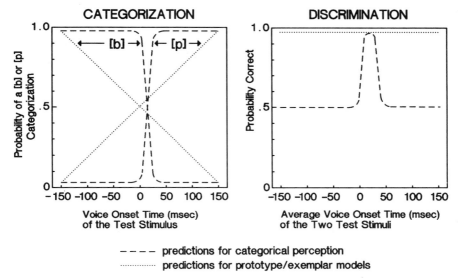

Figure 9.3. Predictions of categorical perception and prototype/exemplar models for phone categorization and discrimination.

Many studies have found that [b] and [p] exhibit categorical perception when VOT varies continuously. Whereas people categorize nearly all bilabial stops having a VOT less than 30 as [b], they categorize nearly all bilabial stops having a VOT greater than 30 as [p]. Numerous studies have also found that many other acoustic cues, besides VOT, exhibit categorical perception (see the collection of papers in Harnad, 1987).

Still stronger evidence for categorical perception comes from discrimination tasks. Imagine that a researcher selects pairs of bilabial stops whose VOT always differs by 20. For example, one pair might have VOTs of − 100 and − 80, and another might have VOTs of 20 and 40. On each trial, a subject hears the two members of a pair in a random order. The subject then hears a test stimulus, which is the same as either the first or second member of the pair. If the pair consists of a − 80 VOT stimulus followed by a − 100 VOT stimulus, the test stimulus might be the − 100 VOT stimulus. The subject's task is to say whether the test stimulus is the same as the first or second pair member. If subjects can tell the difference between the pair members, they should be able to answer correctly, but if the pair members sound the same, subjects' responses should simply reflect guessing (i.e., 50% correct).

Of primary interest is whether subjects can discriminate different phones within a phone category. Can subjects tell the difference between two [b]s, one with a VOT of − 80 and one with a VOT of − 100? If not, then the processing of these phones is indeed categorical. Also of interest is whether discrimination is higher for pairs that straddle the category boundary. Can subjects tell the difference between a 20-VOT stimulus and a 40-VOT stimulus that straddle the 30-VOT boundary between [b] and [p]? According to categorical perception, subjects should discriminate this pair easily, because the two stimuli receive different phonetic categorizations, [b] and [p]. The right panel of Fig. 9.3 summarizes these predictions for categorical perception: Whereas subjects should exhibit no discrimination for pairs within categories, they should exhibit excellent discrimination for pairs between categories.[1]

In contrast, prototype and exemplar models predict that pairs within categories should be discriminable: If subjects categorize an 80-VOT [p] better than a 60-VOT [p] (as the left panel Fig. 9.3 illustrates), then subjects must perceive these stimuli as different. The right panel of Fig. 9.3 shows these predictions of perfect discrimination for prototype and exemplar models.

Across a wide variety of experiments, discrimination data have somewhat supported categorical perception (Harnad, 1987). In general, discrimination is much poorer within categories than between them, when the distance between a pair of stimuli remains constant. In many experiments, however, discrimination is still well above chance within categories. People generally exhibit some ability to discriminate different instances of the same phone, although discrimination remains better between categories than within them.

Theorists believe that within-category discrimination is only possible when acoustic cues for the two phones remain in the cognitive system. If testing occurs while acoustic information remains, subjects can discriminate the original stimuli on the basis of their acoustic differences (e.g., VOT). Thus, if subjects maintain acoustic memories of a 60-VOT [p] and an 80-VOT [p] and then hear an 80-VOT as a test, they can respond correctly. Once phonemic categories replace these acoustic representations, however, subjects cannot discriminate the original stimuli, because the phonemic categories are identical. Thus, if subjects replace the 60-VOT [p] and the 80-VOT [p] with /p/ and /p/, respectively, an 80-VOT test stimulus will not discriminate between them.

As of yet, we have no comprehensive theory of categorical perception. Nevertheless, we have learned that the cognitive system discards acoustic information early in processing, retaining only categorical representations of phonemes. Whatever the nature of the mechanisms responsible, they channel information varying on many continuous acoustic dimensions into the discrete phonemic categories that later retrieve words.

Note that we still haven't considered an additional problem raised earlier:

---

[1] The x-axis in the right panel of Fig. 9.3 represents the average VOT of the two stimuli in a pair. Thus, if a 60-VOT [p] and an 80-VOT [p] constitute the two stimuli in a pair, their average VOT is 70, and the probability of subjects making a correct discrimination lies above 70 on the x-axis.

The acoustic cues that specify phonemes are often of *low quality*. Recall that when people hear words from continuous speech in isolation, they can only recognize about half of them. In many cases, the acoustic cues that specify a word are not of sufficiently good quality to produce its categorization. We shall return to this problem later in discussing immediacy of interpretation (**9**.4), after we explore the roles of lexical access and sentence processing in comprehension. As we shall see, lexical, syntactic, and semantic mechanisms exert powerful top-down effects on speech perception, helping to overcome the tremendous problem of low quality information that bottom-up categorization faces.

9.2 LEXICAL ACCESS

As phoneme categories become are assigned to speech sounds, they access (retrieve) words. How does this occur? The *cohort model* provides one possible account (Marslen-Wilson, 1987; Marslen-Wilson & Tyler, 1980). According to this model, people use each successive phoneme from a word to narrow down the cohort of possible words until a single word remains. Consider the access of *rose*. Upon first identifying an /r/ in the speech stream, one activates the large cohort of words beginning with this phoneme, including *ranger, rosary, river, rogue, rambunctious, road, rose*, and so forth. On next identifying an /o/, one narrows the cohort down to the smaller set of words beginning with /ro/, including *rogue, road, rose*, and so forth. On next identifying /z/, the cohort is narrowed down to the still smaller set of words beginning with /roz/, including *rosary* and *rose*. If no more phonemes follow, then only *rose* remains, which becomes the categorization of /roz/. If another word follows, such as *garden*, then *rose* is still the categorization, because no word corresponds to /rozg/ or contains it initially. Instead, the initial /g/ in *garden* begins the cohort activation and selection process anew. As we shall see later (**9**.4.1), the cohort model not only accounts for bottom-up processing in lexical access, but also for the top-down effects that occur pervasively during immediacy of interpretation. For an alternative model of speech perception, see McClelland and Elman (1986). For further discussion of lexical access during speech perception, see a special issue of the journal *Cognition* (1987, Vol. 25, No. 1).

So far in this chapter, we have only considered the language processing that occurs during spoken language, but people also process language visually during reading. To what extent do the phenomena in spoken language occur in written language? In many ways, the processing of speech and writing are similar, sharing a wide variety of cognitive mechanisms. Many of the phenomena observed for spoken language also occur for written language. Where the two forms of language differ most obviously is in the perception of their elementary units: Whereas speech relies on the categorization of phones, reading relies on the categorization of orthographic symbols for letters. In reading "rose," for example, one must categorize orthographic symbols for "r," "o," "s," and "e." Once these letters have been recognized, they access the lexical unit for *rose*. Because I have already discussed the visual categorization of letters in written words (**2.5**, Fig. 2.9), I do not pursue this topic further here.

In the next section, however, I digress to address a phenomenon that is unique to reading: the phonological recoding of orthographic symbols during lexical access. I then return to phenomena in lexical access that occur in speech as well as in reading, and all of the remaining phenomena that I address in this chapter will be relevant to both forms of language as well. For further discussion of letter and word perception in reading, see Crowder (1982b), Just and Carpenter (1987), McClelland and Rumelhart (1981), Rayner (1983), and Rumelhart and McClelland (1982). For similarities between speech and reading in lexical access, see Bradley and Forster (1987) and D.P. Hayes (1988).

9.2.1 Phonological Recoding in Reading

As one categorizes orthographic letters during normal reading, are they recoded phonologically? Sometimes, people experience phonological recoding subjectively, "hearing" the idiosyncratic speech characteristics of the author as they read (especially if the reader has heard the author speak). Many forms of phonological recoding are possible. In *pre-access recoding*, one recodes the letters of a written word into phonological representations, which then access words, just as in speech perception. Orthographic information does not access words directly but only serves to activate the phonemes that do. Alternatively, in *post-access recoding*, orthographic information accesses words directly, with phonological recoding only occurring *after* lexical access has taken place, if at all. As we shall see, both types of phonological access probably occur to some extent.

Consider, first, the evidence for pre-access recoding. In an experiment by Meyer, Schvaneveldt, and Ruddy (1974), subjects performed the lexical decision task (**4.1.2**). On each trial, subjects received a visual string of letters and had to decide as quickly as possible whether it formed a word (e.g., "light" vs. "laght"). If subjects recoded each word phonologically to access its representation in memory, then the letter-to-phoneme conversion rules that produced this recoding should have become primed in the process (**2.5**). Consider the lexical access of "grown." If subjects recoded the "ow" in "grown" to the phoneme /o/, then the "ow" to /o/ conversion rule that produced this recoding should have become primed. Most importantly, the priming of this conversion rule should have interfered with the subsequent access of any word that required a different "ow" conversion rule, such as the "ow" to /aw/ rule needed to recode "crown." Subjects' expectation that "ow" recodes to /o/, acquired from categorizing "grown," should have inhibited the alternative recoding to /aw/, thereby causing "crown" to be categorized slowly. If subjects did not recode "grown" phonologically, then this change in conversion rules should not have mattered, and they should not have experienced any difficulty in categorizing "crown." In support of pre-access recoding, however, Meyer et al. did indeed find that changes in conversion rules from word to word interfered with lexical access.

Findings from other lexical decision studies provide further support for the presence of pre-access recoding. When subjects receive a non-word that sounds like a word (e.g., "nite"), they take longer to decide that it is not a word than for a non-word that does not sound like a word (e.g., "nipe;" H. Rubenstein, S.S. Lewis, & M.A. Rubenstein, 1971)). Interference occurs because phonological information activates a real word, *night*, thereby leading subjects toward an incorrect response, at least initially.

Interestingly, a similar phenomenon appears to occur during speech perception: As people listen to a speaker talk, they generate visual information for written language unconsciously (Seidenberg & Tanenhaus, 1979). As a result, interference occurs when two words spoken sequentially represent the same phoneme with different orthographic information. For example, subjects judge that "sleaze" rhymes with "cheese" slower than they judge that "freeze" rhymes with "breeze." Because the orthographic information for the same phoneme differs for "sleaze" and "cheese," interference occurs from one to the other.

Other evidence, however, suggests that pre-access recoding plays little, if any, role in reading. An example from Foss and Hakes (1978) illustrates how lexical access can occur without pre-access recoding: When reading "$" people probably don't recode it phonologically, because "$" does not have a phonemic representation. The ability to access the meaning of "$" directly indicates that phonological recoding is not necessary for accessing the meanings of written symbols. LaBerge and Samuels (1974) argue further that direct mappings from written language to meaning occur through the process of automatization: To the extent that a word's written form cooccurs frequently and consistently with its meaning, an automatized relation develops between them (**4.1.2**). As a result, written words can access their meanings directly without phonological recoding.

Furthermore, a number of experiments have found evidence against the necessity of pre-access recoding during reading (Forster, 1976; Kleiman, 1975; Slowiaczek & Clifton, 1980; Stanovich & Bauer, 1978). For example, phonological effects on lexical access, such as those discussed a moment ago, sometimes disappear when researchers ask subjects to respond quickly. This suggests that phonological recoding does not control the initial access of a word but only occurs *after* lexical access.

Many theorists prefer a *dual access view* of phonological recoding, believing that both orthographic and phonological information can control lexical access under various circumstances. Most of the time, orthographic information accesses words directly, but when people don't recognize a written word, they use letter-to-phoneme conversion rules to construct a phonemic representation that provides access. Consider the sentence:

To see how tall John had grown in a year, the school nurse measured his hite.

One hesitates initially upon encountering "hite," because the orthographic information doesn't match a word in memory. As orthographic access is failing, however, letter-to-phoneme conversion rules produce a phonological representation that eventually provides access to *height*. In general, theorists believe that both orthographic and phonemic information become active simultaneously during reading: Orthographic information typically becomes available first and controls lexical access, but the slower phonemic information may come into play later, if orthographic access has not yet converged on a word (Foss & Hakes, 1978, chap. 11; Just & Carpenter, 1987, chap. 3).

It is important to note that this process may be somewhat reversed in children learning to read. Because children at this stage know many more spoken words than written words, letter-to-phoneme conversion plays a much more important role. By sounding out letters, children can access a word phonologically that is unfamiliar orthographically. As relations between orthographic information and semantic information become automatized, however, they begin to dominate lexical access.

Although pre-access recoding may only occur occasionally in normal reading, post-access recoding appears to occur extensively. The phonological representation of a word may become available following its access in either of two manners: First, the letter-to-phoneme conversion that began prior to access may finish sometime thereafter, providing a phonological representation of the word. Second, a phonological representation stored with the word may be retrieved from long-term memory after orthographic information has established initial access. A third possibility is that both these processes converge to provide a phonological representation.

Post-access phonological representations play important roles in language comprehension. As we saw in **5**.1.2, phonological representations of words remain longer in working memory than do visual representations. As we also saw, comprehension of written language suffers when phonological representations are disrupted in working memory (5.2.2). Phonological representations in working memory appear central to integrating the words in a sentence. Because phonological representations are relatively long-lasting, words from a sentence can be represented simultaneously after their visual processing has ended, thereby allowing their meanings to be integrated. In general, phonological representations appear much more important to sentence integration *following* lexical access than to lexical access itself (Kleiman, 1975; Levy, 1978; Slowiaczek & Clifton, 1980; for an alternative view, see Potter & Lombardi, 1990; Von Eckardt & Potter, 1985).

9.2.2 Morphological Versus Direct Access

How does the cognitive system combine letters during reading, or phonemes during speech perception, to access a word? Consider the letter sequence that constitutes "signal" in reading. Perhaps the letters first access the morphemes for *sign* and *-al*, which then combine to access the meaning for *signal* through *morphological access*. Alternatively, *direct access* may occur, with all six letters accessing *signal* directly. Similarly, in speech perception, the access of *signal* could be mediated by its morphemes, or it could be accessed directly from its phonemes.

Some findings suggest the presence of morphological access. Imagine receiving the word "signal" in a lexical decision task. If you process the morpheme for *sign* to access *signal*, then *sign*'s level of activation should increase. As a result, you should process later words containing *sign* faster because less bottom-up information is necessary to activate it. Thus, if *sign* was used to access *signal*, then the priming it received should facilitate its use in later accessing *signature* (**2.5**). Researchers can measure this by seeing if lexical decisions for "signature" are faster when preceded by a word utilizing *sign* (e.g., "signal") than when they are not. On the other hand, if "signal" accesses *signal* directly without using *sign*, then lexical decisions for "signature" should be unaffected by the prior presentation of another word containing "sign." Across a variety of studies, investigators have found that prior activations of a morpheme, such as *sign*, do affect the later processing of words that contain it (MacKay, 1978; Stanners, Neiser, & Painton, 1979; Taft & Forster, 1975, 1976). Lexical access, then, appears to follow morphological structure to some extent.

Other findings provide evidence for direct access. First, readers are somewhat sensitive to word shape, such that violating a word's normal shape makes it a more difficult to identify (E.E. Smith & Spoehr, 1974; F. Smith, 1971). For example, people have more trouble categorizing "hApPiLy" than "happily." Because shape is a global characteristic of a word, its effect on lexical access suggests that the entire word retrieves its meaning directly. Second, readers have more trouble processing individual letters in words as words become more familiar (Healy, 1976). Thus, if subjects scan a text for the letter "r," they are more likely to miss it in a familiar word such as "street" than in an unfamiliar word such as "strife." This suggests that words become increasingly unitized as they become familiar. Third, some researchers have simply failed to find effects of morphological access when looking for them, suggesting the presence of direct access at least under some circumstances (Manelis & Tharp, 1980; G.S. Rubin, Becker, & Freeman, 1979). In general, morphological and direct access both appear to have some control over lexical processing.

9.2.3 Ease of Access

People do not access all words equally easily. In this section, I review three important factors that determine the ease of accessing a word: *length, frequency,* and *recency.*

In both speech perception and reading, long words such as "furniture" take longer to access than short words such as "chair." In general, the time to access a word increases linearly with its length, with each additional phoneme or letter increasing access time by a constant amount. One might believe that this simply reflects word frequency: If frequent words in a language become short and rare words remain relatively long, then short words should become better established in memory and therefore be accessed faster. Indeed, word length does decrease as word frequency increases, but when word frequency is held constant, words are still accessed faster as they become shorter. It is not clear which unit of word length—number of letters, phonemes, or syllables—determines access time, but word length clearly affects ease of access: The less perceptual information that must be processed for a word, the less time it takes to access (Carpenter & Just, 1983; Marslen-Wilson & Tyler, 1980; Zipf, 1935/1965).

As just noted, word frequency also determines ease of access. As a word's frequency increases, the time to access it decreases substantially, both in speech and reading. For example, people access frequent words such as "the" and "telephone" much faster than infrequent words such as "thy" and "telescope." Numerous studies have clearly demonstrated the importance of this variable in lexical processing (Bradley & Forster, 1987; Carpenter & Just, 1983; B. Gordon, 1985; Morton, 1969, 1979; Rayner, 1983).

Theorists have proposed a variety of mechanisms to account for the effect of frequency on lexical access. Because the frequency effect is similar to the base rate effect we considered earlier (2.3.2), and because prototype and exemplar models both provide accounts of the base rate effect, it is not surprising that prototype and exemplar models both provide accounts of the word frequency effect as well. Consider the prototype for categorizing written instances of a word, such as the representation of "butter" in Fig. 2.9 (an analogous argument exists for the prototypes that categorize the spoken forms of words). According to prototype models, the strength of a word's prototype in memory reflects how frequently it has been processed. As a prototype is used to categorize more and more written instances of a word, its strength in memory increases, such that it becomes active more quickly. In terms of spreading activation models (2.5), frequency could either increase the baseline level of activation for a word's prototype, or it could lower its threshold (see Fig. 2.10). Either way, the prototype requires less activation to rise from its baseline to its threshold, relative to other prototypes in memory.

Exemplar models account for the frequency effect quite differently. According to these models, the number of exemplars in long-term memory for a word—either written or spoken—reflects the number of exemplars categorized on previous occasions. As one processes increasing numbers of a word's written exemplars, for example, increasing numbers of memories for them are stored. This could produce a frequency effect in at least two ways: First, if the total number of exemplar memories retrieved for a word determines access time, then words having more memories should be accessed faster, because people retrieve more memories for them. Second, if high similarity between the word being categorized and a single word in memory produces rapid access, then words having more memories should, again, be accessed faster. As the number of memories for a word increases, they tend to cover the variety of possible exemplars more completely. Because the chances of a new exemplar matching a previous memory increase with frequency, people access new exemplars of high frequency words faster than new exemplars of low frequency words. Note that this unintentional use of exemplars is essentially the same as implicit memory (6.3.3). On each account, subjects unintentionally retrieve similar word memories from previous categorizations to guide lexical access.

Recency is a third factor that determines the ease of lexical access. Upon encountering "telescope" again here, you probably accessed it faster than when you read it three paragraphs ago. Indeed, such recency effects can overcome large differences in frequency (D.L. Scarborough, Cortese, & H.S. Scarborough, 1977). Thus, the time to access "telephone" a second time (a word you also read three paragraphs ago) is probably not much less, if any, than the time it just took you to access the second presentation of "telescope," even though "telephone" is much higher in frequency than "telescope."

Prototype and exemplar models readily account for recency effects. According to prototype models, activating a word's prototype increases its strength temporarily, such that subsequent uses soon thereafter require less activation. Again, this increase in strength could reflect either an elevated baseline or a lowered threshold. Until the word's prototype returns to its original state, either alteration can produce a recency effect.

Exemplar models can account for recency by assuming that recently stored word exemplars are stronger or more accessible in memory than older word exemplars. If a word has recent exemplar memories, it has more accessible memories than do words having no recent memories. As a result, the recent word is processed more quickly, thereby producing a recency effect. Again, this unintentional use of exemplars is essentially the same as implicit memory.

Before concluding this section, it is important to note that expectation also affects ease of access: When one expects a particular word, it is accessed much faster than when it is not expected (**2**.4). In fact, these top-down effects often surpass other access effects in magnitude. I defer discussion of this topic until the section on immediacy of interpretation (**9**.4).

9.2.4 Content of Access

Once lexical access occurs, what information becomes available? As discussed in **9**.2.1, phonological information may become available for written words. As suggested in **8**.5, information about grammatical class (e.g., noun, verb) and syntactic requirements may become available as well (e.g., a verb may require an agent and a theme). However, most researchers have focused on the retrieval of semantic information following access.

In general, theorists believe that accessing a word activates its *sense*. As discussed in **8**.6.3, a word's sense may contain a categorization rule, perhaps including a definition, a prototype, and some exemplars (**2**.3.1). In addition, a word's sense may contain much information relevant to conceptualizing a category, including information that enables people to understand, predict, and interact with its category members (**7**.2.1). As we saw in **7**.2.3, however, not all of the knowledge available for a category becomes active on a given occasion. Within the subset that does become active, much information appears to be context-dependent, only being activated because of its relevance in the current context. However, some knowledge appears to be context-independent, being activated automatically for the category across all contexts. Because these topics received discussion in previous sections, I do not discuss them further here. We have already considered many of the issues that concern content of access.

Once a word's sense becomes active, it may then initiate a search for the word's referent, if there is one (**8**.6.3, Fig. 8.5). Thus, "stallion" in a sentence could refer to a live stallion, a painting of a stallion, or a blood sample of a stallion, depending on the current referents in common ground (**8**.7.2). Although the sense of "stallion" is important to its meaning, its referent is important as well. For this reason, care should be taken not to equate meaning exclusively with the content of lexical access. Instead, the referent discovered through this content may also be central to meaning. Under these conditions, the content of access plus the referent constitute meaning. Reference receives further discussion in **9**.6.1.

Resolving lexical ambiguity.   How does lexical access proceed for an ambiguous word, such as "oranges" in:

After studying color chips at the paint store, Peggy selected several <u>oranges</u>.

According to the *selective access view*, only the *color* sense of *orange* becomes active in this sentence, because only this sense is relevant. Its *fruit* sense, as in "Peggy peeled several oranges," does not become active, because it is irrelevant. In contrast, the *multiple access view* proposes that both senses are active initially, regardless of whether they are relevant. Soon thereafter, the sense that is irrelevant in the current context becomes inactive, leaving only the relevant sense active.

Much work has addressed this issue. In one paradigm, subjects listen, on headphones, to a text that contains ambiguous words. For example, a text might contain the sentence:

> Upon entering their mountain cottage, Archie was surprised to find yellows, reds, and <u>oranges</u> everywhere.

As subjects listen to such sentences, they simultaneously perform lexical decisions on letter strings presented visually on a computer screen. Immediately following the ambiguous word (e.g., "oranges"), subjects receive one of four strings: a *relevant probe*, namely, a word that conveys the sense of the ambiguous word relevant in the sentence (e.g., "color"); an *irrelevant probe*, a word that conveys the sense of the ambiguous word irrelevant in the sentence (e.g., "fruit"); a *neutral* probe, a word not related to either sense of the ambiguous word (e.g., "truck"); or a *non-word* (e.g., "monex).

According to the selective access view, the reaction times for relevant, irrelevant, and neutral probes should be ordered as follows:

> relevant < irrelevant = neutral

For the sentence containing "oranges," subjects should respond to "color" faster than "fruit," because only the sense for *color* ever becomes active—the sense for *fruit* remains inactive. Moreover, subjects should take just as long to process "fruit" as they take to process an unrelated word such as "truck." In contrast, the predictions for the multiple access view are:

> relevant = irrelevant < neutral

Subjects should respond equally fast to "color" and "fruit," because both senses of *orange* become active initially. Responses to "truck" should be slower, because it is not related to either sense.

A variety of studies have found evidence for multiple access (Gorfein, 1989; Marslen-Wilson, 1989; Seidenberg, Tanenhaus, Leiman, & Bienkowski, 1982; Swinney, 1979; Tanenhaus, Leiman & Seidenberg, 1979). Often, people access both senses of an ambiguous word initially as they encode it. These studies have also found, however, that multiple access is short–lived. In assessing the time course of these activation effects, re-searchers have found that the irrelevant sense becomes inactive a few hundred milliseconds after subjects read the ambiguous word. Context quickly con-verges on the relevant sense to keep it active and inhibits the irrelevant sense. Although multiple access occurs initially, selective access occurs eventually.

9.3 SENTENCE PROCESSING

Once people identify words through lexical access, they must integrate them into constituents (**8**.5.1). Ultimately, they need to extract propositions from these constituents and integrate them into an evolving referent model (**8**.7.5). I first review evidence for the importance of constituent analysis in sentence processing, and then address the roles of syntactic and semantic strategies in constituent analysis.

9.3.1 Constituent Analysis

If the goal of sentence analysis is to extract propositions (**8**.7.4), then language structure should facilitate this process. One way to mark a propo-sition is to package it as a constituent in a sentence (**8**.5.1). Consider:

The weary intern played the Beethoven piano sonata.

This sentence contains the propositions:

INTERN   **PLAY**   ┌ **SONATA**
(ENERGY LEVEL = weary)   (AGENT = ↑)   │ (INSTRUMENT = piano)
                              (THEME = ↓)   (COMPOSER = Beethoven)

As can be seen, the constituent for the first noun phrase in the sentence contains the *INTERN* proposition; the constituent for the second noun phrase contains the *SONATA* proposition; and the constituent for the verb contains the *PLAY* proposition, which integrates the propositions for *IN-TERN* and *SONATA* as its arguments. Propositions often correspond to constituents in this manner, although they sometimes do not, as we shall see. Once people identify a constituent, however, they often assume that it contains a proposition (H.H. Clark & E.V. Clark, 1977, pp. 45–72).

Much evidence indicates that people rely heavily on constituent analysis to extract propositions from sentences. Compare the ease of reading the fol-lowing two versions of the same sentence:

On his new home	On his new home court
court for the first time, the	for the first time,
three-time all star was	the three-time all star
shooting twenty-foot	was shooting
jump shots that	twenty-foot jump shots
were all net.	that were all net.

Whereas each line in the right-hand version is aligned with constituent boundaries, each line in the left-hand version violates them. As a result, forming the constituents in the left-hand version is more difficult, which in turn makes the extraction of its propositions more difficult. When the markings for constituent boundaries are misleading or unclear, people have trouble extracting propositions (R. Graf & Torrey, 1966).

Consider another type of evidence for the importance of constituents in sentence processing. Caplan (1972) constructed pairs of sentences that ended with the same words, as the last four words of these two sentences illustrate:

When the sun warms the Earth after the rain clouds soon disappear.
When a high pressure front approaches rain clouds soon disappear.

The important property of each sentence pair was that the first of its common words ended a constituent in one sentence but began a constituent in the other: Whereas "rain" ends a constituent in the first sentence ("after the rain"), it begins a constituent in the second ("rain clouds soon disappear"). Imagine reading one of these sentences, receiving a target word, and having to decide if the target occurred in the sentence. When the target is "rain," does the position of the constituent containing "rain" affect reaction time? If the time to recognize "rain" depends only on how much time has elapsed since its presentation, then reaction times for the two sentences should not differ, because "rain" is equidistant from the end of each, followed by exactly the same words. If people process a sentence constituent by constituent, though, its later constituents should be more active in working memory than its earlier ones. As a result, "rain" should be more active in the second sentence than in the first, because it occurs in a more recent constituent. Across a variety of studies, researchers have indeed found that words in recent constituents are more active than words in earlier constituents, when the elapsed time between the word and the test is held constant (see also Ammon, 1968; Jarvella, 1971, 1979; D.J. Townsend & Bever, 1978). A related literature on "click" studies provide further evidence for the importance of constituents in syntactic processing (J.A. Fodor & Bever, 1965; J.A. Fodor, Bever, & Garrett, 1974; Garrett, Bever, & J.A. Fodor, 1966; Holmes & Forster, 1970; Reber, 1973). As all of these studies demonstrate, people process sentences constituent by constituent.

What is the role of working memory in constituent analysis? As we just saw, early constituents in a sentence tend to be less active than recent ones, but have early constituents been purged completely from working memory? Perhaps they have, if their propositions have been extracted, and they serve no other purpose. As we saw in 5.2.2, however, working memory maintains a verbatim representation of the two most recently processed sentences (Glanzer et al., 1981; Glanzer et al., 1984; but see Potter & Lombardi, 1990; Von Eckardt & Potter, 1985). Consequently, working memory contains more than a sentence's most recently processed constituent. Although this constituent may be the most active, working memory also maintains earlier constituents of the sentence, as well as constituents from the previous sentence, to facilitate the integration of propositions within and between sentences (8.7.5, 9.6.1).

The properties of working memory place strong constraints on the syntactic structures that people can process easily. For example, people have trouble with sentences in which words from the same proposition do not lie within the same constituent, as in:

The plumber, who installed exquisite new plumbing in the renovated house, was overworked and underpaid.

Processing this sentence is difficult, because the reader must construct the following proposition from two constituents that are separated by several other constituents in working memory:

PLUMBER
    (WORK LOAD = too much)
    (INCOME = too little)

Extracting this proposition is much easier when one constituent contains it, as in:

The overworked underpaid plumber installed exquisite new plumbing in the renovated house.

Sentences containing center-embedded clauses are particularly hard to understand, because corresponding noun and verb phrases in the outer constituents are separated in working memory, as in:

The tricycle that John whom his godmother spoiled rides everywhere has an obnoxious horn.

A variety of studies have shown that propositions become increasingly difficult to extract as speakers distribute them increasingly over a sentence's constituents (Bever, 1970; J.A. Fodor et al., 1974; Ford, 1983; Kimball, 1973; Larkin & Burns, 1977).

9.3.2 Syntactic Strategies

Given the importance of constituents for propositional analysis, what cognitive mechanisms might be responsible for their formation? In this section, I consider various syntactic strategies that appear important in English. None of these strategies is guaranteed to work or to be error-free. Rather, each strategy provides some information about constituent structure, which, when combined with information produced by other strategies, typically converges on the correct analysis. Also note that these strategies operate unconsciously. As many theorists have observed, people are usually oblivious to the syntactic processing of sentences. Highly proceduralized mechanisms, such as automatized productions, appear to implement these strategies (**4**.1.2).

Many psychologists believe that people use a wide variety of syntactic strategies to process a sentence's constituents. These strategies generally serve five goals:

1. Anticipate the constituent structure of a sentence.
2. Identify the beginning and end of each constituent.
3. Specify the type of each constituent.
4. Integrate the words within each constituent.
5. Integrate the constituents within a sentence.

Over the years, theorists have suggested a wide variety of strategies that serve these goals. In the following five subsections, I review some of their proposals.

Anticipating sentence structure. People use a variety of strategies to anticipate the constituent structure of a sentence (H.H. Clark & E.V. Clark, 1977; J.A. Fodor et al., 1974): First, they expect that the first constituent of a sentence will be a noun phrase. Second, they expect that the sentence will be in the active voice, not the passive. Third, they expect that the first constituent is the main constituent, if the sentence contains more than one. As the result of applying these three strategies, processing is faster for:

The hiker picked up the garbage that was left by some thoughtless campers.

than for:

Left by some thoughtless campers, the garbage was picked up by the hiker.

Note that none of these expectations about sentence structure is a rigid requirement. Clearly, the first constituent of a sentence need not be a noun phrase, a sentence can be passive, and the first clause can be a subordinate. These expectations simply reflect a preference for these structures, perhaps because of their statistical prevalence in a language.

Identifying constituent boundaries.   People use a variety of strategies to determine where constituents begin and end (H.H. Clark & E.V. Clark, 1977; Just & Carpenter, 1987). They assume that determiners (e.g., a, the), quantifiers (e.g., all, many, two), and pronouns (e.g., I, you, they) signal the beginning of a noun phrase. They assume that auxiliaries (e.g., is, was, will, would) signal the beginning of a verb phrase. They assume that relative pronouns (e.g., that, who), complementizers (e.g., for, to), and subordinating conjunctions (e.g., if, because, when) signal the beginning of a new clause. Whenever people encounter one of these words, they usually expect that a new constituent is beginning.

People use these same strategies to identify the ends of constituents: Upon encountering a cue that signals the beginning of a new constituent, they assume that the just-previous constituent has ended. Punctuation (e.g., period, comma) also signals the end of a constituent.

Not all constituents are marked clearly: A noun phrase can begin with an adjective (e.g., graceful birds) or a verb (e.g., plummeting birds), although neither necessarily begins a noun phrase (e.g., many graceful plummeting birds). Similarly, a noun phrase may not end with the first noun it contains (e.g., the bird house). When one strategy fails to identify a boundary, other strategies converge upon it. Thus, a verb following "the bird house" signals the end of the noun phrase and the start of a verb phrase. In this way, the redundancy of cues usually produces accurate constituent boundaries.

Identifying constituent types.   A variety of strategies are used in determining the type of each constituent (H.H. Clark & E.V. Clark, 1977; Just & Carpenter, 1987). All of the strategies for identifying the start of a constituent also provide information about the type of constituent: People assume that determiners and quantifiers indicate a noun phrase, that auxiliaries signal verb phrases, and that prepositions signal prepositional phrases. People use other strategies as well. First, they assume that content words provide information about constituent type. Upon discovering a noun in a constituent, they assume it to be a noun phrase; similarly, the presence of a verb suggests a verb phrase. Second, people assume that affixes provide information about constituent type. A word affixed with "-ing" is assumed to be a verb and to lie within a verb phrase. Again, these strategies are not foolproof, as when a verb form lies within a noun phrase (e.g., the sinking dock). In general, though, these strategies provide good predictions about type of constituent.

Integrating words in a constituent. Once one has identified a new constituent and its type, the words within it must be integrated. As we shall see in **9.**4, this process often takes place word by word, rather than at the end of the constituent. Many psychologists believe that the strategies for integrating a constituent resemble phrase structure rules, such as those in Fig. 8.2 (Bock, 1987, pp. 350–359; J.A. Fodor et al., 1974; J.D. Fodor & Frazier, 1980; Frazier & J.D. Fodor, 1978; Johnson–Laird, 1983, chaps. 12 & 13; Kimball, 1973; Wanner, 1980). Consider the simplified rule in Fig. 8.2 for noun phrases:

NP → (det) + (adj)* + noun + (PP)*

If one identifies the current constituent as a noun phrase, an attempt can be made to integrate its words according to the expectations that this rule expresses. On encountering "the," one expects the next word to be an adjective or a noun; on encountering a noun, one expects either a prepositional phrase or the beginning of a new constituent. In this way, information about word order and grammatical category from the NP rule guides the integration of words in the constituent. Other phrase structure rules, such as the ones for verb phrases and prepositional phrases, similarly facilitate the organization of their respective constituents.

Integrating the constituents of a sentence. Once the processing of a constituent is complete, it must be integrated with any prior constituents that were processed earlier. Some theorists view syntactic analysis as containing two stages, one in which constituents are formed, and one in which constituents are later assembled (J.D. Fodor & Frazier, 1980; Frazier & J.D. Fodor, 1978; Wanner, 1980).

At various points in processing a sentence, people often expect to encounter a particular type of constituent. As we saw earlier, people have expectations about a sentence prior to processing it (e.g., expect a sentence to begin with a noun phrase). At later points in processing, phrase structure rules generate further expectations about upcoming constituents. After encoding an initial noun phrase, one might expect a prepositional phrase, because an indefinite number of them can terminate a noun phrase (see the NP rule in Fig. 8.2). A verb phrase might also be expected, because one is needed to complete the sentence (see the S rule). If a prepositional phrase does occur, followed by a verb phrase, they are integrated with the noun phrase, according to the NP and sentence rules. When a newly processed constituent fits expectations derived from phrase structure rules, people know where to attach it (H.H. Clark & E.V. Clark, 1977).

Some constituents are expected less than others. A variety of syntactic cues signal the presence of less expected constituents and provide information about where to attach them. Consider the following sentence:

Because he loved to sail, Dan moved to the Caribbean.

"Because" signals that the first clause is subordinate to the main clause, which is to come later. Upon encountering "because," you suspend your initial expectation that the first clause will be the main clause and adopt an expectation that a subordinate clause follows immediately. Once you have finished processing the subordinate clause, you once again expect the main clause. Consider another example:

Juliana bought a house that overlooked a river.

In this sentence, "that" signals a relative clause, which modifies the preceding noun phrase. Upon encountering "overlooked a river," you know that it should be attached to "a house." A wide variety of other strategies enable people to attach many kinds of constituents in many different ways (H.H. Clark & E.V. Clark, 1977).

9.3.3 Semantic Strategies

In this section, I review semantic strategies that underlie sentence processing in English and then discuss their possible relations to syntactic strategies. Just as for syntactic strategies, none of these semantic strategies is guaranteed to work or be error-free. Instead, they generally converge, along with syntactic strategies, to produce the correct constituent analysis and to extract propositions. Semantic strategies, like syntactic strategies, appear to operate unconsciously and be highly automatized.

Frame modification.   The purpose of semantic processing is to extract the propositions of a sentence and integrate them into a continually evolving referent model (**8**.7.4, **8**.7.5). As we saw earlier, this is essentially conceptual combination at the level of sentences (**7**.2.4, **8**.6.2). Frame modification provides one account of this process (**7**.2.2; see also G.N. Carlson & Tanenhaus, 1988; Garnsey, Tanenhaus, & R.M. Chapman, 1989; Just & Carpenter, 1987; Tanenhaus, Boland, Garnsey, & G.N. Carlson, 1989; Tanenhaus & M.M. Lucas, 1987).

According to this view, certain words in a sentence activate frames during sentence processing. As these frames become active, other words and constituents in the sentence modify frame attributes to form propositions. Two particular kinds of frames appear central to this process: frames for nouns and frames for verbs. Consider the following sentence:

Two friendly dogs with spots chased fireflies quietly around midnight.

Frames for four nouns (*dog, spot, firefly, midnight*) and one verb (*chase*) are relevant to processing this sentence, each providing an organizational structure for assembling propositions. As you identify each new word or constituent in a sentence, you attempt to integrate its information into an existing frame. If no frame is available, you generate inferences about how this information may modify a future frame. For example, on reading "Two" at the start of the sentence just mentioned, you have not yet activated a frame. However, you infer that a noun is forthcoming and that its attribute for *quantity* will have a value of *two*. Similarly, on next encountering "friendly," you infer that the forthcoming noun will be animate and that its attribute for *disposition* will be *friendly*. Once you encounter "dogs," you activate the frame for *dog* and insert the values for *quantity* and *disposition*. Not only does the frame for *dog* serve to assemble prior information extracted from the sentence, it also serves to assemble information extracted subsequently. For example, when you reach the constituent "with spots," you insert the value *spotted* into the attribute for *appearance*. At this point, the frame for *dog* looks like this:

DOG
   (QUANTITY = two)
   (DISPOSITION = friendly)
   (APPEARANCE = spotted)

As you modify the frame for *dog*, you assume that it will eventually fill a thematic role of a verb not mentioned thus far. On encountering "chase," you activate the frame for the active form of *chase*, which specifies that its subject is the agent and that its direct argument is the theme. Because *dog* satisfies the criteria for agenthood (e.g., *animacy*), its frame modifies *chase*'s thematic role for an agent. On next encountering "fireflies," you activate the frame for *firefly* and insert it into *chase*'s thematic role for a theme.

The subsequent constituents for "quietly" and "around midnight," are also integrated into the frame for *chase*. In contrast to the agent and the theme, however, the attributes that these later constituents modify are not obligatory: The sentence need not contain explicit values for them (**8.5.2**). Nevertheless, when constituents provide optional values, verb frames can often accommodate them. Upon the completion of processing, the integrated collection of frames looks like this:

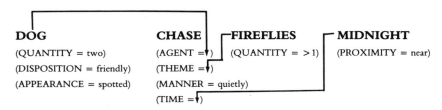

DOG   **CHASE**   ┌**FIREFLIES**   ┌**MIDNIGHT**
(QUANTITY = two)   (AGENT =▼) │ (QUANTITY = >1) │ (PROXIMITY = near)
(DISPOSITION = friendly)   (THEME =▼)
(APPEARANCE = spotted)   (MANNER = quietly)
                           (TIME =▼)

How do people know where to insert words and constituents into available frames? A variety of strategies serve this purpose. First, grammatical category provides information about frame modification. For example, adjectives provide values for noun frames. On encountering an adjective, one can assume that it modifies an attribute in a noun frame that will later be active (as for "friendly" above) or that is already active (as in "The dogs were large"). On encountering a prepositional phrase, one assumes that it modifies either a noun frame or a verb frame (as for "with spots" and "around midnight," respectively). An adverb is assumed to modify an attribute of a verb (as for "quietly" above) or the *value* of a frame attribute (when it modifies an adjective, as in "very friendly," or another adverb, as in "very quietly").

Second, the position of a word or a constituent often provides information about the frame it modifies. Consider the following two sentences:

The rancher <u>on the sidewalk</u> loaded hay.
The rancher loaded hay <u>on the sidewalk</u>.

Whereas "on the sidewalk" modifies the frame for *rancher* in the first sentence, it modifies the frame for *load* in the second sentence. The same prepositional phrase modifies different frames, depending on its position in the sentence. As we saw in **8.5.2**, position can also provide information about the thematic role that a constituent modifies, as in:

The mailman chased the dog.

The active form of *chase* specifies that its subject is the agent and that its direct argument is the theme. In this particular sentence, position is especially important, because of the unusual proposition that the sentence expresses. A reader who did not use position information to guide frame instantiation might conclude erroneously that the dog chased the mailman, following general expectations.

Third, prepositions, in association with particular verbs, often provide information about modification. Compare:

John sang on the Ferrari.
John sang for the Ferrari.

Whereas "on" indicates that *Ferrari* modifies the location of *sing*, "for" indicates that *Ferrari* modifies its goal. The same preposition may provide different information about modification depending on the verb, as in:

Robyn avoided the ticket <u>by</u> acting truly sorry.
Robyn never drove her Lotus <u>by</u> the police station again.

When "by" follows "avoid," its object is an instrument (i.e., *acting truly sorry*), but when "by" follows "drive," its object is a location (i.e., *the police station*).

Fourth, the meaning of a word provides information about modification. Compare:

The poodle slept under the tree <u>with fleas</u>.
The poodle slept under the tree <u>with friends</u>.
The poodle slept under the tree <u>with acorns</u>.

Here, the object of the final prepositional phrase determines the frame it modifies. When the object is *fleas*, the phrase modifies the frame for *poodle*. When the object is *friends*, the phrase modifies the frame for *sleep*. When the object is *acorns*, the phrase modifies the frame for *tree*. Because the frames for *poodle*, *sleep*, and *tree* specify the semantic information that is relevant to them, they disambiguate the syntactically ambiguous constituent.

Inference. People often add information to frames that a sentence does not state explicitly (**8**.7.4, **8**.7.5). Consider:

After a hard week's work in Geneva, Mike <u>flew</u> home to Boston.

You infer that *jet*, not *helicopter*, modifies the implicit instrument, even though the sentence does not mention this information (Corbett & Dosher, 1978; Just & Carpenter, 1978; McKoon & Ratcliff, 1981; Paris & Lindauer, 1976). Similarly, consider:

After a good night's sleep, Gene <u>awoke</u> feeling refreshed.
After <u>surfing</u> for three hours, Jimmy <u>played</u> volleyball.
After <u>driving</u> the president to the White House, the chauffeur napped.

In the first sentence, you infer that *morning*, not *afternoon*, modifies the *time* at which Gene awoke. In the second sentence, you infer that *beach*, not *desert*, modifies *location*. In the third sentence, you infer that *limousine*, not *pick-up truck*, modifies *theme*. All of these examples illustrate people's proclivity for modifying thematic roles left unspecified in a sentence. Whenever an agent, object, instrument, location, time, or some other thematic role remains implicit, people may infer a value for it. As we saw earlier, default values in frames enable these inferences (**7**.2.2, **8**.7.4).

People also make a variety of other inferences during comprehension. Scripts for event sequences (**4**.2.1, **10**.6.2) allow people to infer unstated actions for an event, as in:

Sam ordered the most expensive entree on the menu and left dissatisfied.

Although this sentence does not state that Sam *ate the entreé* or *paid for the entreé*, people infer that these actions occurred (Barsalou & Sewell, 1985; Bower et al., 1979; Graesser, S.E. Gordon, & Sawyer, 1979; Graesser, Woll, Kowalski, & D.A. Smith, 1980; Schank & Abelson, 1977). Knowledge about events also allows people to infer their initiating conditions and final outcomes, as in:

Sam threw his restaurant guide onto the roaring fire.

Although this sentence does not state the initiating event, people infer that Sam viewed the restaurant guide as useless and didn't want it any more. Although this sentence does not state the final outcome, people further infer the destruction of the restaurant guide (Bransford & M.K. Johnson, 1973; M.K. Johnson, Bransford, & Solomon, 1973; Kintsch, 1974).

So far, we have only considered inferences about verbs and the events that they represent. However, people also frequently make inferences about nouns, for example, instantiating them with a specific exemplar, as in:

The <u>fish</u> attacked the swimmer.

Although this sentence does not state the specific type of fish in the event, people often draw an *instantiation inference* and assume the fish to be a shark (R.C. Anderson & Ortony, 1975; R.C. Anderson et al., 1976; Garnham, 1979, 1981; Gumenik, 1979). For conceptual combination (**7**.2.4), we considered another type of inference involving nouns, as in:

The wooden <u>spoon</u> fell behind the stove.

Although *composition* is the only attribute for *spoon* that this sentence modifies explicitly (through *wooden*), people generally infer that *large* modifies *size* as well. When a sentence modifies one attribute of a noun frame, people often infer commonly correlated values for other attributes (Medin & Shoben, 1988; G.L. Murphy, 1988).

People also perform instantiation inferences for adjectives. Consider the meaning of the adjective *good* in:

To prepare all of the vegetables, Jim needed a <u>good</u> knife.
After a hard day's work, Jan relaxed in a <u>good</u> chair.
To change the light bulb, Yvonne looked for a <u>good</u> chair.

People instantiate *good* differently, depending on the frame it modifies. Whereas a good knife is presumably one whose blade is sharp, a good chair for relaxing is comfortable. Furthermore, even a *good chair* is instantiated differently, depending on context: Whereas a chair good for relaxing is comfortable, a chair good for changing a light bulb is movable, sturdy, and plain. *Good* selects different ideal values on attributes that are salient in the current context. In this regard, *good* operates in a fashion similar to the way ideals determine typicality (7.3.2; Barsalou, 1985, 1991, 1992; Katz, 1964). People instantiate many other adjectives differently, depending on what they modify, as in:

The horse was <u>tall</u>.
The skyscraper was <u>tall</u>.

Tall for a horse is not tall for a skyscraper (Rips & Turnbull, 1980).

Finally, people instantiate adverbs differently, depending on what they modify, as in:

The tortoise travelled <u>quickly</u>.
The hare travelled <u>quickly</u>.

The velocity at which turtles and hares travel "quickly" is well known to differ.

When do people actually draw inferences? Intuitively, they seem to draw them immediately upon reading a sentence, and some experiments have indeed found that people draw inferences right away. Other experiments, however, have found that people don't draw inferences immediately, but only draw them later when queried explicitly about them. Consider:

With dubious expectations, Rene tasted the cafe's pasta salad.

One might only infer later that the instrument was a fork, if asked what utensil Rene used. Drawing inferences at retrieval as they become relevant is essentially the process of reconstruction (6.3.2).

It is unlikely that people draw every possible inference initially, given the potential explosion of inferences that could arise. On the other hand, some inferences are essential to understanding a sentence, and others are so probable that well-learned productions generate them automatically (4.1.2). Depending on a variety of factors, inferences may occur during comprehension or later during reconstruction. For further discussion of this issue, see Garnham (1982), McKoon and Ratcliff (1989), Potts and Keenan (1988), Singer (1981), and Thorndyke (1976).

Relations between syntax and semantics. Both syntactic and semantic strategies are necessary for sentence processing. Without role assignments from syntactic strategies, one couldn't tell who the agent is in:

> The embezzler tailed the detective.

If syntax is ignored and only semantics is used in comprehending this sentence, one would probably conclude that the detective was tailing the embezzler, given the greater likelihood of this event. Syntactic strategies prevent this mistake and allow people to assign thematic roles correctly. Conversely, semantic strategies are also essential, as in:

> The medical researcher fought the battle on antibiotics.
> The ailing patient fought the battle on antibiotics.

Without semantic strategies, one would not know that "on antibiotics" is more likely to modify "battle" in the first sentence than in the second.

How do syntax and semantics interact during sentence processing? One possibility is that syntactic strategies play the central role in *forming* constituents, whereas semantic strategies play the central role in *assembling* them. As syntactic strategies identify noun phrases, prepositional phrases, verb phrases, and clauses, semantic strategies integrate propositions from these constituents into frames. Clearly, this generalization is oversimplified, in that semantics can influence constituent formation, and syntax can influence constituent assembly, but in general, syntax and semantics may play these roles.

A related issue is whether syntactic and semantic processing proceed independently, or whether they interact. One possibility is that semantic processing does not begin until syntactic processing has completed. As we shall see in the next section on immediacy of interpretation, this view is clearly false. Another possibility is that syntactic and semantic strategies operate simultaneously but don't affect each other, but consider the following sentences:

> The dissidents met at the warehouse by the diplomat were nervous.
> The passengers met at the airport by the diplomat were nervous.

After reading the underlined words in the first sentence, *met* appears initially to be an active verb, but as this "garden path" sentence unfolds, you discover that *met* is passive. Although the second sentence has the same syntactic structure, the garden path effect does not occur, because its underlined words immediately suggest the passive interpretation. As these two examples illustrate, the meanings of particular words constrain syntactic processing, determining whether the sentence appears active or passive initially. One might conclude that semantic processing therefore affects the outcome of syntactic processing. However, theorists can account for such findings with models in which syntax and semantics are autonomous, and they have not been able to resolve this issue empirically. Although syntactic and semantic strategies are both essential to sentence processing, much remains to be learned about the particular forms they take and the nature of their interaction. For a review of this debate see Garnham (1985, chap. 8). Also see Crain and Steedman (1985), Ferreira and Clifton (1986), Forster (1979), Frazier and Rayner (1987), Marslen-Wilson (1987), Rayner, M. Carlson, and Frazier (1983), Taraban and McClelland (1988), and Tyler and Marslen-Wilson (1977).

9.4 IMMEDIACY OF INTERPRETATION

So far, nearly all of the language processing we have considered is bottom-up: As people encounter linguistic information, their perceptual systems categorize phonemes in speech or letters in reading. Once these perceptual units have been identified, they access words. Once words have been identified, syntactic and semantic strategies integrate them into constituents and extract propositions. Does language processing only proceed in this bottom-up manner, or does it also utilize top-down processing?

The extreme bottom-up view, often implicit in linguists' theories of language, is that sentence processing occurs serially in stages. First, phonological processes identify the words in a sentence. Once *all* of the words in the sentence are known, syntactic processing produces a phrase marker (8.5.1). When the phrase marker is complete, semantic processes determine its meaning through something like truth functional semantics (8.6.2). According to this *serial model* of sentence processing, analysis proceeds in discrete, non-overlapping stages. In contrast, the extreme top-down view, *immediacy of interpretation*, is that all types of analysis occur from the beginning of the sentence. As the listener encodes a sentence phoneme by phoneme, syntactic processing incrementally develops constituents, and semantic processing continuously extracts propositions. Syntactic processing doesn't wait until all of the sentence's words have been identified, and semantic processing doesn't wait until a phrase marker is complete (Marslen-Wilson & Tyler, 1980).

An artificial intelligence system called HEARSAY (Reddy, 1975, 1980) illustrates immediacy of interpretation in language comprehension.

HEARSAY contains a *blackboard*, much like working memory in the human cognitive system (**5**.2). As HEARSAY processes a sentence, its different modules post hypotheses about words, constituents, and meanings on the blackboard. For example, the lexical module might post a hypothesis about the presence of a particular word, the syntactic module might post a hypothesis about the presence of a particular type of constituent, and the semantic module might post a hypothesis about the presence of a particular proposition. As each module posts its hypotheses, it simultaneously has access to the hypotheses of other modules, which it uses to revise its own hypotheses. As phonemes from the sentence enter HEARSAY one by one, each module continually revises its hypotheses about the content of the sentence. Once all of the modules halt, their final hypotheses combine to produce an interpretation of the sentence. Because all of HEARSAY's modules develop hypotheses from the beginning of the sentence, HEARSAY embodies immediacy of interpretation. In addition, HEARSAY's modules are interactive, not autonomous, in that each affects the output of the others. For a similar comprehension system, see Thibadeau, Just, and Carpenter (1982).

What about humans? Earlier I suggested that top-down processing occurs during the assembly of constituents, when phrase structure rules generate expectations about constituents they need (**9**.3.2), and when verbs generate expectations about their thematic roles (**9**.3.3). However, do all top-down effects only occur relatively late during constituent assembly, as these examples suggest? Or do such effects also occur earlier, perhaps during the identification of words, or possibly even during the identification of phonemes?

9.4.1 Lexical Access

Numerous investigators have found that syntactic and semantic processing have powerful effects on the identification of words (Ehrlich & Rayner, 1981; Fischler & P.A. Bloom, 1979; Schuberth & Eimas, 1977; Stanovich & West, 1981, 1983; Tulving, G. Mandler, & Baumal, 1964). Imagine reading one of the following sentence frames:

> Andrew ate the ice cream with a _____.
> Oliver touched the slimy moss with a _____.
> Anna ate the spinach salad with a _____.

Immediately after hearing one of these sentence frames, imagine reading "spoon" in a lexical decision test (**4**.1.2, **9**.2.1). If the serial model is correct, people should verify that "spoon" is a word equally quickly in all three frames. Even though the syntax and semantics of the first frame predict "spoon," these expectations should only act *after* all of the words in the sentence, including "spoon," have been identified. However, many studies have found that expectations from syntax and semantics produce substantial benefits in word recognition. People are much better at recognizing words that syntax and semantics predict than words that syntax and semantics do not predict. For example, people recognize "spoon" faster in the first sentence frame than in the second. Moreover, people have difficulty recognizing words that syntax and semantics predict should not occur. Thus, people recognize "spoon" slower in the third sentence frame than in the second.

These results, together with related findings we shall consider shortly, clearly demonstrate that interpretation is immediate. As you read each word in a sentence, you update syntactic hypotheses about the sentence's constituents and semantic hypotheses about its meaning. In turn, these hypotheses make predictions about words yet to be encountered. Syntactic hypotheses may predict that a noun, verb, or adjective will appear at a particular point. Semantic hypotheses may predict that a particular agent, object, or instrument will appear at a particular point. To the extent that subsequent words satisfy these expectations, their processing proceeds more rapidly. To the extent that subsequent words violate these expectations, their processing proceeds more slowly. These effects of top-down processing are exactly analogous to those we discussed in 2.4 and 2.5 for the categorization of visual scenes. Immediacy of interpretation pervades the cognitive system.

Marslen-Wilson and Tyler (1980) demonstrated that both syntactic and semantic expectations reduce the amount of phonological information that people need to identify a spoken word. In their experiment, subjects received a target word and listened for it in a subsequent sentence. Sometimes the target occurred in the sentence, and sometimes it did not. For example, subjects might listen for "stream" in one of the following sentences:

NORMAL: Julia pitched her <u>tent</u> in the forest beside a small <u>stream</u>.
ANOMALOUS: Julia drove her <u>tent</u> in the ozone beside a disturbing <u>stream</u>.
RANDOM: Beside in drove <u>tent</u> disturbing Julia the her a ozone <u>stream</u>.

On hearing the target, subjects pressed a button as quickly as possible. As you can see, the target "stream" is embedded in three different kinds of sentences. In the normal sentence, both syntax and semantics predict the target. In the anomalous sentence, only syntax predicts the target. In the random sentence, neither syntax nor semantics predicts the target. Marslen-Wilson and Tyler also manipulated the target's position in the sentence from early to late. Whereas "tent" is an early target in the above examples, "stream" is late.

Sentence type had large effects on subjects' ability to recognize targets. Subjects were fastest to recognize targets in normal sentences, next fastest in anomalous sentences, and slowest in random sentences. Whereas the anomalous sentences illustrate the beneficial effect of syntax on recognition, the normal sentences illustrate the added effect of semantics. Analysis of word length provided additional insight into lexical access (**9.2.3**): In random sentences, the time to recognize a word increased with its length. However, the time to recognize a word in anomalous sentences was less likely to correlate with its length, and even less likely in normal sentences. This decreasing importance of word length suggests that subjects identified the target words before they had fully heard them. In fact, additional analyses found that the time to recognize a word in anomalous and normal sentences was much less than the duration of the word itself. Whereas the average length of the targets was 369 msec, the average time to recognize a target in normal sentences was about 200 msec! By utilizing syntactic and semantic expectations, subjects identified words on the basis of incomplete phonemic information. Finally, the effects of syntax and semantics grew as targets occurred later in the sentence. As syntactic and semantic information accumulated over the course of sentence processing, subjects identified words faster, and the time to identify a word depended less and less on its length. These results clearly indicate that syntactic and semantic processing proceed simultaneously with phonological processing during lexical access. As the cognitive system processes a sentence phoneme by phoneme, it updates hypotheses about the sentence's syntactic and semantic structure (see also Marks & G.A. Miller, 1964; G.A. Miller & Isard, 1963).

9.4.2 Phoneme and Letter Perception

Do the top-down effects of semantic and syntactic processing end at the lexical level of analysis, or do they also affect the processing of phonemes during speech perception and the processing of letters during reading? Many investigators have found that top-down processing extends to these lower levels of analysis as well.

The phonemic restoration effect. Imagine hearing the following sentence, with the first [s] in "legislatures" having been deleted and replaced with a cough (i.e., "*"):

> The state governors met with their respective legi*latures convening in the capital city.

Although no acoustic cues for this [s] remain, people still "hear" it, restoring the phoneme experientially, because semantic and lexical knowledge provide strong expectancies that an [s] should occur. Moreover, studies sometimes find that people can't tell that a phoneme is actually missing. Phonemic restoration even occurs when the information that produces the expectancy *follows* the missing phoneme, as in:

It was found that the _eel was on the <u>axle</u>.
It was found that the _eel was on the <u>orange</u>.

On encountering "_eel," people hear "wheel" in the first sentence and "peel" in the second. It is unlikely that people restore the phoneme in these examples immediately, because many different phonemes can precede "eel," as in <u>wh</u>eel, <u>p</u>eel, <u>m</u>eal, and <u>h</u>eel. Instead, people probably restore the phoneme later, once the final word in the sentence produces an expectation (Samuel, 1981, 1987; R.M. Warren, 1970; R.M. Warren, Obusek, & Akroff, 1972; R.M. Warren & R.P. Warren, 1970).

Phoneme monitoring.   Imagine being asked to press a button as soon as you hear a [k] while listening to the following sentence:

Judy fastened her seat belt and drove her <u>c</u>ar onto the sluggish freeway.

Are you faster to identify the [k] upon reaching "car" in this sentence than in:

Barbara finally faced reality and hauled her <u>c</u>ar to the junk yard.

When syntactic and semantic processing produce expectations about words, people can indeed identify phonemes within them faster. Because you expect "car" in the first sentence, you process its [k] faster than when "car" occurs unexpectedly in the second sentence. Results from a variety of studies on phoneme monitoring document the clear presence of top–down effects (Foss, 1982; Foss & Blank, 1980; Foss & Gernsbacher, 1983; Foss & Swinney, 1973; Morton & Long, 1976).

The word superiority effect.   Top–down effects also occur in the perception of letters during reading. Imagine having one of the following three strings flashed very briefly on a screen in front of you:

xxxk   sork   cork

Immediately after seeing the string, imagine being presented with an arrow below where the "k" had been and having to decide whether "k" or "n" had appeared in that position (note that either letter forms a word for the third string and a pronounceable non–word for the second string). If top–down processing does not affect letter perception, then "k" should be identified equally well in all three strings. However, the ability to identify the "k" correctly improves from "xxxk" to "sork" to "cork." One explanation is that representations of possible words become active and prime their letters, before the letters are fully categorized (2.5): As *c*, *o*, *r*, and *k* become active, they prime *cork*, which in turn feeds activation back to *c*, *o*, *r*, and *k*, thereby facilitating the categorization of "k." In contrast, because *x*, *x*, *x*, and *k* don't activate a word representation, they don't receive any top-down assistance. Pronounceable non-words like "sork" receive weak top-down help from similar words such as *sore*, *sort*, *cork*, and *pork*, but not as much as from a word that matches the string perfectly. Results from a variety of studies on letter categorization document the clear presence of top-down effects (McClelland & Rumelhart, 1981; Reicher, 1969; Rumelhart & McClelland, 1982; Wheeler, 1970).

Overcoming the poor quality of information in speech and hand-writing. Recall from our discussion of speech perception that people can only recognize about half of the words from normal speech when they hear them in isolation (9.1). Similarly, when individual letters are extracted from normal handwriting and appear in isolation, their identity is often impossible to ascertain. In general, the quality of the perceptual information available to bottom-up processing during spoken and written language is quite poor. If people had to rely solely on bottom-up information, comprehension would fail frequently. The results in this section, and many others like them, however, demonstrate clearly that top-down processing assists bottom-up processing at all levels of analysis. Although no one source of information is sufficient to produce comprehension, together they capitalize on the redundancy in language to converge on the correct interpretation most of the time.

9.4.3 Interpretations of Immediacy

Before leaving this topic, it is important to consider two specific accounts of how top-down processing might produce immediacy of interpretation. According to the *interactive view*, top-down processing directly affects phoneme categorization during speech perception, letter categorization during reading, and lexical access during both. As syntactic and semantic expectations develop, they prime representations for particular phonemes, letters, and words. Once these representations become primed, less bottom-up information is necessary to categorize them, and categorization proceeds more rapidly than it would on the basis of bottom-up information alone (2.5; see Fig. 2.11). Top-down processing interacts directly with bottom-up processing, because it alters the activation of lower-level detectors (Marslen-Wilson & Tyler, 1980; Reddy, 1975, 1980; Thibadeau et al., 1982).

The *redundant outputs view* accounts for immediacy of interpretation quite differently. According to this view, top-down processing has no effect whatsoever on the rate at which phoneme categorization, letter categorization, and lexical access proceed. Top-down processing does not prime lower level detectors. Lower level detectors do not receive assistance from top-down processing but proceed completely independently of the detectors above them. Most importantly, though, top-down processing simultaneously provides *separate* information about the presence of phonemes, letters, and words. As we shall see, the availability of these redundant sources of information can explain immediacy of interpretation.

Consider categorization of the phoneme that begins a word toward the end of a sentence. Independent information about this phoneme accumulates simultaneously from bottom-up and top-down processing. Based on auditory information, a phoneme detector begins to produce bottom-up information about the identity of the phoneme. Simultaneously, syntactic and semantic expectations from previous words already identified in the sentence begin to prime a particular word, which in turn primes its phonological representation, including its initial phoneme. Most importantly, this phoneme representation being primed by top-down processing is *not* the same as the phoneme detector that performs bottom-up processing of the letter. Instead, these are two separate phoneme representations, whose respective activations proceed independently, having no effect on each other (see **9**.2.1 for discussion of this distinction in pre- and post-access phonological recoding).

Most importantly, the rates at which bottom-up and top-down processing produce information about the phoneme may differ. Counterintuitively, top-down processing may produce faster awareness of the phoneme than bottom-up processing. Top-down processing has a head start, because expectations about the phoneme exist prior to its occurrence in the speech stream. The listener may already expect the word containing the phoneme and have primed its phonemic representation, thereby priming the critical phoneme. As the speaker articulates the phoneme, bottom-up processing begins to extract information about it and activate possible phoneme categories. If one of these initial categories matches the phoneme primed by top-down processing, the listener may respond that the phoneme is present. Even though bottom-up processing has not yet finished and has not ruled out other phoneme categories, the converging evidence from top-down processing is enough to convince the listener that the phoneme is present. The response is faster than it would be if no top-down expectation existed, because completing bottom-up processing would take additional time.

In this way, the redundant outputs view accounts for immediacy of interpretation without requiring that top-down processing affect bottom-up processing. Although the syntactic and semantic systems have no effect on the phonological system, immediacy of processing can nevertheless occur for phoneme categorization. Immediacy of interpretation for letter categorization and lexical access can be explained in a similar manner (Forster, 1979; see also Foss & Blank, 1980; Foss & Swinney, 1973; Marcel, 1983a, 1983b).

The redundant outputs view provides a rather roundabout and involved account of top–down processing. Nevertheless, it explains the critical results and is consistent with a modular view of cognition accepted by many theorists (e.g., J.A. Fodor, 1983). It also demonstrates how difficult it can be to distinguish theoretical positions on the basis of behavioral data (J.R. Anderson, 1978; Barsalou, 1990b; Palmer, 1978; J.T. Townsend, 1971, 1990).

9.5 SENTENCE MEMORY

What is the outcome of sentence processing? What information does sentence processing store in long-term memory? One kind of information that people typically do *not* store is information about a sentence's syntactic structure. In an experiment that had substantial impact, Sachs (1967, 1974) found that memory for a sentence's syntax is very poor. Subjects listened to passages containing sentences such as:

A wealthy manufacturer, Mathew Boulton, sought out the young inventor.

After various delays, subjects then received a test sentence that was either the original sentence or a different sentence, such as this passive version:

The young inventor was sought out by a wealthy manufacturer, Mathew Boulton.

Subjects' task was to state whether the test sentence had occurred earlier in the text. When the test sentence occurred immediately after the original sentence, subjects always knew that the passive transformation had not been presented. If the test sentence was presented 25 seconds later, however, subjects could not determine whether they had heard the passive transformation or the original sentence, because they had lost information about the sentence's syntax very quickly. In contrast, subjects were always able to reject test sentences with a different meaning, such as:

The young inventor sought out the wealthy manufacturer, Mathew Boulton.

Although subjects had lost information about the sentence's syntax after 25 seconds, they still retained its *gist*. Numerous investigators have since replicated these findings (e.g., J.R. Anderson, 1974; Hanson & Bellugi, 1982; Wanner, 1974).

Under certain conditions, however, people *do* remember syntactic information. If they know that they will be tested on verbatim memory for sentences, they can remember them word for word (Graesser & G. Mandler, 1975; Johnson-Laird & Stevenson, 1970; D.C. Rubin, 1988; Wallace & D.C. Rubin, 1988a, 1988b). Thus, people learn to recite poetry, theatrical scripts, and their national anthem. Sometimes people also remember the specific wording of statements that play important roles in conversations. Upon hearing praise or criticism, people often rehearse the statement because of its perceived importance, thereby establishing syntactic structure in long-term memory. Similarly, people often remember the specific wording of jokes, either because of rehearsal or because specific wording is central to telling a joke well (Bates, Kintsch, Fletcher, & Giuliani, 1980; Bates, Masling, & Kintsch, 1978; Keenan, MacWhinney, & Mayhew, 1977; Kintsch & Bates, 1977). In general, though, people remember little, if anything, about the syntactic structure of sentences.

9.5.1 Extracting Propositions

Upon discovering that people typically don't remember syntactic information, theorists began to explore the information that people do remember. What is the nature of the gist that remains for a sentence? What constitutes its content? A number of theorists suggested that *propositions* constitute gist (**8.7.4**). Consider the proposition that underlies the gist of the following three sentences:

The voter called up the senator.
The voter called the senator up.
The senator was called up by the voter.

These sentences constitute *paraphrases* of the same proposition, namely:

CALL
(AGENT = voter)
(THEME = senator)

This proposition represents the gist common to the paraphrases, while failing to capture the syntactic structure that distinguishes them. Because propositions represent the gist that people tend to remember from sentences, and omit the information that people tend to forget, they provide a good account of sentence memory. In this section, I review evidence for this view.

An experiment by Kintsch and Keenan (1973) demonstrated that the ease of understanding a sentence depends on the ease of extracting its propositions. Compare the following two sentences:

Romulus, the legendary founder of Rome, took the women of Sabine by force.

Cleopatra's downfall lay in her foolish trust in the fickle political figures of the Roman world.

Although these two sentences have roughly the same number of words, the first contains fewer propositions than the second, according to Kintsch and Keenan's analysis. If sentence processing aims to extract propositions, then people should take longer to understand the second sentence than the first, because they must extract more propositions. Kintsch and Keenan indeed found that the time to process a sentence increased with its number of propositions.

In a tour de force, J.R. Anderson and Bower (1973) provided a wide variety of evidence for the importance of propositions in sentence processing. In one of their experiments, subjects first learned a sentence such as:

The farmer who flew the plane was friendly.

This sentence contains the following propositions:

FARMER   **FLY**
(DISPOSITION = friendly)   (AGENT =)
                                    (THEME = plane)

Subjects then received one of the following sentences:

The <u>farmer</u> who bought the sandals was <u>friendly</u>.

FARMER   **BUY**
(DISPOSITION = friendly)   (AGENT =)
                                    (THEME = sandals)

The lawyer who bought the <u>plane</u> was <u>friendly</u>.

LAWYER   **BUY**
(DISPOSITION = friendly)   (AGENT =)
                                    (THEME = plane)

On the surface, these second sentences are equally similar to the first sentence, because each shares two words with it (i.e., the underlined words). More deeply, however, the second sentence about the farmer shares one proposition with the first sentence, namely:

FARMER
(DISPOSITION = friendly)

In contrast, the sentence about the lawyer shares no propositions with the first sentence. Anderson and Bower predicted that learning the second sentence about the farmer should be easier than learning the sentence about the lawyer, because one proposition in the farmer sentence was learned earlier. Alternatively, if propositions are not important to sentence processing, then the two sentences should be remembered equally well, because each shares the same number of words with the first sentence. In clear support of propositional analysis, Anderson and Bower found that subjects learned the second sentence more easily when they had learned one of its propositions earlier. Even though the repeated proposition was distributed over the first and last constituents in each sentence (e.g., "The farmer . . . was friendly"), subjects extracted it.

An experiment by Ratcliff and McKoon (1978) further demonstrates the importance of propositions in comprehension (the implications of this study for retrieval were discussed in **6.3.1**). Imagine reading the following sentence and storing three propositions for it:

Smoke filled the lodge as the ranger burned newspapers.

BURN	**CAUSE**	**FILL**
(AGENT = ranger)	(CONDITION = ▼)	(SUBSTANCE = smoke)
(THEME = newspapers)	(OUTCOME = ▼)	(CONTAINER = lodge)

After reading several such sentences, you receive a series of target words and must state whether each occurred in any of the earlier sentences. Imagine receiving *lodge* as one of these targets and verifying that it had occurred earlier, and then receiving either *smoke* or *ranger* as the next target. Although these two words were equally close to *lodge* in the original sentence (three words away), *smoke* belongs to the same proposition as *lodge*, whereas *ranger* does not. If you stored the original sentence propositionally, then recognizing *lodge* should prime its proposition, which in turn should prime *smoke*. As a result, *smoke* should be easier to recognize than *ranger*, which is in a different proposition and receives less priming. Ratcliff and McKoon did indeed find that their subjects took less time to recognize a second word from the same proposition than to recognize a word from a new proposition. This finding offers further evidence that people extract propositions from sentences during comprehension.

The propositions that people store for a sentence are not necessarily the ones it conveys explicitly. People often transform propositions to simpler and more direct forms. Consider the following sentence and its propositional representation:

The cat is not a female.

FALSE   ┌──────**CAT**
    (PROPOSITION = ↑)   (SEX = female)

After reading such a sentence, people often confuse it on a memory test with the equivalent, but simpler, version:

The cat is a male.

CAT
    (GENDER = male)

They, thus, construct propositional representations that are simpler and more direct than those stated explicitly (Fillenbaum, 1966; Just & Carpenter, 1976).

9.6 DISCOURSE PROCESSING

The purpose of communication is to describe, evaluate, and control a state of affairs (8.7.3). At all points during a conversation, speakers and listeners coordinate their common ground, such that they share a common understanding of the state of affairs, or what I have called a *referent model*. Over the course of a conversation, a referent model evolves as conversationalists add, delete, and modify propositions. In this section, I review empirical findings that address this process.

9.6.1 Establishing Common Ground and Controlling Focus

For communication to succeed initially, conversationalists must establish the topic that they will be discussing. From then on, they must constantly coordinate their common ground to include the referents to which they will be referring. As we saw in **8.7.2**, physical, linguistic, and cultural co-presence all play central roles in establishing common ground. Within common ground, a referent model represents the specific referents under discussion (**8.7.5**). In a variety of studies, researchers have demonstrated how conversations go awry when an initial referent model is not established properly. Consider the following passage from Bransford and M.K. Johnson (1973):

> The procedure is actually quite simple. First, you arrange things into different groups. Of course one pile may be sufficient depending on how much there is

to do. If you have to go somewhere else due to lack of facilities that is the next step, otherwise you are pretty well set. It is important not to overdo things. That is, it is better to do too few things at once than too many. In the short run this may not seem important but complications can easily arise. A mistake can be expensive as well. At first the whole procedure will seem complicated. Soon, however, it will become just another facet of life. It is difficult to foresee any end to the necessity for this task in the immediate future, but then one can never tell. After the procedure is completed one arranges the materials into groups again. Then they can be put into their appropriate places. Eventually they will be used once more and the whole cycle will have to be repeated. However, this is part of life. (p. 400)

If you have never seen this passage before, you probably have no idea what it's about, because you can't establish an initial referent model. If I tell you that the passage is about *doing laundry*, though, you retrieve knowledge of relevant entities from memory to establish reference. For example, "procedure" in the first sentence refers to *doing the laundry*, and "things" in the second sentence refers to *clothing, linen,* and so on. For numerous expressions throughout the passage, entities associated with doing the laundry provide referents. Consider another passage:

Rocky slowly got up from the mat, planning his escape. He hesitated a moment and thought. Things were not going well. What bothered him most was being held, especially since the charge against him had been weak. He considered his present situation. The lock that held him was strong but he thought he could break it. He knew, however, that his timing would have to be perfect. Rocky was aware that it was because of his early roughness that he had been penalized so severely—much too severely from his point of view. The situation was becoming frustrating; the pressure had been grinding on him far too long. He was being ridden unmercifully. Rocky was getting angry now. He felt he was ready to make his move. He knew that his success or failure would depend on what he did in the next few seconds. (R.C. Anderson, Reynolds, Schallert, & Goetz, 1977, p. 372)

Most people think this passage is about a jail escape, but when wrestlers read it, they think it is about wrestling. Depending on the referent model that becomes active initially, people establish different referents for the same referring expressions. As these examples illustrate, the referent models that become active initially in discourse processing are central to comprehension (see also Bransford & McCarrell, 1974; Dooling & R. Lachman, 1971; Perfetti & Goldman, 1976; Sulin & Dooling, 1974).

Once conversationalists establish an initial referent model, they integrate propositions from subsequent sentences into it. As we saw in **8**.7.5, one of the central problems in discourse theory is explaining how people integrate propositions to produce discourse coherence. Ultimately, they try to insure that they leave no propositions unintegrated and that they establish critical relations between propositions (Glenberg & Epstein, 1985).

Because the potential number of referents in a referent model is large, establishing reference is not always easy or successful. As we saw in **8**.7.5, a pronoun, such as "it," could refer to any number of referents, and one must use various strategies to identify its specific referent in a referent model. To limit the number of possible referents under consideration, people establish a *focus*, namely, a small subset of referents in the referent model to which speakers are likely to refer in upcoming sentences. As a conversation progresses, the referents in focus constantly change as new ones become relevant and others become irrelevant. Referents in focus appear to be stored phonologically in working memory, at least to some extent, given that disruptions of working memory hinder the integration of new propositions (**5**.2.2).

Recency is one important factor that determines the referents in focus. Consider the following passage:

> Frank and Harriet dropped their dog off at the kennel before leaving California and heading for Montana. The kennel had been founded by a retired couple from New York, but was now run by the husband of a geologist. He had tried his luck at professional baseball and failed, prior to meeting his wife while he was hiking and she was collecting geological specimens in Yosemite.

The referents in focus include those mentioned most recently, such as *Yosemite* and *geological specimens*, and the reader expects the next sentence to be about one of them. Consequently, a sentence about a referent in focus is integrated into the referent model easily:

> Yosemite had been unusually rainy that summer.

Whereas a sentence about a referent not in focus is surprising and takes longer to integrate:

> Frank and Harriet visited Montana every summer for its pristine beauty and superb fishing.

Many researchers have indeed found that sentences about recent referents in focus are easier to integrate than sentences about earlier referents out of focus (Carpenter & Just, 1977a, 1977b; H.H. Clark & Sengul, 1979; Ehrlich & Rayner, 1983; Just & Carpenter, 1980; Malt, 1985).

Other factors besides recency also determine the referents in focus. For example, people often identify *themes* that they believe will continue to be relevant and maintain related referents in working memory through rehearsal. Consider the passage:

> The <u>wedding</u> was to occur on a patio overlooking the mountain valley below. The air was cool and dry as the sun set in the clouds. As the <u>bride</u> and groom stood against the railing, the minister began the ceremony.

Wedding is introduced at the start of the first sentence, but it is not mentioned again in the rest of this sentence, nor in the second sentence. Nevertheless, readers are not surprised by *bride* in the third sentence, and in fact expect it, as priming effects in several studies have shown. Although *wedding* is no longer recent, rehearsal has nevertheless maintained it in focus. Moreover, rehearsal has maintained the activation of *wedding's* associates, such as *bride*, even though the text never mentioned them explicitly. Referents that are thematically relevant to the current topic become active in working memory and remain active until the topic is no longer relevant (A. Anderson, Garrod, & Sanford, 1983; Foss, 1982; Morrow, 1985a, 1985b; Morrow, Bower, & Greenspan, 1989; Morrow, Greenspan, & Bower, 1987; Sharkey & D.C. Mitchell, 1985).

At any given point in a discourse, the current focus contains recent and thematically relevant information in the referent model. However, a particular referring expression, or *anaphor*, could potentially refer to any one of these focal referents (**8**.7.5). Consequently, additional strategies are needed to identify the speaker's intended referent. Investigators have identified a number of strategies that people use to facilitate this process. The following list, adapted from a review by Just and Carpenter (1987, p. 207), summarizes these strategies:

Recency. On encountering a possible anaphor, favor the most recent referent in focus (G.L. Murphy, 1985), as in:

> Dorothea ate pie; <u>Ethel</u> ate cake. Later <u>she</u> had coffee.

Salience. On encountering a possible anaphor, favor the referent in focus that is most salient grammatically (Carpenter & Just, 1977a, 1977b; H.H. Clark & Sengul, 1979; Ehrlich & Rayner, 1983; Malt, 1985), as in:

> It was <u>Paula</u> who met Melissa; <u>she</u> wanted to discuss politics.

Gender. On encountering a possible anaphor, favor a referent that maintains consistency of gender (Corbett & Chang, 1983), as in:

> <u>Gus</u> and Sharon left when <u>he</u> became unhappy.

Number. On encountering a possible anaphor, favor a referent that maintains consistency of number, as in:

When the cup and plates fell, it broke.

Grammatical role. On encountering a possible anaphor, favor a referent that maintains grammatical role (Grober, Beardsley, & Caramazza, 1978; G.L. Murphy, 1985; Sheldon, 1974), as in:

Floyd saw Bert, and then he drove away.

Knowledge. On encountering a possible anaphor, favor a referent that seems plausible based on general knowledge (Caramazza, Grober, Garvey, & Yates, 1977; Hirst & Brill, 1980), as in:

The rabbi and the Pope met for lunch; he was accompanied by his wife.

Although these examples only illustrate strategies for pronouns, they also apply to other anaphoric devices, including repetition and definite description (**8.7.5**).

Much additional research has explored the time course of anaphora (Corbett, 1984; Corbett & Chang, 1983; Ehrlich & Rayner, 1983; Just & Carpenter, 1978, 1980). On encountering an anaphor, one often pauses while establishing co-reference. The amount of time taken to process an anaphor depends on the ease of establishing co-reference, with difficult co-references taking longer. During this time, one may activate more than one possible referent in the discourse model, if more than one satisfies the strategies just described. Eventually, the referent is selected that satisfies the most strategies. Thus, if two referents match on gender but one is more recent, people consider both initially but eventually select the more recent one. When a satisfactory referent cannot be found, processing of the sentence continues past the anaphor, and another attempt to find its referent occurs upon reaching the end of the sentence.

Speakers attempt to facilitate anaphora by selecting referring expressions that they believe uniquely identify referents in the common ground (H.H. Clark & Schaefer, 1989; H.H. Clark, Schreuder, & Buttrick, 1983; H.H. Clark & Wilkes-Gibbs, 1986; Isaacs & H.H. Clark, 1987; Schober & H.H. Clark, 1989). As we saw in **8.7.2**, the knowledge activated for an expression (its sense) provides clues about what the referent might be (Fig. 8.5). When these clues are insufficient and reference fails, speakers and listeners follow various conventions in attempting to establish it, such as expanding a referring expression to contain more information. For example, a speaker might expand a failed reference in "Please hand me the *glue*" to "Please hand me the *epoxy glue on the top shelf.*" Furthermore, speakers often request verification that reference has succeeded (e.g., "know what I mean?"), and listeners often provide such verification (e.g., by nodding).

9.6.2 Discourse Memory

As one processes a discourse, what information about it becomes stored in long-term memory? As we just saw for sentence memory (**9.5**), people typically do not store the syntactic structure of a sentence but store only its propositions. In this section, I explore issues concerning memory for the propositions that people extract from a discourse.

As each sentence in a discourse is processed, its propositions are integrated into an evolving referent model. Once the propositions are integrated, is semantic information about individual sentences lost, similar to syntactic information, or is semantic information retained about which sentences contained which propositions? Consider the following discourse:

Marshall, who lived near Portland, owned a Volvo.   (1)
The Volvo had a digital stereo.   (2)
Marshall had a friend named Rick, who also lived near Portland.   (3)
Rick bought the Volvo from Marshall.   (4)

Figure 9.4 shows a referent model that incorporates all of the propositions from this discourse. Figure 9.4 also indicates the sentences that provided the information for each proposition in the referent model (i.e., the superscripted numbers in the referent model). For example, Sentences 1, 3, and 4 provided information about *Marshall*, Sentences 3 and 4 provided information about *Rick*, and Sentence 2 provided information about the *digital stereo*. If subjects

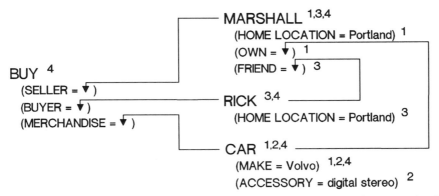

Figure 9.4. Example of sentence integration during discourse processing. The superscripted numbers indicates the sentences that provided the information for each proposition

store information about which propositions came from which sentences—the numbers in Fig. 9.4—then they should be able to state that they did not read these sentences :

> Marshall owned a Volvo, which had a digital stereo.
> Marshall had a friend named Rick, who bought the Volvo from him.

Rather, they should see that these test sentences combine propositions from multiple sentences in the original text. Moreover, upon receiving sentences 1, 2, 3, and 4, subjects should be able to recognize that they had seen these sentences previously. As it turns out, subjects can perform neither type of judgment: They can neither reject the above sentences that did not occur in text, nor identify the sentences that did. Instead, they generally guess when making their memory judgments. Nevertheless, subjects are able to reject sentences that are inconsistent with the discourse model as a whole, such as:

> Marshall bought the Volvo from Rick.

Once people extract a sentence's propositions and integrate them into a referent model, they typically discard the sentence and all of the syntactic and semantic information that individuates it. The only remnant of the sentence that remains is the propositional gist it adds to the integrated discourse model. As a result, people can identify sentences consistent with the discourse model but not the sentences that led to its construction (Barclay, 1973; Bransford & Franks, 1971; Reitman & Bower, 1973).

As we saw earlier, people often perform inferences during sentence processing (**9**.3.3). They perform similar inferences during discourse processing as well. Consider the sentences:

> Edna left her surfboard at the shop overnight for repairs. Just before daylight, an electrical fire broke out in the shop and burned it to the ground.

Following a delay, people are likely to believe, mistakenly, that they had also read:

> Edna's surfboard burned in the fire at the shop.

As discussed earlier, researchers can't always be sure whether people draw an inference while understanding a discourse, or whether they only draw it later when it becomes relevant (**9**.3.3). Some inferences may be warranted so strongly, or may be so necessary for understanding later text, that they are drawn immediately. Other inferences, drawn later at retrieval, underlie the process of *reconstruction* (**6**.3.2).

A wide variety of integrative inferences are possible during comprehension, much along the lines of those described earlier for sentence processing (**9**.3.3). Inferences may establish spatial, temporal, and causal relationships between events; inferences may provide specific instantiations of general terms; and inferences may provide enabling conditions and outcomes. In most cases, frames provide the source of these inferences (**6**.1.3, **7**.2.2). Because speakers often omit many necessary propositions from their sentences, listeners frequently must draw the respective inferences to ensure that their referent models are properly integrated. Speakers don't usually omit such information to be uncooperative. They simply assume that listeners can compute these inferences themselves and would rather not be burdened with hearing them stated explicitly (i.e., see Grice's maxim of quantity in **8**.7.1). In addition, speakers often omit information in cases where they wish to be subtle and not state a controversial or indelicate proposition directly. To the extent that such inferences are computed while comprehending a discourse, they become part of the referent model established for it.

Because all propositions within a referent model are not equally memorable, theorists have tried to identify what makes some propositions more memorable than others. According to the *content* view, people remember some propositions well, because they convey certain types of information. In stories, for example, people remember propositions that describe initiating events, major goals, and final outcomes better than propositions that describe psychological states and minor goals (Cirilo & Foss, 1980; Kintsch, Kozminsky, Streby, McKoon, & Keenan, 1975; J.M. Mandler & N.S. Johnson, 1977; McKoon, 1977; Stein & Glenn, 1979; Thorndyke, 1977). According to the *structural* view, people remember some propositions well, because of their centrality in the referent model. Propositions may be central, either because they are associated to many subordinate propositions, or because they fall within a causal chain that represents a critical event sequence. Memory for central propositions benefits from both repetition and organization (**6**.1.1, **6**.1.3): Every time central propositions are associated to another proposition, the repetition they experience strengthens them in memory, and the newly associated proposition provides another organizational pathway into it during retrieval (**6**.3.1). Furthermore, people are likely to rehearse central propositions together in working memory as thematic information (see the discussion of focus in **9**.6.1). Together, the increased repetition and organization that central propositions receive make them more memorable than propositions that receive less repetition and integration. In general, theorists have come to prefer the structural view over the content view: Some types of content tend to be more central across discourses than others, thereby becoming more memorable (Kintsch & van Dijk, 1978; Omanson, 1982; van Dijk & Kintsch, 1983).

9.6.3 Processing Speech Acts

The intended meaning of a sentence is not necessarily its literal meaning. Imagine that a friend has just walked onto your porch with muddy shoes and is about to enter the house. You say sarcastically:

I hope that you're planning to wear those shoes in the house.

Clearly, your intended message goes beyond the literal meaning of the utterance, implying that your friend needs to remove his shoes before entering. As we saw in **8**.7.1 and **8**.7.3, such inferences occur frequently following (cooperative) violations of the cooperative principle and in indirect speech acts.

What do people remember about sentences like these? Do they remember their literal content, their implied content, or both? Researchers have found that both may be remembered. Depending on the circumstances, people may add propositions for both the literal and implied meanings of a sentence to a referent model (Jarvella & Collas, 1974).

Is it always necessary to compute a sentence's literal meaning prior to computing its implied meaning? Some studies have found that people skip computing the literal meaning, because the context generates such a strong expectancy about the implied meaning. Imagine that someone at dinner is watching you use the pepper grinder and then utters when you're finished:

Can you pass the pepper?

In this context, the literal question about your ability to pass the pepper is bypassed, because the intended request is so salient. As this example illustrates, many indirect requests are almost idiomatic. Given the frequent cooccurrence of their surface form and implied meaning, it is not surprising that people activate the implied meaning automatically (**4**.1.2). In these cases, people only store propositions about the implied meaning in the referent model and not the literal meaning (Gibbs, 1979, 1981, 1983, 1984, 1986, 1989).

People do not always ignore literal meaning, however. Imagine that someone calls a merchant on the telephone and asks:

Would you mind telling me what time you close tonight?

The merchant could provide two kinds of information in response: First, she could respond to the literal question and state whether she minds providing the information. Second, she could respond to the indirect request and state what time her business closes. If she bypasses the literal meaning and only processes the intended message, then she should not begin her utterance by saying "yes" or "no" in response to the literal question. Instead, she should only provide the closing time. If she also processes the literal meaning, though, she may preface the closing time by stating whether she minds providing it. To test this, H.H. Clark (1979) had a research assistant call local merchants and ask them their closing times. He found that merchants often responded to the literal meaning of the request, as well as to the indirect request (e.g., "No, 10 o'clock"). Under some conditions, people do compute the literal meaning of indirect speech acts and respond to them. Whether they compute both the literal and implied meaning of a sentence, or whether they only compute the implied meaning, depends on current circumstances and the nature of the utterance. In either case, people are likely to include propositions for at least the implied meaning in the evolving referent model.

9.7 SPEECH PRODUCTION

Language production has generally received less attention than language comprehension. Reviews of language research always discuss comprehension first and allocate much less space to production, as this chapter illustrates. Yet, research on production has been quite successful, perhaps more so than work on comprehension. Whereas theorists have only developed a rough account of comprehension, a fairly precise account of production was developed by Fromkin (1971, 1973) and Garrett (1975, 1980, 1988) in the early 1970s. Although more recent work has produced significant new insights into the mechanisms of speech production, much of the original Fromkin-Garrett framework remains. Moreover, findings from language production demonstrate the importance of linguistic units at least as convincingly as findings from language comprehension. As we shall see, research on production has provided clear evidence for the psychological importance of constituents, words, morphemes, semantic properties, phonemes, and articulatory features. In this section, I only discuss language production in speech, but a full treatment would also have to consider language production in writing and typing (Bereiter, Burtis, & Scardamalia, 1988; Rosenbaum, 1990; Rumelhart & Norman, 1982).

To develop a theory of language production, early theorists utilized an empirical methodology that was particularly clever and opportunistic. Because of the difficulties inherent in studying production under controlled laboratory conditions, early theorists depended almost completely on naturally occurring speech errors from real-world conversations. As we shall see shortly, such speech errors turn out to be highly informative, providing rich insights into the cognitive mechanisms that produce speech. Although naturally occurring speech errors have played the primary role in motivating theories of speech production, researchers are increasingly discovering ways to perform carefully controlled, laboratory experiments that assess these theories more rigorously. For further discussion of these theories and related work, see H.H. Clark and E.V. Clark (1977, chaps. 6 & 7), Foss and Hakes (1978, chaps. 6 & 7), and Levelt (1989). Also see Bock (1987), Dell (1986), and MacKay (1987).[2]

9.7.1 Levels of Processing in Production

Theorists generally assume that cognitive operations at multiple levels of processing enter into the production of an utterance. Beginning with an abstract proposition, a speaker must find words and syntactic structures to express it. The speaker must then construct a phonological representation of these words and eventually a linear sequence of articulated speech sounds. The following seven steps roughly capture the levels of processing that many theorists believe underlie speech production:

LEVEL 1. Formulate a message.   The speaker determines the propositions to be conveyed in the current utterance.

Consider the propositional representation at Level 1 of Fig. 9.5. The speaker intends to say something about a farmer currently mowing alfalfa. At this point, the speaker has only a conceptual representation of the utterance and nothing more.

LEVEL 2. Formulate an abstract sentential representation.   The speaker retrieves semantic representations of content words that express the message formulated at Level 1, and then retrieves a syntactic frame for the verb and assigns sentential roles to the semantic representations of content words (e.g., subject, direct argument).

Consider the abstract sentential representation at Level 2 of Fig. 9.5. The speaker first retrieves semantic representations of the content words (i.e., *farmer, mow, hay*). Note that these semantic representations are not necessarily the same as their conceptual counterparts in the propositional representation (as the different fonts for the content words at Levels 1 and 2 indicate). Whereas the conceptual representations at Level 1 may not be associated with particular words, the semantic representations at Level 2 are. To illustrate this, Fig. 9.5 contains a conceptual representation of *alfalfa*

---

[2] I am indebted to Kathryn Bock for discussion and guidance on this topic.

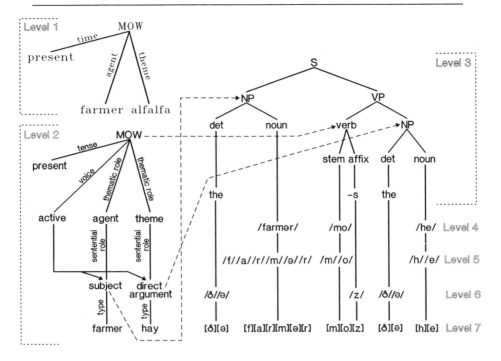

Figure 9.5. Illustration of the seven levels of processing in speech production.

in the propositional representation but a semantic representation of *hay* in the sentential representation. Whereas the speaker conceptualized alfalfa at Level 1, the more general word *hay* is retrieved to represent it at Level 2.

The speaker also retrieves the active-voice verb frame for *mow*, which states that the subject of the verb will be the agent and that the direct argument will be the theme (**8.5.2**). The speaker then inserts the semantic representations of the content words into the verb frame (i.e., *farmer* is the subject, and *hay* is the direct argument).

LEVEL 3. Construct a phrase marker. Using the abstract sentential representation from Level 2 as a guide, the speaker constructs a phrase marker for the sentence (**8.5.1**). The speaker then maps sentential roles from the sentential representation into the phrase marker. Finally, the speaker inserts semantic representations of function words and affixes into the phrase marker.

Consider the phrase marker at Level 3 of Fig. 9.5. Using the subject, verb, and direct argument from the sentential representation as guides, the speaker constructs a noun phrase for the subject and a verb phrase for the verb and its direct argument. As the dashed lines illustrate, the speaker maps the sentential roles for the subject and the direct argument into the relevant constituents as the phrase marker develops. Finally, the speaker inserts semantic representations of the necessary function words and affixes into the phrase marker. These include semantic representations of the determiners that precede farmer and hay (e.g., the, the) and the present tense, singular affix that follows mow (i.e., -s).

LEVEL 4. Formulate phonological representations of content words. Using the abstract sentential representation at Level 2 as a guide, the speaker retrieves a phonological representation for each content word and inserts it into the proper slot of the phrase marker constructed at Level 3.

Consider the phonological representations of the content words at Level 4 of Fig. 9.5. For each content word in the sentential representation at Level 2, the speaker retrieves a phonological representation, such as /mo/ for *mow* and /he/ for *hay*. As these examples illustrate, the phonemic and phonetic notation at this and the remaining levels of Fig. 9.5 do not correspond identically to their orthographic counterparts in written words (e.g., /he/ vs. "hay"). The speaker then inserts each phonological representation into the phrase marker, assigning /mo/ to the verb stem of the verb phrase and /he/ to the noun in the second noun phrase.

LEVEL 5. Spell out the initial phonological representation. For each phonological representation of a content word at Level 4, the speaker spells it out as a series of individual phonemes.

In Fig. 9.5, consider the spell–out at Level 5 of the phonological representations at Level 4. As you can see, the speaker specifies the phonological form of each content word as a series of phonemes. For example, the speaker spells out /mo/ as /m/ /o/ and /he/ as /h/ /e/.

LEVEL 6. Finalize the phonological representation. For each semantic representation of a function word and affix inserted into the phrase marker at Level 3, the speaker retrieves a phonological representation and spells it out.

In Fig. 9.5, consider the phonological representations at Level 6 of the function words and affixes at Level 3. For each of the determiners preceding *farmer* and *hay* (i.e., *the, the*), and for the present tense, singular affix following *mow* (i.e., -s), the speaker retrieves a phonological representation and spells it out, as in spelling out the -s following *mow* with /z/.

LEVEL 7. Formulate phonetic segments. For each phoneme spelled out at Levels 5 and 6, the speaker specifies the articulatory features of the phone that expresses it.

Look at the phonetic representations at Level 7 of Fig. 9.5. The speaker replaces each phoneme at Levels 5 and 6 with a phonetic representation that will guide its articulation, specifing, for example, that the /m/ beginning /mo/ is the *unvoiced bilabial stop*, [m].

Although this brief overview summarizes the levels of processing that theorists have identified in language production, it simplifies many of the subtleties and key points in more technical analyses. For example, these seven levels do not necessarily operate as strict serial stages of processing, as this analysis suggests, nor does each level operate independently of the others. Instead, recent work has demonstrated important interactions between these levels. For example, the phonological representation of a word at Level 4 may affect the retrieval of semantic representations at Level 2. Such results illustrate that these levels do not necessarily occur one after another, with each level waiting until the prior levels complete. Instead, multiple levels often proceed simultaneously, with complex interactions occurring between them (Dell, 1986; Dell & Reich, 1981).

9.7.2 Evidence from Speech Errors

What evidence exists for these seven levels of processing in production? As we shall see, speech errors provide compelling support for this analysis, revealing these specific levels of processing. Note that the errors I present constitute a small fragment of the evidence that linguists and psychologists have marshaled to support this view.

Consider the first level of processing, where the speaker formulates a message. Sometimes a speaker will say something and then realize that the utterance does not express the original propositions in the message. Intending to express the proposition at Level 1 in Fig. 9.5, a speaker might utter incorrectly:

The farmer mows the corn.

Immediately upon uttering this sentence, the speaker might realize the error and say, "I mean the hay," indicating awareness of the original proposition. If the speaker had not formulated the proposition at Level 1, the initial utterance would not seem incorrect. Because the speaker is aware of this error, the message formulated initially must differ from the utterance that attempts to express it (Bock, 1987; H.H. Clark & E.V. Clark, 1977, pp. 237-248; Fromkin, 1971, 1973; Garrett, 1980).

Let us look now at the evidence for the second level of processing, where the speaker formulates an abstract sentential representation. At this point in constructing an utterance, the speaker must retrieve semantic representations of content words from memory and assign them to sentential roles. Two kinds of errors, *semantic substitutions* and *word exchanges*, reflect the presence of these retrieval and assignment processes, respectively. In semantic substitutions, the speaker mistakenly retrieves a word whose semantic properties are similar to the concept in the propositional representation, as in:

He rode his bike to school <u>tomorrow</u>.

Whereas the intended word was *yesterday, tomorrow* was retrieved instead. Such substitutions may occur if a semantic property is lost from the formulation of a concept in a proposition (e.g., *past* from *yesterday*), or if a word with a similar semantic representation is highly active for some reason (e.g., it is a high frequency or was used in a recent utterance; **9.2.3**). Because these substitutions interchange semantically related words, they illustrate the speaker's attempt to retrieve semantic representations at this level of processing.

In word exchanges, the speaker assigns two content words to the wrong sentential roles, as in:

<u>Dinner</u> is being served at <u>wine</u>.

When a speaker exchanges complete words, as in this case, the two words almost always belong to the same grammatical class (e.g., two nouns) and can fill the same sentential roles (e.g., both *dinner* and *wine* could be the subject or the indirect argument of a verb). Because of these similarities, the speaker may mistakenly assign the semantic representations of these words to different sentential roles, such that the words eventually show up in different parts of the sentence (e.g., the word that should be the subject appears as the indirect argument, and vice versa). Because the speaker is manipulating semantic representations and sentential roles at this level, the errors involve word units that may end up in different constituents of the final utterance (Bock & Loebell, 1990; Fromkin, 1973; Garrett, 1980).

Evidence for the third level of processing, where the speaker constructs a phrase marker, is provided by *proximity constraints on exchanges*. As we just saw, word exchanges often cross constituent boundaries. In contrast, other types of exchanges, which we shall consider shortly, almost always occur within the same constituent (e.g., stem–morpheme exchanges, sound exchanges). This suggests that word exchanges occur prior to the construction of a phrase marker, whereas other exchanges occur after its construction. Prior to the existence of a phrase marker, the speaker is processing the entire sentence conceptually, not yet working with a temporally organized plan for producing the utterance. Once a phrase marker exists, however, it specifies constituents in a temporal plan. Because the speaker then processes the plan constituent by constituent at each remaining level, errors thereafter remain within constituents. The lack of a proximity constraint on word exchanges initially, followed by the presence of proximity constraints on other types of exchanges later, indicates the construction of a phrase marker at Level 3 (Garrett, 1975, 1980).

Next consider evidence for the fourth level of processing, where the speaker formulates phonological representations for the semantic representations retrieved at Level 2. At this point in constructing an utterance, the speaker must retrieve phonological representations of content words from memory and insert them into the phrase marker constructed at Level 3. Two kinds of errors, *phonological substitutions (malapropisms)* and *stem-morpheme exchanges*, reflect the presence of these retrieval and insertion processes, respectively. In phonological substitutions, the speaker retrieves an incorrect phonological representation whose properties are similar to the intended phonological representation, as in:

He's the kind of soldier a man looks up to and wants to <u>emanate</u>.

Whereas the speaker intended to retrieve "emulate," the phonologically related "emanate" was retrieved instead. Because these substitutions interchange phonologically related words, they illustrate the attempt to retrieve phonological representations at this level of processing.

In stem-morpheme exchanges, the speaker switches two stem morphemes, as in:

She's already <u>trunk</u>ed two <u>pack</u>s.

At Level 3, the phrase marker specified that the verb *pack* would be in the past tense and that the direct argument *trunk* would be plural. Later, at Level 4, the speaker correctly retrieves the phonological representations of the stem morphemes for *pack* and *trunk*. When subsequently attempting to insert these phonological representations into the phrase marker, however, "trunk" is mistakenly inserted into the slot for the verb and "pack" is inserted into the slot for the direct argument. Because the phrase marker is already in place, along with its function words and affixes, the phonological representations of "trunk" and "pack" become associated with the wrong positions and therefore the wrong affixes. Stem-morpheme exchanges, thus, provide evidence for Level 3, as well as Level 4 (Garrett, 1975, 1980; Stemberger, 1985).

Evidence for the fifth level of processing, where the speaker spells out the initial phonological representation, comes from *sound exchanges*. At this point in constructing an utterance, the speaker specifies the individual phonemes that constitute each phonological representation of a content word at Level 4. In a sound exchange, the speaker switches two phonemes from different words, as in:

<u>h</u>eft <u>l</u>emisphere

Sound exchanges are similar to word exchanges and stem-morpheme exchanges, except that they occur for still smaller units of linguistic structure. Whereas exchanges at Levels 2 and 4 switch words and stem morphemes, respectively, sound exchanges at Level 5 switch phonemes. For a sound exchange to occur, the phonological representation constructed at the Level 4 must already be in place. Otherwise, entire words or morphemes would switch—not just one of their phonemes. In the process of spelling out the individual phonemes for the phonological representations of content words, the speaker mistakenly exchanges two of them. Because speakers often exchange individual phonemes in this manner, they appear to spell out the phonological representations of content words one phoneme at a time (Fromkin, 1973; Garrett, 1980; Shattuck-Hufnagel, 1987).

Consider evidence for the sixth level of processing, where the speaker formulates the phonological representation of the utterance further, inserting phonological representations of the function words and affixes that were represented semantically in the phrase marker at Level 3. *Accommodations* to earlier speech errors indicate the presence of Level 6, as in:

There's <u>an</u> island on the restaurant.
week<u>s</u> in the day

In the first example, *restaurant* and *island* exchange at Level 2. Subsequent insertion of the phonological representation for the indefinite article "a" accommodates to this error. If "restaurant" had occurred in the correct position, "a" would have preceded it. When "island" mistakenly replaces "restaurant," however, "an" occurs instead of "a," following the phonological rule that "a" precedes words beginning with a consonant, and "an" precedes words beginning with a vowel. The accommodation of the indefinite article to "island" indicates that the speaker must have inserted the phonological representation of the indefinite article *after* formulating the phonological representation of "island" at Levels 4 and 5. A sixth level of processing must exist to capture how the phonological representations of function words accommodate to the prior phonological representations of content words. Similarly, in the second example *day* and *week* exchange at Level 4. Later insertion of the phonological representation for the plural affix -*s* accommodates to this error: Although the speaker would have specified -*s* as /z/ following "day," it is specified as /s/ following "week," according to the voicing rule discussed in **8.3**. Again, this accommodation provides evidence for a sixth level of speech production. For the accommodation to occur correctly, it must have occurred after the phonological representation of content words at Levels 4 and 5 (Fromkin, 1973; Garrett, 1980).

Finally, evidence for the seventh level of processing, where the speaker specifies phonetic segments, comes from *phonetic feature exchanges*. At this point in constructing an utterance, the speaker specifies the articulatory features of each phone that expresses a phoneme in the phonological representation (**8.2**). In the process, phonetic features may exchange between two phonemes in two different words, as in:

p̪ig and v̪at

The speaker meant to utter "big and fat" but accidentally exchanged voicing in the [b] for "big" with non-voicing in the [f] for "fat." For this error to have occurred, the speaker must already have spelled out the phonemes for /b/ and /f/ correctly at Level 5. Once these phonemes were in place, the speaker's attempt to specify them phonetically led to the exchange of phonetic features (Fromkin, 1973).

As we have seen, speech error data offer strong support for multiple levels of processing in speech production. These natural slips of the tongue provide penetrating glimpses into the cognitive mechanisms that produce linguistic utterances. In addition, speech error data also provide strong support for the psychological validity of the various linguistic units discussed throughout these last two chapters: Whereas word exchanges generally occur across two different constituents, most other speech errors occur within the same constituent. As a result, constituents appear to have an important psychological status in speech production. Similarly, we saw from stem-morpheme errors that morphemes behave as independent units, which can move mistakenly. From semantic substitutions, phonological substitutions, sound exchanges, and phonetic feature exchanges, we saw that semantic properties, phonemes, and articulatory features also behave as independent units. Because we saw evidence for all of these units earlier in comprehension, they appear central to the cognitive processes that underlie language in general.

9.8 LANGUAGE AND THOUGHT

Before leaving language and moving to thought in the next chapter, I discuss the relation between them briefly (see also H.H. Clark & E.V. Clark, 1977, chap. 14; Foss & Hakes, 1978, chap. 13; Glucksberg, 1988). According to the Whorf-Sapir hypothesis (Sapir, 1968; Whorf, 1956), language plays a central role in how people think about the world: Because different cultures have different languages, their members must think about the world differently. As a simple example, consider color terms, which vary widely across cultures. Some cultures only have words for *black* and *white*; others only have words for *black*, *white*, and *red*; and still others only have words for *black*, *white*, *red, yellow,* and *green.* English-speaking cultures have many additional color terms, such as *blue, lavender,* and *chartreuse.* According to the Whorf-Sapir view, then, the members of cultures with different color terms should perceive the color spectrum differently. The evidence, however, clearly indicates that members of all cultures perceive colors in basically the same way. Differences in the language of color do not produce differences in the experience of color. Instead, the biological bases of color detection mechanisms in vision constrain all humans to experience color similarly (2.2; Berlin & Kay, 1969; Heider, 1972; Heider & D. Oliver, 1973; G.A. Miller & Johnson-Laird, 1976; Rosch, 1974).

Similarly, consider how people think about plants. Whereas people from plant gathering cultures often have extensive folk vocabularies for plants, people from industrial cultures typically do not. In the absence of frequent contact with nature, people from industrial cultures tend to be less adept at plant naming. Nevertheless, these individuals may be able to think about plants in the same ways as people from plant gathering cultures. For example, people from both types of cultures may perceive the colors, shapes, textures, and structures of plants similarly. In addition, people from industrial cultures can develop linguistic expressions for unnamed plants, such as "the mottled bluish grey plant with clusters of pointed leaves." Even though the two cultures have different linguistic systems for describing a domain, their members may nevertheless be able to think about them similarly.

Alternatively, a strong case exists for thought determining language. On this view, linguistic expressions develop to serve the needs of everyday thought. Consider how thought might produce differences in color terms. In general, large numbers of color terms tend to occur more often in industrial cultures than in non-industrial cultures. As theorists have suggested, the ability to extract colors from natural objects and isolate them in paints and dyes may produce the need to create terms for a wider variety of colors. Because a culture's members must think about and discuss independent color substances, it develops precise and efficient expressions for referring to them (G.A. Miller & Johnson-Laird, 1976). Similarly, consider how thought might produce differences in plant vocabulary. Because plant gathering is central to everyday life in some cultures, its members develop a large number of terms for different types of plants. In these cultures, the requirements of everyday thought produce a specialized vocabulary for referring to plants precisely and efficiently during conversation.

Although language may not determine *what* people think about the world, it may affect how *efficiently* they think about it. The ability to think about a domain efficiently may reflect the extent to which a culture has developed words for all of the concepts in the domain that individuals must manipulate in thought. Thus, members of a plant gathering culture should be able to reason rapidly about plants, because they have a highly developed vocabulary of plant concepts. In contrast, if members of an industrial culture must construct unwieldy linguistic expressions to think about plants, they may find reasoning about plants more difficult. Certainly, not all thought utilizes linguistic expressions: When people use imagery in thought (5.2.3), linguistic expressions may play little role. When language is relevant, it may simply streamline thought, not constrain it.

10

THOUGHT

Several years ago, I met with a community group that wanted to learn more about cognitive psychology and, in particular, its views on human thought. Interestingly, the audience found my inclusion of non-formal and mundane cognitive operations in thought to be inappropriate. They wanted, rather, to include only formal and creative operations, believing thought to consist exclusively of lofty, elegant, and rigorous mental activity. I have since encountered this stereotype about thought elsewhere. My response on these occasions has been to note, first, how rarely most people employ formal thought, not only in their daily lives, but even in situations where it might be expected. As we shall see, human thought often deviates substantially from the formal procedures that logicians, mathematicians, scientists, and educators prescribe. Second, I stress that the cognitive operations typical of people's mental activity are quite powerful, given the impressiveness of their abilities to make decisions, to reason, and to solve problems. Although computers are often much better at formal operations (e.g., numerical analysis, deduction), people are much better decision makers, reasoners, and problem solvers in real-world contexts. Third, I point out that these non-formal, cognitive operations are actually quite complex. Although researchers can implement numerical analysis and logic on computers, they are far from having fully implemented the cognitive operations that underlie human thought. To a large extent, this reflects an incomplete analysis of these operations in cognitive psychology. Once analyses of thought are more complete, researchers may be able to build computers that are comparable to people in their abilities to make decisions, reason, and solve problems. As we shall see, however, people are far from perfect at these tasks, exhibiting numerous biases and limitations. Nevertheless, people are quite successful at coping with the tremendous complexity and variability that they face in their daily lives. Non-formal, unique cognitive operations appear to be much more central to the character of human thought and intelligence than formal operations.

10.1 DEFINITIONS AND THEMES

For the remainder of this chapter, I adopt the following definition: *Thought* involves a series of transformations performed on the contents of working memory, where these transformations and contents are conscious at least to some extent. Note that this definition includes a wide variety of non-purposive activities, such as daydreaming and free association (Johnson-Laird, 1988). Although these are interesting and important phenomena, I do not pursue them further here.

Instead, I address *purposive thought*, which is a series of transformations on the contents of working memory *to achieve a goal*, where these transformations and contents are at least partly conscious. This definition rules out a variety of other cognitive activities that are purposive. For example, simple acts of categorization and memory retrieval, even though purposive, typically do not involve a conscious series of transformations. Similarly, highly automatized procedures, such as tying one's shoes, are purposive, yet proceed with little conscious awareness. On the other hand, difficult categorizations and retrievals that occur over an extended time period do constitute purposive thought, because they require a conscious series of transformations. Similarly, having to undo a knot in order to tie one's shoes requires purposive thought.

This definition of purposive thought includes both formal and non-formal procedures. Clearly, the formal procedures central to logical and mathematical reasoning satisfy it, but so do the non-formal procedures that underlie more typical, mundane thought, as we shall see shortly. Furthermore, I assume that non-purposive thought frequently affects purposive thought. While performing a cognitive procedure to achieve a goal, one's thoughts may wander in spontaneous and unintended manners to produce information that affects purposive processing. For example, while trying to decide whether to have a peach or yogurt for an afternoon snack, a person might be reminded of some peach trees in bloom along his running route. Upon thinking of these trees, he might realize that he has time for a short run during the next hour and therefore should eat the peach, because it is less filling and less likely to interfere with running. A spontaneous, unintentional reminding during the process of selecting a snack ultimately determined its outcome (**4**.2.1, **6**.3.3; Johnson-Laird, 1988).

Three themes shape my discussion of purposive thought: similarity, availability, and framing. Each reflects a fundamental aspect of human information processing that occurs automatically to a large extent, pervading a wide variety of cognitive activities.

Similarity plays an extensive role in human thought (**10**.2). As we have seen at numerous points in this book, people often compare two representations and determine the extent to which their properties are similar. Similarity differs considerably from the types of comparisons found in formal procedures for reasoning. In logic, for example, comparisons between two propositions may assess whether they match perfectly, whether one is a subset of the other, or whether one is the negation of the other.[1] In mathematics, comparisons between two numbers may involve subtraction or division to see which number is larger. Whereas formal comparisons follow strict procedures such as these, similarity proceeds relatively unconstrained, because people can judge similarity using any criteria they please (Goodman, 1955, 1972; Quine, 1969). Nevertheless, similarity often dominates human thought, as people note the similarity between two representations and base their decisions on it.

Availability is another non-formal process that pervades human thought. Availability simply concerns how easily one can retrieve a particular piece of information from long-term memory. Many factors considered in chapter 6 can make information highly available, including multiple repetitions, rehearsal, elaboration, low interference, and highly overlapping retrieval cues. As we shall see, the availability of information and reasoning procedures strongly influences human thought: Those that are most available dominate processing (Kahneman et al., 1982; A. Tversky & Kahneman, 1973).

Finally, *framing* influences human thought extensively. In decision making and reasoning, people often use frames to understand, integrate, and contextualize the information currently under consideration (**7**.2.2, **8**.7.4, **9**.3.3). Unlike formal reasoning procedures in which information is combined according to abstract principles of logic and mathematics, people often prefer to integrate information with frames that reflect their everyday experience (Kahneman & A. Tversky, 1982; A. Tversky & Kahneman, 1980).

I assume that all three of these themes reflect fundamental characteristics of the human cognitive architecture: Similarity reflects the centrality of comparison processes in working memory, availability reflects the centrality of memory retrieval in every phase of cognitive processing, and framing reflects the pervasiveness of frames in organizing comprehension and reasoning.

I continue next with a discussion of *similarity*. Availability and framing do

---

[1] For a formal approach that stresses continuous comparisons, see Zadeh (1965).

not receive similar discussion here, because they have been discussed extensively elsewhere. The memory mechanisms that underlie availability were considered in chapter 6, and the mechanisms that underlie framing were addressed in chapters 7, 8, and 9. After providing a brief account of similarity, I then address the roles of similarity, availability, and framing in four types of thought: *decision making*, in which similarity, availability, and framing are central to information assessment and integration; the two basic forms of reasoning—*induction* and *deduction*—for which similarity, availability, and framing are also central; and finally, *problem solving*, which is perhaps the fundamental human activity and involves all of the previous forms of thought.

10.2   SIMILARITY

We have already seen a number of processes that utilize similarity outside of thought. In categorization, the similarity of a physical entity to a prototype or to exemplars determines the category assignment (2.3.1). In graded structure, exemplars are typical to the extent that they are similar to their category's representation (7.3.2). In retrieval, the memories that become active depend on their similarity to the cue (6.3.1). Other examples of similarity abound in previous chapters. These uses of similarity do not constitute thought, according to my definition, because they are usually fast and unconscious.

Nevertheless, conscious uses of similarity permeate purposive thought. As we shall see, people often compare two representations in working memory to achieve a goal, such as selecting the best of two choices, seeking information to confirm an induction, or determining how closely the current state of the world approximates the goal state. Clearly, not all aspects of these comparisons are conscious, yet the deliberate and sometimes systematic comparison of representations often produces conscious products.

10.2.1 Geometric Spaces

Distance in physical space provides a useful way of thinking about similarity. Just as two entities can be close or far in physical space, two representations can be close or far in conceptual space. Intuitively, people perceive *dog* and *wolf* as close in conceptual space, but *dog* and *radio* as far apart. In physical space, the dimensions that define distance are clear, namely, *vertical extent*, *horizontal extent*, and *depth*. These three dimensions enable measuring the distance between any two entities in physical space (e.g., the distance between a hydrant on the street and the top of a skyscraper). What are the dimensions that define distance in conceptual space?

The technique of *multidimensional scaling*, developed by Shepard (1962a, 1962b, 1974, 1980), provides one way to identify conceptual dimensions. Multidimensional scaling requires *proximity data*, such as similarity ratings or confusion data. For similarity ratings, subjects rate the similarity of all possible pairs of concepts under consideration, perhaps on a scale from 1 to 7. From these data, researchers obtain the average similarity of each concept to every other concept. For confusion data, subjects receive stimuli and categorize them. By counting categorization errors, researchers estimate how likely subjects are to confuse the instances of each concept with the instances of each other concept (see the use of confusion matrices in **5**.1.2 and **9**.1.1). Either type of data produces a continuous measure of how "close" each concept is to every other concept. For ratings, two concepts are closer to the extent that their rated similarity is high. For confusion data, two concepts are similar to the extent that subjects confuse them frequently during categorization.

Multidimensional scaling compiles the proximities for all possible pairs of concepts under consideration and represents them in a geometric space. Consider Fig. 10.1, which shows the two–dimensional conceptual space that Rips, Shoben, and E.E. Smith (1973) obtained for *animals* (spaces having more dimensions are also possible). As can be seen, similarity is inversely related to distance in the space: The greater the similarity between two animals, the

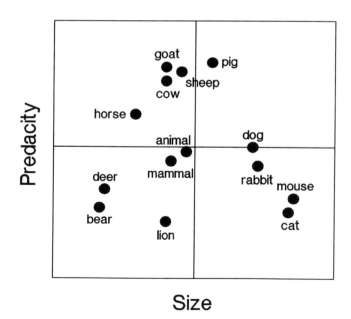

Figure 10.1.   An example of similarity in a geometric space. Adapted from Rips, Shoben, and E.E. Smith (1973), by permission.

shorter the distance between them. Concepts that subjects rated as highly similar (or that would be frequently confused) are close, whereas concepts that subjects rated as dissimilar (or that would be rarely confused) are far apart.

By examining the output of multidimensional scaling, researchers can often identify dimensions that structure the conceptual space. As Fig. 10.1 illustrates, such examination produced the dimensions of *predacity* and *size*. Animals at the bottom of the space are more predatory than animals at the top, and animals at the left of the space are larger than animals at the right. In general, multidimensional scaling provides an exploratory technique for discovering conceptual structure in data. Researchers may have no idea what dimensions structure a conceptual domain, but by collecting proximity data and performing multidimensional scaling, they can discover dimensions of organization. Once these dimensions are identified, they can be used to interpret what similarity means to people. According to Fig. 10.1, for example, two animals are similar to the extent that they are alike in *predacity* and *size*. In this way, multidimensional scaling takes vague, unspecified similarity judgments and provides a specific interpretation of their origin.

Problems with geometric spaces. A. Tversky (1977) and his colleagues have raised several problems for the geometric view of similarity, including violations of minimality, symmetry, the triangle inequality, and nearest neighbors (A. Tversky, 1977; A. Tversky & Hutchinson, 1986; see E.E. Smith, 1990, for a review). As we shall see, these problems all arise from the assumption that distance in a multidimensional space has *metric properties*.

According to the metric property of *minimality*, each concept in a space should be closer to itself than to any other concept. Minimality further entails that each concept should be just as similar to itself as any other concept is to itself. Yet, data from confusion matrices violate these assumptions (A. Tversky, 1977). Counterintuitively, some letters are more likely to be confused with another letter than to be classified correctly (e.g., "Q" is more likely to be called "O" than "Q"). Because these letters are more similar to other letters than they are to themselves, they violate minimality. Additionally, some letters suffer fewer confusions than others (e.g., "O" typically suffers fewer confusions than "Q"). Because letters vary in how similar they are to themselves, they violate minimality further.

According to the metric property of *symmetry*, the order in which people judge two concepts should not affect the distance between them in a geometric space. For example, the distance between *mouse* and *dog* in Fig. 10.1 should be unaffected by whether subjects judge the similarity of *mouse* to *dog* or the similarity of *dog* to *mouse*. In each case, the distance between the two concepts should be identical. However, violations of symmetry occur regularly (A. Tversky, 1977). For example, people judge the similarity of *North*

Korea to *China* as higher than the similarity of *China* to *North Korea*. Similarly, *ovals* are more similar to *circles* than *circles* are to *ovals*.

According to the *triangle inequality*, the distance between any two concepts must be smaller than the sum of the distances from each to a third concept. Thus, the conceptual distance between *Jamaica* and *Russia* must be smaller than the sum of the conceptual distances between *Jamaica* and *Cuba* and between *Russia* and *Cuba*. If the latter two distances are small, the former distance should be at least as small. Yet, similarity data often violate the triangle inequality (A. Tversky, 1977). Although *Cuba* is judged highly similar to both *Jamaica* and *Russia*, *Jamaica* and *Russia* are not considered to be similar at all. Because the distance between *Jamaica* and *Russia* is larger than the sum of their distances to *Cuba*, these similarity relations violate the triangle inequality.[2]

Finally, the geometric view has trouble representing *nearest neighbors*. Consider, again, the concept of *animal*. When people judge the similarity of each exemplar in Fig. 10.1 to its superordinate, *animal*, they typically rate many exemplars as more similar to *animal* than to any other exemplar. For many exemplars, *animal* is their nearest neighbor. However, there is no way to represent this in a two-dimensional geometric space, while simultaneously capturing all of the relations between exemplars (A. Tversky & Hutchinson, 1986). *Animal* cannot be positioned in Fig. 10.1 to represent its nearest neighbor status. If *animal* is close to *lion*, it is necessarily far from *goat* and *dog*. If the space is collapsed toward the center so that all exemplars are very close to *animal*, the exemplars keep getting closer to one another, too, such that *animal* still is not the nearest neighbor of very many exemplars. Moreover, relations between exemplars become lost in the process. As a compromise, *animal* ends up in the middle of the geometric space. There, it is closer on the average to all exemplars than any exemplar is to all other exemplars, but its status as their nearest neighbor is lost.

These problems for the geometric view suggest that people typically do not process similarity geometrically. If they did, their similarity judgments would not violate so many of its fundamental assumptions. Nevertheless, multidimensional scaling provides a very useful technique for discovering structure in data across a wide range of basic and applied domains.

10.2.2 Contrasting Common and Distinctive Properties

An alternative approach views similarity as a contrast between common and distinctive properties. Rather than representing concepts as points in a space structured by continuous dimensions, A. Tversky's (1977) *contrast model*

---

[2] For a way to rescue geometric spaces from violations of minimality, symmetry, and the triangle inequality, see Krumhansl (1978).

simply assumes that feature lists represent concepts (7.2.2). According to the contrast model, two concepts become more similar as the number of *common properties* increases, and as the number of *distinctive properties* decreases. Common properties are properties that two concepts share, such as *eyes* for *tiger* and *horse*. Distinctive properties are properties in one concept that are not in the other. For the pair, *tiger–horse*, the distinctive properties include *claws* for *tiger* and *mane* for *horse*. More specifically, Tversky's contrast model expresses similarity as an algebraic contrast between common and distinctive properties:

$$\text{sim}(x, y) = k_c\, F(C) - k_x\, F(D_x) - k_y\, F(D_y), \qquad k_c, k_x, k_y \geq 0$$

$\text{sim}(x, y)$ represents the similarity of two concepts, x and y; C represents the number of properties common to x and y; D_x represents the number of distinctive properties in x; and D_y represents the number of distinctive properties in y. As you can see, similarity increases as the number of common properties increases and as the number of distinctive properties decreases. The functions, F, weight particular properties according to their salience, importance, and so on, such that some properties count more than others (see also Ortony, 1979). The constants, k_c, k_x, and k_y, weight the importance of common and distinctive properties in various types of judgment, taking on different values for judgments of similarity and judgments of dissimilarity. Thus, when people judge the similarity of two concepts, they weight common properties more heavily than when they judge the dissimilarity of two concepts (i.e., k_c is greater for similarity judgments than for dissimilarity judgments). Conversely, people weight distinctive properties more heavily for dissimilarity judgments than for similarity judgments (i.e., k_x and k_y are greater for dissimilarity than for similarity).

The contrast model solves the problems raised earlier for the geometric view. For minimality, concepts can vary in how similar they are to themselves, depending on their number of properties. As the number of properties for a concept increases, the number of properties common to two instances of that concept increases, while the distinctive properties stay constant at zero. As a result, concepts with many properties are more similar to themselves than are concepts with few properties.[3]

For asymmetry, the order in which people judge two concepts can affect their similarity if the values of k_x and k_y differ. If k_x is greater than k_y, similarity is always greater when the concept having the most distinctive properties is second in the comparison. Under this condition, the second concept receives less focus or attention, giving its greater number of distinc-

---

[3] For simplicity, this argument assumes that different instances of a concept are identical, ignoring the fact that they often vary considerably (7.2.3). Barsalou (1989) addresses the similarity between instances of the same concept that vary.

tive properties less weight. For example, *China* has more distinctive properties than *North Korea*, because most people know more about *China*. The total negative impact of both concepts' distinctive features on similarity is least, therefore, when *North Korea's* smaller number of distinctive features is weighted by the larger k_x, and *China's* larger number of distinctive features is weighted by the smaller k_y. When the order is reversed, *China's* greater number of distinctive features is weighted more, and *North Korea's* smaller number of distinctive features is weighted less, thereby decreasing similarity more overall. In this way, the contrast model captures the asymmetry of similarity judgments.

The contrast model handles violations of the triangle inequality through common properties. Essentially, two concepts can be similar to a third concept for different reasons, while having little in common themselves. For example, *Jamaica* is similar to *Cuba* geographically, and *Russia* was once similar to *Cuba* politically; whereas *Jamaica* and *Russia* have neither geography nor politics in common.

Finally, the contrast model handles the situation where one concept is the nearest neighbor of many others. A superordinate, such as *animal*, shares all of its properties with its subordinates, because each subordinate is likely to subsume these properties through inheritance (7.4.2). As a result, *animal* has no distinctive properties of its own and only differs from its subordinates in their distinctive properties. In contrast, each pair of subordinates also shares the properties common to animals, yet differs on *two* sets of distinctive properties, one for each subordinate. As a result, subordinates are typically less similar to each other than to their superordinate, and the superordinate becomes the nearest neighbor to many exemplars.

10.2.3 The Relevance Problem

Although Tversky's contrast model has enjoyed widespread acceptance, it nevertheless fails to solve one of the fundamental problems facing similarity: How do people determine which properties true of a concept are relevant to a particular similarity comparison? As we saw in 7.3.1, an infinite number of properties are true of any concept (Goodman, 1955, 1972). Thus, the properties true of *chair* include *can be found in Arizona*, *can be a birthday present*, and *can be carried in a truck*. However, these properties are also true of *goat*. Should they count as common to *chair*, *goat*, and to all of the other concepts that share them? If so, and if the infinite number of kindred properties count as well, similarity comparisons become meaningless: As the number of common properties approaches infinity, all concepts become equally similar to each other. Clearly, constraints on the properties relevant to similarity are necessary for this construct to be meaningful.

A number of factors constrain the properties that enter similarity comparisons. First, biologically based, perceptual processes provide constraints (**2.2**). In judging the similarity of two perceived entities, perceptual processes automatically make certain properties available, such as *color, shape*, and *size*. The obligatory nature of these properties essentially constitutes a maximally high level of availability, one of the three themes of this chapter (**10.**1). Properties that perceptual systems provide automatically are highly available and therefore likely to determine similarity.

Availability can take other forms as well, as in Goodman's notion of *entrenchment*: Properties that are highly established in long-term memory (i.e., entrenched) are readily available for similarity judgments. Some properties are so strongly entrenched that their activation is automatic, making them instantly available. Thus, the automatized meaning of "blue" becomes active immediately, even when you are trying to ignore it and state the ink color instead (i.e., the Stroop effect; **4.**1.2). Because the core properties of concepts are well entrenched, they have high availability and are therefore likely to enter similarity judgments through automatic activation (**7.**2.3). Consider the similarity of *apple* and *banana*. Because *fruit* is a well-entrenched core property for each, it becomes activated automatically and contributes to their similarity (Barsalou, 1982, Exp. 2; Barsalou & B.H. Ross, 1986).

In contrast, the activation of less entrenched properties is context-dependent (**7.**2.3). For example, people generally perceive the similarity of *snake* and *raccoon* as relatively low. When *snake* and *raccoon* are judged in the context of *pets*, however, properties relevant to *pets* become active for each, thereby increasing the number of common properties and, in turn, similarity (Barsalou, 1982, Exp. 2). Context increases the availability of less entrenched properties, making them relevant to similarity.

Framing—another of our themes—also constrains the properties that determine similarity. Some properties of an entity are salient, because they reflect important frames in a culture. For Americans, *edible* is a salient property of *cattle*, because they are typically viewed with respect to frames for ranching, stockyards, and butcher shops. In contrast, *edible* is not a salient property of *cattle* in cultures that frame them differently. Properties also become salient in the context of frames that are more abstract and less grounded in daily events. Thus, the mammalian characteristics that *whales* and *porpoises* share reflect some cultures' scientific theories about living organisms (**7.**3.1). In other cultures that don't have these theories, mammalian properties aren't as salient, and *whales* and *porpoises* are perceived as more similar to *fish* than to *mammals*. Thus, many properties are relevant to similarity, because they reflect the frames that organize people's understanding of the world (Carey, 1985; Keil, 1989; Lakoff, 1987; Markman, 1989; G.A. Miller & Johnson-Laird, 1976; G.L. Murphy & Medin, 1985).

Theorists are just beginning to understand the mechanisms that specify the properties relevant to similarity, including biological biases, memory entrenchment, contextual relevance, and frames. Clearly, much remains to be learned about these factors and how they determine similarity. Because the similarity of two concepts on a given occasion depends critically on the properties that represent them, understanding the origins of these properties is essential to understanding similarity.

10.3 DECISION MAKING

Now that we have considered similarity and seen examples of availability and framing, we are ready to address various forms of purposive thought. I begin with decision making. An individual who has to make a decision often begins by attempting to identify the possible *choices*. In selecting a career, for example, someone might consider *nursing, plumbing*, and *computer programming* as possibilities. The decision maker often attempts next to identify the possible *outcomes* that would result from pursuing each choice. Thus, someone might predict that *high job satisfaction, flexible hours*, and *moderate income* would be the outcomes of a career in *nursing*. Assessing the *utility* of each outcome and estimating its *probability* of occurrence come next. For example, the decision maker might believe that *high job satisfaction* has a very high utility and estimate that it has a 90% probability of occurring for nursing. The decision maker weights the utility of each possible outcome by its probability of occurring, and then combines these weighted utilities across outcomes to establish the overall utility of the choice. Finally, the choice having the highest overall utility is selected as the decision.

As this example illustrates, utilities and probabilities are central constructs in decision making. In section **10**.3.1, I review work that addresses people's ability to assess utilities and probabilities; in section **10**.3.2, I review work that addresses people's ability to combine these utilities and probabilities in reaching decisions. As we shall see, people often incorporate similarity, availability, and framing into performing these tasks (Fischoff, 1988; Kahneman et al., 1982; Slovic, Lichtenstein, & Fischoff, 1988).

10.3.1 Assessing Utilities and Probabilities

Utilities. Obviously, the assessment of utility is a subjective matter. Nevertheless, people generally view utility sensibly. For example, people generally view winning $20 as having higher utility than winning $10. Similarly, people generally view losing $15 as having lower utility than losing $5.

An interesting bias characterizes people's assessment of utility. Imagine that you have to decide between Choices A and B:

Choice A.   You accept a bet in which a fair coin is tossed. If the toss comes up heads, you win $10, but if it comes up tails, you lose $10.

Choice B.   You don't take the bet and therefore can't win or lose anything.

Economically, the expected value of these two choices is equal. In Choice A, the expected value is $0, because you have a 50% chance of winning $10 and a 50% chance of losing $10, which averages out to $0. Choice B also has an expected value of $0, because it leads to no change in your economic status. Interestingly, Kahneman and A. Tversky (1979) found that people overwhelmingly select Choice B when faced with this type of decision. Even though the expected values of these two choices are equal, people do not perceive them as having equal utility, but perceive Choice B as having higher utility than Choice A. Kahneman and Tversky interpreted this result as indicating that *losses loom larger than gains*: Subjectively, the utility of losing $10 seems more significant than the utility of winning $10.

E.E. Smith and Osherson (1989) offered an alternative account of this phenomenon. They suggest that people compare the *similarity* of their current situation to each of the possible outcomes in Choice A. If the possible gain constitutes more of a change from the current situation than the possible loss, people select Choice A, but if the possible loss constitutes more of a change, they select Choice B. People will not accept a risk if the loss seems like it would disrupt life more than the gain. One way to measure perceived change is to measure the similarity of the current situation to the future situation. Applying Tversky's contrast model of similarity (10.2.2), Smith and Osherson found that people perceive loss as less similar to their current condition than gain. Because loss constitutes more of a change, people are wary of Choice A and prefer Choice B. Thus, the similarity of a particular choice to one's current condition is one determinant of its subjective utility.

Probabilities.   To some extent, people assess probabilities accurately. In 4.1.1, we saw that people have a natural ability to encode frequency information: Even though they make no effort to acquire information about how often different entities occur, some sort of information about frequency is stored automatically. Frequency information translates readily into probabilities. Thus, if one wants to estimate the probability that checkers in supermarkets are male versus female, probabilities can be constructed from frequency information: The probability that a checker is male is the frequency of male checkers divided by the frequency of male plus female checkers. Although these estimates probably would not be exactly correct, they would likely be at least roughly correct.

In a phenomenon called *probability matching* (Bower & Hilgard, 1981; Estes, 1976), researchers have indeed found that people are excellent estimators of probability. Imagine that subjects view trials that contain either Event X or

Event Y. Further imagine that subjects try to predict, as accurately as possible, whether X will occur on each trial. If X occurs randomly on 75% of the trials, subjects eventually come to select X on 75% of the trials and to select Y on 25% of the trials, having acquired the probability of X and using it to make their selections. Interestingly, subjects' strategy of selecting X on 75% of the trials does not produce optimal performance, because the optimal strategy is to select X on 100% of the trials. If subjects only select X on 75% of the trials, they miss some of the Xs that occur on the other 25% of the trials, because the assignment of X or Y to a given trial is random, and subjects are not always correct. Nevertheless, probability matching illustrates that people can be quite accurate at estimating probabilities. For the related ability to estimate the mean and variance of a probability distribution, see Malmi and Samson (1983).

On the other hand, similarity, availability, and framing can also produce inaccuracy in people's estimates of probability. Of these, availability is perhaps the best documented. In general, people are likely to overestimate the probability of highly available outcomes. If two outcomes are equally probable, but one is more memorable than the other, people judge the more memorable outcome as more probable. In a classic demonstration, A. Tversky and Kahneman (1973) asked subjects whether more four-letter words have "r" as their first letter or as their third letter. Subjects tended to believe that more four-letter words have "r" as their first letter, even though more four-letter words actually have "r" as their third letter. Because it is easier to retrieve words according to their first letter, words with an initial "r" are more available and thus bias probability estimates.

In another study, Tversky and Kahneman presented subjects with people's last names, of which 19 were famous and 20 were not. Subjects received the names mixed in a random order and were instructed to learn them for a later memory test. Subjects later had to estimate, without warning, whether more of the names had been famous or not famous. Subjects tended to believe that more of the names had been famous. Furthermore, when subjects recalled the names, they recalled more famous than non-famous names. As the recall test showed, the famous names were more available in memory than the non-famous names. Consequently, they were also more available during the probability judgments and produced bias. Numerous other studies further document the robust effect of availability on probability estimates (Kahneman et al., 1982).

Similarity biases probability estimates as well. Estimate the probability that a rancher from Wyoming, who is in the market for a vehicle, buys a Toyota. Now estimate the probability that this rancher buys a Toyota truck. Which of your estimated probabilities is larger? According to the laws of probability, the probability of the rancher buying a Toyota is larger than (or at least the same as) the probability of the rancher buying a Toyota truck. Because some ranchers have probably bought Toyotas that are not trucks, ranchers who buy Toyota trucks form a subset of the ranchers who buy Toyotas. As a result, a rancher buying a Toyota truck has a lower probability than a rancher buying any kind of Toyota.

Interestingly, people are often oblivious to this law of probability. Many people perceive a rancher buying a Toyota truck as having a higher probability than a rancher buying a Toyota. A. Tversky and Kahneman (1983) dubbed this the *conjunction fallacy*, because people mistakenly believe that a conjunction of events (Toyota and truck) is more probable than a single event (Toyota). Tversky and Kahneman argued that similarity underlies this bias. Because people believe that American ranchers are not likely to buy foreign vehicles, they do not perceive *ranchers* and *Toyotas* as similar. Because people believe that American ranchers are likely to buy trucks, however, they perceive *ranchers* and *Toyota trucks* as similar. As a result, people believe that ranchers are more likely to buy Toyota trucks than Toyotas. In support of this account, E.E. Smith and Osherson (1989) found that similarity, as measured by Tversky's contrast model (**10.2.2**), explains the higher perceived probability of the conjoined events.

Finally, framing biases probability estimates. L.J. Chapman and J.P. Chapman (1967, 1969) asked clinical psychologists to estimate the probabilities of various events in clinical populations. In one study, clinicians estimated that paranoid clients are more likely to emphasize the eyes in drawing the human figure than are non-paranoid clients. In another comparison, clinicians estimated that homosexual clients are more likely to see genitalia in Rorschach inkblots (which are, by design, ambiguous) than are heterosexuals. When researchers have assessed these probabilities objectively, however, the probability of paranoid clients actually emphasizing eyes in their drawings is no higher than the probability of non-paranoid clients emphasizing them. Similarly, the probability of homosexuals seeing genitalia in inkblots is no higher than the probability of heterosexuals seeing them.

Clinicians' frames about homosexuality and paranoia produced these biases. Such frames often represent characteristics believed to be true for a population, along with a rationale for why they might be true (i.e., stereotypes). For example, the frame for paranoia states that the eyes of paranoid individuals are salient because they are always looking for threats in the environment. When people apply this frame to an individual believed to be paranoid, this stereotypical belief about salient eyes becomes active and is attributed to the individual.

Chapman and Chapman referred to the erroneous beliefs that result from such frames as *illusory correlations*, because these correlations between populations and their perceived characteristics are objectively non-existent. In experimental studies, the Chapmans went on to show that frames can even prevent people from detecting contradictory correlations. For example, imagine that subjects see a set of drawings in which salient eyes occur more frequently in drawings by *non-paranoid* people than in drawings by paranoid people. Even under these conditions, subjects still believe that the drawings by paranoid people are more likely to have salient eyes. Clearly, frames can have a considerable impact on people's estimates of probability.

The *gambler's fallacy* further illustrates the role of framing. Imagine tossing a fair coin six times and obtaining six consecutive tails. What is the probability that the next coin flip will come up heads? Actually, the probability of heads is 50%, just as it was for the first flip, because each flip is *independent* of the others. However, people often predict that the probability of heads is much higher than 50%, because of all the preceding tails. Similarly, people expect to see more alternation in the outcome of athletic events than actually exists, and more alternation in the sex of their children. A common frame that people share for *randomness* specifies that some mechanism insures alternation in random sequences, when, in reality, no such mechanism exists (Kahneman & A. Tversky, 1972; Tune, 1964).

As the findings in this section illustrate, the factors of similarity, availability, and framing often distort people's assessments of utilities and probabilities. The cognitive system is not an unbiased, optimally sensitive estimator of the information used in decision making. Instead, the processing of this information reflects comparison, retrieval, and frame mechanisms central to the human cognitive architecture (**10**.1).

10.3.2 Combining Utilities and Probabilities

Once people have assessed utilities and probabilities, they often attempt to combine them. In this section, I consider two formal procedures for combining this information: the formal utility model and Bayes' Theorem. Although people follow these procedures to some extent, they also deviate from them as similarity, availability, and framing come into play.

Expected utility.   In selecting one of several choices, people often attempt to assess the overall utility of each. In selecting a career, for example, one might attempt to assess the expected utilities of various careers. If these assessments are performed according to the *formal utility model*, probabilities and utilities should be combined as follows:

$$EU(C_1) = P(O_1|C_1)\ U(O_1) + P(O_2|C_1)\ U(O_2) + P(O_3|C_1)\ U(O_3) + \ldots + P(O_n|C_1)\ U(O_n)$$

where $EU(C_1)$ is the expected utility of Choice 1; $P(O_1|C_1)$ is the probability that Outcome 1 will occur, given Choice 1 is taken; $U(O_1)$ is the utility of Outcome 1; $P(O_2|C_1)$ is the probability that Outcome 2 will occur, given

Choice 1 is taken; $U(O_2)$ is the utility of Outcome 2; and so forth, for each of the remaining n outcomes.

Consider an example of how this model represents the expected utility of pursuing a career in nursing. To compute EU(nursing), one must first identify its possible outcomes. Because availability plays a key role in the specific outcomes that people consider, different people may consider different outcomes, and the same person may consider different outcomes on different occasions (**7.2.3**). For whatever outcomes people retrieve, they must estimate probabilities and utilities. Imagine that three possible outcomes for nursing are retrieved: *high job satisfaction, flexible hours*, and *moderate income*. For these outcomes, one might attempt to assess U(SATISFACTION = high), P(SATISFACTION = high|CAREER = nursing), U(HOURS = flexible), P(HOURS = flexible|CAREER = nursing), U(INCOME = moderate), P(INCOME = moderate|CAREER = nursing), and so forth. Having estimated these probabilities and utilities, they are combined according to the simple algebraic rule of the formal utility model. Regardless of the outcomes, probabilities, and utilities considered, this model always combines them in the same way: The expected utility of a choice is the summed utility of its n possible outcomes, each weighted by its probability of occurring. Once the expected utility for each possible choice has been computed, they can be ranked from highest to lowest, and the option having the highest expected utility can be selected (Coombs, Dawes, & A. Tversky, 1970; Edwards, 1954; Winkler & W.L. Hayes, 1975, chap. 9).

People's choices often conform roughly to the formal utility model: When the model specifies that a choice's overall expected utility is high, people's overall subjective utility for the choice tends to be high. Similarly, when the model specifies that a choice's overall expected utility is low, people's overall subjective utility for the choice tends to be low. To some extent, at least, people appear to follow formal prescriptions for reaching decisions.

Fischoff (1988) notes, however, that two interpretive problems accompany this finding. First, success in fitting the formal utility model to subjective behavior may simply represent researchers' judicious selection of outcomes, probabilities, and utilities. Often, researchers have much freedom in specifying these values, and if they look long enough, they can usually find a set that explains people's subjective utilities for a given decision. Such demonstrations, however, do not constitute strong evidence that the formal utility model provides an accurate account of human decision making. People could be combining some other set of outcomes, probabilities, and utilities in a different way that just happens to match researchers' application of the formal utility model. This problem of selecting relevant outcomes, probabilities, and utilities is essentially the same as the relevance problem for similarity (**10.2.3**). In each case, determining the information relevant to a critical process is poorly understood and inadequately constrained, yet understanding the origins of this information is the key issue in understanding the process.

A second problem with the formal utility model is that it only captures the gist of human decision making, missing many idiosyncratic but important details. When decision makers describe their cognitive processing, they often describe operations that differ significantly from the formal utility model. Because different decision makers follow different procedures, however, the idiosyncrasies of these different strategies cancel each other out when researchers assess the model's fit to human data. The formal utility model captures the information that remains—aspects of decision making common to decision makers—and thereby predicts their behavior to some extent. Because of its highly general nature, the formal utility model partially predicts subjective utility, even when it provides a poor account of the underlying cognitive processes in a given individual.

Bayes' theorem. People often have to combine various sources of information to produce a probability estimate. Imagine, for instance, trying to guess the college major of a young woman who is wearing a leather dress and has orange hair. To guess her major, you might estimate the probability that a woman with these characteristics is a drama major, the probability that a woman with these characteristics is an engineering major, and so forth. Once you have estimated the probability of each possible major, you would select the major with the highest probability as your best guess. Each of these probabilities for a major can be represented as $P(O|E)$, namely, the probability of an outcome O (i.e., a major), given the evidence E (i.e., the description of the student). Thus, you might estimate the probability that someone is a drama major, given that this person is a woman wearing a leather dress and orange hair; then you might estimate the probability that someone is an engineering major, given that this person is a woman wearing a leather dress and orange hair, and so on for other majors.

According to Bayes' Theorem, you need to combine two important probabilities to compute $P(O|E)$ for each major: the *base rate*, $P(O)$, and the *likelihood*, $P(E|O)$. The base rate, $P(O)$, is simply the probability of an outcome (see the discussion of base rates in 2.3.2). In our example, the base rate for drama majors is the probability that a student is a drama major (i.e., the proportion of students at the college who are drama majors), and the base rate for engineering majors is the probability that a student is an engineering major. The *likelihood*, $P(E|O)$, is the probability of the evidence given an outcome. In our example, this is the probability that someone is a woman wearing a leather dress and orange hair, given that this person has a particular major. For example, the likelihood for drama majors is the probability that known drama majors are women who wear leather dresses and have orange hair (i.e., the proportion of known drama majors with these characteristics).

Similarly, the likelihood for engineering majors is the probability that known engineering majors are women who wear leather dresses and have orange hair.

According to Bayes' Theorem, the probability of the outcome given the evidence, P(O|E), depends upon the prior probability and the likelihood as follows:

$$P(O|E) = \frac{P(E|O)\ P(O)}{P(E)}$$

As you can see from evaluating the numerator, P(O|E) increases both as the base rate, P(O), increases and as the likelihood, P(E|O), increases. In our example, the probability that a woman wearing a leather dress and having orange hair is a particular major increases with the base rate of the major and the probability that members of the major have these characteristics. The denominator in Bayes' Theorem, P(E), is simply the probability of the evidence. In our example, P(E) is the proportion of students at the college who are women, wear leather dresses, and have orange hair. P(E) remains constant as P(O|E) is computed for each major, because P(E) is defined over the entire college population—not just one major.

To see how Bayes' Theorem works, imagine that the probability of a drama major at this college is .06, that the probability of a drama major being a woman with a leather dress and orange hair is .18, and that the probability of any student being a woman with a leather dress and orange hair is .12. According to Bayes' Theorem, the probability that this student is a drama major is .09, namely:

$$.09 = \frac{(.18)(.06)}{.12}$$

Further imagine that the probability of an engineering major is .41 and that the probability of an engineering major being a woman with a leather dress and orange hair is .08. According to Bayes' Theorem, the probability that this student is an engineering major is .27, namely:

$$.27 = \frac{(.08)(.41)}{.12}$$

If you had followed your intuitions and stereotypes, you might have guessed that this student is more likely to be a drama major, but as this example illustrates, the opposite could be true. Why is this? From examining the example, you can see that the base rate for engineering is much higher than the base rate for drama (.41 vs. .06). Even though the likelihood is higher for drama than for engineering (.18 vs. .08), this difference is not nearly as large as the difference between base rates. As this example illustrates, the base rates and likelihoods compete to predict the major. If the difference in base rates is larger than the difference in likelihoods, the base rates dominate the choice, even when the evidence, as represented by the likelihoods, suggests otherwise (Fischoff, 1988; Winkler & W.L. Hayes, 1975, chap. 8).

Representativeness.   To what extent do people follow Bayes' Theorem when assessing the probability of an outcome, given some evidence? Much work has found that people often focus too much on likelihoods and too little on base rates. Kahneman and A. Tversky (1972) found that people's assessment of a major is influenced too much by the student's characteristics and not enough by the frequency of majors (see also Kahneman et al., 1982). Kahneman and Tversky dubbed this the *representativeness heuristic*, because people perceive the evidence as representative of the outcome. If a student looks like the stereotype of a drama major, then people believe that the student is likely to be a drama major. The representativeness heuristic reiterates our theme of similarity: To the extent that a possible outcome is similar to the evidence, the outcome is seen as likely. In support of this account, E.E. Smith and Osherson (1989) found that the similarity of the outcome to the evidence, as measured by Tversky's contrast model (10.2.2), predicts the extent to which the representativeness bias occurs.

This representativeness strategy makes some sense, given that it uses likelihood information, but Bayes' Theorem also requires that people consider base rates. Consequently, the representativeness heuristic is not an optimal decision strategy. Although people often neglect base rates, a number of investigators have discovered conditions under which people do attend to them. Imagine, first, that a hit-and-run accident involving a cab occurs in a town where 85% of the cabs are green and 15% are blue. Further imagine that a witness says the cab in the accident was blue and that this witness is shown to be 80% accurate at identifying cab color under such circumstances. A. Tversky and Kahneman (1982) found that subjects estimated the probability that the cab in the accident was blue to be around 80%, ignoring the base rates and relying completely on the likelihoods. If subjects had taken the base rates into account, their estimate would have been lower than the 80% value for the likelihood, given that the base rate of blue cabs is only 15%.

A somewhat different scenario, however, produces more sensitivity to base rates. Imagine now that a city has two cab companies, one with blue cabs and one with green cabs. Further imagine that the two companies have similar numbers of cabs but that 85% of the accidents involve the green cab company and 15% of the accidents involve the blue cab company. Again, a witness, who is 80% accurate at observing cab color, reports that the cab in a hit-and-run accident was blue. Under these conditions, subjects now estimate that the cab in the accident had about a 60% chance of being blue. A. Tversky and Kahneman suggested that this sensitivity to base rates occurs because subjects frame the problem with a scenario that makes the base rates relevant (i.e., one cab company has a high accident rate). Alternatively, E.E. Smith and Osherson (1989) suggested that it is similarity that makes the base rates relevant. According to their interpretation, the cab in the accident is similar to the green cab company in the second version, because the green cab company is accident-prone (i.e., *being in accidents* is a common property of the cab in the accident and the cab company). Because of this similarity, subjects take more account of the base rates and are less willing to believe the witness. Subjects' estimates that a blue cab was responsible decrease, as they take both sources of information into account.

In sum, the findings in this section suggest that people follow the pre-scribed procedures of formal decision theory on some occasions to some extent. However, these results also indicate the presence of other important factors in the way people combine utilities and probabilities, namely, simi-larity, availability, and framing. As we shall see, these factors pervade induc-tion, deduction, and problem solving as well.

10.4 INDUCTION

In this section and the next, I turn to the two basic forms of reasoning, induction and deduction, which to many people are the quintessential forms of thought. Induction can take many forms (Greeno & Simon, 1988; J.H. Holland et al., 1986; Holyoak & Nisbett, 1988). In one form, people observe an entity's current behavior and induce a generalization about its future behavior. For example, one might observe a dog chasing a squirrel on one occasion and induce that this dog will chase squirrels on future occasions. In another form of induction, one might observe a few members of a category and attempt to induce a generalization about its other members. For example, you might observe that several dogs chase squirrels and induce that dogs in general chase squirrels. To perform induction, people typically make obser-vations, induce a generalization, and extend it to new situations. Induction is always potentially fallible. Because the potential number of observations that bear on an induction is often indefinitely large, people can't make all possible observations, and they can never be entirely certain that the induction is correct. Although people can be fairly certain that *all zebras have stripes*, they typically do not observe all zebras and therefore cannot be entirely certain that every zebra has this property.

We have already seen numerous examples of induction throughout this book. Prototypes contain generalizations induced from observing exemplars (e.g., dogs have fur; **2.3.1**). A learned automatic production represents the induction that a particular action is the correct response to a particular stimulus (e.g., press the brake pedal on seeing a red light; **4.1.2**). Reconstruction illustrates the use of induced knowledge to fill in forgotten aspects of a remembered episode (e.g., someone falsely remembers taking a taxi from an airport to a hotel, because that is what he usually does; **6**.3.2). Default values in frames represent the induction of values believed to be typical of frame attributes (e.g., the size of a bird is expected to be small; **7**.2.2). The interpretation of linguistic signs reflects the induction of their corresponding linguistic structures (e.g., an /s/ following a noun indicates that the speaker intends the noun to be plural; **8**.4). Inference during language comprehension reflects the induction of propositions likely to be true of particular referent models (e.g., inferring that someone took a jet in a flight from Geneva to Boston; **8**.7.4, **8**.7.5, **9**.3.3, **9**.6.2). As we shall see further on, induction also occurs frequently in problem solving, when people induce solutions from prior problems to solve current problems (**10**.6.2).

Researchers often find it useful to represent an induction problem with an *hypothesis space* and an *observation space* (Greeno & Simon, 1988). A hypothesis space contains the hypotheses that a person could potentially entertain during an induction problem. It is important to note that a hypothesis space does *not* describe a person's cognitive state. Instead, a hypothesis space is an abstract, theoretical tool that theorists use to represent a particular induction problem. During induction, a person may consider *part* of a hypothesis space but rarely all of it, except in cases where the space is small or people are very thorough. On some occasions, people may simply test a single hypothesis to see if it is true or false. For example, someone might decide to test the following hypothesis:

> When the university parking lot contains no empty parking spaces,
> the campus police do not ticket illegally parked cars.

On other occasions, one may test multiple hypotheses in a hypothesis space, attempting to see which fits the observations best. For example, if someone discovers that her long-time adversary is now going out of his way to be nice, she might consider a variety of possible hypotheses, including:

> My adversary has finally seen what a wonderful person I am.
> My adversary has finally seen what a terrible person he has been.
> My adversary is trying to con me into letting down my guard.

An observation space contains the events that a person could potentially observe during an induction problem. An observation space does *not* describe a person's specific experience with the world. Like a hypothesis space, it is an abstract, theoretical tool that theorists use to represent a particular induction problem. People typically do not explore the entire observation space in making an induction, but instead only consider observations that are readily available. In testing the hypothesis that campus police don't ticket illegally parked cars when the lot is full, people make observations when it is convenient to do so. Obviously, they don't make all possible observations, or else they would spend 24 hours a day, 7 days a week, observing the parking lot.

Because the observation space for an induction problem is typically quite large, people have much flexibility in the observations that they decide to make. Often, people seek observations that would *confirm* their hypothesis (**10**.4.3, **10**.5.1). Consider the hypothesis that the campus police do not ticket illegally parked cars when the university parking lot is full. To confirm this hypothesis, people would look for illegally parked cars that do not have parking tickets on them when the lot is full. On observing illegally parked cars without tickets, people's confidence in the hypothesis would increase, because their observations confirm it.

However, another way to test a hypothesis is to seek observations that would *disconfirm* it (**10**.4.3, **10**.5.1). If people seek such observations and never find them, then the hypothesis is judged even more likely to be true. Again, consider the hypothesis that the police do not ticket illegally parked cars when the lot is full. To disconfirm this hypothesis, people would look for illegally parked cars that *have* parking tickets on them when the lot is full. If the hypothesis is false, then people should observe such cases. Rather than looking for illegally parked cars without tickets that confirm the hypothesis, they would be looking for illegally parked cars with tickets that disconfirm it. If they never observe disconfirming cases, they have strong evidence that the hypothesis is true. In general, seeking evidence that disconfirms an induction is at least as important as seeking evidence that confirms it. Shortly, we shall see that people often exhibit a *confirmatory bias*, failing to seek disconfirming evidence.

As we have seen, induction is not foolproof. Although all previous observations may support a hypothesis, new observations may disconfirm it. When revising inductions to accommodate unexpected observations, people often perform two kinds of revision: *generalization* and *specialization*. Consider, again, the induction that the police do not ticket illegally parked cars when the lot is full. If one observes that the police do not even ticket illegally parked cars when the lot is empty, then the induction must be generalized. Information about the lot being full is deleted, producing the more general induction that the police do not ticket illegally parked cars *at all* in this lot. Conversely, if one observes that the police only ticket illegally parked cars when the lot is full in the morning, the induction must be specialized to state that the police do not ticket illegally parked cars when the lot is full *in the afternoon*. As people observe disconfirming events, they constantly update inductions to optimize their predictiveness (J.R. Anderson, 1983; J.H. Holland et al., 1986).

10.4.1 Constraints on Induction

Goodman (1955) observed that the potential number of inductions that follow from a set of observations is infinite. If people attempted to draw all of them, their knowledge would become cluttered with thousands of useless generalizations. For example, observing a zebra with stripes is consistent with the induction that:

All zebras will have stripes until the year 3000 but thereafter become spotted.

Although this induction seems ridiculous, no observations disconfirm it. People could induce an infinite number of equally senseless inductions, by adding an analogous induction for each subsequent year after 3000 (i.e., 3001, 3002, 3003, etc.). Because people typically only draw useful inductions, cognitive processes must somehow constrain the inductive process. As we shall see, similarity, availability, and framing all provide important constraints, as do several other mechanisms.

One way to control induction is to limit the occasions on which it is performed. If people do not attempt to perform induction at every possible opportunity, they may avoid making many unnecessary inductions. Yet, people must perform some inductions in order to adapt continually to their environment. What conditions indicate that a new induction is warranted?

Expectations play a central role in constraining induction. Most of the events that people experience do not violate their expectations (i.e., their prior inductions). For example, on observing a robin with a red breast, one's expectations about robins are not violated, and there is no reason to construct a new induction. Nevertheless, this event is consistent with an infinite number of new inductions, including:

Robins have red breasts until the year 7693 and then green breasts thereafter.
Robins have either red or green breasts.

Although people could make these inductions upon seeing a robin with a red breast, and many others like them, they do not. Because the event is completely consistent with their knowledge, they see no need to revise it. Instead, they only attempt to construct new inductions after they experience an event that violates an expectation. Thus, if one observes a robin with a green breast, this violation of an expectation might well produce a new induction, such as *robins have either red or green breasts*.

Not all new hypotheses arise from unexpected observations in this manner. Sometimes people may have as a goal the discovery of new inductions, as when one tries to understand a new acquaintance's personality, or when a scientist tries to understand a new phenomenon. Nevertheless, many inductions do follow the violation of expectation. Most importantly, the relative rarity of such violations constitutes one important factor that keeps induction under control (J.H. Holland et al., 1986; Schank, 1982).

Temporal contiguity provides another constraint on induction. As animal learning researchers have known for years, organisms often fail to induce relations between stimuli that are not temporally contiguous. If more than several seconds elapse between a predictive stimulus (e.g., a ringing bell) and a desired stimulus (e.g., food), animals do not induce the predictive relation between them (**1.1**). Animals only induce the relation if the food follows the bell immediately.

More generally, the *availability of observations* constrains induction, where temporal contiguity is a special case. If an organism has forgotten events—for lack of temporal contiguity or for any other reason—then these events can not function as observations during induction. Events can only function as relevant observations if they are currently available. If an animal has forgotten the ringing bell by the time food arrives, it will not consider the induction that the bell predicts food. In contrast, if an animal still remembers the ringing bell when food arrives, it may consider this induction. The availability of observations greatly constrains the possible inductions that an organism considers. Because so few observations are available at a given time, the number of inductions suggested is typically small (J.H. Holland et al., 1986; Holyoak et al., 1989).

Similarity provides another constraint on induction. Often, people do not consider making an induction unless they encounter two or more unexpected events that are similar. On perceiving unexpected similar events, one may believe that some systematic regularity underlies them, and try to capture this regularity with an induction. If one does not perceive several unexpected events as similar, however, no attempt will be made to revise current knowledge. For example, a culture may not induce generalizations that encompass *whales* and *dogs* as *mammals*, because *whales* and *dogs* do not appear similar. In contrast, cultures with scientific methods may identify unexpected similarities between *whales* and *dogs* that initiate new inductive inferences about *mammals* (**7.3.1**). Because many unexpected events do not strike people as similar— even when they may be—people do not attempt to induce generalizations about them. In this way, lack of similarity constrains the inductions that people consider. Of course, the key issue becomes: What constitutes the similarities that people perceive? As we have seen, various factors define similarity, including biological predispositions, entrenched knowledge, contextual relevance, and frames (**10.2.3**). Whatever these factors are, they function to make some events appear similar and others dissimilar. To the extent that these factors make many events appear dissimilar, they help keep induction under control.

Frequency provides another constraint on induction. Observing a small number of unexpected similar events may not be sufficient to suggest that an important regularity underlies them for which a new induction is necessary. Instead, these events may simply be viewed as random coincidences. On the other hand, observing many unexpected similar events may eventually be viewed not as random occurrences, but as reflecting a systematic regularity that requires a new induction. Because so many unexpected similar events have occurred, they become observations that must be explained. Thus, if one observes that a golden retriever welcome strangers into a yard on two different occasions, these unexpected similar events may simply be viewed as coincidences. If one observes that several more golden retrievers welcome strangers into a yard, however, so many unexpected events may begin to suggest that some systematic regularity underlies all of them. Because so many of these events occur, they demand an induction, such as:

Golden retrievers are too friendly to be good watchdogs.

To the extent that clusters of frequent, similar, unexpected events don't often occur, frequency also assists in keeping induction under control (J.H. Holland et al., 1986; Jennings, Amabile, & L. Ross, 1982; Nisbett, Krantz, Jepson, & Kunda, 1983).

Finally, *framing* provides a constraint on induction. Once the course of events suggests that an induction is necessary, people's available knowledge greatly constrains or "frames" the hypotheses that they consider: Typically, these hypotheses already exist in knowledge that is currently available, or they are readily derivable from it. Because so many possible hypotheses do not exist in available knowledge or are not readily derivable, they rarely arise during induction. In this way, framing greatly constrains the hypotheses that people consider.

To see this, imagine that a clinical psychologist is trying to diagnose a client's psychological problem. If the psychologist is convinced that inter-personal factors are responsible for his client's problem, he may only enter-tain hypotheses of an interpersonal nature. For example, he might only consider the client's conflict with her parents or with her spouse. Knowledge about interpersonal relations frames the induction problem, such that the only hypotheses considered come from this domain. As a result, the psychol-ogist may fail to consider other plausible hypotheses, for example, a biolog-ical cause of his client's problem, such as an unbalanced diet or a malfunc-tioning thyroid. In general, the knowledge that is currently available frames the problem and limits hypotheses. If different knowledge becomes available at a later time, it will frame the problem in a new way and suggest new hypotheses (**10**.6.1, **10**.6.2).

Framing also prevents people from entertaining hypotheses that are im-plausible: If a hypothesis doesn't follow naturally from people's existing knowledge, they may never consider it. For example, most people would never entertain the hypothesis, *zebras have stripes until the year 3000 and spots thereafter.* Because people have no knowledge that readily explains such a dramatic and arbitrary change, they never consider this hypothesis, nor the infinite number of other hypotheses like it. Instead, they only consider hypotheses that already exist in their knowledge or that are readily derivable from it. Clearly, people's tendency to avoid completely novel hypotheses in this manner has advantages, because it greatly constrains induction. On the other hand, this constraint also has disadvantages, because people may have trouble discovering radically new hypotheses that are correct. If the knowledge necessary for producing the correct hypothesis does not exist in memory, it may never be considered (Goodman, 1955).

Some of the most powerful constraints on framing have a biological basis. After reviewing the animal conditioning literature, Seligman (1970) concluded that organisms are biologically prepared to make some inductions but not others. For example, animals can induce relations between an unusual food they ate and subsequent sickness, even though several hours have elapsed between these two events. In contrast, recall that separating a ringing bell and food by more than a few seconds prevents an animal from inducing their relation. Because inductions about food poisoning are central to survival, organisms have evolved a biological proclivity to frame their illnesses in terms of food. As a result, they consider foods eaten hours ago as hypotheses that might explain their illness. In contrast, because ringing bells have not had a long evolutionary history of predicting food, animals are not predisposed to frame induction problems in terms of them. Instead, animals must rely on temporal contiguity, novelty, similarity, and frequency to suggest ringing bells as a hypothesis. In general, organisms are likely to have numerous biological constraints that facilitate inductions central to early learning and survival.

10.4.2 Hypothesis Testing

As people make observations and raise hypotheses, how do they relate them to one another? Specifically, how do people use observations to evaluate hypotheses, and hypotheses to guide observation? Extensive literatures on hypothesis testing and covariation assessment (**10.4.3**) have addressed these issues.

Theorists once believed that people learn categories from hypothesis testing. According to this view, people actively raise hypotheses about a category's properties and then see if subsequent exemplars of the category exhibit them. As long as all exemplars exhibit the hypothesized property, it is retained in the category rule, but if a single exemplar does not exhibit the property, it is dropped. When learning *robin*, for example, children might test the hypothesis that *red breast* is a defining property.

As we saw earlier, though, most theorists now believe that this is not how category acquisition typically proceeds. Instead, they have become increasingly convinced that the passive and automatic accumulation of non-defining information is much more important. As a category's exemplars are experienced, their properties are passively encoded into prototypes and exemplar memories (**2**.3.1). Rather than actively attempting to identify a rule that defines a category through hypothesis testing, an individual builds up large amounts of non-defining information about the category passively. Even though current models of categorization have little use for hypothesis testing, it may nevertheless play an important role in category learning on some occasions (E.E. Smith & Medin, 1981).

Hypothesis testing appears to play other important roles in cognition as well. When people attempt to determine the cause of an event, they often raise hypotheses about possible causes and test them explicitly (**10**.4.3). For example, one might test hypotheses about why a car won't start or about the cause of a backache. Similarly, when people attempt to solve a problem, they often test hypotheses about the means to a desired goal (**10**.6). Thus, someone might test whether a particular series of actions will make an ailing house plant healthy (Greeno, 1978; Greeno & Simon, 1988).

Much work in psychology has addressed hypothesis testing. In a typical experiment, subjects receive a series of cases, one at a time, such as a *blue square*, then a *blue circle*, then a *red square*, then a *red circle*, then a *blue circle*, then a *red square*, and so forth. A rule, selected by the experimenter, and not divulged to the subject, divides the cases into two groups: cases that satisfy the rule, and cases that do not. Imagine that the rule is:

shapes that are square

Clearly, red squares and blue squares satisfy the rule, whereas red circles and blue circles do not. If you were the subject, your task would be to discover the experimenter's rule. As you receive the cases one at a time, you would develop hypotheses about the rule and test them against future cases. For example, you might hypothesize incorrectly that the rule is *shapes that are blue*. On receiving each case, you state whether it fits your current hypothesis. Thus, if your current hypothesis is *shapes that are blue*, and if the case is a blue square, you would state that the case fits your rule. The experimenter then provides feedback about whether your assessment is correct. For this case, you would be correct but for the wrong reason: The blue square is consistent both with your hypothesis (*shapes that are blue*) and the experimenter's rule (*shapes that are square*). If the next case is a red square, you would say now that this case does not fit your rule, and receive feedback that you are incorrect. At this point, you would probably revise your hypothesis, perhaps to *shapes that are square, shapes that are either square or red*, or some other hypothesis. Eventually, you may converge on the correct rule and no longer make errors (Bourne, 1966, 1970, 1974; Bruner, Goodnow, & G.A. Austin, 1956; E.G. Hunt, J. Martin, & Stone, 1966; Trabasso & Bower, 1968).

In searching a hypothesis space for new hypotheses, people exhibit a variety of biases. In this type of experiment, most people initially seek a *common property*, namely, a property shared by every case that satisfies the rule. As a result, people find it easier to learn a rule such as *shapes that are square* than a rule such as *shapes that are either square or red*. This latter rule is more difficult, because neither *square* nor *red* is common to all cases that satisfy the rule. *Disjunctive rules* like this one are often not considered, at least initially, because people are looking for a single common property. When multiple properties define a rule, people exhibit a bias for *conjunctive rules*, finding it easier to learn conjunctions (*things that are both square and red*) than disjunctions (*things that are either square or red*), which in turn are easier to learn than biconditionals (*things that are both square and red or neither*) (Bourne, 1970; Medin, Wattenmaker, & Hampson, 1987; Medin, Wattenmaker, & Michalski, 1987).

On discovering that a hypothesis is wrong, subjects must either abandon or revise it. *Intradimensional shift* is one strategy they often adopt, shifting their hypothesis from one value of an attribute to another (Erickson, 1971; H.H. Kendler & T.S. Kendler, 1959; T.S. Kendler & H.H. Kendler, 1970; Sutherland & Mackintosh, 1971). When the hypothesis, *things that are blue*, is incorrect, a subject is more likely to shift to things that are *red* than to *things that are square*. Rather than switching to a new attribute, subjects stay with the old attribute but try a new value.

Sometimes people attempt to search a hypothesis space systematically. For example, subjects who perform intradimensional shifts are in some sense systematically seeing what values of a particular attribute, if any, are part of the rule. If *blue* is not in the rule, then subjects may systematically try other colors to see if any of them are. Once subjects have exhausted *color*, they may switch to a new attribute, such as *shape*, and similarly examine its values. Eventually, subjects may examine all of the attributes in the hypothesis space systematically (Bruner et al., 1956).

On the other hand, sometimes subjects' search of the hypothesis space is not so systematic, exhibiting instead more of an opportunistic, bottom-up character. Every time such subjects disconfirm a hypothesis, they may examine the current case, retrieve available cases from memory, and construct a new rule that fits them. Once again, we see the importance of availability, because new hypotheses reflect cases that are currently available. A potential problem with this strategy is that subjects may not remember that they once

disconfirmed their new hypothesis and try it again. Researchers have generally found, however, that subjects remember rejected hypotheses and don't
reconsider them later (T.D. Wickens & Millward, 1971).

10.4.3 Assessing Covariation and Causality

As we just saw, people may abandon a hypothesis as soon as a single case
disconfirms it. Importantly, this learning strategy assumes that a hypothesis
is only useful if it is *never* disconfirmed and is unconditionally true. However,
many hypotheses are useful, even if they are *sometimes* disconfirmed and,
therefore, only partially true. Even though these hypotheses are sometimes
disconfirmed, they are true often enough to provide useful predictions. For
example, cloudiness does not always mean rain, but it often does. If weather
forecasters had to ignore weather indicators that the weather has disconfirmed on a single occasion, they would have no indicators at all! Because so
many important relations are not necessarily true but are statistically probable, the ability to assess covariation is central to induction. On discovering
covariation between two events, people add this relation to their knowledge
and use it to predict future events. Even though such knowledge is not a rule,
because it sometimes fails, it is correct often enough to be an improvement
over no knowledge at all. Note that the prototype and exemplar models in
2.3.1 exhibit this property, because they often provide accurate categorizations but not always.

Covariations include both positive and negative contingencies between
events. In positive contingencies, the presence of one event predicts the
presence of the other, as when cloudiness predicts rain. In negative contingencies, the presence of one event predicts the absence of the other, as when
the absence of a student from school predicts an illness. For positive contingencies, the amount of contingency can vary from 0 (no contingency) to 1
(perfect contingency), with values between 0 and 1 representing intermediate
amounts of contingency. Analogously for negative contingencies, the
amount of contingency can vary from 0 (no contingency) to -1 (perfect
contingency). Theorists typically use values that range from 1 to 0 to -1,
because many statistical measures of covariation use values in this range.

Simple contingency. Many types of contingency are possible. For
example, people can assess the contingency between two continuous attributes, such as the relation between a person's *height* and *weight*. Sometimes
these relations are linear, and sometimes they are non–linear. For example,
the relation between *distance* and *driving time* is linear when speed remains
constant: For each additional mile traveled, driving time increases by a fixed
amount. In contrast, the non–linear relation between *test performance* and
arousal takes the shape of an inverted U: Test performance is low at low

arousal, high at moderate arousal, but then drops back down to low at high arousal (Yerkes & Doddson, 1908). People can also assess the contingency between two dichotomous attributes, where a dichotomous attribute is one that has only two values (e.g., *male* and *female* for *gender*). For example, people can assess the contingency between *gender* and *major political party* (assuming that *major political party* has only two values, such as *Democrat* and *Republican*). People can also assess the contingency between a dichotomous attribute and a continuous attribute (e.g., the relation between *gender* and *height*), or the contingency between two attributes that each have many discrete, non-ordered values (e.g., the relation between *occupation* and *religion*). Statistics texts present many formal procedures for computing these various contingencies (e.g., Guilford & Fruchter, 1973; W.L. Hayes, 1973).

So far, researchers have primarily studied people's ability to assess the contingency between two dichotomous attributes. Imagine trying to assess the hypothesis that:

> Couples with children are likely to have pets,
> whereas couples without children are unlikely to have pets.

As Fig. 10.2 illustrates, the formal way to assess this relation requires establishing a 2 × 2 contingency table. Cell A represents the number of couples observed to have both children and pets, D represents the number of couples observed to have neither, and B and C represent the number of couples having one but not the other. One formal statistic for assessing this contingency is the *phi coefficient*, ϕ, where:

$$\phi = \frac{AD - BC}{\sqrt{(A+B)(C+D)(A+C)(B+D)}}$$

		PETS present	PETS absent
CHILDREN	present	A	B
	absent	C	D

Figure 10.2. A 2 x 2 table for assessing simple contingency. A, B, C, and D represent frequencies of occurrence.

As the contingency between children and pets becomes increasingly positive, ϕ approaches 1; when no contingency exists between children and pets, ϕ approaches 0; as the contingency between children and pets becomes increasingly negative, ϕ approaches -1. The ϕ coefficient produces a rigorous and precise measure of contingency that takes all possible sources of statistical information—A, B, C, and D—into account (Guilford & Fruchter, 1973; W.L. Hayes, 1973).

Strategies for assessing contingency.   Clearly the formula for ϕ requires much more formal computation that most people are willing or able to perform in working memory. As we shall see instead, people use a variety of much simpler strategies to construct contingency estimates. Although these strategies sometimes produce a reasonable degree of accuracy, they can also produce substantial bias.

The simplest strategy is to assess the prevalence of cases in cell A of Fig. 10.2. If people perceive many instances of couples having both children and pets, they may conclude that a positive contingency exists between them. Clearly, this strategy can produce biased estimates. For example, if the values of B, C, and D are just as high as the value of A, then no contingency exists between children and pets, regardless of how large A is. Similarly, if B and C are more prevalent than A, a negative contingency between children and pets may exist. Even though the number of cases for A is large, concluding that they represent a positive contingency could well be incorrect. Nevertheless, people frequently adopt this strategy.

A slightly better strategy is to assess the prevalence of cases in cells A and D of Fig. 10.2. If people perceive many instances of couples having both children and pets and of couples having neither, they may perceive a contingency. Again, this strategy can lead to error, if the prevalence of cases in B and C is equal to the prevalence of cases in A and D (no contingency), or if B and C are larger than A and D (a negative contingency). Nevertheless, this strategy is often used as well.

A much better strategy is to compare the prevalence of cases in A and D to the prevalence of cases in B and C. Although this strategy is not formally equivalent to the ϕ coefficient, it is about as optimal as an intuitive strategy can be, and people do adopt it under some circumstances. Researchers have found that people adopt still other strategies as well, such as computing the difference between A and B. For further discussion of the strategies that people use to assess contingency, and for experiments that demonstrate these strategies, see Beyth-Marom (1982), Einhorn and Hogarth (1978), and Shaklee and Tucker (1980). For a general review, see Shustack (1988).

Biases in contingency judgments.   As people attempt to assess the nature of a contingency, a variety of biases come into play. People's proclivity to focus on cells A and D in Fig. 10.2 often reflects *confirmatory bias*. Consider the following hypothesis once again:

Couples with children are likely to have pets,
whereas couples without children are unlikely to have pets.

In this hypothesis, the phrase, *couples with children are likely to have pets*, describes observations in cell A of Fig. 10.2; similarly, *couples without children are unlikely to have pets* describes observations in cell D. Because the hypothesis happens to be stated this way, people often seek the observations that it describes explicitly (A and D). To test the hypothesis, people count the number of *couples with children who have pets* that they know, as well as the number of *couples without children who do not have pets*. In this way, people attempt to confirm their hypothesis by looking for the observations that it predicts. In the process, they ignore other important observations that could disconfirm the hypothesis, such as many *couples with children who don't have pets* (B) or many *couples without children who have pets* (D).

Similarity often appears responsible for confirmatory bias. Because the cases in cells A and D are similar to the hypothesis, people focus on them the most. Relevant observations in cells B and C receive less consideration because they are less similar to the hypothesis. On the other hand, some hypotheses contain attribute descriptions that minimize the role of similarity. For these hypotheses, people often attend to a broader range of evidence. Consider the attribute descriptions in the following hypothesis:

Gender covaries with political party.

Because these attribute descriptions do not state particular attribute values, they provide no basis for a confirmatory bias, and people consider observations from the four cells more evenly. In contrast, consider the attribute descriptions in:

Men are likely to be Republicans.

Because this hypothesis states particular attribute values explicitly, it is likely to engender confirmatory bias. People are likely to focus on the number of *Republican men* that they know and ignore *Democratic men, Republican women,* and *Democratic women* (Beyth-Marom, 1982).

Availability also biases contingency estimates. Try to assess whether there is a contingency between gender and college education. To assess this relation, people often retrieve memories of particular individuals, noting their gender and whether they went to college. Optimally, people should consider as many individuals as possible. Because the ability to retrieve information is limited, however, people only consider a subset of the relevant cases and are likely to produce a biased estimate. In contrast, when people receive a complete contingency table that specifies the frequency of observations in each cell, availability is less of a factor, and estimates become more accurate. Even under these conditions, however, the non-optimal strategies that we considered earlier remain prevalent (Beyth-Marom, 1982).

Finally, *framing* biases contingency estimates. As we saw earlier, L.J. Chapman and J.P. Chapman (1967, 1969) found that clinicians perceived illusory correlations between paranoia and salient eyes, and between homosexuality and genitalia, even when these contingencies did not exist objectively (**10.3.1**). People often perceive contingencies erroneously, when they have false but strong beliefs that they exist. On observing even an occasional case that matches a preconceived belief, people's conviction in it grows. In contrast, people often discount cases that disconfirm a preconceived belief, viewing them as being exceptions or errors. People may also ignore disconfirming cases, simply because they don't want to revise their beliefs. As many experiments have shown, framing often dominates the process of covariation assessment.

Assessing causality.   Covariation does not imply causality. If people observe that couples who have children also have pets, they cannot necessarily conclude that one of these two events causes the other. People can't conclude that having children causes couples to have pets, because perhaps having pets causes people to have children. Certainly, one of these two causal scenarios could be true, but a known covariation between *children* and *pets* does not distinguish between them. Furthermore, neither could be true, if some third attribute causes people to have both children and pets. For example, the key could be how much people like to care for dependents. In general, an attribution of causality is only justified when the purported cause is known to precede the purported effect, and when possible third attributes have been ruled out.

Nevertheless, people often perceive causation when it is not justified. Consider the following questions:

How accurately does a son's height (A) predict his father's height (B)?
How accurately does a father's height (B) predict his son's height (A)?

Formally, these two contingencies have equal strength, because a covariation between A and B is always equivalent to the covariation between B and A, by definition. Yet, when A. Tversky and Kahneman (1980) asked people questions like these, many believed that a father's height predicts his son's height better than a son's height predicts his father's. People appear to frame these two questions with a causal scenario that describes how fathers transmit genes to their sons. As a result, they perceive the dependencies causally rather than as simple contingencies.

When causal mechanisms do underlie a contingency, people may try to induce what they are. Typically, several different causal factors produce the occurrence of a single event. A fire, for example, results from a joint set of causes, including heat, fuel, and oxygen. Similarly, a combined set of environmental and physiological conditions could produce a headache. How do people discover causal relations under such conditions? First, they usually focus only on *unusual conditions* and ignore common ones (J.H. Holland et al., 1986; Shustack, 1988; **10**.4.1). In explaining a fire, someone might focus on the presence of an unusual source of heat and never note the importance of oxygen. Second, people often exhibit *confirmatory bias* (C.J. Downing, R.J. Sternberg, & B.H. Ross, 1985; Shustack & R.J. Sternberg, 1981; **10**.4.1). If they suspect that one attribute causes another, they only consider that causal relation and fail to test whether any other attribute also plays a causal role. In explaining a headache, someone might believe that an environmental event was responsible and thereby fail to consider a dietary influence. Third, people often overestimate the importance of a cause, exhibiting a bias for *minimal causation* (Shaklee & Fischoff, 1982). Once they discover one causal attribute, they assume it to be completely responsible for the outcome, even when other causal attributes necessarily contribute. Fourth, if people do look beyond a single causal attribute, they exhibit a bias toward *focused sampling*, focusing their attention on other attributes correlated with the known cause (Billman & Heit, 1988; J.D. Martin & Billman, 1991). People tend to believe that a somewhat redundant, cooccurring pattern of causes—not an unrelated set of causes—is responsible for an outcome.

10.4.4 Category-Based Induction

Categories often play a central role in induction. On discovering that an entity exhibits a new property, people may use a category to guide how far they project the property to other known entities. Imagine that someone discovers his Toyota Celica has a four-cylinder engine. Should he conclude that only his Toyota Celica has this property? If he decides to generalize the property to additional entities, how far should he go? Should he conclude that all Toyota Celicas have four-cylinder engines? Should he extend the generalization still further to all Toyotas? To all cars? To all vehicles? As we shall see, people use categories to constrain their inductions.

Children as young as two years old use categories to constrain induction (Gelman & Coley, 1990; Gelman & Markman, 1986, 1987; Wellman & Gelman, 1988). In one of Gelman's studies, two-year olds were presented with an exemplar of a category (e.g., a black cat) and told that it possessed a property (e.g., could see in the dark). The children then received two additional stimuli. One stimulus was perceptually similar to the initial exemplar (e.g., a black skunk that looked like the cat), whereas the other stimulus was not (e.g., a white cat that did not look much like the black cat). The children were asked whether the skunk or the white cat was more likely to the ability to see in the dark. Not surprisingly, the children generally selected the black skunk, because it looked more like the black cat.

In a second condition, as the children viewed the stimuli, the experimenter referred to both the black cat and the white cat as "a cat," and to the black skunk as "a skunk." Again, the children were told that the black cat could see in the dark. When they were asked whether the black skunk or the white cat was more likely to see in the dark, these children generally selected the white cat. Because the experimenter had used the same verbal label for the two cats to indicate their common category membership, the children perceived them as much more similar than when the experimenter did not name them, in the first condition.

As these findings illustrate, even very young children believe that categories should guide induction. Two entities may appear superficially different, as in the color of their fur, but if they are believed to be from the same category, they are perceived as sharing the same fundamental properties (e.g., the ability to see in the dark). People of all ages tend to assume that natural categories circumscribe set of entities that share deep causal mechanisms in nature (7.3.1).

A number of factors determine how readily people perform category-based inductions. For example, the typicality of the exemplar exhibiting a new property is important. Consider the following two inductive arguments:

Dogs have a left aortic arch.	Whales have a left aortic arch.
Mammals have a left aortic arch.	Mammals have a left aortic arch.

In each argument, the first line is the premise, and the second is the conclusion. Of interest is whether the typicality of the exemplar in the premise influences how readily people generalize *left aortic arch* to all of the other mammals in the conclusion. Rips (1975) found that people were more likely to generalize a new property from typical exemplars, like *dog*, than from atypical exemplars, like *whales*. In general, the typicality of the exemplar exhibiting a new property has a substantial effect on how readily people generalize it to the category.

Osherson, E.E. Smith, Wilkie, Lopez, and Shafir (1990) proposed that *coverage* underlies this effect of typicality: As coverage increases, so does people's willingness to generalize the property in the premise. Osherson et al. define coverage, for the two arguments we are considering, as the average similarity between the exemplar in the premise (*dog* or *whale*) and each exemplar of the category in the conclusion (*cat, horse, lion, mouse, walrus,* etc. in *mammals*). Typical exemplars have high coverage because they are similar to most exemplars of their category, whereas atypical exemplars have low coverage because they are dissimilar (7.3.2). Thus, *mammals* is covered better by *dog* than by *whale*, because *dog* has a higher average similarity to other mammals.

The following pair of arguments demonstrates that coverage—not typicality—is indeed the critical factor in argument strength:

| Dogs have a left aortic arch. | Dogs have a left aortic arch. |
Cats have a left aortic arch.	Whales have a left aortic arch.
Mammals have a left aortic arch.	Mammals have a left aortic arch.

If typicality is critical to argument strength, the left argument should be stronger, because the average typicality of *dog* and *cat* in *mammal* is higher than the average typicality of *dog* and *whale*. If coverage is critical, however, the argument on the right should be stronger, because *dog* and *whale* together cover *mammal* better than do *dog* and *cat*. To see this, consider the similarity between the exemplars in the premise and other *mammals*, in particular, *raccoon* and *walrus*. For the left argument, both *dog* and *cat* are similar to *raccoon*, but neither is similar to *walrus*. As a result, *dog* and *cat* do a good job of covering *raccoon* but a poor job of covering *walrus*. For the right argument, *dog* is similar to *raccoon*, and *whale* is similar to *walrus*. As a result, *dog* and *whale* together do a good job of covering both *raccoon* and *walrus*. In general, coverage is poor for the first argument, because everything that *dog* covers, *cat* covers about as well. Coverage is better for the second argument, because *dog* and *whale* cover very different sets of mammals. When subjects judge the strength of these two arguments, they rate the right as being stronger, because coverage, not typicality, is important.

Coverage explains why people are less willing to generalize from an exemplar to increasingly abstract categories. Compare:

Chimpanzees have a left aortic arch.	Chimpanzees have a left aortic arch.
Primates have a left aortic arch.	Mammals have a left aortic arch.

People judge the argument on the left as stronger than the argument on the right. To see why, consider how well *chimpanzee* covers *primate* versus *mammal*. *Mammal* contains many other categories besides *primate*, including *dog, horse,* and *whale,* which are not very similar to *chimpanzee*. Thus, *chim-*

panzee does an inferior job of covering *mammal* than *primate*, and inductive strength is lower.

Consider one final pair of arguments:

Horses have a left aortic arch.	Horses have a left aortic arch.
Donkeys have a left aortic arch.	Rabbits have a left aortic arch.

People judge the argument on the left as stronger than the argument on the right. In both arguments, *mammal* is the category that the premise covers, because it is the most specific category that contains the exemplars in the premise and the conclusion. Coverage is equal, because *horse* covers *mammal* equally well for both arguments. Because coverage is not responsible for the difference in argument strength here, something else must be. Osherson et al. suggest that the similarity of the exemplar in the premise to the exemplar in the conclusion determines argument strength in arguments like this. Because *horse* and *donkey* are more similar to each than are *horse* and *rabbit*, the left argument is stronger. As these examples illustrate, various forms of similarity play central roles in how people perform category–based induction (see also A.M. Collins & Michalski, 1989).

10.4.5 Analogy

People can often induce knowledge about a domain without having to extract it through observation. Imagine that you begin a new job at an office complex whose spatial layout is unusual and complicated. One way to induce knowledge about the layout would be to explore the office complex on foot. In the process of observing the layout, you would develop hypotheses about it and test them through further observation. On experiencing disconfirmation, you would revise your hypotheses as needed, until your knowledge supports error-free navigation.

Alternatively, someone who has worked at the complex a while could simply explain to you that the layout is analogous to a starfish. On hearing this analogy, you might transfer knowledge about starfish to the office complex. Thus, the knowledge that a starfish has a circular body, with five legs extending from it radially and symmetrically, would lead to the belief that the office complex contains a central circular building, with five tapered buildings extending from it in a radially symmetric pattern.

A critical issue is knowing how far to extend an analogy. Clearly, people do not transfer everything they know when drawing an analogy from one domain to another, as from a starfish to an office complex. Clearly, the office complex is not alive, it does not live underwater, and beachcombers cannot gather it. Furthermore, the information that people do transfer may not fit the new domain perfectly. For example, the spatial configuration of the starfish may only approximate the layout of the office complex. Rather than being circular, the central building may be square; rather than being tapered, the extended buildings may be rectangular; rather than being arranged symmetrically, the five extended buildings may be asymmetric. As you initially explore the office complex, your initial predictions about circularity, tapering, and symmetry may generate false predictions that lead to minor revisions of your knowledge. Nevertheless, the approximate correctness of the analogy may provide much useful information that greatly facilitates navigation.

As this example illustrates, analogy is a powerful source of induction. If an analogy is reasonably accurate, it can save people a tremendous amount of time inducing generalizations about a new domain because they don't have to rely as much on observation. We shall return to analogy later in the discussion of problem solving (**10**.6.2). For discussion of analogy and the related topic of metaphor, see Gentner (1989), Gentner and A.L. Stevens (1983), Glucksberg and Keysar (1990), J.H. Holland et al. (1986), Holyoak and Thagard (1989a, 1989b), Lakoff (1987), Lakoff and M. Johnson (1980), Ortony (1979), and Vosniadou and Ortony (1989).

10.5   DEDUCTION

To many people, deduction is the apex of human thought. Its rigorous methods epitomize rationality and provide the foundation of logic (Copi, 1978; Mates, 1972; McCawley, 1981; Quine, 1972; Schoenfield, 1973) and mathematics (Courant & Robbins, 1941). *Uncertainty* underlies the difference between deduction and induction. In a valid inductive argument, the conclusion follows from the premises, but with some uncertainty. Consider the inductive argument:

The sky is filled with clouds.
The wind is blowing.
_____

It will rain.

Although rain is likely to follow clouds and wind, it may not. For this reason, weather forecasters typically associate some measure of uncertainty with their predictions (e.g., a 70% chance of rain). In a valid deductive argument, though, the conclusion follows from the premises with complete certainty: If the premises are true, and if a rule of deductive inference produces the conclusion, then deductive logic guarantees that the conclusion is true.

Deduction is *truth preserving*. It is this guarantee of truth that provides deduction with its power and elegance. Consider the deductive argument:

> Amy is taller than Patty.
> Patty is taller than Kelly.
>
> ---
>
> Amy is taller than Kelly.

If the premises of this argument are true, the deductive rule of *transitivity* guarantees that the conclusion is true as well. Note that transitivity doesn't apply to all relations, as we saw earlier for similarity and the triangle inequality (10.2.2). For other violations of transitivity, see Johnson-Laird (1983, chap. 3).

People sometimes follow the prescriptions of logic quite naturally. As many researchers have shown, people often recognize and use transitivity. They also follow logical prescriptions frequently in their use of connectives (Johnson-Laird, 1983, chap. 3). Consider the connective, *and*, in the expression:

> Luke loves Katie and Katie loves Luke.

According to propositional logic, this expression is true only if both underlined constituents are true simultaneously. If either is false (e.g., if Katie doesn't love Luke), the expression is false. Similarly, consider the inclusive sense of the connective, *or*, in the expression:

> The student is working or the student is eating.

According to propositional logic, this expression is true only if at least one of the underlined constituents is true. If both are false (e.g., if the student is bowling), the expression is false. Clearly, people sometimes understand *and* and *or* in their logically prescribed forms. However, people often interpret them in non-logical ways as well, as in:

> The burglar became scared and ran.

Because knowledge about burglaries frames this use of *and*, people interpret it as implying a causal relation between being scared and running, thereby exceeding its logical interpretation. People often similarly fail to understand other connectives according to the rules of deductive logic. As we shall see next for conditional reasoning, people sometimes do not interpret *if* in the formally prescribed manner. Similarity, availability, and framing adulterate the purity of everyday deduction.

10.5.1 Conditional Reasoning

In conditional reasoning, one must evaluate conditional statements containing *if*, such as:

If Chris is home, he will answer the phone.

Conditional statements enable various types of deductive inference. *Modus ponens* is one type of deductive inference that can be performed on a conditional statement. Consider:

If A, then B.	If Chris is home, then he will answer the phone.
A	Chris is home.
B	Chris answers the phone.

The argument on the right illustrates the abstract form of modus ponens on the left. If one believes that the conditional statement is true (the first premise), and if its antecedent currently holds in the world (the second premise), then modus ponens guarantees that the conclusion is true. Intuitively, it is hard to imagine not following modus ponens, and, indeed, this is one deductive rule that people appear to follow regularly (Rips, 1988).

Modus tollens is another fundamental form of deductive inference. Consider:

If A, then B.	If Chris is home, then he will answer the phone.
Not B	Chris does not answer the phone.
Not A	Chris is not home.

The argument on the right illustrates the abstract form of modus tollens on the left. If one believes that the conditional statement is true (the first premise), and if its consequent does not currently hold in the world (the second premise), then modus tollens guarantees that the antecedent does not hold either. Whereas people often use modus ponens, they frequently fail to use modus tollens.

To see people's differential use of modus ponens and modus tollens, consider the *selection task* (Wason & Johnson-Laird, 1972). In the selection task, subjects evaluate a conditional statement, such as:

If a card has a vowel on one side,
then it has an even number on the other side.

Subjects receive four cards, each having a letter on one side and a number on the other, but they can only see one side. For example:

| E | | K | | 2 | | 5 |

The subjects' task is to select the two cards, which when turned over would determine if the conditional statement is true or false. Which two cards should subjects select here?

Turning over both the E card and the 5 card provides sufficient evidence for evaluating the truth of the conditional statement—the other sides of the K and 2 cards have no bearing on its truth whatsoever. Turning over the E card tests modus ponens: If a vowel is on one side of the card (E), then an even number must be on the other side. If not, then the conditional statement is false. Turning over the 5 card tests modus tollens: If an odd number is on one side of the card (5), then a vowel must not be on the other side. If there is, the conditional statement is false. If both modus ponens and modus tollens hold, then this conditional statement is true. In this type of experiment, nearly all subjects turn over the E card to test modus ponens. However, subjects rarely turn over the 5 card to test modus tollens. Although people often use modus ponens in conditional reasoning, they rarely use modus tollens.

People also frequently turn over the 2 card in the selection task, even though it does not provide a diagnostic test of the conditional statement. If people turn over this card and find a consonant, the statement could still be true. The statement is false only if there is a vowel on one side and an odd number on the other. The tendency to make this mistake is called *affirming the consequent*. The following argument illustrates this error, where the ★ prior to the conclusion indicates invalidity:

If A, then B.
B
_____

★A

Affirming the consequent reflects the incorrect belief that conditional statements are *symmetrical*: Because A implies B, B implies A. People fail to realize that this is not true and that B can accompany not-A.

Denying the antecedent constitutes a similar error, as this argument illustrates:

If A, then B.
Not A
_____

★Not B

In the selection task, people believe incorrectly that if a vowel is not on one side (the K card), then an even number is not on the other. As we just saw, however, the conditional statement is false only if there is a vowel on one side and an odd number on the other. Again, people believe incorrectly that the conditional statement is symmetrical: If not-A is true, then not-B must also be true. People fail to realize that not-A can accompany B.

The predisposition to select the E card and the 2 card in the selection task reflects *confirmatory bias* (**10**.4.3): People select the E card, expecting to see an even number on the other side (modus ponens), and they select the 2 card, expecting to see a vowel on the other side (affirming the consequent). Both selections are confirmatory, because people seek observations that match the conditional statement (i.e., observations that relate vowels and even numbers). However, people could also test the statement by trying to disconfirm it. If the statement is true, then attempts to disconfirm it should fail. For example, selecting the 5 card and not finding a vowel on the other side would fail to disconfirm the statement, such that it remains true. In general, though, people often believe that the way to test a conditional statement is to obtain evidence that confirms it. Because they focus on the similarity of the evidence to the statement, they once again exhibit a similarity bias (**10**.4.3). For further discussion of the selection task, see Cheng and Holyoak (1985), Johnson-Laird (1983), and Rips (1988).

Not surprisingly, people perform better on the selection task when they evaluate a conditional statement that is framed in a familiar context. To see this, consider the argument about Chris answering the phone again:

If Chris is home, then he will answer the phone.

Imagine that you must determine the validity of this statement on the basis of turning over two of the following four cards:

Chris is home.	Chris is not home.	Chris answers the phone.	Chris does not answer the phone.

Under these conditions, most people still follow modus ponens by selecting the first card, but they become more likely to pursue disconfirmation by picking the fourth card (modus tollens). Similarly, they are less subject to confirmation bias and do not select the third card as frequently. Unlike the unfamiliar task of assessing relations between letters and numbers, reasoning about a familiar task produces more sophisticated selections.

What is it about unfamiliar contexts that produces poor reasoning? Perhaps people know the rules of deductive logic and attempt to follow them, but other factors interfere. In this spirit, Rips (1988) suggested that people have trouble remembering the premises of an unfamiliar argument such that they err in evaluating it. Similarly, he suggested that the multiple meanings of *if* interfere with its logical use, and also that people know the importance of attempting disconfirmation but fail to remember this. Familiar contexts minimize the roles of these interfering factors and allow people to use deductive rules more competently: They remember premises from familiar arguments better and thus make fewer errors in applying deductive rules to them; they process *if* logically when it is framed in a familiar context that eliminates irrelevant meanings; and their knowledge of a familiar context suggests evidence that could disconfirm a statement, thereby making disconfirmation more available.

Pragmatic reasoning schemas.   Some theorists have argued that people do not use rules of deductive logic at all when processing conditional statements in familiar contexts. These theorists propose, instead, that people reason about familiar contexts using frames developed from everyday experience (7.2.2). For example, Cheng and Holyoak (1985) have suggested that people develop *pragmatic reasoning schemas* to process conditional statements in familiar contexts (see also Cheng, Holyoak, Nisbett, & L.M. Oliver, 1986). Consider an example of a pragmatic reasoning schema, the *permission schema*, which applies to any context in which people must reason about an action and its preconditions. Essentially, the permission schema is a frame with two attributes, one for an action, *A*, and one for a precondition of the action, *P*:

Rule 1.   If *A* is taken, then *P* must be satisfied.
Rule 2.   If *A* is not taken, then *P* need not be satisfied (but may be).
Rule 3.   If *P* is satisfied, then *A* may be taken (but need not be).
Rule 4.   If *P* is not satisfied, then *A* may not be taken.

The permission schema bears important analogical properties to the rules of deductive logic, even though the analogy is far from exact. Rule 1 is analogous to modus ponens, because the presence of the antecedent (the action was taken) implies the presence of the consequent (the precondition was met). Rule 4 is analogous to modus tollens, because the absence of the consequent (the precondition was not met) implies the absence of the antecedent (the action could not be taken). Because the schema states both of these rules explicitly, they are highly available and support optimal reasoning. In contrast, the content of Rules 2 and 3 prevents errors in reasoning: Rule 2 prevents denying the antecedent, because the absence of the antecedent (the action was not taken) does not deny the presence of the consequent (the precondition could have been met). Similarly, Rule 3 prevents affirming the consequent, because the presence of the consequent (the precondition was met) does not imply the presence of the antecedent (the action might not have been taken). Whereas Rules 1 and 4 state clear dependencies, Rules 2 and 3 state no dependency. As a result, people can see that only Rules 1 and 4 are useful in testing the validity of a conditional statement. Because the permission schema states this information explicitly, people are likely to test conditional statements that concern permission optimally. Note that the permission schema would not help people process conditional statements that don't concern possession. However, people may have other pragmatic reasoning schemata that apply to these domains.

Cheng and Holyoak proposed that people retrieve the permission schema whenever they must assess a conditional relation between an action and its preconditions. For example, imagine having to evaluate the following statement about the action of *riding the subway* and its precondition of *having the necessary fare*:

If James rides the subway, then he has $1.00 for the fare.

Further imagine receiving the following four cards and performing the selection task:

James rides the subway.	James does not ride the subway.	James has $1.00.	James does not have $1.00.

Because this problem addresses an action and its precondition, people apply the permission schema. Because Rules 1 and 4 provide unambiguous tests, people typically turn over the first and fourth cards, expecting:

If James rides the subway, then he has $1.00.
If James does not have $1.00, then he can't ride the subway.

In contrast, because Rules 2 and 3 aren't informative, people typically don't turn over the second and third cards, realizing:

If James does not ride the subway, then he may or may not have $1.00.
If James has $1.00, then he may or may not ride the subway.

The permission schema, because it makes all four relations between the action and its precondition highly available, enables people to reason optimally. Framing the problem with the proper conceptual knowledge facilitates reasoning. In unfamiliar situations, no such frames apply, and people have to fall back on the domain–independent rules of deductive inference, such as modus ponens and modus tollens. If they do not know these rules, then confirmatory bias may constitute their best attempt at an appropriate strategy.

10.5.2 Categorical Syllogisms

Quantifiers, such as *all* and *some*, are also fundamental elements of logic, along with the various connectives that we have considered thus far. In exploring how people process quantifiers, researchers have focused primarily on *categorical syllogisms*, perhaps because they constitute a reasonably small and well-structured domain of arguments. Consider the following syllogisms, where * indicates an invalid conclusion:

All Ys are Xs.	All Xs are not Ys.	Some Ys are Xs.
All Zs are Ys.	All Ys are not Zs.	All Zs are not Ys.
———————	———————	———————
All Zs are Xs.	*All Xs are not Zs.	Some Xs are not Zs.

As can be seen, each syllogism contains two premises and a conclusion. In all syllogisms, one term must occur in the first premise and the conclusion (X), a second term must occur in the second premise and the conclusion (Z), and a third term must occur in both premises (Y). The order of the two terms in each statement can vary (e.g., the order of X and Y). Each statement can be quantified with either *all* or *some* and is either positive or negative, producing four statement types, as illustrated by *all Xs are Ys, some Xs are Ys, all Xs are not Ys*, and *some Xs are not Ys*.

One formal method for solving categorical syllogisms is to construct *Euler circles* (Erickson, 1974; Johnson-Laird & Bara, 1984). Consider the application of Euler circles to the syllogism in Fig. 10.3. For each premise, we draw circles to represent each of the possible *set relations* that could exist between its two terms. As Fig. 10.3 illustrates, two different set relations are possible for the first premise, *all Ys are Xs*. The circle for Y embedded in the circle for X represents the first of these two set relations. Because the circle for Y lies completely within the circle for X, *all Ys are Xs*, but because the circle for X extends beyond the circle for Y, *some Xs are not Ys* (i.e., those Xs inside the circle for X but outside the circle for Y). However, the first premise could also mean something else. To see this, consider the coextensive circles for X and Y at the top-right of Fig. 10.3. Because these two circles overlay each other exactly, *all Xs are Ys* and *all Ys are Xs*. In other words, there is no difference between sets X and Y.

As these two different set relations indicate, the first premise is ambiguous. According to its first interpretation, the set of Xs is larger than the set of Ys and contains all Ys. According to the second interpretation, the set of Xs is identical to the set of Ys. Although the first premise could refer to either of these two states of affairs, it cannot refer to both. Only one possible set relation exists in the world at a given point in time. Because we don't know

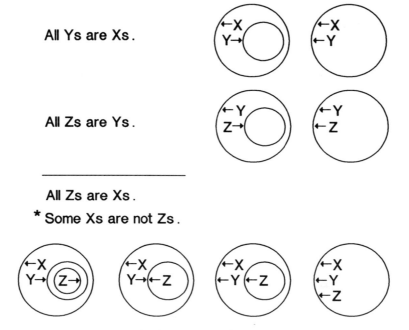

All Ys are Xs.

All Zs are Ys.

All Zs are Xs.

* Some Xs are not Zs.

Figure 10.3.   An example of a syllogism and its accompanying Euler circles.

which set relation currently holds, however, we must take both into account when evaluating a syllogism that contains this premise.

As Fig. 10.3 further illustrates, the second premise of this syllogism, *all Zs are Ys*, is also ambiguous. Just like the first premise, it has two different interpretations. According to the first interpretation, the set of Ys is larger than the set of Zs and contains all Zs. According to the second interpretation, the set of Ys is identical to the set of Zs.

Once we have represented all possible interpretations of each premise alone, we are ready to represent all possible interpretations of the two premises combined. To construct these interpretations, we combine each possible interpretation of the first premise with each possible interpretation of the second premise. Consider the four sets of circles at the bottom of Fig. 10.3. As can be seen, each set of circles represents one combination of the two premises (i.e., one possible relationship between sets X, Y, and Z). Consider the first set of circles on the left, which results from combining the first interpretation of the first premise with the first interpretation of the second premise. According to this interpretation, the set of Xs completely contains the set of Ys and is larger than the set of Ys. In addition, the set of Ys completely contains the set of Zs and is larger than the set of Zs. Now look at the fourth set of circles, furthest to the right, which results from combining the second interpretation of the first premise with the second interpretation of the second premise. According to this interpretation, all three sets are identical.

Once we have represented all possible interpretations of the two premises, we are ready to test the conclusion. The argument is valid if the conclusion is consistent with *every* possible interpretation of the combined premises (i.e., every possible relationship between sets X, Y, and Z). Consider the first conclusion in Fig. 10.3, *all Zs are Xs*. To test this conclusion, we assess the relation between Zs and Xs in every interpretation of the combined premises. Because the circle for Z never extends beyond the circle for X in any of the four interpretations, the relation, *all Zs are Xs*, is consistent with all of them. Consequently, the argument containing the two premises and this conclusion is valid.

In contrast, if a conclusion is inconsistent with *any* interpretation of the combined premises, then the argument is invalid. Consider the second conclusion in Fig. 10.3, *some Xs are not Zs*. As can be seen, this conclusion is consistent with the first three interpretations of the two premises but not with the fourth. Because every X is also a Z in the fourth interpretation, the relation, *some Xs are not Zs*, is not true. Consequently, the argument containing the two premises and this conclusion is invalid.

The syllogism in Fig. 10.3 is one of the simplest. Constructing Euler circles for some of the more complicated syllogisms produces a significant increase in the number and complexity of the interpretations that people must consider. As a result, most people are unlikely to solve complex syllogisms using Euler circles. However, people often do report using such circles in solving syllogisms, so this method may constitute at least a partial strategy.

To study syllogistic reasoning, researchers present subjects with syllogisms, assess how likely they are to solve each syllogism correctly, and rank the syllogisms from easiest to most difficult. In general, as the Euler circles for a syllogism become more complex, subjects are more likely to draw inaccurate conclusions. This suggests that people attempt to construct all possible set relations for each premise and the conclusion, as formal theories prescribe. Because of processing limitations, though, people fail to consider all possible set relations—especially for complex problems with many possibilities. Thus, if subjects only construct the first three interpretations of the combined premises in Fig. 10.3 and fail to construct the last, they will mistakenly construe the conclusion, *some Xs are not Zs*, as valid.

Other researchers have argued that people do not use formal methods, such as Euler circles, to solve syllogisms. For example, Johnson-Laird (1983) suggested that people use mental models instead (7.2.2; see also Johnson-Laird & Bara, 1984; Johnson-Laird & Steedman, 1978). According to this view, people use the first premise to construct an initial model of the situation described in the problem and then use the second premise to develop the model further. To test the conclusion, people see whether the conclusion is inconsistent with their final model of the situation in any way. If not, they accept the syllogism as valid. This procedure is simpler than Euler circles and may lie within the power of normal human computation.

People often exhibit various types of bias in solving syllogisms. In *atmosphere bias*, the similarity of a conclusion to its premises affects people's judgments of validity. According to this non-formal strategy, a conclusion is similar to a premise, if they share either *some* or *not*. When a conclusion and at least one premise are similar in this manner, people tend to judge the argument as valid. When a conclusion and a premise are not similar in this manner, people tend to judge the argument as invalid. Consider the following invalid syllogisms:

Some Xs are Ys.	All Xs are not Ys.	Some Xs are Ys.
Some Ys are Zs.	All Ys are not Zs.	Some Ys are Zs.
★Some Xs are Zs.	★All Xs are not Zs.	★All Xs are Zs.

People often conclude that the first two arguments are valid and that the third is invalid. Whereas the similarity of the conclusion to the premises biases people to perceive the first two arguments as valid, dissimilarity in the third argument prevents this bias from occurring. Once again, we see the effect of similarity on thought (Johnson-Laird, 1983; Rips, 1988; Woodworth & Sells, 1935).

Conversion bias constitutes another weakness in people's ability to perform syllogistic reasoning. Conversion bias reflects faulty comprehension of the premises during the initial construction of an argument. Rather than constructing all possible set relations for a premise, people may convert it into a simpler set of relations. Consider the premise, *all Xs are Ys*, in Fig. 10.4. As this figure illustrates, people often construct only the set relation on the left, failing to construct the less obvious set relation on the right. They also often fail to construct some of the less obvious set relations for *some Xs are Ys* and for *some Xs are not Ys*, shown in Fig. 10.4. As a result, people often make errors on syllogisms that have these premises. Because they fail to take all possible interpretations of the premises into account, they miss an interpretation that is inconsistent with the conclusion. Conversion bias further illustrates the role of availability in human thought. Because some set relations are highly available, people mistakenly assume that these represent *all* of the relevant possibilities (Ceraso & Provitera, 1971; Revlis, 1975; Rips, 1988).

In summary, people follow the formal prescriptions of deductive logic to some extent. During conditional reasoning, they may apply transitivity, connectives, and modus ponens properly. When assessing syllogisms, people may attempt to generate set relations as exhaustively as they can. On the

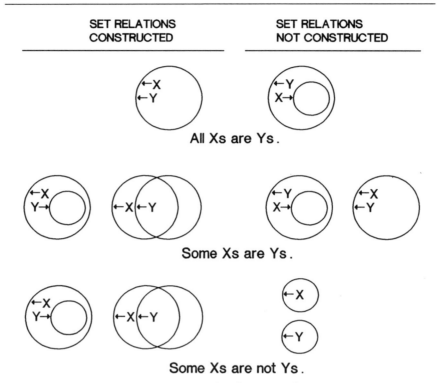

Figure 10.4.   Examples of conversion bias.

other hand, similarity, availability, and framing once again function extensively.

10.6   PROBLEM SOLVING

Life is full of problems, and people spend much of their time trying to solve them. They have scheduling problems, trying to be in the right place at the right time. They have interpersonal problems, trying to establish and maintain relationships. They have physical and psychological problems, trying to keep their bodies and minds in shape. They have educational problems, having to acquire and impart knowledge. They have occupational problems, having to achieve the goals of their daily work.

What, then, distinguishes problem solving from the other forms of thought that we have considered so far, namely, decision making, induction, and deduction? Roughly speaking, problem solving addresses how people use thought to transform or arrange the physical world to achieve a goal. In trying to get into good physical condition, one has to determine a set of actions that will transform his or her body from its current state into a more desirable state. In trying to schedule errands, one has to arrange them in a way that will minimize time and effort. However, problems frequently involve the other forms of thought that we have considered thus far. For example, problem solving often requires decision making: At each point in problem solving, people must choose among the possible actions they could perform. Problem solving often requires induction: Generalizations about previous problems are often useful in predicting actions that will work in future problems. Problem solving often requires deduction: In reasoning about actions that can solve a problem, people often process conditional statements to determine the implications of a particular state or action. In other words, decision making, induction, and deduction are all tools for problem solving. People frequently use these cognitive skills to transform and arrange the physical world as they strive to achieve their goals.

Greeno (1978) proposed a taxonomy of problems that captures important distinctions among them (see also Greeno & Simon, 1988). In *comprehension problems*, people must discover the structure of a domain, so that they can understand its operation and predict its behavior. In relationships, for example, individuals often try to understand other people's values and motives so that they can understand and predict their actions. Similarly, people might want to understand how a bureaucratic institution works, so that they can avoid red tape. Because comprehension problems typically constitute induction, I do not pursue them here (see **10**.4).

In *transformation problems*, people have to identify a series of actions that will transform a current state into a known goal state. Typically in such problems, the goal state is specified clearly, and the problem is to identify a series of transformations that will achieve it. For example, one might want to identify a series of actions that will produce a perfect souffle, or a series of actions that will repair a lawn mower.

In *arrangement problems*, people have to identify a set of relations among entities that will optimize desirable constraints. Typically in these problems, a goal state is not specified clearly, and the problem is to specify one that is optimal. For example, one might want to arrange the furniture in a room so as to support certain activities without impeding travel through it. Similarly, one might want to arrange a bouquet to optimize symmetry, texture, color, and other aesthetic criteria.

Many problems require combinations of comprehension, transformation, and arrangement. For example, designing an automobile involves first comprehending people's needs and then arranging the various aspects of automobile technology to achieve them. Similarly, chess involves transforming the board to achieve checkmate while simultaneously trying to arrange pieces in an optimal defensive configuration.

Another important distinction in problem solving concerns *problem famil-iarity*. Problems vary from being completely novel, to being somewhat familiar, to being so familiar that people are experts at solving them. This distinction of problem familiarity cuts across problem types: Novel prob-lems, familiar problems, and domains of expertise may all require compre-hension, transformation, and arrangement. In the remainder of this section, I begin with a discussion of how people solve novel problems, I then address how they solve familiar problems, and finally I address how they become expert problem solvers.

10.6.1 Solving Novel Problems

Solving a novel problem is often a frustrating experience. Because its solution may not be readily available, one has to try various alternatives in hopes of finding one that works. As a result, the solving of a novel problem typically exhibits the following performance characteristics:

Long solution times. People often take a very long time to solve a novel problem. Because they don't know what they're doing, they spend ex-tended periods of time trying out possible solutions and rejecting them.

Backtracking. In trying out a possible solution, people often discover at some point that it won't work. Rather than starting from scratch, they retrace their steps to an earlier point in the solution and pursue an action that was previously rejected in favor of the one that failed. For example, in trying to find someone's office in a large building, people don't return to the front door when the search down a particular corridor fails. Instead, they would backtrack to some previous choice point (e.g., the elevator) and try another option (e.g., a different corridor).

Concentration. Solving a novel problem typically requires all of people's limited resource for strategic processing (**4.2.2**). Because automatized pro-cedures and existing frames don't apply to the current problem, people must use executive productions to combine knowledge in new manners (**5**). As a result, little of the strategic resource remains for performing a secondary task, such as conversation or listening to music.

Failure. Solving a novel problem often ends in failure, at least tempo-rarily. Because people may have little idea of how to solve the problem, and because of the cognitive effort required, they ultimately may be unable to find a solution.

Non-optimal solutions. When people do find solutions to novel problems, the solutions are often not optimal. In trying to find someone's office in a complicated building for the first time, one may eventually discover a path, but it may not be the shortest. On returning frequently, more efficient paths may be discovered.

As we shall see, these performance characteristics typically characterize novel problem solving in a domain. As we shall also see in later sections, these characteristics disappear as people become experienced problem solvers.

Relevance.   Much of the frustration in solving a novel problem stems from not knowing which aspects of the problem are relevant to its solution. Because so many objects and relations exist in the problem context, it is not obvious which to transform or arrange to facilitate a solution. Essentially, this is the same problem of relevance that we have seen before (7.3.1, **10.2.3, 10.4.1**).

Duncker (1945) used the "radiation problem" to illustrate the importance of relevance in problem solving, adapted as follows:

> Imagine that a patient enters a hospital with a malignant tumor in his stomach that will eventually kill him if not removed. Although no surgical procedure for removing the tumor exists, a kind of ray could destroy it. At high intensities, the ray will destroy the malignant tissue, but will also destroy healthy tissue. At lower intensities, the ray will not harm healthy tissue, but neither does it destroy malignant tissue. Develop a procedure for using the ray that will destroy the tumor but not damage healthy tissue.

In trying to solve this problem, people exhibit all of the performance characteristics just described for novel problems: They spend considerable time, they backtrack, they concentrate, they fail, and they find non-optimal solutions. For example, people suggest cutting away healthy tissue so that the ray reaches the tumor directly, or they suggest treating the healthy tissue with some chemical that prevents it from being damaged. Although these solutions might work, they are not optimal. The first requires major surgery, and the second requires an unknown chemical.

Why do initial attempts at solving the radiation problem often fail? They fail because subjects have not focused their attention on a relevant aspect of the problem that can be transformed or arranged to produce a solution. People believe initially that the healthy tissue is relevant. As a result, they focus their attention on transformations of the tissue that would protect it from the ray (e.g., cutting the tissue away, treating it chemically). Instead, stop for a moment and view the ray as a relevant aspect of the problem that could be transformed or rearranged to produce a solution. How could the ray be transformed? What aspects of the ray can be varied? Which of these variations will protect healthy tissue and destroy the tumor?

The answer is to aim many rays of low intensity at the tumor from different directions, such that their convergence produces a high intensity only in the malignant tissue. People often fail to see this solution, at least initially, because they fail to see the relevance of transforming the ray. As a result, people continue to make two implicit assumptions about it: (a) use only one ray machine, (b) use only high intensity rays. Once people start considering the ray as relevant, they question these assumptions, transform the ray, and discover the solution. Duncker predicted that making the ray more salient in the problem description would cause people to view it as relevant and discover the correct solution more easily. By simply mentioning the ray earlier in the problem to make it more available, he produced faster solutions.

As the radiation problem illustrates, people often flounder while solving novel problems because they fail to consider relevant aspects, focusing their attention instead on aspects that don't matter or that are only part of the solution. Failure to know the relevant aspects is hardly blameworthy. After all, the problem is novel. On the other hand, good advice for those trying to solve novel problems is to consider as many possible aspects of a problem as are potentially relevant, not focusing on some to the neglect of others. Because irrelevant aspects are often highly available, and because relevant aspects may be relatively unavailable, people should be as open-minded as possible in searching for solutions.

A related problem is *functional fixedness*. As we just saw for the radiation problem, people often draw implicit assumptions that interfere with finding a solution. Even when they consider relevant aspects of the problem, they may fail to view it in a way that is relevant to solving the problem. For example, they might consider the ray as relevant but never consider more than one. Duncker illustrated this problem of functional fixedness with the "candle problem," adapted as follows:

> On a table before you are a candle, some matches, a box of tacks, a hammer, some string, some pliers, and other objects. Your task is to hang the candle stably on a wall so that the candle burns safely and properly.

Just as with the radiation problem, people exhibit the non-optimal performance characteristics of novel problem solving. They make errors, they backtrack, and they try non-optimal solutions. For example, people try nailing the candle to the wall, or they try hanging the candle against the wall with string. Both of these solutions are obviously not optimal, because they could burn down the building! The correct solution is to empty the tacks from the box, use the hammer and tacks to nail the box to the wall, and to place the candle on the box away from the wall.

People generally fail to consider this solution, at least initially, because they remain fixed on the current function of the box. As long as they view the box's function as containing tacks, they fail to consider it as a platform on which to place the candle. To overcome functional fixedness, one must question the function of each problem aspect that is considered. If this isn't done, available functions irrelevant to the problem will keep coming to mind, and less available but relevant functions will not.

In summary, Duncker's demonstrations illustrate the importance of relevance in novel problem solving. If people don't consider the relevant aspects of a problem, and if they don't view these aspects in the relevant ways, they will fail. For subsequent work that has addressed these issues under the heading of "problem representation," see Greeno and Simon (1988).

Search. As we just saw, people must often search for possible solutions when solving a novel problem. Newell and Simon (1972) developed a model called the *General Problem Solver* (GPS) that illustrates the importance of search in novel problem solving. GPS contains three general components. First, it contains an *information processing system*, which can be viewed as a cognitive model of a human problem solver. Roughly speaking, this information processing system, which I will call the *problem solver*, contains executive productions (**4.2**.1) that operate on information in working memory (**5**), while transferring information to and from long-term memory (**6, 7**).

Second, GPS contains a *model of the external task environment*. This model typically includes a description of the physical entities relevant to the problem, constraints on how the problem solver can manipulate these entities, and an externally provided goal to achieve (i.e., the problem). Typically, GPS' model of the task environment does not represent the entire environment that a human problem solver might experience, but only represents those aspects of the environment that are relevant to the current problem.

Third, GPS contains a *problem space*. A problem space represents the set of all possible states in which the problem solver can be while solving a problem. Note that the problem space is a theoretical construct, much like the hypothesis and observation spaces we considered for induction (**10**.4). Rather than being a description of the problem solver's current cognitive state, the problem space is a theoretical tool. When solving a problem, the problem solver typically does not explore or represent the entire problem space. Instead, only a small region of the problem space may be explored while solving a problem, and still smaller regions of the problem space are represented at any given point in time.

Each state in the problem space contains the following information about the problem solver and the task environment:

1. The current goal of the problem solver.
2. The current state of the task environment.
3. Operators (i.e., actions) known by the problem solver that can transform the current state of the task environment into some other

state. Each operator is a production rule, with initiating conditions and an action (**4**.1. **4**.2.1)
4. Procedures known by the problem solver for selecting operators (i.e., algorithms and heuristics).

At each point in solving a novel problem, the problem solver selects an operator and applies it to the current state of the task environment. Upon applying the operator, the problem solver moves from one state in the problem space into another state: As the environment changes, the operators that can be applied may change, as may the procedures for choosing among operators. Hopefully, the new state of the task environment is closer to the goal than was the previous state. If not, the problem solver can backtrack to a previous state and try another operator that hasn't been applied to that state previously. Essentially, then, the problem solver searches for a path through the problem space. Beginning with the initial state, the problem solver seeks a series of intermediate states that lead to the goal state. If the problem solver cannot find such a path during its search, it fails to solve the problem. If the problem solver does find a path, it succeeds, although the path may not be optimally efficient.

To see how GPS represents novel problem solving, consider its account of how people solve the following instance of Luchins' (1942) "water jug problem," adapted as follows:

> In front of you are three empty water jugs. Jug A has a capacity of 21 oz., Jug B has a capacity of 127 oz., and Jug C has a capacity of 3 oz. Your goal is to have one jug contain 85 oz. At any time, you can fill a jug from the water faucet, but you must always fill the jug full. You can pour the contents of one jug into another jug, but you must either empty the jug being poured, or completely fill the jug being filled. You can empty a jug into the sink, but you must always empty the jug completely.

This problem description provides information about the task environment, including relevant entities, constraints on their manipulation, and the goal. For example, Jug A is a relevant entity, filling a jug from the faucet is a possible operation, and obtaining 85 oz. is the goal. Figure 10.5 illustrates a very small subset of the states in the problem space. Note that Fig. 10.5 only includes partial information about each of the states in the problem space, excluding the possible operators at each state and the procedures for choosing among them. Instead, each state only represents information about the task environment. For example, the initial state 0,0,0 indicates that all three jugs are empty at the start of the problem. Its three immediate descendents represent the three subsequent states possible, given the available operators. If you fill Jug A, you enter state 21,0,0; if you fill Jug B, you enter state

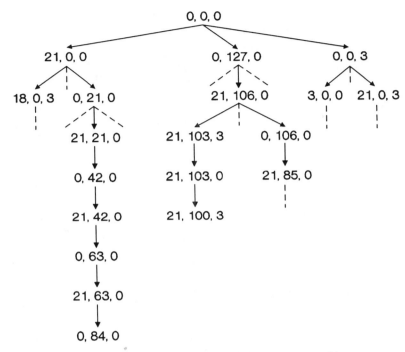

Figure 10.5. A partial problem space for a water jug problem.

0,127,0; and if you fill Jug C, you enter state 0,0,3. Similarly, the immediate descendents of these three states represent the next set of subsequent states that are possible. Thus, if you filled Jug A initially and are therefore at 21,0,0, you could next pour some of Jug A into Jug C to produce 18,0,3, or you could pour all of Jug A into Jug B to produce 0,21,0. To solve a problem, you search for a path that begins with the initial state and ends with the goal state. If the goal is to obtain 85 oz. of water, you must discover a path from 0,0,0 to any state in which Jug B has 85 oz. (because Jug B is the only jug large enough to hold that much water). The path from 0,0,0 to 0,127,0 to 21,106,0 to 0,106,0 to 21,85,0 constitutes one possible solution.

As Fig. 10.5 illustrates, the problem space for this water jug problem is potentially infinite. Given the immense number of paths through this space, how do people search for a path that provides a solution? In general, *algorithms* and *heuristics* guide search. An algorithm is a procedure that, in principle, guarantees a solution. Consider *forward search*, in which people apply operators to the current state and attempt to reach the goal state. In Fig. 10.5, forward search would begin at 0,0,0 and attempt to move through the space toward a goal state (e.g., 21,85,0). *Breadth-first search* and *depth-first search* constitute two algorithmic forms of forward search. Consider how breadth-first search would work in Fig. 10.5. Beginning at 0,0,0, you explore every state that could possibly follow from it in the problem space (i.e., 21,0,0, 0,127,0, and 0,0,3). You do not proceed any further in the problem space (e.g., 18,0,3) until you have examined every descendent of 0,0,0 and not found a solution. If none of these states provides a solution, you then test all of the descendents of these states before proceeding any further in the problem space. For example, you would test 18,0,3, 0,21,0, 21,106,0, 3,0,0, and 21,0,3, among others. If none of these states provides a solution, you would then test all of the descendents of these states, and so forth. Search is breadth-first, because the entire "breadth" of possibilities is tested at the current level in the search space before performing any test at the next level.

In principle, breadth-first search is algorithmic. Because you will eventually examine every path through the problem space, a solution is guaranteed, assuming that one exists and that sufficient time exists to find it. In practice, however, if the search space is large or infinite, you will not have the time or the resources to discover a solution. Imagine a search space in which each state has 10 descendents. The initial state leads to 10 descendents, which lead to 100 descendents, which lead to 1000 descendents, which lead to 10,000 descendents, and so forth. Because of the various limitations on human cognition, it is extremely unlikely that you would perform breadth-first search much beyond the second level of this search space.

Alternatively, you could perform *depth-first search*. In this type of search, you follow a single path through a problem space, until it either succeeds or fails. Imagine that you begin solving the problem in Fig. 10.5 by moving from 0,0,0 to 0,127,0. If you are performing depth-first search, you would not consider any other descendents of 0,0,0 at this point (i.e., 21,0,0 or 0,0,3). Instead, you would next test a descendent of 0,127,0, such as 21,106,0. Once you had tested 21,106,0, you would not consider any other descendents of 0,127,0, such as 0,124,3. Instead, you would test a descendent of 21,106,0, such as 21,103,3. As you arrive at each successively deeper state along this path, you would determine if it provides a solution. If so, you are finished; if not, you would proceed one level deeper in the search space. Once a path ends without having led to a solution, you backtrack to the state tested at the previous level and follow every possible path from it, in a depth-first manner. Thus, imagine that you end a path at 21,103,3, deciding for some reason that continuing further is unlikely to produce a solution. At this point, you would backtrack to 21,106,0 and might next proceed down the path beginning with 0,106,0. If none of these paths from 21,106,0 yields a solution, you would continue to back track until you eventually reached 0,0,0, at which point you would try another previously untaken path from there.

In principle, depth-first search is also algorithmic. Because you will eventually consider every path through the problem space, a solution is guaranteed, assuming that one exists and that sufficient time is available to find it. In practice, however, if the search space is large or infinite, once again, you will not have the time or the resources to discover a solution. Furthermore, depth-first search runs into problems when every path is potentially infinite, as in Fig. 10.5, because search will follow one path forever without ever backtracking. Under such conditions, you may decide to terminate search at some arbitrary level, if you have not found a solution, and begin to backtrack. For example, if you have not found a solution upon reaching any tenth descendent of 0,0,0, you might always begin to backtrack, rather than looking for a solution deeper in the problem space

A similar class of algorithms exists for *backward search*. In backward search, you begin with the goal state and search for a path from it back to the current state. Imagine that the goal is 0,85,0 and that the current state is 0,0,0. In performing backward search, you first search for states that could have produced 0,85,0. In the process, you might discover 21,64,0 and 0,82,3, among many others. If one of these states constitutes the current state, you have found a path from the goal state to the current state, and you can then apply the operator(s) that produced the backward path—in reverse order—to reach the goal. If none of these states is the current state, however, you must search further back. From 21,64,0, you might discover 21,61,3, 0,64,0, and so forth. If one of these states is the current state, you have found a solution; if not, you must continue to search.

Analogous to forward search, backward search can be breadth-first or depth-first. In breadth-first search, you examine every possible state that could have led to the goal state before proceeding any further toward the current state. In depth-first search, you examine a complete path, beginning with the goal, and only backtrack on encountering failure or on performing an arbitrary number of searches. Similar to forward search, backward search may require tremendous amounts of time and computational resources, making it impractical.

As we have seen, the fundamental problem with breadth-first and depth-first search in either direction is that they may require a tremendous amount of time and processing capacity. If a problem space is large, as it often is, searching it successfully may be infeasible. Consequently, people often use *heuristics* instead of algorithms to guide search, where a heuristic is a procedure that is likely to converge quickly on a solution but that may also fail. Whereas algorithms guarantee a solution, heuristics do not. Often, heuristics are successful strategies that people have induced from their previous problem solving experience (**10**.4). Even though heuristics don't guarantee a solution, they often provide solutions faster than algorithms, and they almost always provide significant improvement over random search. In terms of Duncker's observations about novel problem solving, heuristics are useful because they specify aspects of a problem that are likely to be *relevant* (**7**.3.1, **10**.2.3, **10**.4.1).

One simple heuristic that people often use is *difference reduction*, which states:

> Select the operator that reduces the difference between the current state and the goal state by the largest amount.

According to this heuristic, one should select the operator that makes the subsequent state most similar to the goal state. Once again, we see the importance of similarity in human thought. To see how difference reduction works, consider the problem space in Fig. 10.5, and imagine that you wish to obtain 100 oz. If you use difference reduction, you would attempt to find the operator that reduces the difference between the empty jugs and the goal state by the largest amount. If you fill Jug A, the difference between it and the goal state, |21 − 100|, is 79; if you fill Jug B, the difference between it and the goal state, |127 − 100|, is 27; and if you fill Jug C, the difference between it and the goal state, |3 − 100|, is 97. To maximize difference reduction, you should first fill Jug B, because this will produce the subsequent state that is most similar to the goal state. Once you have filled Jug B, you assess the differences again. To maximize difference reduction at this point, you would pour 21 oz. from Jug B into Jug A, thereby reducing Jug B to 106 oz. and bringing it closest to the goal state. After pouring 3 oz. from Jug B into Jug C twice, you would obtain 100 oz. and have solved the problem.

The difference reduction method can lead problem solvers astray, however. Consider the problem of obtaining 84 oz. As Fig. 10.5 illustrates, your first move should be to fill Jug B, because this produces the greatest similarity between the next state and the goal state. Subsequently, you should pour Jug B into Jug A twice, thereby achieving 85 oz. in Jug B. What should you do next? Although you are only 1 ounce away from the solution, you are actually a long way from a solution in the problem space. Most importantly, the use of difference reduction has caused you to miss a relatively simple solution. As Fig. 10.5 illustrates, you can obtain 84 oz. by filling Jug A and pouring it into Jug B four times (i.e., 4 × 21 = 84). Although difference reduction can sometimes obscure a solution, its success on other occasions makes it a prevalent heuristic (Atwood & Polson, 1976; Greeno, 1974).

A more powerful heuristic is *means-ends analysis* (Newell & Simon, 1972; see also Greeno & Simon, 1988). To apply this heuristic, you would first attempt to find the most important difference between the current state and the goal state. Identifying the most important difference is a difficult problem in itself and once again constitutes the relevance problem that continues to rear its head (7.3.1, **10.2.3**, **10.4.1**). Assuming that you have some means of identifying the most important difference, you find it and establish a *subgoal* to remove it. This establishment of a subgoal initiates a search for an operator that will eliminate the difference. Once an operator is found, its conditions of application are compared to the current state. If its conditions are met, the operator is applied, and the most important difference is eliminated. If no further differences remain between the current state and goal state, the problem is solved. Otherwise, the difference reduction process repeats itself for each remaining difference.

What happens, though, if the conditions for one of these difference reduction operators doesn't match the current state? At this point, means–ends analysis is applied to differences between the current state and the conditions of this operator. Reducing these differences requires the application of additional operators, and applying these additional operators may require means–ends analysis again. Means–ends analysis can continue to be applied within itself *recursively* as long as is necessary (similar to the recursion inherent in forward and backward search, as well as in phrase structure rules; 8.5.1). The general goal is to remove differences, which enable the removal of other differences, which enable the removal of still other differences, and so forth, until no differences remain between the current state and the goal state. Although the means–ends heuristic is quite powerful, it may fail when an operator cannot be found to eliminate a difference. Under these conditions, backtracking may produce operators that can.

To see how means–ends analysis works, imagine that you have some spare time and want to take a quick trip to the Bahamas. The most critical difference is the one between your current location and your desired location: You can't be in the Bahamas, because you are (presumably) somewhere else. To reduce this difference, you could take a plane trip, but if you don't have a plane reservation and are not at an airport, the conditions for this difference reduction operator don't match your current conditions. You can reduce these differences, though, by applying a second operator for making a plane reservation and a third operator for driving to the airport. If the conditions for these two difference reduction operators are met (e.g., you have a telephone and a car), you can apply them to your current situation, and the differences that prevented you from applying the operator for a plane flight no longer exist. Now that you have a reservation and are at the airport, you can take a flight to the Bahamas and eliminate the original difference, thereby achieving your goal.

10.6.2 Mechanized Problem Solving

As we have seen, novel problem solving is difficult because people must search a problem space with little guidance. If people know what is relevant, or if they have a useful heuristic, they may discover a solution quickly. What do people learn once they have solved a problem successfully? What happens when they encounter a similar problem again later? Because novel problem solving requires concentration, solutions receive extensive processing and become stored in memory (6.1). On encountering a similar problem later, one may therefore be *reminded* of the prior problem and apply its solution to the current problem (**4.2.1**). Furthermore, on noticing similarities between these related problems, a *script* for solving them may begin to develop in memory (**4.2.1**; see also Medin & B.H. Ross, 1989; Schank, 1982). As the script becomes increasingly available, problem solving becomes more mechanical and less creative, because one simply applies a well-known solution to the problem and no longer needs to search through the problem space.

As we shall see, however, the remindings that produce a script don't always occur. Even though people have the solution to a current problem already stored in memory, they often are not reminded of it. As a result, people treat the current problem as novel, search a problem space again for solutions, and don't develop a script for this type of problem. Consider the following problem from an experiment by Gick and Holyoak (1980), adapted as follows:

> An army wishes to attack the center of a city, which has roads leading into it like the spokes of a wheel. These roads are mined in a special way: If only a few people, such as the town folk, travel along a road at a time, the mines won't detonate. The mines will explode only if a large group of people, such as an army, is travelling down the road. How should the army attack the city so that the mines don't detonate?

Think about this problem and see if you can construct a solution. If you can't, here's a hint: Can you think of a prior problem in this chapter whose solution might apply? If you still can't construct a solution, consider the solution from Duncker's radiation problem. Now the way to attack the city should be evident: Send a small a number of soldiers down each road, such that they arrive simultaneously at the center of the town and don't detonate the mines in the process. Both the radiation problem and the mine problem have the same abstract solution: Multiple forces that are low in magnitude must converge.

Interestingly, Gick and Holyoak found little evidence that people remember the radiation problem spontaneously and draw the analogy (**10**.4.5). Subjects who received the radiation problem just prior to the mine problem were no more likely to solve the mine problem than those who had not received the radiation problem previously. Numerous studies since have similarly found that people are often not reminded of previous problems, even when they are potentially useful. On the other hand, when the relevance of a prior problem is pointed out, people usually retrieve and apply it successfully. As a result of this processing, a script for the common solution begins to become established in memory. To the extent that this script is also useful on later occasions, it becomes increasingly available and facilitates solving other problems of its type (Bassok, 1990; Bassok & Holyoak, 1989; Catrambone & Holyoak, 1989; Gentner, 1989; Gick & Holyoak, 1980, 1983;

Holyoak & Koh, 1987; Holyoak & Thagard, 1989a, 1989b; Kolodner, 1988; Novick, 1988; B.H. Ross, 1984, 1987, 1989a, 1989b; B.H. Ross & Kennedy, 1990; Schank, 1982).

Clearly, the increasing availability of a script is highly desirable in problem solving. Once people have a script for solving a particular type of problem, the performance characteristics of novel problem solving begin to disappear: People solve problems faster, they no longer backtrack, they don't need to concentrate as much, and they never fail. However, the increasing availability of a script also has its drawbacks. As Luchins (1942) noted, a highly available script *mechanizes* problem solving. Because a script is likely to work and easy to apply, people use it mechanically whenever they can and stop thinking creatively. Luchins worried that if education were to focus on the rote learning of scripts, thought would become overly mechanized and insufficiently creative.

In a classic experiment, Luchins demonstrated the acquisition of scripts and the subsequent mechanization of problem solving. Consider the series of water jug problems in Fig. 10.6. For each problem, the middle three columns contain the capacities of Jugs A, B, and C, and the right-hand column contains the goal quantity to be obtained. Try solving the first problem. Once you have solved it, try solving all of the remaining problems. If you solved the first problem, you discovered that the solution is:

Problem	Capacity (oz.)			Goal
	Jug A	Jug B	Jug C	
1	21	127	3	100
2	14	163	25	99
3	18	43	10	5
4	9	42	6	21
5	20	59	4	31
6	23	49	3	20
7	15	39	3	18
8	28	76	3	25

Figure 10.6. Water jug problems from Luchins (1942) that illustrate mechanized problem solving.

1. Fill Jug B and pour it into Jug C.
2. Empty Jug C.
3. Pour Jug B into Jug C again.
4. Pour Jug B into Jug A.
5. Jug B now contains the required amount.

As you began working on the second problem, you probably discovered rather quickly that the solution for the first problem also solves the second problem. Upon reaching the third problem, the first thing you probably tried was the solution that worked for the first two problems. After solving the fourth, fifth, and sixth problems with the same solution, you probably had a well-established five-step script for it. To apply this script, you simply bind its attributes to values in the current problem, where the attributes are Jugs A, B, and C in the five steps, and the values are the capacities in Fig. 10.6.

Note what happens when you reach the seventh problem, however. Although applying the script works, you miss an easier solution:

1. Fill Jug A and pour it into Jug B.
2. Fill Jug C and pour it into Jug B.
3. Jug B now contains the required amount.

As this illustrates, your problem solving has become mechanized. Because you have stopped being creative, you miss a more efficient solution. What happens when you reach the eighth problem? Because the same script solved the first seven problems successfully, you might also try applying it to the eighth. However, the script now fails to provide a solution. More importantly, it obscures an alternative solution that is quite simple:

1. Fill Jug A and pour it into Jug C.
2. Jug A now contains the required amount.

Many of Luchins' subjects experienced substantial difficulty in solving this eighth problem, and some even failed to solve it. In another condition of Luchins' experiment, subjects received the seventh and eighth problems without having received the first six problems beforehand. Not surprisingly, these subjects found the simple solutions to the seventh and eighth problems quickly and easily. Although mechanization has benefits, it also has costs.

10.6.3 Automatized Problem Solving

People never stop getting better at solving a familiar problem. Results from a wide range of studies have found that the time to solve a familiar problem continues to decrease, even after thousands and thousands of trials. This phenomenon is known as the *power law of practice*, because the relation of problem solving speed to amount of practice generally conforms to a mathematical power function. As 10.7 illustrates, the time to perform a familiar problem decreases most rapidly during initial practice, with the rate of improvement becoming smaller and smaller over time, approaching asymptote. Nevertheless, this improvement never stops, because people continue getting faster, even after thousands and thousands of trials (Newell & Rosenbloom, 1981).

What underlies this improvement? J.R. Anderson (1983) has suggested that a transition from strategic to automatized processing is responsible (**4.3**; see also Laird et al., 1986; Logan, 1988; Newell, 1990). To see how this might work, consider the example in Fig. 10.8. Imagine that someone visits Michigan, and after wearing sandals all of his life, must learn to tie shoelaces. From tying them a few times, he develops a script that lists the steps in their correct order (see Fig. 10.8). As described in **4.2.1** and **7**.1, this script is passive and declarative in nature, because it can't control the cognitive system itself, but requires executive productions for its implementation. At each point in tying shoelaces, executive productions determine what needs to be done and implement the appropriate step in the script.

After several weeks of practice, the script for tying shoelaces begins to automatize. Productions begin to form, as adjacent steps from the frame are processed contiguously in working memory. More specifically, the *consistent mapping* from each step to its subsequent step produces an automatized relation between them (**4.1.2.**). Figure 10.8 illustrates the initial productions that develop during early automatization. For example, P2 fires on detecting the outcome of P1, P3 fires on detecting the outcome of P2, P4 fires on

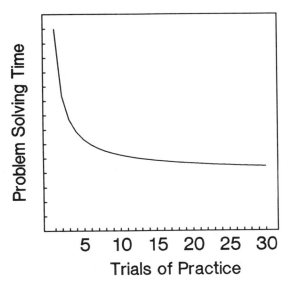

Figure 10.7. The general form for the power law of practice.

SCRIPT FOR TYING SHOELACES

(1) Have the goal to tie shoelaces.
(2) Cross lace R under lace L.
(3) Form a loop with lace R on the left.
(4) Wrap lace L around the base of the R loop.
(5) Push lace L through the opening below the R loop.
(6) Pull lace L through the opening to form a loop.

EARLY AUTOMATIZATION

P1:   have the goal to tie shoelaces   ⟶ cross lace R under lace L
P2:   lace R crossed under lace L   ⟶ form a loop with lace R on the left
P3:   lace R formed in a loop on the left   ⟶ wrap lace L around the base of the R loop
P4:   lace L wrapped around the base of the R loop   ⟶ push lace L through the opening below the R loop
P5:   lace L pushed through the opening below the R loop   ⟶ pull lace L through the opening to form a loop
P6:   lace L pulled through the opening to form a loop   ⟶ pull laces L and R tight

LATE AUTOMATIZATION

P7:   have the goal to tie shoelaces   ⟶   cross lace R under lace L
                                          +   form a loop with lace R on the left
                                          +   wrap lace L around the base of the R loop
                                          +   push lace L through the opening below the R loop
                                          +   pull lace L through the opening to form a loop
                                          +   pull laces L and R tight

Figure 10.8.   The automatization of tying one's shoelaces.

detecting the outcome of P3, and so forth. Because these productions are automatized, they proceed more rapidly than strategic execution of the script. With practice, the strength of these productions increases and performance continues to improve, following the power law of practice.

Just as adjacent statements from the script combine to form simple productions, adjacent productions later combine to form larger productions. Again, the essential idea is that consistent mapping between adjacent productions automatizes the relation between them. Initially, one of these larger productions may only combine two of the original productions, but after extensive practice, consistent mapping between larger and larger productions eventually produces a single production for the entire process (P7 in Fig. 10.8). This production continues to strengthen with further practice, such that performance continues to improve, albeit increasingly slowly.

The process of automatization is availability taken to the limit: With sufficient practice, productions become so automatized that they become available instantly, even when people have no intention of retrieving them (as in the Stroop effect, **4**.1.2, and context-independent properties, **7**.2.3). Moreover, automatization is often accompanied by decreasing availability of the original script. Ask a friend how she ties her shoes. Because your friend's script for tying shoes has become unavailable, and because she cannot examine her automatized productions for tying shoes, she cannot retrieve declarative descriptions of the steps (**7**.1). Instead, your friend is likely to use visual imagery in working memory to simulate tying her shoes (5.2.3). As she simulates each step, she encodes it linguistically and then expresses it verbally to answer your question. Unless the declarative script for a solution is processed frequently, it becomes increasingly unavailable in memory. An exception is teachers, who often retain these declarative representations in order to describe solutions explicitly to their students.

As performance evolves from novel problem solving, to mechanized problem solving, to automatized problem solving, the characteristics of novel problem solving disappear: People become increasingly fast at solving problems, they rarely fail or need to backtrack, and their solutions become increasingly optimal. In addition, people can perform secondary tasks while problem solving (e.g., talking), because automatization frees strategic resources (4.2.2). Whereas watching a novice is often painful, watching an expert is usually a pleasure.

CONCLUSION

As we have seen, the three themes that we considered initially—similarity, availability, and framing—pervade human thought. All three themes appear in every form of thought that we have considered, including decision making, induction, deduction, and problem solving. Each theme reflects a fundamental mechanism in the architecture of human cognition: Similarity reflects comparison processes in working memory, availability reflects the retrieval properties of long-term memory, and framing reflects the omnipresence of frames in organizing experience. Clearly, the cognitive architecture leaves its signature across the spectrum of human thought.

Understanding human thought is of great scientific interest in its own right, given its unique and powerful properties. However, understanding human thought has always held much promise for more practical concerns as well. For this reason, researchers have often studied thought as it occurs in natural domains (Chi, Glaser, & Farr, 1988; Greeno & Simon, 1988). Traditionally, work on decision making has addressed important issues in economic and political arenas. More recently, researchers have begun to explore induction, deduction, and problem solving in educational domains, such as geometry and physics, and in occupational domains, such as medicine and electronic troubleshooting. To some extent, much of this work can be viewed as applied cognitive science, yet this work also makes major contributions to basic science, through the discovery of new methods and mechanisms. Because of the great potential that the technical era holds for education and job performance, and because of the serious challenges that we face socially and economically, these developments hold much promise.

11

APPROACHES TO COGNITIVE PSYCHOLOGY

Human beings were not created for the convenience of experimental psychologists.

—George Miller[1]

According to a common stereotype, a science develops in a logical and organized manner: Although different scientists study different phenomena within the science, they use a common methodology to explore them. Although different scientists develop different aspects of theory, they contribute pieces to a single developing theory. Although new discoveries continually appear, each builds upon previous discoveries systematically and coherently. As a science evolves, each new piece of the puzzle falls into place.

Unfortunately, this scientific fairy tale is more fiction than fact, especially in cognitive psychology. Clearly, some sciences are more stable than others, but even physics, which is perhaps the most stable, contains controversies and different approaches. Philosophers of science often observe that revolution in science is no less common than cumulative evolution (Kuhn, 1970; see also Bechtel, 1988b, McCauley, 1986). Controversy is particularly extensive in young sciences, as researchers struggle to find an approach that works. Unfortunately, the leaders of a new science typically don't know a methodology that will produce systematic and coherent accumulation, nor can they

---

[1] Personal communication, April 21, 1988. For Miller's central role in establishing cognitive psychology, see Hirst (1988) and Barsalou and E.E. Smith (1990).

see the general outline of a theory that will guide future research and persist for future theorists to articulate more precisely.

Instead, the apple falls close to the tree: The early work in a science reflects the biases of those who perform it. As we saw in **1**.1, cognitive psychology evolved from work in linguistics, information theory, and computer science. As a result, initial discoveries typically reflected these origins. Early researchers did not design a grand scheme to guide cognitive psychology through its development (although some might have believed that their particular approach would provide that role). Rather, early researchers applied insights from their immediate work to make initial headway. Their accomplishments were substantial and are reflected extensively in current work. No one doubts the significance of the original contributions that initiated modern cognitive psychology.

Unanticipated shifts ensued, however, as cognitive psychology flourished: Few still believe that either applied information theory or the digital computer provide an accurate view of human cognition (**1**.1). Few foresaw the importance of the parallel, neural-like models that appear to have so much potential (**2**.5, **4**.4). Few imagined that Chomsky's (1957) transformational grammar would fail as an account of human language (**1**.1). Few anticipated the importance of the non-formal operations that pervade human knowledge and thought (**7**.1, **7**.4.2, **10**.1).

Conversely, it would be unfair to say that cognitive psychology is completely splintered. In general, cognitive psychologists share several fundamental assumptions. First, cognitive psychologists generally believe that humans are processors of information. Clearly, humans process information much differently than current computers, but information processing nevertheless appears fundamental to human nature (**1**.2). Second, cognitive psychologists generally believe that internal constraints govern human information processing. To understand human information processing, researchers must assess the internal mechanisms that underlie it, and not simply examine observable stimulus–response pairs, as in behaviorism. Third, cognitive psychologists generally believe that cognitive constructs have scientific utility. By employing these constructs, cognitive psychologists can develop a powerful science: They can explain data from a wide variety of research, produce hypotheses to guide future research, and develop applications of social and technological value. Moreover, cognitive constructs contribute to the understanding of intelligence, because they provide an explanatory account of the mechanisms that produce it (**1**.2).

Even though cognitive psychologists share fundamental assumptions, they nevertheless differ in their approaches, both methodologically and theoretically. In the following sections, I briefly characterize what I perceive as the dominant approaches, although other cognitive psychologists might characterize the field differently. Note that many researchers do not fit neatly into any particular approach and that many researchers straddle more than one. After presenting these approaches, I argue that they are neither mutually exclusive nor at odds with one another. Rather, these approaches are complementary, each playing a necessary role in the development of a strong science.

11.1 THE ECOLOGICAL APPROACH

Proponents of the ecological approach argue that cognitive psychologists must understand the physical environment if they are to understand cognition (Gibson, 1950, 1966; Neisser, 1976, 1982, 1984; Neisser & E. Winograd, 1988). Because humans evolved on the Earth's surface, their brains developed biological mechanisms to process information in this environment that is essential to surviving in it. Ecological psychologists argue that cognitive psychologists should use this adaptive relation to their advantage: By understanding the information in the environment that humans evolved to process, cognitive psychologists can constrain their exploration of cognition. Rather than searching for cognitive mechanisms in a vacuum, cognitive psychologists can seek specific mechanisms that process important environmental information. Without an account of the environmental information that people process, the search for cognitive mechanisms is constrained inadequately.

Ecological psychologists also stress the importance of studying natural behaviors. Much like ethologists, who study the behavior of non-human animals in their natural environment, ecological psychologists believe that cognitive psychologists should study the behavior of humans as they perform their daily activities. Without such observation, the search for cognitive mechanisms is again constrained inadequately.

Ecological psychologists are sometimes critical of mainstream research in cognitive psychology, arguing that many laboratory paradigms are too artificial and simplified to be informative about important cognitive mechanisms. When cognitive psychologists study people's simple reactions to artificial stimuli in controlled laboratory paradigms, they often ignore many aspects of the environment and people's normal activity in it. Ecological psychologists are concerned that the theories developed from such paradigms will only explain performance on laboratory tasks and provide a limited and distorted view of human cognition in the natural world.

Critics of the ecological approach, on the other hand, worry that it is too descriptive. Because of its focus on the environment and natural activity, it provides little theory about cognitive mechanisms. Without such guidance, the ecological approach runs the risk of not knowing which environmental phenomena are important to study and which are not. Critics also worry that lack of theory may produce a relatively unorganized catalogue of descriptive results (Potter, 1983).

Nevertheless, the ecological approach has had considerable impact on the development of cognitive psychology and cognitive science. In particular, many researchers who study perception and movement have adopted Gibson's (1950, 1966) vision of the ecological approach (2.1), as have researchers who study computational vision in artificial intelligence (e.g., Marr, 1982). In both areas, researchers are attempting increasingly to relate analyses of the environment to the cognitive mechanisms that process it. Similarly, much work in mainstream cognitive psychology has begun to study more naturalistic behaviors in more ecological environments, especially research on memory (Neisser, 1988; D.C. Rubin, 1987) and thought (Chi et al., 1988).

11.2   THE LABORATORY APPROACH

The laboratory approach dominates cognitive psychology, as the bulk of work reviewed in this book illustrates. As noted earlier, however, many cognitive psychologists adopt two or more approaches in their research. In particular, many practitioners of the ecological, formal, and computational approaches are also practitioners of the laboratory approach.

The basic tack of the average cognitive psychologist is to identify a phenomenon of interest and develop a carefully controlled laboratory paradigm for studying it. To draw firm conclusions about the cognitive mechanisms responsible for the phenomenon, it is necessary to establish tight control over all of the variables that influence it. Examples of variables that might be controlled include those described throughout this book, such as presentation duration, associative strength, similarity, context, and many, many others. To measure the effects of these controlled variables, laboratory researchers observe how they influence uncontrolled variables, such as reaction time, accuracy, and ratings.

One of the first things that graduate students in cognitive psychology learn is to conduct carefully controlled experiments. This heritage of experimental psychology remains central, because its methodology provides a powerful epistemological tool. Laboratory researchers take pride in their ability to isolate critical relations between experimental variables. Given the incredible complexity and variability of human behavior, not to mention the awareness and cleverness of human subjects, this is no small feat. Indeed, the principles of experimental design and statistical analysis needed to overcome these problems are at least as sophisticated as those in any other science.

The goal of studying a phenomenon in a controlled laboratory setting is to develop an information processing model of it. Typically, a laboratory researcher considers several possible models and derives their specific predictions of how the phenomenon should behave under various conditions.

Once the predictions of each model are known, an experiment is designed to assess predictions that differ. Models whose predictions fit an experiment's results gain acceptance; models whose predictions fail lose credibility. Theoretically, laboratory researchers are quite conservative, typically only including a cognitive mechanism in an information processing model if they have empirical evidence for it.

Critics are often impatient with laboratory researchers' passion for experimental control. As we saw in **11**.1, ecological psychologists worry that laboratory paradigms won't generalize to more natural environments and activities. Yet, consider where physics would be today if it had constrained itself to ecological phenomena, such as earthquakes and tidal waves. Clearly, the accomplishments of physics reflect the use of highly controlled laboratory paradigms. By isolating fundamental mechanisms and submitting them to careful scrutiny, physicists produced major scientific accomplishments. Why shouldn't this also be true in cognitive psychology? In fact, it is hard to imagine how cognitive psychologists could demonstrate the fundamental mechanisms of cognition convincingly in any other way.

Those who take the computational approach (**11**.4), on the other hand, often become impatient with the theoretical conservatism of laboratory researchers. Computationalists often complain that laboratory researchers spend too much time assessing specific cognitive mechanisms that play only a small role in the grand scheme of things. More colloquially, computationalists worry that laboratory researchers lose the forest for the trees (Newell, 1973). In response, laboratory researchers argue that grand theories of computation suffer from insufficient verification. To them, a substantiated account of a specific mechanism has more value than an unsubstantiated account of a general computational system.

Clearly, the laboratory approach has been immensely successful. Without it, many cognitive phenomena would not be understood as well as they are today. Future applications of the laboratory approach will certainly be central to the growth of cognitive psychology: Laboratory paradigms will play essential roles in assessing the specific mechanisms of more general, computational theories, and they may eventually isolate and demonstrate the critical mechanisms of cognition.

11.3   THE FORMAL APPROACH

Many laboratory researchers focus primarily on the empirical side of laboratory paradigms, seeking to chart relations between the variables that underlie a phenomenon. In contrast, practitioners of the formal approach typically focus on the theoretical side of laboratory paradigms, striving to develop rigorous and elegant accounts of these relations between variables.

Since the inception of modern cognitive psychology, the formal approach has played a central role in modeling cognitive phenomena. In an area known as *mathematical psychology*, theorists have developed an impressive and extensive collection of mathematical tools for constructing theories. Across virtually every area of cognitive psychology, these tools have produced elegant accounts of particular phenomena. In other areas, theorists have also developed *logics* to model phenomena of interest.

Formalists are sometimes critical of non-formalists. They are critical of the ecological approach, because its descriptive data are difficult to model, and they are critical of laboratory researchers, who often construct qualitative accounts of their findings rather than quantitative ones. In general, formalists tend to believe that formal models should guide research. If cognitive psychologists are to gain respect within the scientific community, they must develop and assess formal accounts of cognitive processes.

Critics of the formal approach, in contrast, sometimes suggest that its proponents suffer from "physics envy," a deep-seated fear of rejection by physical scientists. Similarly, critics often suggest that formalists are more interested in formalism than in cognitive psychology, focusing more on the formal properties of a model than on the cognitive phenomena it represents. Furthermore, these critics argue that a strong insistence on following formal modeling is a bit like looking only where the light is good for something you have dropped on a dark street: If cognitive psychologists restrict their research to simple, systematic, and well-understood phenomena for which formal modeling is currently tractable, they will fail to explore numerous other phenomena of much importance. Because so many critical phenomena remain poorly understood, if not ignored, we must be willing to explore them, even if we can't bring our most rigorous methods to bear on them initially.

Clearly, formal modeling is an essential and invaluable part of any science. Most cognitive psychologists believe that formal modeling should be pursued whenever it is possible and appropriate. Most believe that developing a completely formalized science is the ultimate goal.

11.4 THE COMPUTATIONAL APPROACH

Cognitive psychologists from the computational approach simulate cognitive phenomena on computers. Whereas formalists are often satisfied if they can find a mathematical relation between critical variables, computationalists are satisfied only if they can build a system that implements the underlying cognitive mechanisms. Constructing a working simulation provides the ultimate test of a theory. A theorist might believe that a particular theory provides a complete and consistent account of the empirical findings from some ecological or laboratory paradigm. On implementing this theory in a computational simulation, however, the theorist might discover that the theory lacks critical mechanisms, or that its existing mechanisms are incompatible in some way. Attempts to simulate a theory often illustrate a theory's weaknesses and lead to a revised theory that is more complete and consistent. Most computationalists believe that theorists should implement their theories as simulations for these reasons. Once theorists have implemented a theory, they can compare results from the simulation to the empirical results that motivated it. If the fit is good, then the simulation provides one possible account of the results, although not necessarily the best one.

Another advantage of the computational approach is that it allows cognitive psychologists to test theories that they can't test otherwise. Often, a cognitive theory is so complex and interactive that formalists are unable to derive its predictions from mathematical analysis. Even though formalists may be able to define a theory's initial representations and processes, they may lack the analytic tools to predict its intermediate and final states. This information may only be obtainable by presenting the initial set of stimulus conditions to a simulation of the theory, allowing it to run, and observing the outcome. Eventually, formalists may develop analytic procedures for deriving these predictions, but until they do, cognitive psychologists must rely on simulations to evaluate the performance of the theory and its relation to data.

One disadvantage of the computational approach is that building a simulation often requires including mechanisms that have not received empirical support. As we saw in **11.2**, laboratory researchers are often dubious of computational models for this reason. Because a working computational theory often contains so many untested assumptions—added because the simulation would not run without them—why should cognitive psychologists believe that it provides a good account of human cognition? In response, computationalists reply that at least they have a working model of the process, which may be more impressive than any partial theory that laboratory researchers have.

Ultimately, this issue boils down to whether it is computational sufficiency or psychological realism that is more important. If the goal of cognitive psychologists is to construct *any* computational system that is sufficient to simulate a phenomenon, then they succeed by building a working simulation. At this point in cognitive science, sufficient models are indeed a major contribution, given the difficulty of constructing simulations that approximate the common sense of a frog, much less of a human. On the other hand, if the goal of cognitive psychologists is to construct a psychologically plausible account of a phenomenon, then they succeed when a theory only includes mechanisms that have received empirical support. Even though the resulting account may not be sufficient to produce a fully working computational system, it nevertheless serves a useful scientific function in representing scientific knowledge to date. Moreover, such accounts are probably an accurate account of cognitive phenomena at some abstract computational level.

In general, computationalists often seem to be the most open-minded of all the researchers described so far. They readily adopt insights from the ecological and laboratory approaches in developing and constraining their theories. When applicable, they use tools from the formal approach to perform analytic assessments of their simulations. Computationalists, by virtue of their interests, also rely heavily on work from artificial intelligence, adapting new techniques and technologies to human simulations.

11.5 COMPLEMENTARITY OF APPROACHES

Although these four approaches are often critical of each other, they are actually complementary. Each is necessary for a complete science.

Obviously, cognitive psychology must have a strong descriptive base. If cognitive psychologists do not develop an accurate account of human activities and the environments in which they occur, their theories will be distorted. Moreover, careful descriptive analysis is likely to suggest the presence of important cognitive mechanisms. Thus, when one initiates research in a new area, common sense calls for a descriptive analysis of the relevant situations and activities. Cognitive psychologists should not go straight into the laboratory with an intuitive account of the important variables and begin testing them. Otherwise, they are likely to discover later that they failed to consider essential variables that would have been obvious had they performed a descriptive analysis. For these reasons, the ecological approach is an essential component of cognitive psychology.

Patterns within a descriptive account are likely to suggest underlying cognitive mechanisms that produce them. As cognitive psychologists develop hypotheses about these mechanisms, the laboratory approach provides the requisite tools for testing them under controlled conditions. Without experimental assessment, conclusions drawn from a descriptive analysis are little more than conjecture. To develop confidence in underlying mechanisms, cognitive psychologists must demonstrate control over them in the laboratory. In an experimental science, control constitutes proof of understanding.

Similarly, the laboratory approach provides a natural context for testing mechanisms in computational theories. As computationalists become increasingly adept at constructing sufficient accounts of cognitive tasks, they will probably become increasingly concerned with converging on a particular account that is as close to the empirical data as possible. Hopefully, cognitive psychologists will eventually develop a grand computational scheme—built only from empirically supported mechanisms—that exhibits the power of human intelligence.

Both the formal and the computational approaches are essential to theory development. As researchers gain laboratory control over a phenomenon and chart the relevant variables, they provide information that motivates and constrains theory. Computationalists can begin to build working models of the phenomenon, and formalists can begin to develop analytic accounts of these models. In the process, both are likely to discover unresolved issues and competing models that subsequent ecological and laboratory research can address.

A strong science needs both data and theory. In cognitive psychology, the ecological and laboratory approaches provide rich sources of data, and the formal and computational approaches provide strong sources of theory. Rather than being competitors for the "right" way to perform cognitive psychology, each of these approaches serves a necessary and important scientific function. In any science, observation, laboratory research, formal analysis, and simulation provide complementary and integral aspects of the scientific process. It makes no sense to eschew any of these approaches from any science. Given the tremendous complexity of human cognition, an *eclectic approach* to understanding it is likely to prove most successful in the long run. Practitioners of each approach should be open to the methods and findings of the other approaches, rather than dismissing them on the basis of a superficial and prejudiced examination (Bechtel, 1985).

Cognitive psychology has already benefited tremendously from the eclecticism that lies at the heart of cognitive science. One could argue that the most substantial and influential contributions to cognitive psychology have come through interactions with other disciplines. As we have seen throughout this book, cognitive psychology has borrowed heavily from linguistics, artificial intelligence, philosophy, and the other cognitive sciences, as well as from the neurosciences. Undoubtedly, cognitive psychology will continue to borrow and to contribute as well. As many theorists have noted, the problems that cognitive psychologists face in explaining human intelligence are so complex as to require contributions from many disciplines. Cognitive psychology stands to benefit from eclecticism at many levels of scientific activity.

11.6 CONCLUSION

Cognitive psychology is a young science. Whereas other experimental sciences have existed for hundreds of years, experimental psychology is about 100 years old, and modern cognitive psychology is about 30. Cognitive psychologists are far from having a powerful theory of cognition, yet they have made much progress in understanding a wide variety of cognitive phenomena. In 30 years, their understanding of categorization, control, memory, knowledge, language, and thought has grown considerably. From thousands of experiments, cognitive psychologists have learned much about these phenomena. Often these understandings are more descriptive than analytic, but at least cognitive psychologists have some idea of what they need to explain. More importantly, cognitive psychologists have discovered how complex these phenomena are, and they have become aware of significant problems that they must solve before explaining them.

Even though cognitive psychologists do not yet have a comprehensive theory, they have nevertheless made considerable theoretical progress. Theorists have explored a wide variety of formal systems and learned much about their potential for modeling cognitive mechanisms. As empirical knowledge of cognition increases, and as theoretical tools become more sophisticated, ambitious theories of cognition should be increasingly successful. Because human cognition is one of the most complicated topics ever explored scientifically, and because cognitive psychologists have only been studying it for 30 years, we should be patient in judging cognitive psychology, as it works to prove that it has the potential for explaining human intelligence.

Regardless of whether cognitive psychology succeeds in its current form, we should remember that the questions it asks are incredibly important. We should not banish these questions from our intellectual horizon—as did the behaviorists—just because they are difficult to address scientifically, and demand new approaches. Rather than being fearful of what the other sciences may think, we should welcome the challenge to address some of the most intriguing questions imaginable. What is the nature of perception, memory, language, and thought? What is the nature of knowledge and the processes that operate on it? What is the nature of human intelligence?

REFERENCES

Abbott, V., Black, J.B., & Smith, E.E. (1985). The representation of scripts in memory. *Journal of Memory and Language, 24,* 179–199.

Adams, R.D., & Victor, M. (1989). *Principles of neurology* (4th ed.). New York: McGraw-Hill.

Alba, J.W., Chromiak, W., Hasher, L., & Attig, M.S. (1980). Automatic encoding of category size information. *Journal of Experimental Psychology: Human Learning and Memory, 6,* 370–378.

Alba, J.W., & Hasher, L. (1983). Is memory schematic? *Psychological Bulletin, 93,* 203–231.

Ammon, P.R. (1968). The perception of grammatical relations in sentences: A methodological exploration. *Journal of Verbal Learning and Verbal Behavior, 7,* 869–875.

Anderson, A., Garrod, S.C., & Sanford, A.J. (1983). The accessibility of pronominal antecedents as a function of episode shifts in narrative text. *Quarterly Journal of Experimental Psychology, 35A,* 427–440.

Anderson, J.R. (1974). Verbatim and propositional representation of sentences in immediate and long-term memory. *Journal of Verbal Learning and Verbal Behavior, 13,* 149–162.

Anderson, J.R. (1976). *Language, memory, and thought.* Hillsdale, NJ: Lawrence Erlbaum Associates.

Anderson, J.R. (1978). Arguments concerning representations for mental imagery. *Psychological Review, 85,* 249–277.

Anderson, J.R. (1981). The relationship between response latency and response accuracy. *Journal of Experimental Psychology: Human Learning and Memory, 7,* 326–343.

Anderson, J.R. (1983). *The architecture of cognition.* Cambridge, MA: Harvard University Press.

Anderson, J.R. (1990). *Cognitive psychology and its implications* (3rd ed.). New York: Freeman.

Anderson, J.R., & Bower, G.H. (1972). Recognition and retrieval processes in free recall. *Psychological Review, 79,* 97–123.

Anderson, J.R., & Bower, G.H. (1973). *Human associative memory.* Washington, DC: Winston.

Anderson, J.R., & Bower, G.H. (1974). A propositional theory of recognition memory. *Memory & Cognition, 2,* 406–412.

Anderson, R.C., & Ortony, A. (1975). On putting apples into bottles: A problem of polysemy. *Cognitive Psychology, 7,* 167–180.

Anderson, R.C., & Pichert, J.W. (1978). Recall of previously unrecallable information following a shift in perspective. *Journal of Verbal Learning and Verbal Behavior, 17,* 1–12.

Anderson, R.C., Pichert, J.W., Goetz, E.T., Schallert, D.L., Stevens, K.V., & Trollip, S.R. (1976). Instantiation of general terms. *Journal of Verbal Learning and Verbal Behavior, 15,* 667–679.

Anderson, R.C., Reynolds, R.E., Schallert, D.L., & Goetz, E.T. (1977). Frameworks for comprehending discourse. *American Educational Research Journal, 14,* 367–381.

Anderson, S.R. (1974). *The organization of phonology.* New York: Academic.

Anglin, J.M. (1983). Extensional aspects of the preschool child's word concepts. In T.B. Seiler & W. Wannenmacher (Eds.), *Concept development and the development of word meaning* (pp. 247–266). New York: Springer-Verlag.

Anthony, B.J., & Graham, F.K. (1983). Evidence for sensory-selective set in young infants. *Science, 220,* 742–744.

Armstrong, S.L., Gleitman, L.R., & Gleitman, H. (1983). On what some concepts might not be. *Cognition, 13,* 263–308.

Atkinson, R.C., Herrnstein, R.J., Lindzey, G., & Luce, R.D. (1988a). *Stevens' handbook of experimental psychology: Vol. 1. Perception and motivation.* New York: Wiley.

Atkinson, R.C., Herrnstein, R.J., Lindzey, G., & Luce, R.D. (1988b). *Stevens' handbook of experimental psychology: Vol. 2. Learning and cognition.* New York: Wiley.

Atkinson, R.C., & Juola, J.F. (1974). Search and decision processes in recognition memory. In D.H. Krantz, R.C. Atkinson, & P. Suppes (Eds.), *Contemporary developments in mathematical psychology.* New York: Freeman.

Atkinson, R.C., & Shiffrin, R.M. (1968). Human memory: A proposed system and its control processes. In K.W. Spence & J.T. Spence (Eds.), *Advances in the psychology of learning and motivation* (Vol. 2). New York: Academic.

Atwood, M.E., & Polson, P.G. (1976). A process model for water jug problems. *Cognitive Psychology, 8,* 191–216.

Austin, J.L. (1962). *How to do things with words.* Oxford: Oxford University Press.

Baddeley, A.D. (1982). Domains of recollection. *Psychological Review, 89,* 708–729.

Baddeley, A.D. (1986) *Working memory.* Oxford: Clarendon.

Baddeley, A.D., & Hitch, G.J. (1974). Working memory. In G.H. Bower (Ed.), *The psychology of learning and motivation: Advances in research and theory* (Vol. 8, pp. 47–90). New York: Academic.

Baddeley, A.D., & Lieberman, K. (1980). Spatial working memory. In R. Nickerson (Ed.), *Attention and performance VIII* (pp. 521–539). Hillsdale, NJ: Lawrence Erlbaum Associates.

Bahrick, H.P. (1983). Memory and people. In J. Harris (Ed.), *Everyday memory, actions and absentmindedness.* New York: Academic.

Bahrick, H.P. (1984). Semantic memory content in permastore: Fifty years of memory for Spanish learned in school. *Journal of Experimental Psychology: General, 113,* 1–29.

Bahrick, H.P., Bahrick, P.O., & Wittlinger, R.P. (1975). Fifty years of memory for names and faces: A cross-sectional approach. *Journal of Experimental Psychology: General, 104,* 54–75.

Banks, W.P. (1970). Signal detection theory and human memory. *Psychological Bulletin, 74,* 81–99.

Barclay, J.R. (1973). The role of comprehension in remembering sentences. *Cognitive Psychology, 4,* 229–254.

Barclay, J.R., Bransford, J.D., Franks, J.J., McCarrell, N.S., & Nitsch, K. (1974). Comprehension and semantic flexibility. *Journal of Verbal Learning and Verbal Behavior, 13,* 471–481.

Barnes, M. (1987). *The effects of reading context on access to world knowledge.* Unpublished doctoral dissertation, McMaster University, Hamilton, Ontario.

Barsalou, L.W. (1982). Context-independent and context-dependent information in concepts. *Memory & Cognition, 10,* 82–93.

Barsalou, L.W. (1983). Ad hoc categories. *Memory & Cognition, 11,* 211–227.

Barsalou, L.W. (1985). Ideals, central tendency, and frequency of instantiation as determinants of graded structure in categories. *Journal of Experimental Psychology: Learning, Memory, and Cognition, 11,* 629–654.

Barsalou, L.W. (1987). The instability of graded structure in concepts. In U. Neisser (Ed.), *Concepts and conceptual development: Ecological and intellectual factors in categorization* (pp. 101–140). New York: Cambridge University Press.

Barsalou, L.W. (1988). The content and organization of autobiographical memories. In U. Neisser & E. Winograd (Eds.), *Remembering reconsidered: Ecological and traditional approaches to the study of memory* (pp. 193–243). New York: Cambridge University Press.

Barsalou, L.W. (1989). Intra-concept similarity and its implications for inter-concept similarity. In S. Vosniadou & A. Ortony (Eds.), *Similarity and analogical reasoning* (pp. 76–121). New York: Cambridge University Press.

Barsalou, L.W. (1990a). Access and inference in categorization. *Bulletin of the Psychonomic Society, 28,* 268–271.

Barsalou, L.W. (1990b). On the indistinguisability of exemplar memory and abstraction in category representation. In T.K. Srull & R.S. Wyer (Eds.), *Advances in social cognition* (Vol. 3, pp. 61–88). Hillsdale, NJ: Lawrence Erlbaum Associates.

Barsalou, L.W. (1991). Deriving categories to achieve goals. In G.H. Bower (Ed.), *The psychology of learning and motivation: Advances in research and theory* (Vol. 27, 1–64). New York: Academic Press.

Barsalou, L.W. (1992). Frames, concepts, and conceptual fields. In E. Kittay & A. Lehrer (Eds.), *Frames, fields, and contrasts: New essays in semantic and lexical organization.* Hillsdale, NJ: Lawrence Erlbaum Associates.

Barsalou, L.W., & Billman, D. (1989). Systematicity and semantic ambiguity. In D. Gorfein (Ed.), *Resolving semantic ambiguity* (pp. 146–203). New York: Springer-Verlag.

Barsalou, L.W., & Medin, D.L. (1986). Concepts: Fixed definitions or context-dependent representations? *Cahiers de Psychologie Cognitive, 6,* 187–202.

Barsalou, L.W., & Ross, B.H. (1986). The roles of automatic and strategic processing in sensitivity to superordinate and property frequency. *Journal of Experimental Psychology: Learning, Memory, and Cognition, 12,* 116–134.

Barsalou, L.W., & Sewell, D.R. (1984). *Constructing categories from different points of view* (Emory Cognition Report No. 2). Emory University, Atlanta, GA.

Barsalou, L.W., & Sewell, D.R. (1985). Contrasting the representation of scripts and categories. *Journal of Memory and Language, 24,* 646–665.

Barsalou, L.W., Sewell, D.R., & Ballato, S.M. (1986). *Assessing the stability of category representations with graded structure.* Unpublished manuscript.

Barsalou, L.W., & Smith, E.E. (1990). One pillar in the making of cognitive science [Review of *One pillar in the making of cognitive science* by W. Hirst]. *Contemporary Psychology, 35,* 574–575.

Barsalou, L.W., Spindler, J.L., Sewell, D.R., Ballato, S.M., & Gendel, E.M. (1987). *Assessing the stability of category representations with property generation.* Unpublished manuscript.

Bartlett, F.C. (1932). *Remembering: A study in experimental and social psychology.* New York: Cambridge University Press.

Bassok, M. (1990). Transfer of domain-specific problem solving procedures. *Journal of Experimental Psychology: Learning, Memory, and Cognition, 16,* 522–533.

Bassok, M., & Holyoak, K.J. (1989). Interdomain transfer between isomorphic topics in algebra and physics. *Journal of Experimental Psychology: Learning, Memory, and Cognition, 15,* 153–166.

Bates, E., Kintsch, W., Fletcher, C., & Giuliani, V. (1980). On the role of pronominalization and ellipsis in texts: Some memory experiments. *Journal of Experimental Psychology: Human Learning and Memory, 6,* 676–691.

Bates, E., Masling, M., & Kintsch, W. (1978). Recognition memory for aspects of dialogue. *Journal of Experimental Psychology: Human Learning and Memory, 4,* 187–197.

Bechtel, W. (1985). Realism, instrumentalism, and the intentional stance. *Cognitive Science, 9,* 473–498.

Bechtel, W. (1988a). *Philosophy of mind: An overview for cognitive science.* Hillsdale, NJ: Lawrence Erlbaum Associates.

Bechtel, W. (1988b). *Philosophy of science: An overview for cognitive science.* Hillsdale, NJ: Lawrence Erlbaum Associates.

Bechtel, W., & Abrahamsen, A. (1990). *Connectionism and the mind: An introduction to parallel processing in networks.* Oxford: Basil Blackwell.

Beck, A.T. (1976). *Cognitive therapy and the emotional disorders.* New York: International Universities Press.

Begg, I., Maxwell, D., Mitterer, J.O., & Harris, G. (1986). Estimates of frequency: Attribute or attribution? *Journal of Experimental Psychology: Learning, Memory, and Cognition, 12,* 496–508.

Begg, I., Snider, A., Foley, F., & Goddard, R. (1989). The generation effect is no artifact: Generating makes words distinctive. *Journal of Experimental Psychology: Learning, Memory, and Cognition, 15,* 977–989.

Bellezza, F.S. (1982). *Improve your memory.* Englewood Cliffs, NJ: Prentice-Hall.

Bellezza, F.S. (1984a). Reliability of retrieval from semantic memory: Common categories. *Bulletin of the Psychonomic Society, 22,* 324–326.

Bellezza, F.S. (1984b). Reliability of retrieval from semantic memory: Noun meanings. *Bulletin of the Psychonomic Society, 22,* 377–380.

Bellezza, F.S. (1984c). Reliability of retrieval from semantic memory: Information about people. *Bulletin of the Psychonomic Society, 22,* 511–513.

Bereiter, C., Burtis, P.J., & Scardamalia, M. (1988). Cognitive operations in constructing main points in written comprehension. *Journal of Memory and Language, 27,* 261–278.

Berlin, B., Breedlove, D.E., & Raven, P.H. (1974). *Principles of Tzeltal plant classification.* New York: Academic.

Berlin, B., & Kay, P. (1969). *Basic color terms: Their universality and evolution.* Berkeley: University of California Press.

Bever, T.G. (1970). The cognitive basis for linguistic structures. In J.R. Hayes (Ed.), *Cognition and the development of language.* New York: John Wiley & Sons.

Beyth-Marom, R. (1982). Perception of correlation reexamined. *Memory & Cognition, 10,* 511–519.

Biederman, I. (1981). On the semantics of a glance at a scene. In M. Kubovy & J.R. Pomerantz (Eds.), *Perceptual organization* (pp. 213–253). Hillsdale, NJ: Lawrence Erlbaum Associates.

Biederman, I. (1987). Recognition-by-components: A theory of human image understanding. *Psychological Review, 94,* 115–147.

Biederman, I., Rabinowitz, J.C., Glass, A.L., & Stacy, E.W., Jr. (1974). On the information extracted from a glance at a scene. *Journal of Experimental Psychology, 103,* 597–600.

Billman, D., & Heit, E. (1988). Observational learning from internal feedback: A simulation of an adaptive learning model. *Cognitive Science, 12,* 587–626.

Blaxton, T.A. (1989). Investigating dissociations among memory measures: Support for a transfer-appropriate processing framework, *Journal of Experimental Psychology: Learning, Memory, and Cognition, 15,* 657–668.

Bloom, B.S. (1974). Time and learning. *American Psychologist, 29,* 682–688.

Bloom, F.E., & Lazerson, A. (1988). *Brain, mind, and behavior* (2nd ed.). New York: Freeman.

Bobrow, D.G., & Winograd, T. (1977). An overview of KRL, a knowledge representation language. *Cognitive Science, 1,* 3–46.

Bobrow, S.A., & Bower, G.H. (1969). Comprehension and recall of sentences. *Journal of Experimental Psychology, 80,* 455–461.

Bock, J.K. (1987). Co-ordinating words and syntax in speech plans. In A.W. Ellis (Ed.), *Progress in the psychology of language* (Vol. 3, pp. 337–390). Hillsdale, NJ: Lawrence Erlbaum Associates.

Bock, J.K., & Loebell, H. (1990). Framing sentences. *Cognition, 35,* 1–39.

Boff, K.P., Kaufman, L., & Thomas, J.P. (1986). *Handbook of perception and human performance: Vol. 1. Sensory processes and perception.* New York: Wiley.

Boring, E.G. (1953). A history of introspectionism. *Psychological Bulletin, 50,* 169–189.

Boring, E.G. (1957). *A history of experimental psychology* (2nd ed.). New York: Appleton-Century-Crofts.

Borkenau, P. (1990). Traits as ideal-based and goal-derived social categories. *Journal of Personality and Social Psychology, 58,* 381–396.

Bourne, L.E., Jr. (1966). *Human conceptual behavior.* Boston: Allyn & Bacon.

Bourne, L.E., Jr. (1970). Knowing and using concepts. *Psychological Review, 77,* 546–556.

Bourne, L.E., Jr. (1974). An inference model of conceptual rule learning. In R. Solso (Ed.), *Theories in cognitive psychology.* Hillsdale, NJ: Lawrence Erlbaum Associates.

Bousfield, W.A. (1953). The occurrence of clustering in the recall of randomly arranged associates. *Journal of General Psychology, 49,* 229–240.

Bousfield, W.A., & Cohen, B.H. (1953). The effects of reinforcement on the occurrence of clustering in the recall of randomly arranged associates. *Journal of Psychology, 36,* 67–81.

Bower, G.H. (1972a). Mental imagery and associative learning. In L.W. Gregg (Ed.), *Cognition in learning and memory* (pp. 51–88). New York: Wiley.

Bower, G.H. (1972b). Stimulus sampling theory of encoding variability. In A.W. Melton & E. Martin (Eds.), *Coding processes in human memory* (pp. 85–123). Washington, DC: Winston.

Bower, G.H. (1981). Mood and memory. *American Psychologist, 36,* 129–148.

Bower, G.H., Black, J.B., & Turner, T.J. (1979). Scripts in memory for text. *Cognitive Psychology, 11,* 177–220.

Bower, G.H., Clark, M.C., Lesgold, A.M., & Winzenz, D. (1969). Hierarchical retrieval schemes in recall of categorized word lists. *Journal of Verbal Learning and Verbal Behavior, 8,* 323–343.

Bower, G.H., & Hilgard, E.R. (1981). *Theories of learning* (5th ed.). Englewood Cliffs, NJ: Prentice Hall.

Bradley, D.C., & Forster, K.I. (1987). A reader's view of listening. *Cognition, 25,* 103–134.

Bransford, J.D., & Franks, J.J. (1971). The abstraction of linguistic ideas. *Cognitive Psychology, 3,* 331–350.

Bransford, J.D., & Johnson, M.K. (1973). Considerations of some problems of comprehension. In W.G. Chase (Ed.), *Visual information processing.* New York: Academic Press.

Bransford, J.D., & McCarrell, N.S. (1974). A sketch of a cognitive approach to comprehension: Some thoughts about understanding what it means to comprehend. In W.B. Weimer & D.S. Palermo (Eds.), *Cognition and the symbolic processes* (pp. 377–399). Hillsdale, NJ: Lawrence Erlbaum Associates.

Bresnan, J.W. (1978). A realistic transformational grammar. In M. Halle, J.W. Bresnan, & G.A. Miller (Eds.), *Linguistic theory and psychological reality.* Cambridge, MA: MIT Press.

Bresnan, J.W. (Ed.). (1982). *The mental representation of grammatical relations.* Cambridge, MA: MIT Press.

Broadbent, D.E. (1958). *Perception and communication.* London: Pergamon.

Brooks, L.R. (1968). Spatial and verbal components of the act of recall. *Canadian Journal of Psychology, 22,* 349–368.

Brooks, L.R. (1978). Nonanalytic concept formation and memory for instances. In E. Rosch & B.B. Lloyd (Eds.), *Cognition and categorization.* Hillsdale, NJ: Lawrence Erlbaum Associates.

Brooks, L.R. (1987). Decentralized control of categorization: The role of prior processing episodes. In U. Neisser & E. Winograd (Eds.), *Remembering reconsidered: Ecological and traditional approaches to the study of memory* (pp. 141–174). New York: Cambridge University Press.

Brown, F.M. (Ed.). (1987). *The frame problem in artificial intelligence.* Los Altos, CA: Morgan Kaufmann.

Brown, J. (1968). Some tests of a decay theory of immediate memory. *Quarterly Journal of Experimental Psychology, 10,* 12–21.

Brown, J. (1968). Reciprocal facilitation and impairment of free recall. *Psychonomic Science, 10,* 41–42.

Brown, R. (1986). *Social psychology* (2nd ed.). New York: Macmillan.

Bruce, V., & Green, P. (1990). *Visual perception: Physiology, psychology, and ecology* (2nd ed.). Hillsdale, NJ: Lawrence Erlbaum Associates.

Bruner, J.S., Goodnow, J.J., & Austin, G.A. (1956). *A study of thinking.* New York: Wiley.

Byrne, B. (1974). Item concreteness vs. spatial organization as predictors of visual imagery. *Memory & Cognition, 2,* 53–59.

Cantor, N., & Mischel, W. (1977). Traits as prototypes: Effects on recognition memory. *Journal of Personality and Social Psychology, 35,* 38–48.

Cantor, N., & Mischel, W. (1979) Prototypes in person perception. In L. Berkowitz (Ed.), *Advances in experimental social psychology* (Vol. 12, pp. 3–52). New York: Academic.

Caplan, D. (1972). Clause boundaries and recognition latencies for words in sentences. *Perception & Psychophysics, 12,* 73–76.

Caramazza, A., Grober, E.H., Garvey, C., & Yates, J. (1977). Comprehension of anaphoric pronouns. *Journal of Verbal Learning and Verbal Behavior, 16,* 601–609.

Card, S.K., Moran, T.P., & Newell, A. (1983). *The psychology of human-computer interaction.* Hillsdale, NJ: Lawrence Erlbaum Associates.

Carey, S. (1985). *Conceptual change in childhood.* Cambridge, MA: MIT Press.

Carlson, G.N., & Tanenhaus, M.K. (1988). Thematic roles and language comprehension. In W. Wilkins (Ed.), *Syntax and semantics: Vol. 21. Thematic relations* (pp. 263–288). New York: Academic.

Carlson, N.R. (1986). *Physiology of behavior* (3rd ed.). Boston: Allyn & Bacon.

Carpenter, P.A., & Just, M.A. (1977a). Integrative processes in comprehension. In D. LaBerge & J. Samuels (Eds.), *Basic processes in reading: Perception and comprehension.* Hillsdale, NJ: Lawrence Erlbaum Associates.

Carpenter, P.A., & Just, M.A. (1977b). Reading comprehension as eyes see it. In M.A. Just & P.A. Carpenter (Eds.), *Cognitive processes in comprehension.* Hillsdale, NJ: Lawrence Erlbaum Associates.

Carpenter, P.A., & Just, M.A. (1983). What your eyes do while your mind is reading. In K. Rayner (Ed.), *Eye movements in reading: Perceptual and language processes.* New York: Academic Press.

Carpenter, P.A., & Just, M.A. (1988). The role of working memory in language comprehension. In D. Klahr & K. Kotovsky (Eds.), *Complex information processing: The impact of Herbert A. Simon.* Hillsdale, NJ: Lawrence Erlbaum Associates.

Catrambone, R., & Holyoak, K.J. (1989). Overcoming contextual limitations in problem-solving transfer. *Journal of Experimental Psychology: Learning, Memory, and Cognition, 15,* 1147–1156.

Ceraso, J., & Provitera, A. (1971). Sources of error in syllogistic reasoning. *Cognitive Psychology, 2,* 400–410.

Chaffin, R. (1992). The concept of a semantic relation. In E. Kittay & A. Lehrer (Eds.), *Frames, fields, and contrasts: New essays in semantic and lexical organization.* Hillsdale, NJ: Lawrence Erlbaum Associates.

Chaplin, W.G., John, O.P., & Goldberg, L.R. (1988). Conceptions of states and traits: Dimensional attributes with ideals as prototypes. *Journal of Personality and Social Psychology, 54,* 541–557.

Chapman, L.J., & Chapman, J.P. (1967). Genesis of popular but erroneous psychodiagnostic observations. *Journal of Abnormal Psychology, 73,* 193–204.

Chapman, L.J., & Chapman, J.P. (1969). Illusory correlation as an obstacle to the use of valid psychodynamic signs. *Journal of Abnormal Psychology, 74,* 272–280.

Charniak, E., & McDermott, D. (1985). *Introduction to artificial intelligence.* Reading, MA: Addison-Wesley.

Chase, W.G., & Ericsson, K.A. (1981). Skilled memory. In J.R. Anderson (Ed.), *Cognitive skills and their acquisition* (pp. 141–190). Hillsdale, NJ: Lawrence Erlbaum Associates.

Chase, W.G., & Simon, H.A. (1973). The mind's eye in chess. In W.G. Chase (Ed.), *Visual information processing.* New York: Academic.

Chater, N., Lyon, K., & Myers, T. (1990). Why are conjunctive categories overextended? *Journal of Experimental Psychology: Learning, Memory, and Cognition, 16,* 497–508.

Cheng, P.W., & Holyoak, K.J. (1985). Pragmatic reasoning schemas. *Cognitive Psychology, 17,* 391–416.

Cheng, P.W., Holyoak, K.J., Nisbett, R.E., & Oliver, L.M. (1986). Pragmatic versus syntactic approaches to training deductive reasoning. *Cognitive Psychology, 18,* 293–328.

Cherry, E.C. (1953). Some experiments on the recognition of speech, with one and two ears. *Journal of the Acoustical Society of America, 25,* 975–979.

Cherry, E.C., & Taylor, W.K. (1954). Some further experiments on the recognition of speech with one and two ears. *Journal of the Acoustical Society of America, 26,* 554–559.

Chi, M.T.H., Glaser, R., & Farr, M.J. (Eds.). (1988). *The nature of expertise.* Hillsdale, NJ: Lawrence Erlbaum Associates.

Chiesi, H.L., Spilich, G.J., & Voss, J.F. (1979). Acquisition of domain-related information in relation to high- and low-domain knowledge. *Journal of Verbal Learning and Verbal Behavior, 18,* 257–273.

Chomsky, N. (1957). *Syntactic structures.* The Hague: Mouton.

Chomsky, N. (1959). [Review of *Verbal Behavior* by B.F. Skinner]. *Language, 35,* 26–58.

Chomsky, N. (1965). *Aspects of a theory of syntax.* Cambridge, MA: MIT Press.

Chomsky, N. (1968). *Language and mind.* New York: Harcourt Brace Jovanovich.

Chomsky, N. (1975). *Rules and representations.* New York: Columbia University Press.

Chomsky, N. (1981). *Lectures on government and binding.* Dordrecht: Foris.

Chomsky, N., & Miller, G.A. (1963). Introduction to the formal analysis of natural languages. In D. Luce, R. Bush, & E. Galanter (Eds.), *Handbook of mathematical psychology* (Vol. 2, pp. 269–321). New York: Wiley.

Churchland, P.M. (1990). *A neurocomputational perspective: The nature of mind and the structure of science.* Cambridge, MA: MIT Press.

Churchland, P.S. (1986). *Neurophilosophy.* Cambridge, MA: MIT Press.

Cirilo, R.K., & Foss, D.J. (1980). Text structure and reading time for sentences. *Journal of Verbal Learning and Verbal Behavior, 19,* 96–109.

Clark, H.H. (1979). Responding to indirect speech acts. *Cognitive Psychology, 11,* 430–477.

Clark, H.H., & Chase, W.G. (1974). Perceptual coding strategies in the formation and verification of descriptions. *Memory & Cognition, 2,* 101–111.

Clark, H.H., & Clark, E.V. (1977). *Psychology and language.* New York: Harcourt Brace Jovanovich.

Clark, H.H., & Clark, E.V. (1978). When nouns surface as verbs. *Language, 55,* 767–811.

Clark, H.H., & Marshall, C. (1981). Definite reference and mutual knowledge. In A. Joshi, B. Webber, & I. Sag (Eds.), *Elements of discourse understanding* (pp. 10–63). New York: Cambridge University Press.

Clark, H.H., & Schaefer, E.F. (1989). Contributing to discourse. *Cognitive Science, 13,* 259–294.

Clark, H.H., Schreuder, R., & Buttrick, S. (1983). Common ground and the understanding of demonstrative reference. *Journal of Verbal Learning and Verbal Behavior, 22,* 245–258.

Clark, H.H., & Sengul, C.J. (1979). In search of referents for nouns and pronouns. *Memory & Cognition, 7,* 35–41.

Clark, H.H., & Wilkes-Gibbs, D. (1986). Referring as a collaborative process. *Cognition, 22,* 1–39.

Cofer, C.N. (1967). Does conceptual organization influence the amount retained in immediate free recall? In B. Kleinmuntz (Ed.), *Concepts and the structure of memory* (pp. 181–214). New York: Wiley.

Cohen, C.E. (1981). Person categories and social perception: Testing some boundaries of the processing effects of prior knowledge. *Journal of Personality and Social Psychology, 40,* 441–452.

Cohen, J.D., Dunbar, K. & McClelland, J.L. (1990). On the control of automatic processes: A parallel distributed account of the Stroop effect. *Psychological Review, 97,* 332–361.

Cole, M., & Cole, S.R. (1989). *The development of children.* New York: Freeman.

Collins, A.M., & Loftus, E.F. (1975). A spreading activation theory of semantic processing. *Psychological Review, 82,* 407–428.

Collins, A.M., & Michalski, R. (1989). The logic of plausible reasoning: A core theory. *Cognitive Science, 13,* 1–50.

Collins, A.M., & Quillian, M.R. (1969). Retrieval time from semantic memory. *Journal of Verbal Learning and Verbal Behavior, 8,* 240–248.

Conrad, C. (1972). Cognitive economy in semantic memory. *Journal of Experimental Psychology, 92,* 149–154.

Conrad, C. (1978). Some factors involved in the recognition of words. In J.W. Cotton & R. Klatzky (Eds.), *Semantic factors in cognition.* Hillsdale, NJ: Lawrence Erlbaum Associates.

Conrad, R. (1964). Acoustic confusions in immediate memory. *British Journal of Psychology, 55,* 75–84.

Conrad, R. (1972). Short-term memory in the deaf: A test for speech coding. *British Journal of Psychology, 63,* 173–180.

Coombs, C.H., Dawes, R.M., & Tversky, A. (1970). *Mathematical psychology: An elementary introduction.* Englewood Cliffs, NJ: Prentice-Hall.

Cooper, E.C., & Pantle, A.J. (1967). The total time hypothesis in verbal learning. *Psychological Bulletin, 68,* 221–234.

Cooper, L.A. (1976). Demonstration of a mental analogue of an external rotation. *Perception & Psychophysics, 19,* 296–302.

Copi, I.M. (1978). *Introduction to logic.* New York: Macmillan.

Corbett, A.T. (1984). Prenominal adjectives and the disambiguation of anaphoric nouns. *Journal of Verbal Learning and Verbal Behavior, 23,* 683–695.

Corbett, A.T., & Chang, F.R. (1983). Pronoun disambiguation: Accessing potential antecedents. *Memory & Cognition, 11,* 283–294.

Corbett, A.T., & Dosher, B.A. (1978). Instrument inferences in sentence encoding. *Journal of Verbal Learning and Verbal Behavior, 17,* 479–491.

Corman, C.N., & Wickens, D.D. (1968). Retroactive inhibition in short-term memory. *Journal of Verbal Learning and Verbal Behavior, 7,* 16–19.

Corteen, R.S., & Wood, B. (1972). Autonomic responses to shock-associated words in an unattended channel. *Journal of Experimental Psychology, 94,* 308–313.

Courant, R., & Robbins, H. (1941). *What is mathematics?* New York: Oxford University Press.

Craik, F.I.M., & Lockhart, R.S. (1972). Levels of processing: A framework for memory research. *Journal of Verbal Learning and Verbal Behavior, 11,* 671–684.

Craik, F.I.M., & Tulving, E. (1975). Depth of processing and the retention of words in episodic memory. *Journal of Experimental Psychology: General, 104,* 268–294.

Craik, F.I.M., & Watkins, M.J. (1973). The role of rehearsal in short-term memory. *Journal of Verbal Learning and Verbal Behavior, 12,* 599–607.

Crain, S., & Steedman, M.J. (1985). On not being led up the garden path: The use of context by the psychological parser. In D. Dowty, L. Karttunen, & A. Zwicky (Eds.), *Natural language parsing.* New York: Cambridge University Press.

Crowder, R.G. (1976). *Principles of learning and memory.* Hillsdale, NJ: Lawrence Erlbaum Associates.

Crowder, R.G. (1982a). The demise of short-term memory. *Acta Psychologica, 50,* 291–323.

Crowder, R.G. (1982b). *The psychology of reading: An introduction.* Oxford: Oxford University Press.

Cruse, D.A. (1977). The pragmatics of lexical specificity. *Journal of Linguistics, 13,* 153–164.

Culicover, P. (1976). *Syntax.* New York: Academic.

Curtiss, S. (1977). *Genie: A psycholinguistic study of a modern-day "wild-child."* New York: Academic.

Daneman, M., & Carpenter, P.A. (1980). Individual differences in working memory and reading. *Journal of Verbal Learning and Verbal Behavior, 19,* 450–466.

Davies, G.M., & Thomson, D.M. (Eds.). (1988). *Memory in context: Context in memory.* New York: Wiley.

DeJong, G., & Mooney, R. (1986). Explanation-based learning: An alternative view. *Machine Learning, 1,* 145–176.

de Kleer, J., & Brown, J.S. (1984). A qualitative physics based on confluences. *Artificial Intelligence, 24,* 7–83.

Delattre, P.C., Liberman, A.M., & Cooper, F.S. (1955). Acoustic loci and transitional cues for consonants. *Journal of the Acoustical Society of America, 27,* 769–773.

Dell, G.S. (1986). A spreading activation theory of retrieval in sentence production. *Psychological Review, 93,* 283–321.

Dell, G.S., & Reich, P.A. (1981). Stages in sentence production: An analysis of speech error data. *Journal of Verbal Learning and Verbal Behavior, 20,* 611–629.

Dellarosa, D. (1988). A history of thinking. In R.J. Sternberg & E.E. Smith (Eds.), *The psychology of human thought* (pp. 1–18). New York: Cambridge University Press.

Dennet, D.C. (1978). *Brainstorms.* Cambridge, MA: MIT Press.

Deutsch, J.A., & Deutsch, D. (1963). Attention: Some theoretical considerations. *Psychological Review, 70,* 80–90.

Domjan, M., & Burkhard, B. (1986). *The principles of learning and behavior.* Monterey, CA: Brooks-Cole.

Dooling, D.J., & Lachman, R. (1971). Effects of comprehension on retention of prose. *Journal of Experimental Psychology, 88,* 216–222.

Dougherty, J.W.D. (Ed.). (1985). *Directions in cognitive anthropology.* Urbana, IL: University of Illinois Press.

Downing, C.J., Sternberg, R.J., & Ross, B.H. (1985). Multicausal inference: Evaluation of evidence in causally complex situations. *Journal of Experimental Psychology: General, 114,* 239–263.

Downing, P. (1977). On the creation and use of English compound nouns. *Language, 53,* 810–842.

Dowty, D.R., Wall, R.E., & Peters, S. (1981). *Introduction to Montague semantics.* Dordrecht: Reidel.

Duncker, K. (1945). On problem solving. *Psychological Monographs, 58,* 1–110.

Eagle, M., & Leiter, E. (1964). Recall and recognition in intentional and incidental learning. *Journal of Experimental Psychology, 68,* 58–63.

Eckman, P. (1982). *Emotion in the human face.* Cambridge, England: Cambridge University Press.

Eckman, P., & Oster, H. (1979). Facial expressions of emotion. *Annual Review of Psychology, 30*, 527–554.

Edwards, W. (1954). The theory of decision making. *Psychological Bulletin, 51*, 380–417.

Egan, D.E., & Schwartz, B.J. (1979). Chunking in recall of symbolic drawings. *Memory & Cognition, 7*, 149–158.

Egeth, H.E., Virzi, R.A., & Garbart, H. (1984). Searching for conjunctively defined targets. *Journal of Experimental Psychology: Human Perception and Performance, 10*, 32–39.

Ehrlich, S.F., & Rayner, K. (1981). Contextual effects on word perception and eye movements during reading. *Journal of Verbal Learning and Verbal Behavior, 20*, 641–655.

Ehrlich, S.F., & Rayner, K. (1983). Pronoun assignment and semantic integration during reading: Eye movements and immediacy of processing. *Journal of Verbal Learning and Verbal Behavior, 22*, 75–87.

Eibl-Eibesfeldt, I. (1972). *Ethology: The biology of behavior* (2nd ed.). New York: Holt, Rinehart & Winston.

Eich, J.E. (1980). The cue-dependent nature of state-dependent retrieval. *Memory & Cognition, 8*, 157–173.

Eich, J.E. (1985). Context, memory, and integrated item/context imagery. *Journal of Experimental Psychology: Learning, Memory, and Cognition, 11*, 764–770.

Einhorn, H.J., & Hogarth, R.M. (1978). Confidence in judgment: Persistence of the illusion of validity. *Psychological Review, 85*, 395–416.

Elio, R., & Anderson, J.R. (1981). The effects of category generalizations and instance similarity on schema abstraction. *Journal of Experimental Psychology: Learning, Memory, and Cognition, 7*, 397–417.

Ellis, H.C., & Hunt, R.R. (1989). *Fundamentals of human memory and cognition* (4th ed.). Dubuque, IA: William C. Brown.

Erickson, J.R. (1971). Problem shifts and hypothesis behavior in concept identification. *American Journal of Psychology, 84*, 101–111.

Erickson, J.R. (1974). A set analysis theory of behavior in formal syllogistic reasoning tasks. In R.L. Solso (Ed.), *Theories in cognitive psychology: The Loyola symposium.* Hillsdale, NJ: Lawrence Erlbaum Associates.

Ericsson, K.A., & Simon, H.A. (1984). *Protocol analysis: Verbal reports as data.* Cambridge, MA: MIT Press.

Estes, W.K. (1976). The cognitive side of probability learning. *Psychological Review, 83*, 37–64.

Estes, W.K. (1986). Array models for category learning. *Cognitive Psychology, 18*, 500–549.

Farah, M.J. (1988). Is visual imagery really visual? Overlooked evidence from neuropsychology. *Psychological Review, 95*, 307–317.

Farah, M.J., Hammond, K.M., Levine, D.N., & Calvanio, R. (1988). Visual and spatial mental imagery: Dissociable systems of representation. *Cognitive Psychology, 20*, 439–462.

Fehr, B., & Russell, J.A. (1984). Concept of emotion viewed from a prototype perspective. *Journal of Experimental Psychology: General, 113*, 464–486.

Ferreira, F., & Clifton, C. (1986). The independence of syntactic processing. *Journal of Memory and Language, 25*, 348–368.

Fillenbaum, S. (1966). Memory for gist: Some relevant variables. *Language and Speech, 9*, 217–227.

Fillmore, C.J. (1968). The case for case. In E. Bach & R. Harms (Eds.), *Universals in linguistic theory* (pp. 1–88). New York: Holt, Rinehart & Winston.

Fillmore, C.J. (1977). The case for case reopened. In P. Cole & J.M. Sadock (Eds.), *Syntax and semantics: Vol. 8. Grammatical relations* (pp. 59–81). New York: Academic.

Fillmore, C.J. (1985). Frames and the semantics of understanding. *Quaderni di Semantica, 6*, 222–255.

Finke, R.A. (1989). *Principles of mental imagery.* Cambridge, MA: MIT Press.

Fischler, I., & Bloom, P.A. (1979). Automatic and attentional processes in the effects of sentence contexts on word recognition. *Journal of Verbal Learning and Verbal Behavior, 18,* 1–20.

Fischoff, B. (1988). Judgment and decision making. In R.J. Sternberg & E.E. Smith (Eds.), *The psychology of human thought* (pp. 153–187). New York: Cambridge University Press.

Fiske, S.T., & Taylor, S.E. (1991). *Social cognition* (2nd ed.). New York: McGraw-Hill.

Fitts, P.M., & Posner, M.I. (1967). *Human performance.* Belmont, CA: Brooks Cole.

Flavell, J.H. (1985). *Cognitive development* (2nd ed.). Englewood Cliffs, NJ: Prentice-Hall.

Fodor, J.A. (1975). *The language of thought.* New York: T.Y. Crowell.

Fodor, J.A. (1983). *The modularity of mind: An essay on faculty psychology.* Cambridge, MA: Bradford Books, MIT Press.

Fodor, J.A., & Bever, T.G. (1965). The psychological reality of linguistic segments. *Journal of Verbal Learning and Verbal Behavior, 4,* 414–420.

Fodor, J.A., Bever, T.G., & Garrett, M.F. (1974). *The psychology of language: An introduction to psycholinguistics and generative grammar.* New York: McGraw-Hill.

Fodor, J.A., & Pylyshyn, Z.W. (1988). Connectionism and cognitive architecture: A critical analysis. *Cognition, 28,* 3–71.

Fodor, J.D., & Frazier, L. (1980). Is the human sentence processing mechanism an ATN? *Cognition, 8,* 417–459.

Forbus, K.D. (1984). Qualitative process theory. *Artificial Intelligence, 24,* 7–83.

Ford, M. (1983). A method for obtaining measures of local parsing complexity throughout sentences. *Journal of Verbal Learning and Verbal Behavior, 22,* 203–218.

Forster, K.I. (1976). Accessing the mental lexicon. In R.J. Wales & E. Walker (Eds.), *New approaches to language mechanisms.* Amsterdam: North-Holland.

Forster, K.I. (1979). Levels of processing and the structure of the language processor. In W.E. Cooper & E.C.T. Walker (Eds.), *Sentence processing: Psycholinguistic studies presented to Merrill Garrett.* Hillsdale, NJ: Lawrence Erlbaum Associates.

Foss, D.J. (1982). A discourse on semantic priming. *Cognitive Psychology, 14,* 590–607.

Foss, D.J., & Blank, M.A. (1980). Identifying the speech code. *Cognitive Psychology, 12,* 1–31.

Foss, D.J., & Gernsbacher, M.A. (1983). Cracking the dual code: Toward a unitary model of phoneme identification. *Journal of Verbal Learning and Verbal Behavior, 22,* 609–632.

Foss, D.J., & Hakes, D.T. (1978). *Psycholinguistics: An introduction to the psychology of language.* Englewood Cliffs, NJ: Prentice-Hall.

Foss, D.J., & Swinney, D.A. (1973). On the psychological reality of the phoneme: Perception, identification, and consciousness. *Journal of Verbal Learning and Verbal Behavior, 12,* 246–257.

Foulke, E., & Sticht, T. (1969). Review of research on the intelligibility and comprehension of accelerated speech. *Psychological Bulletin, 72,* 50–62.

Frazier, L., & Fodor, J.D. (1978). The sausage machine: A new two-stage parsing model. *Cognition, 6,* 291–325.

Frazier, L., & Rayner, K. (1987). Resolution of syntactic category ambiguities: Eye movements in parsing lexically ambiguous sentences. *Journal of Memory and Language, 26,* 505–526.

Frege, G. (1952). On sense and reference. In P.T. Geach & M. Black (Eds. and Trans.), *Philosophical writings of Gottlob Frege.* Oxford: Basil Blackwell. (Original work published 1892)

Freud, S. (1933). *New introductory lectures on psychoanalysis* (W.J.H. Sprout, Trans.). New York: Norton.

Fromkin, V.A. (1971). The non-anomolous nature of anomolous utterances. *Language, 47,* 27–52.

Fromkin, V.A. (Ed.). (1973). *Speech errors as linguistic evidence.* The Hague: Mouton.

Gallistel, C.R. (1990). *The organization of learning.* Cambridge, MA: MIT Press.

Gardiner, J.M., Gregg, V.H., & Hampton, J.A. (1988). Word frequency and generation effects. *Journal of Experimental Psychology: Learning, Memory, and Cognition, 14,* 687–693.

Garnham, A. (1979). Instantiation of verbs. *Quarterly Journal of Experimental Psychology, 31,* 207–214.

Garnham, A. (1981). Anaphoric reference to instances, instantiated, and non-instantiated categories: A reading-time study. *British Journal of Psychology, 72,* 377–384.

Garnham, A. (1982). Testing psychological theories about inference making. *Memory & Cognition, 10,* 341–349.

Garnham, A. (1985). *Psycholinguistics: Central topics.* New York: Routledge.

Garnsey, S.M., Tanenhaus, M.K., & Chapman, R.M. (1989). Evoked potentials and the study of sentence comprehension. *Journal of Psycholinguistic Research, 18,* 51–60.

Garrett, M.F. (1975). The analysis of sentence production. In G.H. Bower (Ed.), *The psychology of learning and memory: Advances in research and theory* (Vol. 9, pp. 133–177). New York: Academic.

Garrett, M.F. (1980). The limits of accomodation. In V.A. Fromkin (Ed.), *Errors in linguistic performance* (pp. 263–271). New York: Academic.

Garrett, M.F. (1988). Processes in language production. In F.J. Newmeyer (Ed.), *Linguistics: The Cambridge survey: Vol. 3. Language: Psychological and biological aspects.* New York: Cambridge University Press.

Garrett, M.F., Bever, T.G., & Fodor, J.A. (1966). The active use of grammar in speech perception. *Perception & Psychophysics, 1,* 30–32.

Gazdar, G., Klein, E., Pullum, G., & Sag, I. (1985). *Generalized phrase structure grammar.* Oxford: Basil Blackwell.

Gelman, S.A., & Coley, J.D. (1990). The importance of knowing a dodo is a bird: Categories and inferences in 2-year-old children. *Developmental Psychology, 26,* 796–804.

Gelman, S.A., & Markman, E.M. (1986). Categories and induction in young children. *Cognition, 23,* 183–208.

Gelman, S.A., & Markman, E.M. (1987). Young children's inductions from natural kinds: The role of categories and appearance. *Child Development, 58,* 1532–1541.

Gentner, D. (1989). The mechanisms of analogical reasoning. In S. Vosniadou & A. Ortony (Eds.), *Similarity and analogical reasoning* (pp. 199–241). New York: Cambridge University Press.

Gentner, D., & Stevens, A.L. (Eds.). (1983). *Mental models.* Hillsdale, NJ: Lawrence Erlbaum Associates.

Geschwind, N. (1972). Language and the brain. *Scientific American, 226,* 76–83.

Gibbs, R. (1979). Contextual aspects in understanding indirect requests. *Discourse Processes, 2,* 1–10.

Gibbs, R. (1981). Your wish is my command: Convention and context in interpreting indirect requests. *Journal of Verbal Learning and Verbal Behavior, 20,* 431–444.

Gibbs, R. (1983). Do people always process the literal meanings of indirect requests? *Journal of Experimental Psychology: Learning, Memory, and Cognition, 9,* 524–533.

Gibbs, R. (1984). Literal meaning and psychological theory. *Cognitive Science, 8,* 275–304.

Gibbs, R. (1986). What makes some indirect speech acts conventional? *Journal of Memory and Language, 25,* 181–196.

Gibbs, R. (1989). Understanding and literal meaning. *Cognitive Science, 13,* 243–251.

Gibson, J.J. (1950). *The perception of the visual world.* Boston: Houghton Mifflin.

Gibson, J.J. (1966). *The senses considered as perceptual systems.* Boston: Houghton Mifflin.

Gick, M.L., & Holyoak, K.J. (1980). Analogical problem solving. *Cognitive Psychology, 12,* 306–355.

Gick, M.L., & Holyoak, K.J. (1983). Schema induction and analogical transfer. *Cognitive Psychology, 15,* 1–38.

Gillund, G., & Shiffrin, R.M. (1984). A retrieval model for both recognition and recall. *Psychological Review, 91,* 1–67.

Glanzer, M., Dorfman, D., & Kaplan, B. (1981). Short-term storage in the processing of text. *Journal of Verbal Learning and Verbal Behavior, 20,* 656–670.

Glanzer, M., Fischer, B., & Dorfman, D. (1984). Short-term storage in reading. *Journal of Verbal Learning and Verbal Behavior, 23,* 467–486.

Glass, A.L., & Holyoak, K.J. (1975). Alternative conceptions of semantic memory. *Cognition, 3,* 313–339.

Glass, A.L., & Holyoak, K.J. (1986). *Cognition* (2nd ed.). New York: Random House.

Glenberg, A.M., & Epstein, W. (1985). Calibration of comprehension. *Journal of Experimental Psychology: Learning, Memory, and Cognition, 11,* 702–718.

Glenberg, A.M., Smith, S.M., & Green, C. (1977). Type I rehearsal: Maintenance and more. *Journal of Verbal Learning and Verbal Behavior, 16,* 339–352.

Glover, J.A., & Bruning, R.H. (1990). *Educational psychology: Principles and applications.* Boston: Scott-Foresman/Little-Brown.

Glover, J.A., Ronning, R.R., & Bruning, R.H. (1990). *Cognitive psychology for teachers.* New York: Macmillan.

Gluck, M.A., & Bower, G.H. (1988). Evaluating an adaptive network model of human learning. *Journal of Memory and Language, 27,* 166–195.

Glucksberg, S. (1988). Language and thought. In R.J. Sternberg & E.E. Smith (Eds.), *The psychology of human thought* (pp. 214–241). New York: Cambridge University Press.

Glucksberg, S., & Keysar, B. (1990). Understanding metaphorical comparisons: Beyond similarity. *Psychological Review, 97,* 3–18.

Godden, D.R., & Baddeley, A.D. (1975). Context-dependent memory in two natural environments: On land and underwater. *British Journal of Psychology, 66,* 325–332.

Goldin-Meadow, S. (1982). The resilience of recursion: A study of a communication system developed without a conventional language model. In E. Wanner & L.R. Gleitman (Eds.), *Language acquisition: The state of the art* (pp. 51–77). New York: Cambridge University Press.

Goldstein, A.G., & Chance, J.E. (1971). Recognition of complex visual stimuli. *Perception & Psychophysics, 9,* 237–241.

Goldstein, E.B. (1989). *Sensation and perception* (3rd ed.). Belmont, CA: Wadsworth.

Goodman, N. (1955). *Fact, fiction, and forecast.* Cambridge, MA: Harvard University Press.

Goodman, N. (1972). *Problems and projects* (pp. 437–447). Indianapolis: Bobbs-Merrill.

Goodwin, D.W., & Guze, S.B. (1984). *Psychiatric diagnosis* (3rd ed.). New York: Oxford University Press.

Goolkasian, P. (1981). Retinal location and its effect on the processing of target and distractor information. *Journal of Experimental Psychology: Human Perception and Performance, 7,* 1247–1257.

Gordon, B. (1985). Subjective frequency and the lexical decision latency function: Implications for mechanisms of lexical access. *Journal of Memory and Language, 24,* 631–645.

Gorfein, D. (Ed.). (1989). *Resolving semantic ambiguity.* New York: Springer-Verlag.

Graesser, A.C., Gordon, S.E., & Sawyer, J.D. (1979). Recognition memory for typical and atypical actions in scripted activities: Test of a script pointer + tag hypothesis. *Journal of Verbal Learning and Verbal Behavior, 18,* 319–332.

Graesser, A.C., & Mandler, G. (1975). Recognition memory for the meaning and surface structure of sentences. *Journal of Experimental Psychology: Human Learning and Memory, 104,* 238–248.

Graesser, A.C., Woll, S.B., Kowalski, D.J., & Smith, D.A. (1980). Memory for typical and atypical actions in scripted activities. *Journal of Experimental Psychology: Human Learning and Memory, 6,* 503–515.

Graf, R., & Torrey, J.W. (1966). Perception of phrase structure in written language. *American Psychological Association Proceedings,* 83–84.

Gray, J.A., & Wedderburn, A.A.I. (1960). Grouping strategies with simultaneous stimuli. *Quarterly Journal of Experimental Psychology, 12,* 180–184.

Greenberg, J.H. (1966a). *Language universals.* The Hague: Mouton.

Greenberg, J.H. (1966b). *Universals of language* (2nd ed.). Cambridge, MA: MIT Press.

Greenberg, J.H., & Jenkins, J.J. (1964). Studies in the psychological correlates of the sound system of American English. *Word, 20,* 157–177.

Greene, R.L. (1984). Incidental learning of event frequency. *Memory & Cognition, 12,* 90–95.

Greene, R.L. (1986). The effects of intentionality and strategy on memory for frequency. *Journal of Experimental Psychology: Learning, Memory, and Cognition, 12,* 489–495.

Greene, R.L. (1988). Generation effects in frequency judgment. *Journal of Experimental Psychology: Learning, Memory, and Cognition, 14,* 298–304.

Greeno, J.G. (1974). Hobbits and orcs: Acquisition of a sequential concept. *Cognitive Psychology, 6,* 270–292.

Greeno, J.G. (1978). Natures of problem-solving abilities. In W.K. Estes (Ed.), *Handbook of learning and cognitive processes, Vol. 5: Human information processing* (pp. 239–270). Hillsdale, NJ: Lawrence Erlbaum Associates.

Greeno, J.G., & Simon, H.A. (1988). Problem solving and reasoning. In R.C. Atkinson, R.J. Herrnstein, G.Lindzey, & R.D Luce. (Eds.), *Stevens' handbook of experimental psychology: Vol. 2. Learning and cognition* (pp. 589–672). New York: Wiley.

Greenspan, S.L. (1986). Semantic flexibility and referential specificity of concrete nouns. *Journal of Memory and Language, 25,* 539–557.

Grice, H.P. (1975). Logic and conversation. In P. Cole & J.L. Morgan (Eds.), *Syntax and semantics: Vol. 3. Speech acts* (pp. 41–58). New York: Academic.

Grier, J.W. (1984). *Biology of animal behavior.* St. Louis, MO: Times Mirror/Mosby.

Grober, E.H., Beardsley, W., & Caramazza, A. (1978). Parallel function in pronoun assignment. *Cognition, 6,* 117–133.

Guilford, J.P., & Fruchter, B. (1973). *Fundamental statistics in psychology and education* (5th ed.). New York: McGraw-Hill.

Gumenik, W.E. (1979). The advantage of specific terms over general terms as cues for sentence recall: Instantiation or retrieval? *Memory & Cognition, 7,* 240–244.

Hacking, I. (1983). *Observing and intervening.* New York: Cambridge University Press.

Halpern, A., & Bower, G.H. (1982). Musical expertise and melodic structure in memory for musical notation. *American Journal of Psychology, 95,* 31–50.

Hampton, J.A. (1979). Polymorphous concepts in semantic memory. *Journal of Verbal Learning and Verbal Behavior, 18,* 441–461.

Hampton, J.A. (1982). A demonstration of intransitivity in natural concepts. *Cognition, 12,* 151–164.

Hampton, J.A. (1987). Inheritance of attributes in natural concept conjunctions. *Memory & Cognition, 15,* 55–71.

Hampton, J.A. (1988). Overextension of conjunctive concepts: Evidence for a unitary model of concept typicality and class inclusion. *Journal of Experimental Psychology: Learning, Memory, and Cognition, 14,* 12–32.

Hampton, J.A., & Gardiner, M.M. (1983). Measures of internal category structure: A correlational analysis of normative data. *British Journal of Psychology, 74,* 491–516.

Hanson, V.L., & Bellugi, U. (1982). On the role of sign order and morphological structure in memory for American Sign Language sentences. *Journal of Verbal Learning and Verbal Behavior, 21,* 621–633.

Harnad, S. (1987). *Categorical perception: The groundwork of cognition.* New York: Cambridge University Press.

Hasher, L., & Zacks, R.T. (1979). Automatic and effortful processes in memory. *Journal of Experimental Psychology: General, 108,* 356–388.

Hasher, L., & Zacks, R.T. (1984). Automatic processing of fundamental information. *American Psychologist, 39,* 1372–1388.

Hayes, D.P. (1988). Speaking and writing: Distinct patterns of word choice. *Journal of Memory and Language, 27,* 572–585.

Hayes, P.J. (1979). The logic of frames. In D. Metzing (Ed.), *Frame conceptions and frame understanding* (pp. 46–61). Berlin: Walter de Gruyter.

Hayes, P.J. (1985). The second naive physics manifesto. In J.R. Hobbs & R.C. Moore (Eds.), *Formal theories of the commonsense world.* Norwood, NJ: Ablex.

Hayes, W.L. (1973). *Statistics for the social sciences* (2nd ed.). New York: Holt, Rinehart & Winston.

Hayes-Roth, B., & Hayes-Roth, F. (1977). Concept learning and the recognition and classification of exemplars. *Journal of Verbal Learning and Verbal Behavior, 16,* 321–338.

Healy, A.F. (1976). Detection errors on the word *the*: Evidence for reading units larger than letters. *Journal of Experimental Psychology: Human Perception and Performance, 2,* 235–242.

Heatherington, E.M., & Parke, R.D. (1986). *Child psychology: A contemporary viewpoint* (3rd ed.). New York: McGraw-Hill.

Heider, E.R. (1972). Universals in color naming and memory. *Journal of Experimental Psychology, 93,* 10–20.

Heider, E.R., & Oliver, D. (1972). The structure of the color space in naming and memory for two languages. *Cognitive Psychology, 3,* 337–354.

Heilman, K.M., & Valenstein, E. (Eds.). (1985). *Clinical neuropsychology* (2nd ed.). New York: Oxford University Press.

Henderson, L. (1982). *Orthography and word recognition in reading.* London: Academic.

Hillis, W. (1985). *The connection machine.* Cambridge, MA: MIT Press.

Hintzman, D.L. (1976). Repetition and memory. In G.H. Bower (Ed.), *The psychology of learning and motivation: Advances in research and theory* (Vol. 10). New York: Academic Press.

Hintzman, D.L. (1986). "Schema abstraction" in a multiple-trace memory model. *Psychological Review, 93,* 411–428.

Hintzman, D.L. (1988). Judgments of frequency and recognition memory in a multiple-trace memory model. *Psychological Review, 95,* 528–551.

Hirst, W. (Ed.). (1988). *The making of cognitive science: Essays in honor of George A. Miller.* New York: Cambridge University Press.

Hirst, W., & Brill, G.A. (1980). Contextual aspects of pronoun assignment. *Journal of Verbal Learning and Verbal Behavior, 19,* 168–175.

Hockett, C. (1966). The problem of universals in language. In J.H. Greenberg (Ed.), *Universals of language* (2nd ed., pp. 1–29). Cambridge, MA: MIT Press.

Holland, D., & Quinn, N. (1987). *Cultural models in language and thought.* New York: Cambridge University Press.

Holland, J.H., Holyoak, K.J., Nisbett, R.E., & Thagard, P.R. (1986). *Induction: Processes of inference, learning, and discovery.* Cambridge, MA: MIT Press.

Holmes, V.M., & Forster, K.I. (1970). Detection of extraneous signals during sentence processing. *Perception & Psychophysics, 7,* 297–301.

Holyoak, K.J., & Glass, A.L. (1975). The role of contradictions and counterexamples in the rejection of false sentences. *Journal of Verbal Learning and Verbal Behavior, 14,* 215–239.

Holyoak, K.J., & Koh, K. (1987). Surface and structural similarity in analogical transfer. *Memory & Cognition, 15,* 332–340.

Holyoak, K.J., Koh, K., & Nisbett, R.E. (1989). A theory of conditioning: Inductive learning within rule-based default hierarchies. *Psychological Review, 96,* 315–340.

Holyoak, K.J., & Nisbett, R.E. (1988). Induction. In R.J. Sternberg & E.E. Smith (Eds.), *The psychology of human thought* (pp. 50–91). New York: Cambridge University Press.

Holyoak, K.J., & Thagard, P.R. (1989a). Analogical mapping by constraint satisfaction. *Cognitive Science, 13,* 295–356.

Holyoak, K.J., & Thagard, P.R. (1989b). A computational model of analogical problem solving. In S. Vosniadou & A. Ortony (Eds.), *Similarity and analogical reasoning* (pp. 242–266). New York: Cambridge University Press.

Homa, D. (1984). On the nature of categories. In G.H. Bower (Ed.), *The psychology of learning and motivation: Advances in research and theory* (Vol. 18, pp. 49–94). New York: Academic.

Honig, W.K., & Staddon, J.E.R. (1977). *Handbook of operant behavior.* Englewood Cliffs, NJ: Prentice-Hall.

Hubel, D.H., & Wiesel, T.N. (1959). Receptive fields of single neurones in the cat's striate cortex. *Journal of Physiology, 148*, 574–591.

Hubel, D.H., & Wiesel, T.N. (1962). Receptive fields, binocular interaction, and functional architecture in the cat's visual cortex. *Journal of Physiology, 160*, 106–154.

Hunt, E.G., Martin, J., & Stone, P.I. (1966). *Experiments in induction.* New York: Academic.

Hyde, T.S., & Jenkins, J.J. (1969). Differential effects of incidental tasks on the organization of recall of a list of highly associated words. *Journal of Experimental Psychology, 82*, 472–481.

Hyman, L.M. (1975). *Phonology: Theory and analysis.* New York: Holt, Rinehart & Winston.

Ingram, D. (1989). *First language acquisition: Method, description, and explanation.* New York: Cambridge University Press.

Isaacs, E.A., & Clark, H.H. (1987). References in conversation between experts and novices. *Journal of Experimental Psychology: General, 116*, 26–37.

Jackendoff, R. (1983). *Semantics and cognition.* Cambridge, MA: MIT Press.

Jackendoff, R. (1987). The status of thematic relations in linguistic theory. *Linguistic Inquiry, 18*, 369–411.

Jacoby, L. (1978). On interpreting the effects of repetition: Solving a problem versus remembering a solution. *Journal of Verbal Learning and Verbal Behavior, 17*, 649–667.

Jacoby, L. (1983). Remembering the data: Analyzing interactive processes in reading. *Journal of Verbal Learning and Verbal Behavior, 22*, 485–508.

Jacoby, L.L., & Brooks, L.R. (1984). Nonanalytic cognition: Memory, perception, and concept learning. In G.H. Bower (Ed.), *The psychology of learning and motivation: Advances in research and theory* (Vol. 18). New York: Academic.

Jacoby, L.L., & Hayman, C.A.G. (1987). Specific visual transfer in word identification. *Journal of Experimental Psychology: Learning, Memory, and Cognition, 13*, 456–463.

James, W. (1890). *Principles of psychology.* New York: Holt, Rinehart & Winston.

Jarvella, R.J. (1971). Syntactic processing of connected speech. *Journal of Verbal Learning and Verbal Behavior, 10*, 409–416.

Jarvella, R.J. (1979). Immediate memory and discourse processing. In G.H. Bower (Ed.), *The psychology of learning and motivation: Advances in research and theory* (Vol. 13). New York: Academic Press.

Jarvella, R.J., & Collas, J.G. (1974). Memory for the intentions of sentences. *Memory & Cognition, 2*, 185–188.

Jennings, D.L., Amabile, T.M., & Ross, L. (1982). Informal covariation assessment: Data-based versus theory-based judgments. In D. Kahneman, P. Slovic, & A. Tversky (Eds.), *Judgment under uncertainty: Heuristics and biases* (pp. 211–230). New York: Cambridge University Press.

Johnson, M.K., Bransford, J.D., & Solomon, S. (1973). Memory for tacit implications of sentences. *Journal of Experimental Psychology, 98*, 203–205.

Johnson, M.K., Peterson, M.A., Yap, E.C., & Rose, P.M. (1989). Frequency judgments: The problem of defining a perceptual event. *Journal of Experimental Psychology: Learning, Memory, and Cognition, 15*, 126–136.

Johnson, M.K., & Raye, C.L. (1981). Reality monitoring. *Psychological Review, 88*, 67–85.

Johnson-Laird, P.N. (1983). *Mental models.* Cambridge, MA: Harvard University Press.

Johnson-Laird, P.N. (1988). A taxonomy of thinking. In R.J. Sternberg & E.E. Smith (Eds.), *The psychology of human thought* (pp. 429–458). New York: Cambridge University Press.

Johnson-Laird, P.N., & Bara, B. (1984). Syllogistic inference. *Cognition, 16,* 1–61.

Johnson-Laird, P.N., & Steedman, M.J (1978). The psychology of syllogisms. *Cognitive Psychology, 10,* 64–99.

Johnson-Laird, P.N., & Stevenson, R. (1970). Memory for syntax. *Nature, 227,* 412.

Joliceur, P., Gluck, M., & Kosslyn, S.M. (1984). Pictures and names: Making the connection. *Cognitive Psychology, 16,* 243–275.

Jones, G.V. (1983). Identifying basic categories. *Psychological Bulletin, 94,* 423–428.

Jonides, J., & Naveh-Benjamin, M. (1987). Estimating frequency of occurrence. *Journal of Experimental Psychology: Learning, Memory, and Cognition, 13,* 230–240.

Just, M.A., & Carpenter, P.A. (1976). The relation between comprehending and remembering some complex sentences. *Memory & Cognition, 4,* 318–322.

Just, M.A., & Carpenter, P.A. (1978). Inference processes during reading: Reflections from eye fixations. In J.W. Senders, D.F. Fisher, & R.A. Monty (Eds.), *Eye movements and the higher psychological functions.* Hillsdale, NJ: Lawrence Erlbaum Associates.

Just, M.A., & Carpenter, P.A. (1980). A theory of reading: From eye fixations to comprehension. *Psychological Review, 87,* 329–324.

Just, M.A., & Carpenter, P.A. (1987). *The psychology of reading and language comprehension.* Boston: Allyn & Bacon.

Kahneman, D. (1973). *Attention and effort.* Englewood Cliffs, NJ: Prentice-Hall.

Kahneman, D., & Henik, A. (1981). Perceptual organization and attention. In M. Kubovy & J.R. Pomerantz (Eds.), *Perceptual organization.* Hillsdale, NJ: Lawrence Erlbaum Associates.

Kahneman, D., & Miller, D.T. (1986). Norm theory: Comparing reality to its alternatives. *Psychological Review, 93,* 136–153.

Kahneman, D., Slovic, P., & Tversky, A. (Eds.). (1982). *Judgment under uncertainty: Heuristics and biases.* New York: Cambridge University Press.

Kahneman, D., & Tversky, A. (1972). Subjective probability: A judgment of representativeness. *Cognitive Psychology, 3,* 430–454.

Kahneman, D., & Tversky, A. (1979). Prospect theory. *Econometrica, 47,* 263–292.

Kahneman, D., & Tversky, A. (1982). The simulation heuristic. In D. Kahneman, P. Slovic, & A. Tversky (Eds.), *Judgment under uncertainty: Heuristics and biases* (pp. 201–210). New York: Cambridge University Press.

Kantowitz, B.H., & Roediger, H.L., III (1984). *Experimental psychology: Understanding psychological research* (2nd ed.). New York: West.

Kaplan, R., & Sacuzzo, D. (1984). *Clinical psychology.* Boston: Allyn & Bacon.

Katz, J. (1964). Semantic theory and the meaning of "good." *Journal of Philosophy, 61,* 739–766.

Katz, J. (1972). *Semantic theory.* New York: Harper & Row.

Keenan, J.N., MacWhinney, B., & Mayhew, D. (1977). Pragmatics in memory: A study of natural conversation. *Journal of Verbal Learning and Verbal Behavior, 16,* 549–560.

Keil, F.C. (1979). *Semantic and conceptual development: An ontological perspective.* Cambridge, MA: Harvard University Press.

Keil, F.C. (1989). *Concepts, kinds, and cognitive development.* Cambridge, MA: MIT Press.

Kendler, H.H., & Kendler, T.S. (1959). Reversal and nonreversal shifts in kindergarten children. *Journal of Experimental Psychology, 58,* 56–60.

Kendler, T.S., & Kendler, H.H. (1970). An ontogeny of optional shift behavior. *Child Development, 41,* 1–27.

Kerr, N.H. (1983). The role of vision in "visual imagery" experiments: Evidence from the congenitally blind. *Journal of Experimental Psychology: General, 112,* 265–277.

Kieras, D.E., & Bovair, S. (1984). The role of a mental model in learning to operate a device. *Cognitive Science, 8,* 255–274.

Kimball, J.P. (1973). Seven principles of surface structure parsing in natural language. *Cognition, 2,* 15–47.

Kintsch, W. (1970). *Learning, memory, and conceptual processes.* New York: Wiley.

Kintsch, W. (1974). *The representation of meaning in memory.* Hillsdale, NJ: Lawrence Erlbaum Associates.

Kintsch, W., & Bates, E. (1977). Recognition memory for statements from a classroom lecture. *Journal of Experimental Psychology: Human Learning and Memory, 3,* 150–159.

Kintsch, W., & Keenan, J.M. (1973). Reading rate and retention as a function of the number of propositions in the base structure of a sentence. *Cognitive Psychology, 5,* 257–274.

Kintsch, W., Kozminsky, E., Streby, W.J., McKoon, G., & Keenan, J.M. (1975). Comprehension and recall of text as a function of content variables. *Journal of Verbal Learning and Verbal Behavior, 14,* 196–214.

Kintsch, W., & van Dijk, T.A. (1978). Toward a model of text comprehension and production. *Psychological Review, 85,* 363–394.

Kleiman, G. (1975). Speech recoding in reading. *Journal of Verbal Learning and Verbal Behavior, 14,* 323–329.

Koffka, K. (1935). *Principles of Gestalt psychology.* New York: Harcourt, Brace & World.

Kohler, W. (1940). *Dynamics in psychology.* New York: Liveright.

Kolb, B., & Whishaw, I. (1980). *Fundamentals of human neuropsychology.* New York: Freeman.

Kolodner, J. (1988). *Proceedings of the case-based reasoning workshop.* San Mateo, CA: Morgan-Kaufman.

Kosslyn, S.M. (1975). Information representation in visual images. *Cognitive Psychology, 7,* 341–370.

Kosslyn, S.M. (1980). *Image and mind.* Cambridge, MA: Harvard University Press.

Kosslyn, S.M., Ball, T., & Reiser, B.J. (1978). Visual images preserve metric spatial information: Evidence from studies of image scanning. *Journal of Experimental Psychology: Human Perception and Performance, 4,* 47–60.

Kripke, S. (1972). Naming and necessity. In D. Davidson & G. Harmon (Eds.), *Semantics of natural language* (pp. 253–355). Dordrecht: Reidel.

Krumhansl, C. (1978). Concerning the applicability of geometric models to similarity data: The interrelationship between similarity and spatial density. *Psychological Review, 85,* 445–463.

Kuhn, T.S. (1970). *The structure of scientific revolutions* (2nd ed.). Chicago: University of Chicago Press.

LaBerge, D., & Brown, V. (1989). Theory of attentional operations in shape identification. *Psychological Review, 96,* 101–124.

LaBerge, D., & Samuels, S.J. (1974). Toward a theory of automatic information processing in reading. *Cognitive Psychology, 6,* 293–323.

Lachman, R., Lachman, J.L., & Butterfield, E.C. (1979). *Cognitive psychology and information processing: An introduction.* Hillsdale, NJ: Lawrence Erlbaum Associates.

Ladefoged, P. (1975). *A course in phonetics.* New York: Harcourt Brace Jovanovich.

Ladefoged, P. (1981). *Elements of acoustic phonetics* (2nd ed.). Chicago: University of Chicago Press.

Laird, J.E., Rosenbloom, P.S., & Newell, A. (1986). Chunking in Soar: The anatomy of a general learning mechanism. *Machine Learning, 1,* 11–46.

Lakoff, G. (1987). *Women, fire, and dangerous things: What categories reveal about the mind.* Chicago: University of Chicago Press.

Lakoff, G., & Johnson, M. (1980). *Metaphors we live by.* Chicago: University of Chicago Press.

Lane, H. (1979). *The wild boy of Aveyron.* London: Granada.

Langacker, R.W. (1987). *Foundations of cognitive grammar: Vol. 1. Theoretical prerequisites.* Stanford, CA: Stanford University Press.

Larkin, W., & Burns, D. (1977). Sentence comprehension and memory for embedded structure. *Memory & Cognition, 5,* 17–22.

Lawrence, D.M., & Banks, W.P. (1973). Accuracy of recognition memory for common sounds. *Bulletin of the Psychonomic Society, 1,* 298–300.

Lehrer, A. (1992). Names and naming: A frame approach. In E. Kittay & A. Lehrer (Eds.), *Frames, fields, and contrasts: New essays in semantic and lexical organization.* Hillsdale, NJ: Lawrence Erlbaum Associates.

Lenneberg, E. (1967). *Biological foundations of language.* New York: Wiley.

Levelt, W.J.M. (1989). *Speaking: From intention to articulation.* Cambridge, MA: MIT Press.

Levi, J.N. (1978). *The syntax and semantics of complex nominals.* New York: Academic.

Levy, B.A. (1978). Speech analysis during sentence processing: Reading versus listening. *Visible language, 12,* 81–101.

Lewis, J.L. (1970). Semantic processing of unattended messages using dichotic listening. *Journal of Experimental Psychology, 85,* 225–228.

Lezak, M.D. (1983). *Neuropsychological assessment* (2nd ed.). New York: Oxford University Press.

Liberman, A.M. (1970). The grammars of language and speech. *Cognitive Psychology, 1,* 301–323.

Liberman, A.M., Cooper, F.S., Shankweiler, D.P., & Studdert-Kennedy, M. (1967). Perception of the speech code. *Psychological Review, 74,* 431–461.

Lieberman, P. (1975). *On the origins of language.* New York: Macmillan.

Lindsay, P.H., & Norman, D.A. (1977). *Human information processing.* New York: Academic.

Loftus, E.F. (1975). Leading questions and the eyewitness report. *Cognitive Psychology, 7,* 560–572.

Loftus, E.F., & Loftus, G.R. (1980). On the permanence of stored information in the human brain. *American Psychologist, 35,* 409–420.

Logan, G.D. (1980). Attention and automaticity in Stroop and priming tasks: Theory and data. Cognitive Psychology, 12, 523–553.

Logan, G.D. (1988). Toward an instance theory of automatization. *Psychological Review, 95,* 492–527.

Loken, B., & Ward, J. (1990). Alternative approaches to understanding the determinants of typicality. *Journal of Consumer Research, 17,* 111–126.

Lorayne, H., & Lucas, J. (1974). *The memory book.* New York: Stein & Day.

Luchins, A.S. (1942). Mechanization in problem solving. *Psychological Monographs, 54* (Whole No. 248).

Luria, A.R. (1968). *The mind of a mnemonist.* New York: Basic.

Lyons, J. (1977a). *Semantics* (Vol. 1). New York: Cambridge University Press.

Lyons, J. (1977b). *Semantics* (Vol. 2). New York: Cambridge University Press.

MacKay, D.G. (1973). Aspects of the theory of memory, comprehension, and attention. *Quarterly Journal of Experimental Psychology, 25,* 22–40.

MacKay, D.G. (1978). Derivational rules and the internal lexicon. *Journal of Verbal Learning and Verbal Behavior, 17,* 61–71.

MacKay, D.G. (1987). *The organization of perception and action.* New York: Springer-Verlag.

MacLeod, C.M., & Dunbar, K. (1988). Training and Stroop-like interference: Evidence for a continuum of automaticity. *Journal of Experimental Psychology: Learning, Memory, and Cognition, 14,* 126–135.

MacNeilage, P.F. (Ed.). (1983). *The production of speech.* New York: Springer-Verlag.

MacNeilage, P.F., & Ladefoged, P. (1976). The production of speech and language. In E.C. Carterette & M.P. Friedman (Eds.), *Handbook of perception* (Vol. 7, pp. 75–120). New York: Academic.

Madigan, S.A. (1969). Intraserial repetition and coding processes in free recall. *Journal of Verbal Learning and Verbal Behavior, 8,* 828–835.

Mahoney, M.J. (1974). *Cognition and behavior modification.* Cambridge, MA: Ballinger.

Malmi, R.A., & Samson, D.J. (1983). Intuitive averaging of categorized numerical stimuli. *Journal of Verbal Learning and Verbal Behavior, 22,* 547–559.

Malt, B.C. (1985). The role of discourse structure in understanding anaphora. *Journal of Memory and Language, 24,* 271–289.

Malt, B.C., & Smith, E.E. (1984). Correlated properties in natural categories. *Journal of Verbal Learning and Verbal Behavior, 23,* 250–269.

Mandler, G. (1967). Organization and memory. In K.W. Spence & J.T. Spence (Eds.), *The psychology of learning and motivation* (Vol. 1, pp. 327–372). New York: Academic.

Mandler, G. (1975). *Mind and emotion.* New York: Wiley.

Mandler, G. (1980). Recognizing: The judgment of previous occurrence. *Psychological Review, 87,* 252–271.

Mandler, G. (1985). *Cognitive psychology: An essay in cognitive science.* Hillsdale, NJ: Lawrence Erlbaum Associates.

Mandler, G., & Pearlstone, Z. (1966). Free and constrained concept learning and subsequent recall. *Journal of Verbal Learning and Verbal Behavior, 5,* 126–131.

Mandler, J.M., & Johnson, N.S. (1977). Remembrance of things parsed: Story structure and recall. *Cognitive Psychology, 9,* 111–151.

Mandler, J.M., & Mandler, G. (1964). *Thinking: From association to Gestalt.* New York: Wiley.

Manelis, L., & Tharp, D.A. (1977). The processing of affixed words. *Memory & Cognition, 5,* 690–695.

Marcel, A.J. (1983a). Conscious and unconscious perception: Experiments on visual masking and word recognition. *Cognitive Psychology, 15,* 197–237.

Marcel, A.J. (1983b). Conscious and unconscious perception: An approach to the relations between phenomenal experience and perceptual processes. *Cognitive Psychology, 15,* 238–300.

Markman, E.M. (1989). *Categorization and naming in children.* Cambridge, MA: MIT Press.

Marks, L.E., & Miller, G.A. (1964). The role of semantic and syntactic constraints in the memorization of English sentences. *Journal of Verbal Learning and Verbal Behavior, 3,* 1–5.

Marler, P., & Mundinger, P. (1971). Vocal learning in birds. In H. Moltz (Ed.), *Ontogeny of vertebrate behavior* (pp. 389–449). New York: Academic.

Marr, D. (1982). *Vision.* New York: Freeman.

Marslen-Wilson, W.D. (1987). Functional parallelism in spoken word-recognition. *Cognition, 25,* 71–102.

Marslen-Wilson, W.D. (Ed.). (1989). *Lexical representation and process.* Cambridge, MA: MIT Press.

Marslen-Wilson, W.D., & Tyler, L.K. (1980). The temporal structure of spoken language understanding. *Cognition, 8,* 1–71.

Martin, J.D., & Billman, D. (1991). Representational specificity and concept learning. In D. Fisher & M. Pazzani (Eds.), *Computational approaches to concept formation.* San Mateo, CA: Morgan-Kaufmann.

Mates, B. (1972). *Elementary logic.* New York: Oxford University Press.

Mathews, P.H. (1976). *Morphology: An introduction to the theory of word structure.* New York: Cambridge University Press.

Maxwell, G. (1964). The ontological status of theoretical entites. In H. Feigl & G. Maxwell (Eds.), *Minnesota studies in the philosophy of science: Vol. 3. Scientific explanation, space, and time* (pp. 3–14). Minneapolis: University of Minnesota Press.

Mayer, R.E. (1987). *Educational psychology: An educational approach.* Boston: Little-Brown.

McCarthy, J., & Hayes, P.J. (1969). Some philosophical problems from the standpoint of artificial intelligence. In B. Meltzer & D. Michie (Eds.), *Machine learning 4.* Edinburgh: Edinburgh University Press.

McCauley, R.N. (1986). Intertheoretic relations and the future of psychology, *Philosophy of Science, 53,* 177–199.

McCawley, J.D. (1981). *Everything that linguists have always wanted to know about logic.* Chicago: University of Chicago Press.

McClelland, J.L., & Elman, J.L. (1986). The TRACE model of speech perception. *Cognitive Psychology, 18,* 1–86.

McClelland, J.L., & Rumelhart, D.E. (1981). An interactive activation model of context effects in letter perception: Part 1. An account of basic findings. *Psychological Review, 88,* 375–407.

McClelland, J.L., Rumelhart, D.E., & the PDP Research Group (1986). *Parallel distributed processing: Explorations in the microstructure of cognition: Vol. 2. Psychological and biological models.* Cambridge, MA: MIT Press.

McCloskey, M. (1980). The stimulus familiarity problem in semantic memory research. *Journal of Verbal Learning and Verbal Behavior, 19,* 485–502.

McCloskey, M., & Cohen, N.J. (1989). Catastrophic interference in connectionist networks: The sequential learning problem. In G.H. Bower (Ed.), *The psychology of learning and motivation: Advances in research and theory* (Vol. 24, pp. 109–165). New York: Academic.

McCloskey, M., & Glucksberg, S. (1978). Natural categories: Well-defined or fuzzy sets? *Memory & Cognition, 6,* 462–472.

McCloskey, M., & Glucksberg, S. (1979). Decision processes in verifying category membership statements: Implications for models of semantic memory. *Cognitive Psychology, 11,* 1–37.

McCloskey, M., & Zaragoza, M. (1985). Misleading postevent information and memory for events: Arguments and evidence against memory impairment hypotheses. *Journal of Experimental Psychology: General, 114,* 1–16.

McKoon, G. (1977). Organization of information in text memory. *Journal of Verbal Learning and Verbal Behavior, 16,* 247–260.

McKoon, G., & Ratcliff, R. (1981). The comprehension processes and memory structures involved in instrumental inference. *Journal of Verbal Learning and Verbal Behavior, 20,* 671–682.

McKoon, G., & Ratcliff, R. (1989). Assessing the occurrence of elaborative inferences with recognition: Compatibility checking vs. compound cue theory. *Journal of Memory and Language, 28,* 547–563.

McMullin, E. (1978). Structured explanations. *American Philosophical Quarterly, 15,* 139–147.

Mead, C. (1989). *Analog VLSI and neural systems.* Reading, MA: Addison-Wesley.

Medin, D.L. (1983). Structural principles of categorization. In T. Shepp & T. Tighe (Eds.), *Interaction: Perception, development, and cognition* (pp. 203–230). Hillsdale, NJ: Lawrence Erlbaum Associates.

Medin, D.L., Altom, M.W., Edelson, S.M., & Freko, D. (1982). Correlated symptoms and simulated medical classification. *Journal of Experimental Psychology: Learning, Memory, and Cognition, 8,* 37–50.

Medin, D.L., & Edelson, S.M. (1988). Problem structure and the use of base-rate information from experience. *Journal of Experimental Psychology: General, 117,* 68–85.

Medin, D.L., & Ross, B.H. (1989). The specific character of abstract thought: Categorization, problem solving, and induction. In R.J. Sternberg (Ed.), *Advances in the psychology of human intelligence* (Vol. 5, pp. 189–223). Hillsdale, NJ: Lawrence Erlbaum Associates.

Medin, D.L., & Schaffer, M. (1978). A context theory of classification learning. *Psychological Review, 85,* 207–238.

Medin, D.L., & Schwanenflugel, P.J. (1981). Linear separability in classification learning. *Journal of Experimental Psychology: Human Learning and Memory*355–368.

Medin, D.L., & Shoben, E.J. (1988). Context and structure in conceptual combination. *Cognitive Psychology, 20,* 158–190.

Medin, D.L., & Smith, E.E. (1984). Concepts and concept formation. *Annual Review of Psychology, 35,* 113–138.

Medin, D.L., Wattenmaker, W.D., & Hampson, S.E. (1987). Family resemblance, conceptual cohesiveness, and category construction. *Cognitive Psychology, 19,* 242–279.

Medin, D.L., Wattenmaker, W.D., & Michalski, R. (1987). Constraints and preferences in inductive reasoning: An experimental study of human and machine performance. *Cognitive Science, 11,* 299–339.

Meichenbaum, D.B. (1977). *Cognitive-behavior modification: An integrative approach.* New York: Plenum.

Melton, A.W. (1963). Implications of short-term memory for a general theory of memory. *Journal of Verbal Learning and Verbal Behavior, 2,* 1–21.

Mervis, C.B. (1987). Child-basic object categories and early lexical development. In U. Neisser (Ed.), *Concepts and conceptual development: Ecological and intellectual factors in categorization* (pp. 201–233). New York: Cambridge University Press.

Mervis, C.B., & Rosch, E. (1981). Categorization of natural objects. *Annual Review of Psychology, 32,* 89–115.

Meyer, D.E. (1970). On the representation and retrieval of stored semantic information. *Cognitive Psychology, 1,* 242–299.

Meyer, D.E., & Schvaneveldt, R.W. (1971). Facilitation in recognizing pairs of words. *Journal of Experimental Psychology, 90,* 227–234.

Meyer, D.E., Schvaneveldt, R.W., & Ruddy, M.G. (1974). Functions of graphemic and phonemic codes in visual word recognition. *Memory & Cognition, 2,* 309–321.

Miller, G.A. (1956). The magical number seven plus or minus two: Some limits on our capacity for processing information. *Psychological Review, 63,* 81–97.

Miller, G.A. (1981). *Language and speech.* New York: Freeman.

Miller, G.A., & Chomsky, N. (1963). Finitary models of language users. In D. Luce, R. Bush, & E. Galanter (Eds.), *Handbook of mathematical psychology* (Vol. 2, pp. 419–491). New York: Wiley.

Miller, G.A., & Isard, S.D. (1963). Some perceptual consequences of linguistic rules. *Journal of Verbal Learning and Verbal Behavior, 2,* 217–228.

Miller, G.A., & Johnson-Laird, P.N. (1976). *Language and perception.* Cambridge, MA: Harvard University Press.

Miller, G.A., & Nicely, P.E. (1955). An analysis of perceptual confusions among some English consonants. *Journal of the Acoustical Society of America, 27,* 338–352.

Minksy, M.L. (1977). A framework for representing knowledge. In P.H. Winston (Ed.), *The psychology of computer vision* (pp. 211–277). New York: McGraw-Hill.

Minsky, M.L. (1985). *The society of mind.* New York: Simon & Schuster.

Mitchell, T.M., Keller, R.M., & Kedar-Cabelli, S.T. (1986). Explanation-based generalization: A unifying view. *Machine Learning, 1,* 47–80.

Mohr, B., & Wang, W.S. (1968). Perceptual distance and the specification of phonological features. *Phonetics, 18,* 31–45.

Moray, N. (1959). Attention in dichotic listening: Affective cues and the influence of instructions. *Quarterly Journal of Experimental Psychology, 11,* 56–60.

Moray, N. (1970). *Attention: Selective processes in vision and hearing.* New York: Academic.

Morris, C.D., Bransford, J.D., & Franks, J.J. (1977). Levels of processing versus test-appropriate strategies. *Journal of Verbal Learning and Verbal Behavior, 16,* 519–533.

Morrow, D.G. (1985a). Prominent characters and events organize narrative understanding. *Journal of Memory and Language, 24,* 304–319.

Morrow, D.G. (1985b). Prepositions and verb aspect in narrative understanding. *Journal of Memory and Language, 24,* 390–404.

Morrow, D.G., Bower, G.H., & Greenspan, S.L. (1989). Updating situation models during narrative comprehension. *Journal of Memory and Language, 28,* 292–312.

Morrow, D.G., Greenspan, S.L., & Bower, G.H. (1987). Accessibility and situation models in narrative comprehension. *Journal of Memory and Language, 26,* 165–187.

Morton, J. (1969). Interaction of information in word recognition. *Psychological Review, 76,* 165–178.

Morton, J. (1979). Word recognition. In J. Morton & J.C. Marshall (Eds.), *Psycholinguistics 2: Structure and process.* Cambridge, MA: MIT Press.

Morton, J., & Long, J. (1976). Effect of word transition probability on phoneme identification. *Journal of Verbal Learning and Verbal Behavior, 15,* 43–51.

Murphy, G.L. (1982). Cue validity and levels of categorization. *Psychological Bulletin, 91,* 174–177.

Murphy, G.L. (1985). Processes of understanding anaphora. *Journal of Memory and Language, 24,* 290–303.

Murphy, G.L. (1988). Comprehending complex concepts. *Cognitive Science, 12,* 529–562.

Murphy, G.L., & Brownell, H.H. (1985). Category differentiation in object recognition: Typicality constraints on the basic category advantage. *Journal of Experimental Psychology: Learning, Memory, and Cognition, 11,* 70–84.

Murphy, G.L., & Medin, D.L. (1985). The role of theories in conceptual coherence. *Psychological Review, 92,* 289–316.

Murphy, G.L., & Smith, E.E. (1982). Basic-level superiority in picture categorization. *Journal of Verbal Learning and Verbal Behavior, 21,* 1–20.

Murphy, G.L., & Wisniewski, E.J. (1989). Feature correlations in conceptual representations. In G. Tiberghien (Ed.), *Advances in cognitive science: Vol. 2. Theory and applications* (pp. 23–45). Chichester: Ellis Harwood.

Naveh-Benjamin, M., & Jonides, J. (1986). On the automaticity of frequency encoding: Effects of competing task loads, encoding strategy, and intention. *Journal of Experimental Psychology: Learning, Memory, and Cognition, 12,* 378–386.

Navon, D. (1984). Resources—a theoretical soup stone? *Psychological Review, 91,* 216–234.

Neely, J.H. (1977). Semantic priming and retrieval from lexical memory. Roles of inhibitionless spreading activation and limited-capacity attention. *Journal of Experimental Psychology: General, 106,* 226–254.

Neely, J.H., Schmidt, S.R., & Roediger, H.L., III (1983). Inhibition from related primes in recognition memory. *Journal of Experimental Psychology: Learning, Memory, and Cognition, 9,* 196–211.

Neisser, U. (1967). *Cognitive psychology.* Englewood Cliffs, NJ: Prentice-Hall.

Neisser, U. (1976). *Cognition and reality.* New York: Freeman.

Neisser, U. (1982) *Memory observed: Remembering in natural contexts.* San Francisco: Freeman.

Neisser, U. (1984). Toward an ecologically oriented cognitive science. In T.M. Shlecter & M.P. Toglia (Eds.), *New directions in cognitive science.* Norwood, NJ: Ablex.

Neisser, U., & Winograd, E. (Eds.). (1988). *Remembering reconsidered: Ecological and traditional approaches to the study of memory.* New York: Cambridge University Press.

Nelson, D.L., & McEvoy, C.L. (1979). Encoding context and set size. *Journal of Experimental Psychology: Human Learning and Memory, 5,* 292–314.

Nelson, D.L., Walling, J.R., & McEvoy, C.L. (1979). Doubts about depth. *Journal of Experimental Psychology: Human Learning and Memory, 5,* 24–44.

Nelson, T.O. (1971). Savings and forgetting from long-term memory. *Journal of Verbal Learning and Verbal Behavior, 10,* 568–576.

Nelson, T.O. (1977). Repetition and depth of processing. *Journal of Verbal Learning and Verbal Behavior, 16,* 151–171.

Nelson, T.O. (1978). Detecting small amounts of information in memory: Savings for nonrecognized items. *Journal of Experimental Psychology: Learning, Memory, and Cognition, 4,* 453–368.

Neumann, O. (1987). Beyond capacity: A functional view of attention. In H. Heuer & A.F. Sanders (Eds.), *Perspectives on perception and action* (pp. 361–394). Hillsdale, NJ: Lawrence Erlbaum Associates.

Newell, A. (1973). You can't play 20 questions with nature and win. In W.G. Chase (Ed.), *Visual information processing*. New York: Academic.

Newell, A. (1990). *Unified theories of cognition*. Cambridge, MA: Harvard University Press.

Newell, A., & Rosenbloom, P.S. (1981). Mechanisms of skill acquisition and the law of practice. In J.R. Anderson (Ed.), *Cognitive skills and their acquisition*. Hillsdale, NJ: Lawrence Erlbaum Associates.

Newell, A., & Simon, H.A. (1972). *Human problem solving*. Englewood Cliffs, NJ: Prentice-Hall.

Nickerson, R.S. (1965). Short-term memory for complex meaningful visual configurations: A demonstration of capacity. *Canadian Journal of Psychology, 19*, 155–160.

Nilsson, L.G., Law, J., & Tulving, E. (1988). Recognition failure of recallable unique names: Evidence for an empirical law of memory and learning. *Journal of Experimental Psychology: Learning, Memory, and Cognition, 14*, 266–277.

Nisbett, R.E., Krantz, D.H., Jepson, C., & Kunda, Z. (1983). The use of statistical heuristics in everyday inductive reasoning. *Psychological Review, 90*, 339–363.

Norman, D.A. (1968). Toward a theory of memory and attention. *Psychological Review, 75*, 522–536.

Norman, D.A. (1969). Memory while shadowing. *Quarterly Journal of Experimenal Psychology, 21*, 85–93.

Norman, D.A. (Ed.). (1970). *Models of human memory*. New York: Academic.

Norman, D.A., & Bobrow, D.G. (1975). On data-limited and resource-limited processes. *Cognitive Psychology, 7*, 44–64.

Norman, D.A., & Bobrow, D.G. (1979). Descriptions: An intermediate stage in memory retrieval. *Cognitive Psychology, 11*, 107–123.

Norman, D.A., Rumelhart, D.E., & the LNR Research Group (1975). *Explorations in cognition*. New York: Freeman.

Norman, D.A., & Shallice, T. (1986). Attention to action: Willed and automatic control of behavior. In R.J. Davidson, G.E. Schwartz, & D. Shapiro (Eds.), *Consciousness and self-regulation: Advances in research and theory* (Vol. 4, pp. 1–18). New York: Plenum.

Nosofsky, R.M. (1984). Choice, similarity, and the context theory of classification. *Journal of Experimental Psychology: Learning, Memory, and Cognition, 10*, 104–114.

Novick, L.R. (1988). Analogical transfer, problem similarity, and expertise. *Journal of Experimental Psychology: Learning, Memory, and Cognition, 14*, 510–520.

Oden, G.C. (1987). Concept, knowledge, thought. *Annual Review of Psychology, 38*, 203–227.

Omanson, R.C. (1982). The relation between centrality and story category variation. *Journal of Verbal Learning and Verbal Behavior, 21*, 326–337.

Ortony, A. (1979). Beyond literal similarity. *Psychological Review, 86*, 161–180.

Ortony, A., Clore, G.L., & Collins, A.M. (1988). *The cognitive structure of emotions*. New York: Cambridge University Press.

Ortony, A., & Medin, D.L. (1989). Psychological essentialism. In S. Vosniadou & A. Ortony (Eds.), *Similarity and analogical reasoning* (pp. 179–196). New York: Cambridge University Press.

Osherson, D.N., & Smith, E.E. (1981). On the adequacy of prototype theory as a theory of concepts. *Cognition, 9*, 35–58.

Osherson, D.N., & Smith, E.E. (1982). Gradedness and conceptual combination. *Cognition, 12*, 299–318.

Osherson, D.N., Smith, E.E., Wilkie, O., Lopez, A., & Shafir, E. (1990). Category based induction. *Psychological Review, 97*, 185–200.

Owens, J., Bower, G.H., & Black, J.B. (1979). The "soap opera" effect in story recall. *Memory & Cognition, 7,* 185–191.

Painter, C. (1979). *An introduction to instrumental phonetics.* Baltimore, MD: University Park Press.

Paivio, A. (1971). *Imagery and verbal processes.* New York: Holt, Rinehart & Winston.

Palmer, S.E. (1975a). The effects of contextual scenes on the identification of objects. *Memory & Cognition, 3,* 519–526.

Palmer, S.E. (1975b). Visual perception and world knowledge: Notes on a model of sensory-cognitive interaction. In D.A. Norman, D.E. Rumelhart, & the LNR Research Group, *Explorations in cognition.* San Francisco: Freeman.

Palmer, S.E. (1978). Fundamental aspects of cognitive representation. In E. Rosch & B.B. Lloyd (Eds.), *Cognition and categorization.* Hillsdale, NJ: Lawrence Erlbaum Associates.

Paris, S.G., & Lindauer, B.K. (1976). The role of inference in children's comprehension and memory for sentences. *Cognitive Psychology, 8,* 217–227.

Parsons, L.M. (1987a). Imagined spatial transformations of one's body. *Journal of Experimental Psychology: General, 116,* 172–191.

Parsons, L.M. (1987b). Imagined spatial transformations of one's hands and feet. *Cognitive Psychology, 19,* 178–241.

Penfield, W., & Perot, P. (1963). The brain's record of auditory and visual experience. *Brain, 86,* 595–696.

Perfetti, C.A., & Goldman, S.R. (1976). Discourse memory and reading comprehension skill. *Journal of Verbal Learning and Verbal Behavior, 14,* 33–42.

Peterson, L.R., & Peterson, M.J. (1959). Short term retention of individual verbal items. *Journal of Experimental Psychology, 58,* 193–198.

Pinel, J. (1990). *Biopsychology.* New York: Allyn & Bacon.

Pinker, S., & Prince, A. (1988). On language and connectionism: Analysis of a parallel distributed processing model of language acquisition. *Cognition, 28,* 73–193.

Pisoni, D.B. (1975). Dichotic listening and processing phonetic features. In F. Restle, R.M. Shiffrin, N.J. Castellan, H.R. Lindman, & D.B. Pisoni (Eds.), *Cognitive theory* (Vol. 1, pp. 79–102). Hillsdale, NJ: Lawrence Erlbaum Associates.

Pisoni, D.B., & Luce, P.A. (1987). Acoustic-phonetic representations in word recognition. *Cognition, 25,* 21–52.

Pollack, I., & Pickett, J.M. (1964). Intelligibility of excerpts from fluent speech: Auditory versus structural content. *Journal of Verbal Learning and Verbal Behavior, 3,* 79–84.

Posner, M.I., Boies, S.J., Eichelman, W.H., & Taylor, R.L. (1969). Retention of visual and name codes of single letters. *Journal of Experimental Psychology Monograph, 79* (1, Pt. 2).

Posner, M.I., & Keele, S.W. (1967). Decay of visual information form a single letter. *Science, 158,* 137–139.

Posner, M.I., & Keele, S.W. (1968). On the genesis of abstract ideas. *Journal of Experimental Psychology, 77,* 353–363.

Posner, M.I., Nissen, M.J., & Ogden, W.C. (1978). Attended and unattended processing modes: The role of set for spatial location. In H.L. Pick & E. Saltzman (Eds.), *Modes of perceiving and processing information* (pp. 137–157). Hillsdale, NJ: Lawrence Erlbaum Associates.

Posner, M.I., & Snyder, C.R.R. (1975). Attention and cognitive control. In R.L. Solso (Ed.), *Information processing and cognition.* Hillsdale, NJ: Lawrence Erlbaum Associates.

Posner, M.I., Snyder, C.R.R., & Davidson, B.J. (1980). Attention and the detection of signals. *Journal of Experimental Psychology: General, 109,* 160–174.

Postman, L., & Underwood, B.J. (1973). Critical issues in interference theory. *Memory & Cognition, 1,* 19–40.

Potter, M.C. (1983). Neisser's challenge. *Contemporary Psychology, 28,* 272–274.

Potter, M.C., & Lombardi, L. (1990). Regeneration in the short-term recall of sentences. *Journal of Memory and Language, 29*, 633–654.

Potts, G.R., & Keenan, J.M. (1988). Assessing the occurrence of elaborative inferences: Lexical decision versus naming. *Journal of Memory and Language, 27*, 399–415.

Premack, D. (1976). Language and intelligence in ape and man. *American Scientist, 64*, 674–683.

Premack, D., & Woodruff, G. (1978). Chimpanzee problem solving: A test for comprehension. *Science, 202*, 532–535.

Puff, C.R. (1970). Role of clustering in free recall. *Journal of Experimental Psychology, 86*, 384–386.

Putnam, H. (1970). Is semantics possible? In H.E. Keifer & M.K. Munitz (Eds.), *Language, belief, and metaphysics* (pp. 50–63). New York: State University of New York Press.

Putnam, H. (1973). Meaning and reference. *Journal of Philosophy, 70*, 699–711.

Putnam, H. (1975). The meaning of "meaning." In H. Putnam, *Mind, language, and reality: Philosophical papers* (Vol. 2, pp. 215–271). New York: Cambridge University Press.

Pylyshyn, Z.W. (1973). What the mind's eye tells the mind's brain: A critique of mental imagery. *Psychological Bulletin, 80*, 1–24.

Pylyshyn, Z.W. (1981). The imagery debate: Analogue media versus tacit knowledge. *Psychological Review, 88*, 16–45.

Pylyshyn, Z.W. (1984). *Computation and cognition: Toward a foundation for cognitive science.* Cambridge, MA: Bradford Books, MIT Press.

Quillian, M.R. (1968). Semantic memory. In M.L. Minsky (Ed.), *Semantic information processing.* Cambridge, MA: MIT Press.

Quine, W.Van O. (1969). Natural kinds. In N. Rescher (Ed.), *Essays in honor of Carl G. Hempel* (pp. 5–23). Dordrecht: Reidel.

Quine, W.Van O. (1972). *Methods of logic.* New York: Holt Rinehart, & Winston.

Rabin, M.D., & Cain, W.S. (1984). Odor recognition: Familiarity, identifiability, and encoding consistency. *Journal of Experimental Psychology: Learning, Memory, and Cognition, 10*, 316–325.

Rachlin, H. (1970). *Introduction to modern behaviorism.* San Francisco: Freeman.

Rasmussen, J. (1986). *Information processing and human-machine interaction: An approach to cognitive engineering.* New York: North-Holland.

Ratcliff, R. (1978). A theory of memory retrieval. *Psychological Review, 85*, 59–108.

Ratcliff, R., & McKoon, G. (1978). Priming in item recognition: Evidence for the propositional structure of sentences. *Journal of Verbal Learning and Verbal Behavior, 17*, 403–417.

Ratcliff, R., & McKoon, G. (1988). A retrieval theory of priming. *Psychological Review, 95*, 385–316.

Rayner, K. (Ed.). (1983). *Eye movements in reading: Perceptual and language processes.* New York: Academic.

Rayner, K., Carlson, M., & Frazier, L. (1983). The interaction of syntax and semantics during sentence processing: Eye movements in the analysis of semantically biased sentences. *Journal of Verbal Learning and Verbal Behavior, 22*, 358–374.

Read, S.J., Jones, D.K., & Miller, L.C. (1990). Traits as goal-based categories: The importance of goals in the coherence of dispositional categories. *Journal of Personality and Social Psychology, 58*, 1048–1061.

Reber, A.S. (1973). What clicks may tell us about speech perception. *Journal of Psycholinguistic Research, 2*, 287–288.

Reber, A.S. (1985). *The Penguin dictionary of psychology.* New York: Viking Penguin.

Reddy, D.R. (Ed.). (1975). *Speech recognition.* New York: Academic.

Reddy, D.R. (1980). Machine models of speech perception. In R.A. Cole (Ed.), *Perception and production of fluent speech.* Hillsdale, NJ: Lawrence Erlbaum Associates.

Reder, L.M. (1982). Plausibility judgment versus fact retrieval: Alternative strategies for sentence verification. *Psychological Review, 89,* 250–280.

Reder, L.M. (1987). Strategy selection in question answering. *Cognitive Psychology, 19,* 90–138.

Reder, L.M., & Ross, B.H. (1983). Integrated knowledge in different tasks: Positive and negative fan effects. *Journal of Experimental Psychology: Human Learning and Memory, 8,* 55–72.

Reed, S.K. (1972). Pattern recognition and categorization. *Cognitive Psychology, 3,* 382–407.

Reed, S.K. (1988). *Cognition: Theory and applications* (2nd ed.). Pacific Grove, CA: Brooks-Cole.

Reicher, G.M. (1969). Perceptual recognition as a funciton of the meaningfulness of the stimulus material. *Journal of Experimental Psychology, 81,* 275–280.

Reisberg, D., Baron, J., & Kemler, D.G. (1980). Overcoming Stroop interference: The effects of practice on distractor potency. *Journal of Experimental Psychology: Human Perception and Performance, 6,* 140–150.

Reitman, J.S. (1971). Mechanisms of forgetting in short-term memory. *Cognitive Psychology, 2,* 185–195.

Reitman, J.S. (1974). Without surreptitious rehearsal, information in short-term memory decays. *Journal of Verbal Learning and Verbal Behavior, 13,* 365–377.

Reitman, J.S. (1976). Skilled performance in Go: Deducing memory structures form inter-response times. *Cognitive Psychology, 8,* 336–356.

Reitman, J.S., & Bower, G.H. (1973). Storage and later recognition of exemplars of concepts. *Cognitive Psychology, 4,* 194–206.

Remington, R.W. (1980). Attention and saccadic eye movements. *Journal of Experimental Psychology: Human Perception and Performance, 6,* 726–744.

Repp, B., & Liberman, A.M. (1987). Phonetic category boundaries are flexible. In S. Harnad (Ed.), *Categorical perception: The groundwork of cognition* (pp. 89–112). New York: Cambridge University Press.

Revlis, R. (1975). Syllogistic reasoning: Logical decisions from a complex data base. In R.J. Falmagne (Ed.), *Reasoning: Representation and process in children and adults* (pp. 93–133). Hillsdale, NJ: Lawrence Erlbaum Associates.

Rey, G. (1983). Concepts and stereotypes. *Cognition, 15,* 237–262.

Rifken, A. (1985). Evidence for a basic level in event taxonomies. *Memory & Cognition, 13,* 538–556.

Rips, L.J. (1975). Inductive judgments about natural categories. *Journal of Verbal Learning and Verbal Behavior, 14,* 665–681.

Rips, L.J. (1986). Mental muddles. In M. Brand & R.H. Harnish (Eds.), *The representation of knowledge and belief* (pp. 258–286). Tucson, AZ: University of Arizona Press.

Rips, L.J. (1988). Deduction. In R.J. Sternberg & E.E. Smith (Eds.), *The psychology of human thought* (pp. 116–154). New York: Cambridge University Press.

Rips, L.J. (1989). Similarity, typicality, and categorization. In S. Vosniadou & A. Ortony (Eds.), *Similarity and analogical reasoning* (pp. 21–59). New York: Cambridge University Press.

Rips, L.J., & Conrad, F.G. (1989). Folk psychology of mental activities. *Psychological Review, 96,* 187–207.

Rips, L.J., Shoben, E.J., & Smith, E.E. (1973). Semantic distance and the verification of semantic relations. *Journal of Verbal Learning and Verbal Behavior, 12,* 1–20.

Rips, L.J., & Turnbull, W. (1980). How big is big? Relative and absolute properties in memory. *Cognition, 8,* 145–174.

Robinson, P.W. (1981). *Fundamentals of experimental psychology* (2nd ed.). Englewood Cliffs, NJ: Prentice-Hall.

Roediger, H.L., III, & Neely, J.H. (1982). Retrieval blocks in episodic and semantic memory. *Canadian Journal of Psychology, 36,* 213–242.

Roediger, H.L., III, Neely, J.H., Blaxton, T.A. (1983). Inhibition from related primes in semantic memory retrieval: A reappraisal of Brown's (1979) paradigm. *Journal of Experimental Psychology: Learning, Memory, and Cognition, 9,* 478–485.

Rosch, E. (1974). Linguistic relativity. In A. Silverstein (Ed.), *Human communication: Theoretical perspectives* (pp. 95–121). New York: Halsted.

Rosch, E. (1978). Principles of categorization. In E. Rosch & B. Lloyd (Eds.), *Cognition and categorization.* Hillsdale, NJ: Lawrence Erlbaum Associates.

Rosch, E., & Mervis, C.B. (1975). Family resemblances: Studies in the internal structure of categories. *Cognitive Psychology, 7,* 573–605.

Rosch, E., Mervis, C.B., Gray, W.D., Johnson, D.M., & Boyes-Braem, P. (1976). Basic objects in natural categories. *Cognitive Psychology, 8,* 382–439.

Rosenbaum, D.A. (1990). *Human motor control.* New York: Academic.

Rosenthal, R., & Rosnow, R.L. (1984). *Essentials of behavioral research: Methods and data analysis.* New York: McGraw-Hill.

Ross, B.H. (1984). Remindings and their effects in learning a cognitive task. *Cognitive Psychology, 16,* 371–416.

Ross, B.H. (1987). This is like that: The use of earlier problems and the separation of similarity effects. *Journal of Experimental Psychology: Learning, Memory, and Cognition, 13,* 629–639.

Ross, B.H. (1989a). Distinguishing types of superficial similarities: Different effects on the access and use of earlier problems. *Journal of Experimental Psychology: Learning, Memory, and Cognition, 15,* 456–468.

Ross, B.H. (1989b). Remindings in learning and instruction. In S. Vosniadou & A. Ortony (Eds.), *Similarity and analogical reasoning* (pp. 438–469). New York: Cambridge University Press.

Ross, B.H., & Kennedy, P.T. (1990). Generalizing from the use of earlier examples in problem solving. *Journal of Experimental Psychology: Learning, Memory, and Cognition, 16,* 42–55.

Roth, E.M., & Shoben, E.J. (1983). The effect of context on the structure of categories. *Cognitive Psychology, 15,* 346–378.

Rouse, W.B., & Morris, N.M. (1986). On looking into the black box: Prospects and limits in the search for mental models. *Psychological Bulletin, 100,* 349–363.

Rubenstein, H., Lewis, S.S., & Rubenstein, M.A. (1971). Homographic entries in the internal lexicon: Effects of systematicity and relative frequency of meanings. *Journal of Verbal Learning and Verbal Behavior, 10,* 57–62.

Rubin, D.C. (Ed.). (1987). *Autobiographical memory.* New York: Cambridge University Press.

Rubin, D.C. (1988). Learning poetic language. In F.S. Kessel (Ed.), *The development of language and language researchers: Essays in honor of Roger Brown.* Hillsdale, NJ: Lawrence Erlbaum Associates.

Rubin, G.S., Becker, C.A., & Freeman, R.H. (1979). Morphological structure and its effect on visual word recognition. *Journal of Verbal Learning and Verbal Behavior, 18,* 757–767.

Rumelhart, D.E., & McClelland, J.L. (1982). An interactive activation model of context effects in letter perception: Part 2. The contextual enhancement effect and some tests and extensions of the model. *Psychological Review, 89,* 60–94.

Rumelhart, D.E., McClelland, J.L., & the PDP Research Group (1986). *Parallel distributed processing: Explorations in the microstructure of cognition: Vol 1. Foundations.* Cambridge, MA: MIT Press.

Rumelhart, D.E., & Norman, D.A. (1978). Accretion, tuning, and restructuring: Three modes of learning. In J.W. Cotton & R.L. Klatzky (Eds.), *Semantic factors in cognition* (pp. 37–53). Hillsdale, NJ: Lawrence Erlbaum Associates.

Rumelhart, D.E., & Norman, D.A. (1982). Simulating a skilled typist: A study of skilled cognitive-motor performance. *Cognitive Science, 6,* 1–36.

Rumelhart, D.E., & Norman, D.A. (1988). Representation in memory. In R.C. Atkinson, R.J. Herrnstein, G. Lindzey, & R.D. Luce (Eds.), *Stevens' handbook of experimental psychology: Vol. 2. Learning and cognition* (pp. 511–587). New York: Wiley.

Rumelhart, D.E., & Ortony, A. (1978). The representation of knowledge in memory. In R.C. Anderson, R.J. Spiro, & W.E. Montague (Eds.), *Schooling and the acquisition of knowledge.* Hillsdale, NJ: Lawrence Erlbaum Associates.

Rundus, D. (1971). Analysis of rehearsal processes in free recall. *Journal of Experimental Psychology, 89,* 63–77.

Rundus, D. (1973). Negative effects of using list items as recall cues. *Journal of Verbal Learning and Verbal Behavior, 12,* 43–50.

Sachs, J.D.S. (1967). Recognition memory for syntactic and semantic aspects of connected discourse. *Perception & Psychophysics, 2,* 437–442.

Sachs, J.D.S. (1974). Memory in reading and listening to discourse. *Memory & Cognition, 2,* 95–100.

Salmon, V. (1969). [Review of *Cartesian linguistics* by N. Chomsky]. *Journal of Linguistics, 5,* 165–187.

Samuel, A.G. (1981). Phonemic restoration: Insights from a new methodology. *Journal of Experimental Psychology: General, 110,* 474–494.

Samuel, A.G. (1987). Lexical uniqueness effects on phonemic restoration. *Journal of Memory and Language, 26,* 36–56.

Sapir, E. (1968). Language and environment. In D.G. Mandelbaum (Ed.), *Selected writings of Edward Sapir in language, culture, and personality.* Berkeley, CA: University of California Press.

Savage-Rumbaugh, E.S., Rumbaugh, D.M., & Boysen, S. (1980). Do apes use language? *American Scientist, 68,* 49–61.

Scarborough, D.L., Cortese, C., & Scarborough, H.S. (1977). Frequency and repetition effects in lexical memory. *Journal of Experimental Psychology: Human Perception and Performance, 3,* 1–17.

Schank, R.C. (1975). *Conceptual information processing.* Amsterdam: North-Holland.

Schank, R.C. (1982). *Dynamic memory: A theory of reminding and learning in computers and people.* New York: Cambridge University Press.

Schank, R.C., & Abelson, R.P. (1977). *Scripts, plans, goals, and understanding: An inquiry into human knowledge structures.* Hillsdale, NJ: Lawrence Erlbaum Associates.

Schank, R.C., Collins, G.C., & Hunter, L.E. (1986). Transcending inductive category formation in learning. *The Behavioral and Brain Sciences, 9,* 639–651.

Schieber, S.M. (1986). *An introduction to unification-based approaches to grammar.* Stanford, CA: Center for the Study of Language and Information.

Schneider, W., & Shiffrin, R.M. (1977). Controlled and automatic human information processing: I. Detection, search and attention. *Psychological Review, 84,* 1–66.

Schober, M.F., & Clark, H.H. (1989). Understanding by addressees and overhearers. *Cognitive Psychology, 21,* 211–232.

Schoenfield, J.R. (1973). *Mathematical logic.* Reading, MA: Addison-Wesley.

Schuberth, R.E., & Eimas, P.D. (1977). Effects of context on the classification of words and nonwords. *Journal of Experimental Psychology: Human Perception and Performance, 3,* 27–36.

Schwanenflugel, P.J. (1991). Why are abstract concepts hard to understand? In P.J. Schwanenflugel (Ed.), *The psychology of word meanings.* Hillsdale, NJ: Lawrence Erlbaum Associates.

Schwanenflugel, P.J., Akin, C., & Luh, W.M. (in press). Context availability and the recall of abstract and concrete words. *Memory & Cognition.*

Schwanenflugel, P.J., Harnishfeger, K.K., & Stowe, R.W. (1988). Context availability and lexical decisions for abstract and concrete words. *Journal of Memory and Language, 27,* 499–520.

Schwanenflugel, P.J., & Rey, M. (1986). The relationship between category typicality and concept familiarity: Evidence from Spanish- and English-speaking monolinguals. *Memory & Cognition, 14,* 150–163.

Schwanenflugel, P.J., & Shoben, E.J. (1983). Differential context effects in the comprehension of abstract and concrete verbal materials. *Journal of Experimental Psychology: Learning, Memory, and Cognition, 9,* 82–102.

Schwanenflugel, P.J., & Stowe, R.W. (1989). Context availability and the processing of abstract and concrete words in sentences. *Reading Research Quarterly, 24,* 114–126.

Searle, J.R. (1969). *Speech acts.* New York: Cambridge University Press.

Segal, S.J., & Fusella, V. (1970). Influence of imaged pictures and sounds in detection of visual and auditory signals. *Journal of Experimental Psychology, 83,* 458–474.

Segalowitz, S.J. (Ed.). (1983). *Language functions and brain organization.* New York: Academic.

Seidenberg, M.S., & McClelland, J.L. (1989). A distributed, developmental model of word recognition and naming. *Psychological Review, 96,* 523–568.

Seidenberg, M.S., & Tanenhaus, M.K. (1979). Orthographic effects on rhyme monitoring. *Journal of Experimental Psychology: Human Learning and Memory, 5,* 546–554.

Seidenberg, M.S., Tanenhaus, M.K., Leiman, J.M., & Bienkowski, M. (1982). Automatic access of the meanings of ambiguous words in context: Some limitations of knowledge-based processing. *Cognitive Psychology, 14,* 489–537.

Sekular, R., & Blake, R. (1990). *Perception* (2nd ed.). New York: McGraw-Hill.

Seligman, M.E.P. (1970). On the generality of the laws of learning. *Psychological Review, 77,* 406–418.

Shaklee, H., & Fischoff, B. (1982). Strategies of information search in causal displays. *Memory & Cognition, 10,* 520–530.

Shaklee, H., & Tucker, D. (1980). A rule analysis of judgments of covariation between events. *Memory & Cognition, 8,* 459–467.

Shallice, T. (1988). *From neuropsychology to mental structure.* New York: Cambridge University Press.

Shannon, C.E., & Weaver, W. (1949). *The mathematical theory of communications.* Urbana: University of Illinois Press.

Sharkey, N.E., & Mitchell, D.C. (1985). Word recognition in a functional context: The use of scripts in reading. *Journal of Memory and Language, 24,* 253–270.

Shattuck-Hufnagel, S. (1987). The role of word-onset consonants in speech production planning: New evidence from speech error patterns. In E. Keller & M. Gopnik (Ed.), *Motor and sensory processes of language* (pp. 17–51). Hillsdale, NJ: Lawrence Erlbaum Associates.

Shaver, K.G. (1987). *Principles of social psychology.* Hillsdale, NJ: Lawrence Erlbaum Associates.

Shaw, M., & Shaw, P. (1977). Optimal allocation of cognitive resources to spatial location. *Journal of Experimental Psychology: Human Perception and Performance, 12,* 383–387.

Sheldon, A. (1974). The role of parallel function in the acquisition of relative clauses in English. *Journal of Verbal Learning and Verbal Behavior, 13,* 272–281.

Shepard, R.N. (1962a). The analysis of proximities: Multidimensional scaling with an unknown distance function. Part I. *Psychometrika, 27,* 125–140.

Shepard, R.N. (1962b). The analysis of proximities: Multidimensional scaling with an unknown distance function. Part II. *Psychometrika, 27,* 219–246.

Shepard, R.N. (1967). Recognition memory for words, sentences, and pictures. *Journal of Verbal Learning and Verbal Behavior, 6,* 156–163.

Shepard, R.N. (1972). Psychological representation of speech sounds. In E.E. David & P.B. Denes (Eds.), *Human communication: A unified view* (pp. 67–113). New York: McGraw-Hill.

Shepard, R.N. (1974). Representation of structure in similarity data: Problems and prospects. *Psychometrika, 39,* 373–421.

Shepard, R.N. (1980). Multidimensional scaling, tree-fitting, and clustering. *Science, 210,* 390–398.

Shepard, R.N., & Cooper, L.A. (1982). *Mental images and their transformations.* New York: Cambridge University Press.

Shepard, R.N., & Metzler, J. (1971). Mental rotation of three-dimensional objects. *Science, 171,* 701–703.

Shepard, R.N., & Podgorny, P. (1978). Cognitive processes that resemble perceptual processes. In W.K. Estes (Ed.), *Handbook of learning and cognitive processes* (Vol. 5). Hillsdale, NJ: Lawrence Erlbaum Associates.

Shiffrin, R.M. (1988). Attention. In R.C. Atkinson, R.J. Herrnstein, G. Lindzey, & R.D. Luce (Eds.), *Stevens' handbook of experimental psychology: Vol. 2. Learning and cognition* (pp. 739–811). New York: Wiley.

Shiffrin, R.M., & Schneider, W. (1977). Controlled and automatic information processing: II. Perceptual learning, automatic attending, and a general theory. *Psychological Review, 84,* 127–190.

Shulman, G.L., Remington, R.W., & McLean, J.P. (1979). Moving attention through visual space. *Journal of Experimental Psychology: Human Perception and Performance, 5,* 522–526.

Shulman, H.G. (1970). Encoding and retention of semantic and phonemic information in short-term memory. *Journal of Verbal Learning and Verbal Behavior, 9,* 499–508.

Shulman, H.G. (1971). Similarity effects in short-term memory. *Psychological Bulletin, 75,* 399–415.

Shustack, M.W. (1988). Thinking about causality. In R.J. Sternberg & E.E. Smith (Eds.), *The psychology of human thought* (pp. 92–115). New York: Cambridge University Press.

Shustack, M.W., & Sternberg, R.J. (1981). Evaluation of evidence in causal inference. *Journal of Experimental Psychology: General, 110,* 101–120.

Siegler, R.S. (1986). *Children's thinking.* Englewood Cliffs, NJ: Prentice-Hall.

Singer, M. (1981). Verifying the assertions and implications of language. *Journal of Verbal Learning and Verbal Behavior, 20,* 46–60.

Skinner, B.F. (1953). *Science and human behavior.* New York: Macmillan.

Skinner, B.F. (1957). *Verbal behavior.* New York: Appleton-Century-Crofts.

Slamecka, N.J., & Graf, P. (1978). The generation effect: Delineation of a phenomenon. *Journal of Experimental Psychology: Learning, Memory, and Cognition, 4,* 592–604.

Slobin, D.I. (Ed.). (1985). *The cross-linguistic study of language acquisition.* Hillsdale, NJ: Lawrence Erlbaum Associates.

Slovic, P., Lichtenstein, S., & Fischoff, B. (1988). Decision making. In R.C. Atkinson, R.J. Herrnstein, G. Lindzey, & R.D. Luce (Eds.), *Stevens' handbook of experimental psychology: Vol. 2. Learning and cognition* (pp. 673–738). New York: Wiley.

Slowiaczek, M.L., & Clifton, C. (1980). Subvocalization and reading for meaning. *Journal of Verbal Learning and Verbal Behavior, 19,* 573–582.

Smith, E.E. (1978). Theories of semantic memory. In W.K. Estes (Ed.), *Handbook of learning and cognitive processes* (Vol. 6). Hillsdale, NJ: Lawrence Erlbaum Associates.

Smith, E.E. (1990). Categorization. In D.N. Osherson & E.E. Smith (Eds.), *An invitation to cognitive science* (Vol. 3). Cambridge, MA: MIT Press.

Smith, E.E., & Medin, D.L. (1981). *Categories and concepts.* Cambridge, MA: Harvard University Press.

Smith, E.E., Medin, D.L., & Rips, L.J. (1984). A psychological approach to concepts: Comments on Rey's "Concepts and stereotypes." *Cognition, 17,* 265–274.

Smith, E.E., & Osherson, D.N. (1989). Similarity and decision making. In S. Vosniadou & A. Ortony (Eds.), *Similarity and analogical reasoning* (pp. 60–75). New York: Cambridge University Press.

Smith, E.E., Osherson, D.N., Rips, L.J., & Keane, M. (1988). Combining prototypes: A selective modification model. *Cognitive Science, 12,* 485–528.

Smith, E.E., Shoben, E.J., & Rips, L.J. (1974). Structure and process in semantic memory: A featural model for semantic decisions. *Psychological Review, 81,* 214–241.

Smith, E.E., & Spoehr, K.T. (1974). The perception of printed English: A theoretical perspective. In B.H. Kantowitz (Ed.), *Human information processing: Tutorials in performance and cognition.* Hillsdale, NJ: Lawrence Erlbaum Associates.

Smith, F. (1971). *Understanding reading: A psycholinguistic analysis of reading and learning to read.* New York: Holt, Rinehart & Winston.

Smith, S.B. (1983). *The great mental calculators: The psychology, methods, and lives of calculating prodigies, past and present.* New York: Columbia University Press.

Smith, S.M. (1979). Remembering in and out of context. *Journal of Experimental Psychology: Human Learning and Memory, 5,* 460–471.

Smith, S.M. (1982). Enhancement of recall using multiple environmental contexts during learning. *Memory & Cognition, 10,* 405–412.

Smith, S.M. (1986). Environmental context-dependent recognition memory using a short-term memory task for input. *Memory & Cognition, 14,* 347–354.

Snowdon, C.T., Brown, C.H., & Peterson, M.R. (Eds.). (1982). *Primate communication.* New York: Cambridge University Press.

Solso, R.L. (1988). *Cognitive psychology* (2nd ed.). Boston: Allyn & Bacon.

Sommers, F. (1959). The ordinary language tree. *Mind, 68,* 160–185.

Sommers, F. (1963). Types and ontology. *Philosophical Review, 72,* 327–363.

Sperling, G. (1960). The information available in brief visual presentations. *Psychological Monographs, 74* (No. 11).

Spilich, G.J., Vesonder, G.T., Chiesi, H.L., & Voss, J.F. (1979). Text processing of domain-related information for individuals with high- and low-domain knowledge. *Journal of Verbal Learning and Verbal Behavior, 18,* 275–290.

Squire, L.R. (1987). *Memory and brain.* New York: Oxford University Press.

Squire, L.R., & Butters, N. (Eds.) (1984). *Neuropsychology of memory.* New York: Guilford.

Sroufe, L.A., & Cooper, R.G. (1988). *Child development: Its nature and course.* New York: Knopf.

Standing, L., Conezio, K., & Haber, R.N. (1970). Perception and memory for pictures: single-trial learning of 2560 visual stimuli. *Psychonomic Science, 19,* 73–74.

Stanners, R.F., Neiser, J.J., & Painton, S. (1979). Memory representation for prefixed words. *Journal of Verbal Learning and Verbal Behavior, 18,* 733–743.

Stanovich, K.E., & Bauer, D. (1978). Experiments on the spelling-to-sound regularity effect in word recognition. *Memory & Cognition, 6,* 115–123.

Stanovich, K.E., & West, R.F. (1981). The effect of sentence context on ongoing word recognition: Tests of a two-process theory. *Journal of Experimental Psychology: Human Perception and Performance, 7,* 658–672.

Stanovich, K.E., & West, R.F. (1983). On priming with a sentence context. *Journal of Experimental Psychology: General, 112,* 1–36.

Stein, N.L., & Glenn, C.G. (1979). An analysis of story comprehension in elementary school children. In R.O. Freedle (Ed.), *New directions in discourse processes.* Norwood, NJ: Ablex.

Stemberger, J.P. (1985). An interactive activation model of language production. In A. Ellis (Ed.), *Progress in the psychology of language* (Vol 1, pp. 143–186). Hillsdale, NJ: Lawrence Erlbaum Associates.

Sternberg, S. (1966). High-speed scanning in human memory. *Science, 153,* 652–654.

Sternberg, S. (1969a). The discovery of processing stages: Extensions of Donders' method. In W.G. Koster (Ed.), *Attention and performance II* [Special issue]. *Acta Psychologica, 30,* 276–315.

Sternberg, S. (1969b). Memory scanning: mental processes revealed by reaction time experiments. *American Scientist, 57,* 421–457.

Sternberg, S. (1975). Memory scanning: New findings and current controversies. *Quarterly Journal of Experimental Psychology, 27,* 1–32.

Stevens, S.S. (1975). *Psychophysics: Introduction to its perceptual, neural, and social prospects.* New York: Wiley.

Stigler, J.W., Shweder, R.A., & Herdt, G. (Eds.). (1990). *Cultural psychology: Essays on comparative human development.* New York: Cambridge University Press.

Stroop, J.R. (1935). Studies on interference in serial verbal reactions. *Journal of Experimental Psychology, 18,* 643–662.

Sulin, R.A., & Dooling, D.J. (1974). Intrusion of a thematic idea in retention of prose. *Journal of Experimental Psychology, 103,* 255–262.

Sutherland, N.J., & Mackintosh, N.S. (1971). *Mechanisms of animal discrimination learning.* New York: Academic.

Swinney, D.A. (1979). Lexical access during sentence comprehension: (Re)consideration of context effects. *Journal of Verbal Learning and Verbal Behavior, 18,* 645–659.

Taft, M., & Forster, K.I. (1975). Lexical storage and retrieval of prefixed words. *Journal of Verbal Learning and Verbal Behavior, 14,* 638–647.

Taft, M., & Forster, K.I. (1976). Lexical storage and retrieval of polymorphemic and polysyllabic words. *Journal of Verbal Learning and Verbal Behavior, 15,* 607–620.

Tanenhaus, M.K., Boland, J., Garnsey, S.M., & Carlson, G.N. (1989). Lexical structure in parsing long-distance dependencies. *Journal of Psycholinguistic Research, 18,* 37–49.

Tanenhaus, M.K., Leiman, J.M., & Seidenberg, M.S. (1979). Evidence for multiple stages in the processing of ambiguous words in syntactic contexts. *Journal of Verbal Learning and Verbal Behavior, 18,* 427–440.

Tanenhaus, M.K., & Lucas, M.M. (1987). Context effects in lexical processing. *Cognition, 25,* 213–234.

Taraban, R., & McClelland, J.L. (1988). Constituent attachment and thematic role assignment in sentence processing: Influences on content-based expectations. *Journal of Memory and Language, 27,* 597–632.

Tartter, V.C. (1986). *Language processes.* New York: Holt, Rinehart & Winston.

Terrace, H.S., Petitto, L.A., Sanders, R.J., & Bever, T.G. (1979). Can an ape create a sentence? *Science, 206,* 891–902.

Thagard, P. (1988). *Computational philosophy of science.* Cambridge, MA: MIT Press.

Thibadeau, R., Just, M.A., & Carpenter, P.A. (1982). A model of the time course and content of reading. *Cognitive Science, 6,* 157–203.

Thomson, D.M., & Tulving, E. (1970). Associative encoding and retrieval: Weak and strong cues. *Journal of Experimental Psychology, 86,* 255–262.

Thorndyke, P.W. (1976). The role of inferences in discourse comprehension. *Journal of Verbal Learning and Verbal Behavior, 15,* 437–446.

Thorndyke, P.W. (1977). Cognitive structures in comprehension and memory of narrative discourse. *Cognitive Psychology, 9,* 77–110.

Thorndyke, P.W., & Hayes-Roth, B. (1979). The use of schemata in the acquisition and transfer of knowledge. *Cognitive Psychology, 11,* 82–106.

Titchener, E.B. (1910). *A textbook of psychology.* New York: Macmillan.

Toulmin, S. (1961). *Foresight and understanding: An enquiry into the aims of science.* New York: Harper & Row.

Townsend, D.J., & Bever, T.G. (1978). Interclause relations and clausal processing. *Journal of Verbal Learning and Verbal Behavior, 17,* 509–522.

Townsend, J.T. (1971). A note on the identifiability of parallel and serial processes. *Perception & Psychophysics, 10,* 161–163.

Townsend, J.T. (1990). Serial vs. parallel processing: Sometimes they look like Tweedledum and Tweedledee but they can (and should) be distinguished. *Psychological Science, 1,* 46–54.

Trabasso, T.R., & Bower, G.H. (1968). *Attention in learning.* New York: Wiley.

Treisman, A.M. (1969). Strategies and models of selective attention. *Psychological Review, 76,* 282–299.

Treisman, A.M. (1982). Perceptual grouping and attention in visual search for features and objects. *Journal of Experimental Psychology: Human Perception and Performance, 8,* 194–214.

Treisman, A.M., & Gelade, G. (1980). A feature integration theory of attention. *Cognitive Psychology, 12*, 97–136.

Tsal, Y. (1983). Movements of attention across the visual field. *Journal of Experimental Psychology: Human Perception and Performance, 9*, 523–530.

Tulving, E. (1962). Subjective organization in free recall of "unrelated" words. *Psychological Review, 69*, 344–354.

Tulving, E. (1964). Intratrial and intertrial retention: Notes toward a theory of free recall verbal learning. *Psychological Review, 71*, 219–237.

Tulving, E. (1966). Subjective organization and the effects of repetition in multi-trial free recall verbal learning. *Journal of Verbal Learning and Verbal Behavior, 5*, 193–197.

Tulving, E. (1972). Episodic and semantic memory. In E. Tulving & W. Donaldson (Eds.), *Organization and memory* (pp. 381–403). New York: Academic.

Tulving, E. (1976). Ecphoric processes in recall and recognition. In J. Brown (Ed.), *Recall and recognition*. New York: Wiley.

Tulving, E. (1983). *Elements of episodic memory*. New York: Oxford University Press.

Tulving, E. (1984). Precis of *Elements of episodic memory*. *The Behavioral and Brain Sciences, 7*, 223–268.

Tulving, E., Mandler, G., & Baumal, R. (1964). Interaction of two sources of information in tachistoscopic word recognition. *Canadian Journal of Psychology, 18*, 62–71.

Tulving, E., & Pearlstone, Z. (1966). Availability versus accessibility of information in memory for words. *Journal of Verbal Learning and Verbal Behavior, 5*, 381–391.

Tulving, E., & Thomson, D.M. (1973). Encoding specificity and retrieval processes in episodic memory. *Psychological Review, 80*, 352–373.

Tune, G.S. (1964). Response preferences: A review of some relevant literature. *Psychological Bulletin, 61*, 286–302.

Tversky, A. (1977). Features of similarity. *Psychological Review, 84*, 327–352.

Tversky, A., & Hutchinson, J.W. (1986). Nearest neighbor analysis of psychological spaces. *Psychological Review, 93*, 3–22.

Tversky, A., & Kahneman, D. (1973). Availability: A heuristic for judging frequency and probability. *Cognitive Psychology, 5*, 207–232.

Tversky, A., & Kahneman, D. (1980). Causal schemas in judgments under uncertainty. In M. Fishbein (Ed.), *Progress in social psychology* (Vol. 1, pp. 49–72). Hillsdale, NJ: Lawrence Erlbaum Associates.

Tversky, A., & Kahneman, D. (1982). Evidential impact of base rates. In D. Kahneman, P. Slovic, & A. Tversky (Eds.), *Judgment under uncertainty: Heuristics and biases* (pp. 153–162). New York: Cambridge University Press.

Tversky, A., & Kahneman, D. (1983). Extensional versus intuitive reasoning: The conjunction fallacy in probability judgment. *Psychological Review, 90*, 293–315.

Tversky, B. (1973). Encoding processes in recognition and recall. *Cognitive Psychology, 5*, 275–287.

Tversky, B., & Hemenway, K. (1983). Categories of environmental scenes. *Cognitive Psychology, 15*, 121–149.

Tversky, B., & Hemenway, K. (1985). Objects, parts, and categories. *Journal of Experimental Psychology: General, 113*, 169–193.

Tyler, L.K., & Marslen-Wilson, W.D. (1977). The on-line effects of semantic context on syntactic processing. *Journal of Verbal Learning and Verbal Behavior, 16*, 683–692.

van Dijk, T.A., & Kintsch, W. (1983). *Strategies of discourse comprehension*. New York: Academic.

Von Eckardt, B., & Potter, M.C. (1985). Clauses and the semantic representation of words. *Memory & Cognition, 13*, 371–376.

von Frisch, K. (1974). Decoding the language of the bee. *Science, 185*, 663–668.

Von Wright, J.M., Anderson, K., & Steman, W. (1975). Generalization of conditioned GSRs in dichotic listening. In P.M.A. Rabbitt & S. Dornic (Eds.), *Attention and performance V.* London: Academic.

Vosniadou, S., & Ortony. A. (Eds.). (1989). *Similarity and analogical reasoning.* New York: Cambridge University Press.

Waldrop, M.W. (1987). The workings of working memory. *Science, 237*, 1564–1567.

Wallace, W.T., & Rubin, D.C. (1988a). Memory of a ballad singer. In M.M Gruenberg, P.E. Morris, & R.N. Sykes (Eds.), *Practical aspects of memory: Current research and issues: Vol. 1. Memory in everyday life* (pp. 257–262). New York: Wiley.

Wallace, W.T., & Rubin, D.C. (1988b). The wreck of the old 97: A real event remembered in song. In U. Neisser & E. Winograd (Eds.), *Remembering reconsidered: Ecological and traditional approaches to the study of memory* (pp. 283–310). New York: Cambridge University Press.

Wanner, E. (1974). *On remembering, forgetting, and understanding sentences.* The Hague: Mouton.

Wanner, E. (1980). The ATN and the sausage machine: Which one is baloney? *Cognition, 8*, 209–225.

Warren, R.M. (1970). Perceptual restoration of missing speech sounds. *Science, 167*, 392–393.

Warren, R.M., Obusek, C., & Akroff, J.M. (1972). Auditory induction: Perceptual synthesis of absent sounds. *Science, 196*, 1149–1151.

Warren, R.M., & Warren, R.P. (1970). Auditory illusions and confusions. *Scientific American, 223*, 30–36.

Wason, P.C., & Johnson-Laird, P.N. (1972). *Psychology of reasoning: Structure and content.* Cambridge, MA: Harvard University Press.

Watkins, M.J., & Kerkar, S.P. (1985). Recall of a twice-presented item without recall of either presentation: Generic memory for events. *Journal of Memory and Language, 24*, 666–678.

Watson, J.B. (1930). *Behaviorism.* New York: Norton.

Wattenmaker, W.D., Dewey, G.I., Murphy, T.D., & Medin, D.L. (1986). Linear separability and concept learning: Context, relational properties, and concept naturalness. *Cognitive Psychology, 18*, 158–194.

Waugh, N.C., & Norman, D.A. (1965). Primary memory. *Psychological Review, 72*, 89–104.

Wellman, H.M., & Gelman, S.A. (1988). Children's understanding of the non-obvious. In R. Sternberg (Ed.), *Advances in the psychology of human intelligence* (pp. 99–135). Hillsdale, NJ: Lawrence Erlbaum Associates.

Wertheimer, M. (1982). *Productive thinking.* Chicago: University of Chicago Press. (Original work published 1945)

Wheeler, D.D. (1970). Processes in word recognition. *Cognitive Psychology, 1*, 59–85.

Whitney, P., McKay, T., & Kellas, G. (1985). Semantic activation of noun concepts in context. *Journal of Experimental Psychology: Learning, Memory, and Cognition, 11*, 126–135.

Whorf, B. (1956). *Language, thought, and reality.* Cambridge, MA: MIT Press.

Wickelgren, W.A. (1965). Acoustic similarity and retroactive interference in short-term memory. *Journal of Verbal Learning and Verbal Behavior, 10*, 316–321.

Wickens, C.D. (1984). *Engineering psychology and human performance.* Columbus, OH: Charles E. Merrill.

Wickens, D.D. (1972). Characteristics of word encoding. In A.W. Melton & E. Martin (Eds.), *Coding processes in human memory* (pp. 191–215). Washington, DC: Winston.

Wickens, D.D., Born, D.G., & Allen, C.K. (1963). Proactive inhibition and item similarity in short-term memory. *Journal of Verbal Learning and Verbal Behavior, 2*, 440–445.

Wickens, T.D., & Millward, R.B. (1971). Attribute elimination strategies for concept identification with practiced subjects. *Journal of Mathematical Psychology, 8*, 453–480.

Wilkins, W. (Ed.). (1988). *Syntax and semantics: Vol. 21. Thematic relations.* New York: Academic.

Williams, K.W., & Durso, F.T. (1986). Judging category frequency: Automaticity or availability? *Journal of Experimental Psychology: Learning, Memory, and Cognition, 12,* 387–396.

Williams, M.D., & Hollan, J.D. (1981). The process of retrieval from very long-term memory. *Cognitive Science, 5,* 87–119.

Winkler, R.L., & Hayes, W.L. (1975). *Statistics: Probability, inference, and decision.* New York: Holt, Rinehart & Winston.

Winograd, T. (1975). Frame representations and the declarative-procedural controversy. In D.G. Bobrow & A.M. Collins (Eds.), *Representation and understanding: Studies in cognitive science.* New York: Academic.

Winston, M.E., Chaffin, R., & Herrmann, D. (1987). A taxonomy of part-whole relations. *Cognitive Science, 11,* 417–444.

Winston, P.H. (Ed.). (1975). *The psychology of computer vision.* New York: McGraw-Hill.

Wish, M., & Carroll, J.D. (1974). Application of individual differences scaling to studies of human perception and judgment. In *Handbook of perception* (Vol. 2, pp. 449–491). New York: Academic.

Wittgenstein, L. (1953). *Philosophical investigations* (G.E.M. Anscombe, Trans.). New York: Macmillan.

Woodworth, R.S., & Sells, S.B. (1935). An atmosphere effect in formal syllogistic reasoning. *Journal of Experimental Psychology, 18,* 451–460.

Yerkes, R.M., & Doddson, J.D. (1908). The relation of strength of stimulus to rapidity of habit-formation. *Journal of Comparative Neurological Psychology, 18,* 459–482.

Zacks, R.T. (1969). Invariance of total learning time under different conditions of practice. *Journal of Experimental Psychology, 82,* 441–447.

Zadeh, L.A. (1965). Fuzzy sets. *Information and Control, 8,* 338–353.

Zadeh, L.A. (1982). A note on prototype theory. *Cognition, 12,* 291–297.

Zipf, G.K. (1965). *The psychology of language.* Cambridge, MA: MIT Press. (Original work published 1935)

Author Index

SUBJECT INDEX